the

BoweryBoys

ADVENTURES in OLD NEW YORK

an unconventional exploration of Manhattan's
historic neighborhoods, secret spots
and colorful characters

GREG YOUNG & TOM MEYERS

Ulysses Press

Published in the United States by:
Ulysses Press
P.O. Box 3440
Berkeley, CA 94703
www.ulyssespress.com

ISBN: 978-1-61243-557-2
Library of Congress Control Number: 2015952114

Printed in the United States by United Graphics

10 9 8 7 6 5 4 3 2 1

Acquisitions editor: Keith Riegert
Project editor: Casie Vogel
Managing editor: Claire Chun
Editor: Lauren Harrison
Proofreaders: Kathy Kaiser, Renee Rutledge, Caety Klingman
Indexer: Sayre Van Young
Front cover design: Thomas Cabus
Interior design and layout: what!design @ whatweb.com
Interior photographs: see page 490

Dedicated to Carey Ballard and Elizabeth Meyers Hendrickson

TABLE OF CONTENTS

Have a Great New York Week

(Whether You Live Here or Not) by Greg Young

The scene: Straus Square, specifically the top-floor apartment of a somewhat shabby tenement building on the square's northwest corner.

It was here on a rather hot evening in 2007 that Tom Meyers and I, good friends for many years, drank a bit of wine, opened up my new laptop, plugged in a karaoke microphone, and started recording a podcast on a whim.

That is obviously not the most remarkable thing about Straus Square.

Straus Square is an irregular plaza on the Lower East Side, formed by the collision of five streets at the southwest corner of Seward Park. The intersection they form is named for Nathan Straus (1848–1931), the German Jewish merchant king who launched Macy's Department Store with his brother Isidor. When Isidor died on the *Titanic* in 1912, Nathan got in touch with his Jewish roots, handing over most of his fortune to the cause of creating a Jewish state.

Even that is not the most remarkable thing about Straus Square.

In the nineteenth century, Straus Square was referred to informally as "Tweed Plaza," named for the most famously corrupt character in the city's history — William "Boss" Tweed. Born down at 1 Cherry Street[1] in 1823 to a Scottish

---

1   Thirty years earlier, America's first presidential mansion — the home of George Washington — was at 1 Cherry Street. So you could say the neighborhood went a little downhill.

chair maker, Tweed mastered the shady and labyrinthine world of New York politics and became a savior to the impoverished residents of the Lower East Side, all the while padding both his pockets and those of his cronies with robust kickbacks and bribes.

In 1870, on the eve of Tweed's downfall, supporters conspired to erect a statue on this very spot to honor their besieged hero. (They hoped to make something that would accentuate his marvelous girth so that future generations of birds would have ample room to nest.) The statue was never built, of course, and Tweed was soon locked up at the Ludlow Street Jail just three blocks north. But the name Tweed Plaza lingered around for decades, not unlike a whiff of one of Tweed's cigars.[2]

On the southern side of Straus Square is the gentlemanly Forward Building, a slab of frosted architectural might, the headquarters (from 1912 to 1972) of the influential *Jewish Daily Forward*. Today it's luxury condos, of course. Next door to the Forward is the still-festive 169 Bar with its colorful vintage sign. The tavern has served booze off and on since 1916 and was nicknamed the "Bloody Bucket" in the 1950s for reasons that, we fear, were probably quite literal.

---

2   The old New York City County Courthouse on Chambers Street, the most flagrant example of Tweed's excess, built upon a foundation of corruption and erected with absurdly lavish materials, is unofficially called the Tweed Courthouse, thus proving that if you can perform your crime boldly enough, you'll at least be remembered.

Across the street, inside Seward Park (opened in 1903 and one of the first public playgrounds in America), sits the magnificent Seward Park Library, a vital educational outlet for an overcrowded immigrant neighborhood when it opened its doors in 1909, thanks to funding from Andrew Carnegie. It sits back in the park like an antique trophy, the most decorative structure in Nathan's square.

Straus and Tweed and Carnegie and Jewish culture and hipster bars. I bring them up to illustrate what it takes to make a place: an overlapping cast of characters, many unknown to each other, striving to make the world great— or maybe just to finish the day with a little change in their pocket. Pick a corner, and you'll find a thousand people from history standing there—Jewish "newsies," seamstresses, tired cabbies, tourists, men with iPods.[3]

Straus Square is remarkable because it has collected those stories and preserved them—in architecture and street names, from manhole covers to rooftop water towers. History here is active and alive.

And it was here, in 2007, pretty much oblivious to many of those forces, that *The Bowery Boys: New York City History* podcast was born.

THE AUDIO HISTORY OF EVERYTHING

A podcast is a curious, intangible thing, a specialized take on a radio show and captured like a lightning bug in a jar. Given the endless length of digital airspace, independent podcasters have the power to change the world, to have their bite-size manifestos spread all over the planet, delivered instantaneously and more pervasively than a radio or television signal. But changing the world is hard work, so most of us choose a more modest scope of subjects for our podcasts, like discussing sports or knitting or episodes of *The Walking Dead.*

The podcast format was still very new in 2007—only about 6,000 existed at the time. Today there are a great many podcasts, approximately a googolplex, approaching a near-infinite stream of people talking about things that interest them. Due to the relative ease of podcasting, Tom and I decided that tipsy June evening to add to the number of podcasts, determining quickly that ours should be something about New York City.

---

3   That would be me in January 2006 when I was mugged in Straus Square for that very iPod.

Although both of us were born outside Manhattan—Tom in northern Ohio, me in southwest Missouri—we had become very distinct products of New York by that time, shaped by its buildings and rattling subway cars.

Some might have even called us New Yorkers.

The first episode of our writhing little newborn of a podcast was devoted to Canal Street and Collect Pond; the latter was a source of freshwater in the eighteenth century that became so foul with industrial waste that it had to be drained into Manhattan's two rivers in the early nineteenth century (via canals, giving us the name of today's Canal Street). That's right—we couldn't just begin our show talking about the Statue of Liberty. No, give us toxic water! By the second show, we had found our official name—the Bowery Boys, named for a set of dapper 1850s thugs who styled their hair with soap and terrorized Irish neighborhoods while looking, generally, very foppish.[4] The actual Bowery, its southern portion now packed with Chinese-language awnings and worn-out jewelry stores, sat just a few blocks west of us.

City Hall.

---

4   There's also a wacky troupe of theater—and later, film—stars from the 1930s, '40s, and '50s called the Bowery Boys that included Leo Gorcey, Huntz Hall, Bobby Jordan, and others.

Each time we sat down to record, we became lost in a city of rich characters and surprises, with each story taking a different turn on the kaleidoscope — from the tricornered silhouette of the Revolutionary War to the crackling, crimson terror of the Great Fire of 1835. The glitz of the Chrysler Building and the majestic permanence of Green-Wood Cemetery. The Flatiron, the Woolworth, Trinity Church, and old Penn Station. Astors and Vanderbilts. Olmsted and Vaux. Studio 54 and Saks Fifth Avenue. And Robert Moses, of course, the twentieth-century parks commissioner who dreamed up great urban solutions, bridges, and parkways — while inflicting more urban collateral damage than a multitude of King Kongs.

Children at May Day party, Battery Park, New York.

In our podcast we tackle these subjects and more, conversing as though hanging out at a bar or all-night diner, perhaps Edward Hopper's imaginary late-night cafe in *Nighthawks* or McSorley's Old Ale House on a slow day. Or — most likely, I'm afraid — that swanky new craft-cocktail bar that just opened on the corner. (In reality, a live bar-corner conversation of such intensity and spittle would probably drive other customers from said bar and lead to its closure.)

As our listenership grew, we quickly discovered that it wasn't just New Yorkers tuning in, but also countless others who had fallen in love with the city in a myriad of ways — through vacations, school trips, movies, daydreams, photos. New York City's history was really everyone's to enjoy.

HISTORY AND YOU!

Walking through the city, history isn't experienced in chronological order. New skyscrapers stand next to century-old concert halls. Colonial-era farmhouses nestle in the shadows of 1960s housing projects. Neighborhoods that once provided inexpensive first homes to new immigrants are now overwhelmed by trendy nightclubs and artisan wine bars. Times Square looks like a scene from *Blade Runner* now, yet it contains some of the oldest operating theaters in America. Outlandishly priced Fifth Avenue boutiques reside inside the very mansions of those who might have shopped there one hundred years ago.

Anyone who is or becomes a New Yorker interacts with the ragged fabric of its history whether they like it or not. We're affected by the decisions made by people long dead, live in spaces other people built, walk down sidewalks and travel through tunnels that someone long ago decided should be put right at that precise spot and not, for instance, *over there*.

Many people never give the name John Randel, Jr., much thought, but he was the surveyor of New York's visionary grid plan and the reason it's so difficult to get a crosstown cab to move faster than 5 miles per hour. For many, the Empire State Building is the symbol of the city and its most photogenic building. Why does it sit right *there*? Because the Astors, a bickering and ludicrously wealthy family, built dueling hotels on that block at the peak of the Gilded Age—the original Waldorf-Astoria—that came to be considered outmoded when the skyscraper boom arrived in Midtown in the 1920s. The aforementioned Robert Moses—builder of highways and parks, destroyer of small worlds—made countless decisions that still affect the daily lives of New Yorkers.

But New York keeps changing, keeps rising, so New Yorkers don't experience their city's history in an easily digestible fashion. Often, they don't experience it at *all*, as the speed and intensity of city life turn it into one big blur. But behind those walls and under our heels (whether they be Adidas or Manolo Blahnik) lives old New York.

WHAT IS OLD NEW YORK?

There has always been a somewhat vague and romantic notion of New York's past. Even people from the period we might today call old New York hearkened back to the Founding Fathers, or even back to the old Dutch families of New Amsterdam. "[T]he New-Yorker, to whom the great structures have ceased to be novelties, looks with equal interest on the few architectural relics of the past, the old-time, modest houses which still remain on the modern thoroughfares," said one newspaper[5] in 1902, the same year the Flatiron Building—probably the most romantic building in New York—opened. In 1926, the Museum of the City of New York presented a runaway

---

5   *New York Tribune*, May 4, 1902.

smash exhibition called "Old New York," which attracted thousands to its old quilts and daguerreotypes of famous opera singers.

When history-gazing was more of a casual, parasol-twirling affair, looking for old New York may have required something of a selective memory. How fond could one be of an old building that could remind us of slavery, of racism and riot, of the subjugation of women, of disease, or of corruption? Today we make an effort to remember both sides of history, the darkness and the light, making the buildings that survive today more than just landmarks. They're a profound link to past struggles.

Nostalgia for pretty much anything can be found on the streets of New York today—retro video arcades, bars with disco and punk nights, swing dancing lessons, Bushwick dandies with straw hats, soda fountains with $15 egg creams (prices, of course, are almost never throwbacks). But nostalgia is not really history; it's selective remembering, a sentimental coloring of the past.

Lenox Avenue at 135th Street, Harlem, on March 23, 1939.

While it's certainly present in the pages that follow, we hope we've kept it in check. We're visiting memorials, sites of tragedy, and disasters. How nostalgic can one get for the "good old days" when the city was overcome with yellow fever? Not very.

So what is Old New York? For this book, we've loosely defined it as the pre-1898 border of New York City, which was Manhattan Island. Obviously, history runs just as deep in the other four boroughs. Take Brooklyn, which contains, of note, one of the oldest homes in America—the Wyckoff House of Canarsie, dating to the 1650s—not to mention the fine homes of Brooklyn Heights. Staten Island (or Richmond, if we're being accurate) has Fort Wadsworth and the Conference House and all of Historic Richmond Town. Queens has the relics of Steinway and Jamaica. The Bronx has hints of its Dutch past in its very name.

But it's in Manhattan that the past is at its most concentrated, especially around iconic spots that have changed American history—Wall Street, the Brooklyn

Bridge, the Bowery, Central Park, Fifth Avenue, Times Square, Harlem. Through the efforts of New York City's Landmark Preservation Commission, building off the momentum of past preservationists and a million happy accidents of survival, history lines nearly every street in Manhattan.

The sites mentioned in this book are mostly from the pre-1898 years—expanded to encompass the Gilded Age period that stretched into the 1920s. In some cases, we simply couldn't ignore significant stories from the recent past. A single block, after all, can tell a multitude of stories.

THE ADVENTURE BEGINS

Before you is a story of New York City told from tip to top, neighborhood by neighborhood, and point to point. It's a historical treasure hunt in which the prize at the end, if we do our job right, is a better connection with the thousands of people who have walked these streets before you. The good news is, you can start at the beginning and explore the entire length of Manhattan, from the islands of New York Harbor to the northernmost point. Or you can come up with your own path.

These adventures of old New York are divided into neighborhoods. Many of these designations trace back to original Dutch or British names (Harlem, Murray Hill); others have modern portmanteaus created to bolster real estate values (SoHo, Tribeca).

Immigrants on Ellis Island.

Each chapter begins with a brief overview of a neighborhood's history called "Situate the Reader" (playing off a regular feature in our podcasts). Following that is a history of the neighborhood told through the perspective of several places, streets, and objects. We focus on a few less obvious sights, or on the surprising details of the more iconic landmarks.

You will see a host of unusual themes and exquisite quirks rise from the hundreds of "Points of Interest" covered in the book. We hope a new New York City emerges in the search for the old one—a city of cat and owl statues, medieval and Egyptian carvings, strange signs, fairy-tale corners and alleyways, hints of Freemasonry, various places George Washington slept, mysterious obelisks. And everywhere — secret cemeteries.

So welcome to this unique Bowery Boys adventure! We hope that you enjoy the journey and that you find a rich new world of characters and experiences at spots around town that you might *think* you already know.

And we have one small piece of advice: Stick with the book for a while, but then just get lost. Beneath this little scavenger hunt through history awaits another — one that you'll find on your own, with all its surprises and joys provided by the millions of New Yorkers before us who already forged their own adventures. But first start with this....

A SHORT HISTORY OF MANHATTAN

The Lenape Indians called this canoe-shaped island Mannahatta, a modest slip of a thing next to larger Sewanhaka (Long Island), but rich with natural life from its southern marshes to its northern heights. The end of their dominion over the island was nigh the moment scouts sighted English explorer Henry Hudson and his *Halve Maen* sail into the harbor. Hudson worked for the Dutch, and by 1625, the Dutch West India Company had founded a settlement at the southernmost tip. New Amsterdam, as it was called, was a chaotic and often dissolute place, even after 1647, when stern director-general Peter Stuyvesant enforced a semblance of governance and security.

When the Dutch were unceremoniously booted from their settlement by invading British forces in 1664, Stuyvesant chose to stay put in America, as did many Dutch. For more than a hundred years, England monitored their distant holding — now renamed, like the entire colony, New York — via appointed governors and the oversight of its Trinity Church, chartered in 1697.

But Colonial Americans united against vast English injustices, eventually inciting rebellion. When representatives voted in Philadelphia on July 2, 1776, to declare their independence from England, General George Washington amassed an army in New York. He and the Continental Army were no match for the massive British troops, and for the entire duration of the Revolutionary War, the British held the city and based themselves here until their expulsion in November 1783 (Evacuation Day).

Until the early nineteenth century, the city of New York was geographically limited to the bottom fifth of Manhattan island. But the Commissioners' Plan of 1811 encouraged northward expansion, stamping a grid of streets and avenues onto most of the undeveloped island. And just in the nick of time too, for waves of immigrants (first Irish and German, then Eastern European and Italian) began landing on the city's shore in the 1830s and didn't abate for nearly a century. They brought a rush of new languages, cultures, and cuisines, turning the city into a crowded and exciting metropolis.

Transportation advancements, especially the railroad, made travel to the city easier, although the dominant method of street transportation inside New York would remain horse-drawn varieties into the twentieth century. In the late nineteenth century, a manufacturing and trading boom and the development of a new financial economy helped create a society of millionaires mere blocks from the most ramshackle of tenements.

The unhygienic accommodations of so many people in such tight quarters prompted the construction of the Croton Aqueduct, an elaborate water delivery system, and the planting of massive Central Park, which wasn't originally part of the grid plan. Local authorities attempted improvements by forming city police and fire departments, and by establishing sanitation and social services. However, these were often infiltrated by corrupt political "machines," such as Tammany Hall, who lined their pockets at the public's expense.

New York City from Met Life Tower, looking south toward Battery and New York Harbor.

New Yorkers were not of one mind during the Civil War; violent riots in the summer of 1863 almost destroyed the city, pitting Irish against blacks, Southern sympathizers against Lincoln supporters. Neighborhoods such as Five Points and the Tenderloin seethed with vice and gang activity. Often the only recourse was wholesale demolition, couched conveniently in terms of colossal city projects, such as the Brooklyn Bridge and New York's civic center (and later the construction of the Lincoln Tunnel). As the city moved northward, the upper classes tracked up Fifth Avenue while the entertainment district headed up Broadway to Longacre Square, renamed in 1904 after its newest tenant, the *New York Times.*

Meanwhile, across the East River sat America's third biggest city — Brooklyn — sharing resources and sometimes competing for resources with Manhattan. In 1898, it begrudgingly entered the fold of Greater New York alongside the Bronx, Queens, and Staten Island.

Most of these disparate neighborhoods were soon connected by a series of underground subways, which linked the five boroughs with ferries and elevated railroads. The trains of Grand Central, previously hampering the growth of upper Manhattan, caused a development boom when Manhattan (literally) covered its tracks, creating miles of new real estate and a new thoroughfare, Park Avenue, mere blocks from where the Fifth Avenue elites had already settled. Farther north, New York's African American community, seeking refuge from tense conflicts in Hell's Kitchen and other neighborhoods, resettled into the old Dutch village of Harlem, building America's most important black neighborhood.

Advancements in construction were creating a skyline downtown of marvelous stone and steel towers, lifted by new elevators and twinkling at night with electric lights. Manhattan was the crucible for reform movements, many conceived in the wake of horrific tragedies like the *General Slocum* disaster and the Triangle Shirtwaist Factory fire. Prohibition was also considered a "reform," but it mostly fostered a not-so-clandestine network of speakeasies and an underworld of crime. The affluence of Wall Street kept New York roaring through the 1920s—until the stock market crashed in 1929, hurtling country and city alike into the dire straits of the Depression.

Fortunately, massive projects, both private and public, kept many employed through the hard times—from the Empire State Building to Rockefeller Center. But the greatest engine of change belonged to something much tinier and four-wheeled: the automobile. City planners like Robert Moses, so influential in rebuilding city parks, pushed through the construction of driver-friendly bridges and roads both inside and outside of New York, which made it easier than ever for middle-class residents to exit for the suburbs. New York's once-thriving ports corroded with the rise of container shipping and interstate highway trucking; an elevated railroad linking west side businesses arrived too late.

New York in the late 1960s and '70s became a symbol of America's urban decay. It was out of money, weakened by failing infrastructure, and defined by many on the outside by its perceived debauchery—its 42nd Street theaters, once showcases of mainstream entertainment, now flickered with pornography. Yet lower rents and laissez-faire attitudes also spurred artistic innovation (from CBGB to off-Broadway theater), energizing Manhattan's art scene. The "cleanup" of the 1990s saw crime rates drop dramatically and new construction projects rise, sending residential and business rents skyrocketing and causing distinct shifts in neighborhood demographics that threatened the city's cherished diversity.

On September 11, 2001, when the World Trade Center was attacked and destroyed, the world turned again toward Manhattan. People were again reminded of its strength and vitality, of the city born almost four centuries earlier, just blocks from the WTC site. Fifteen years later, New York is again itself, at once its past and future.

***

About the Map: Our points of interest are plotted on a 1917 map produced by C. S. Hammond & Co. (from the New York Public Library Digital Collections). Note that many "modern" city elements aren't indicated, as they hadn't yet been built (for example, Rockefeller Center and Seventh Avenue in the Village). How many other differences can you spot?

MANHATTAN
SITUATE THE READER
-The Neighborhoods-

Numbers marked below refer to chapters in the book.

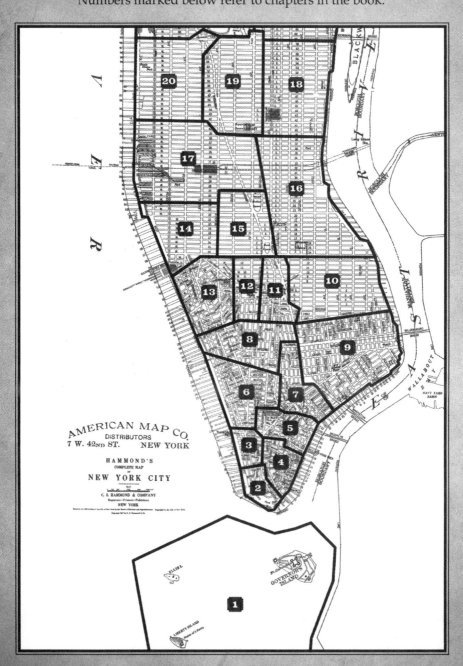

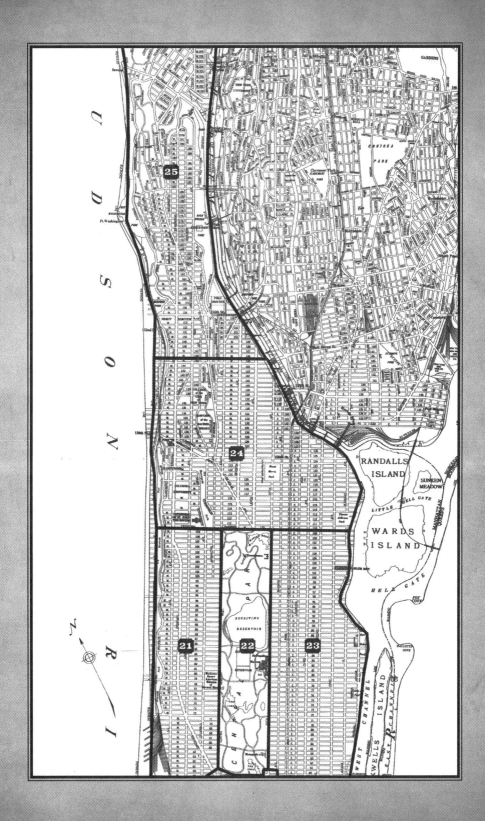

THE NEW COLOSSUS

Emma Lazarus wrote the poem "The New Colossus" in 1883 on a rather urgent mission. France had just given the United States an enormous gift, called "Liberty Enlightening the World," better known as the Statue of Liberty. The only hitch: It lacked a base to stand on. Through newspaper campaigns and fundraisers (such as the one at which an audience first heard Lazarus's poem), citizens eventually raised $270,000, enough money to fit Miss Liberty with a smart new pedestal designed by Richard Morris Hunt.

Twenty years after Lazarus wrote the poem, the verses were etched into bronze and placed onto a lower level of the pedestal. Her words have represented the voice of Lady Liberty ever since:

Not like the brazen giant of Greek fame,

With conquering limbs astride from land to land;

Here at our sea-washed, sunset gates shall stand

A mighty woman with a torch, whose flame

Is the imprisoned lightning, and her name

Mother of Exiles. From her beacon-hand

Glows world-wide welcome; her mild eyes command

The air-bridged harbor that twin cities frame.

"Keep, ancient lands, your storied pomp!" cries she

With silent lips. "Give me your tired, your poor,

Your huddled masses yearning to breathe free,

The wretched refuse of your teeming shore.

Send these, the homeless, tempest-tossed to me,

I lift my lamp beside the golden door!

Chapter 1///
New York Harbor

Those ships have sailed: A sketch of New York Harbor by British army officer Thomas Davies, 1776.

SITUATE THE READER
–New York Harbor–

In 1609 Henry Hudson discovered what the Native Americans of the region had known for more than 6,000 years—the value of what would one day be called New York Harbor. Hudson was the talk of the town (or rather, the wigwam); no European explorer had dared enter since Giovanni da Verrazzano briefly tipped his ship into the legendary Narrows in 1524.[1]

Hudson and the men of his vessel the *Halve Maen* were sailing on behalf of his employer, the Dutch East India Company. The harbor and the so-called North River (today renamed for Mr. Hudson) would prove vital to the success of that first Dutch settlement, New Amsterdam.[2] Fifty-five years after Hudson's journey, the more powerful British Crown would snatch up the territory from the Dutch, eager to control its valuable ports, prized network of waterways, and strategic position among its other North American colonies.

Soon this same harbor would help define the American dream and make New York one of the richest cities in the world. With the opening of the Erie Canal in the 1820s, connecting the Hudson River with the American inlands via the Great Lakes, New York Harbor became a gateway of domestic and international commerce, and a symbol of American progress.

Soon something even bigger than trade was enriching New York's shores. It was here that millions of immigrants reached their new home, greeted after 1886 by a new beacon of opportunity and rebirth, the Statue of Liberty. Immigrants at Ellis Island gazed across the harbor to that astounding city of dreams and imagined possibilities they thought impossible in their home countries. America the beautiful.

---

1   For his efforts, they named that big bridge linking Staten Island to Brooklyn for him in 1964.

2   While Hudson worked for the Dutch *East* India Company, the New Amsterdam settlement belonged to the similarly named Dutch *West* India Company.

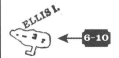

ELLIS I.

MA Ft.Columbus GOVERNORS ISLAND

6-10

LIBERTY ISLAND
Statue of Liberty

1-5

POINTS OF INTEREST

1 Captain Kidd's Buried Treasure

2 The Smallest Statue of Liberty of All

3 Lady's Got Back

4 Tribute to the Forty States

5 The Fort Beneath Her Feet

6 Stand Here

7 The Sound Experience of Ellis Island

8 The Explosive Island

9 The Writing on the Wall

10 The VIP Bridge to New Jersey

MA Governors Island

Adventures on Governors Island

Of the three small islands that sit in New York Harbor between Staten Island and Manhattan, two of them (Ellis Island and Liberty Island) have been embedded into the American consciousness as icons of freedom and opportunity. The third, Governors Island, is often overlooked by both visitors and residents.

However, for much of the city's history, this ice-cream-cone shaped island,[3] separated from Brooklyn by the richly named Buttermilk Channel, has been critically important to the nation's defense. Fortunately, its most treasured historical landmarks are still around more than 200 years after they were constructed.

Chillin' out on Governors Island, painted by Frederick Catherwood.

In 1624, when the Dutch brought the first settlers to the New World to establish what would become New Netherland, they deposited eight men on this small island, which they named Noten (Nut) Island. It was a convenient spot, just a short rowing distance from the future settlements of New Amsterdam and Breukelen. But it would be the British who would give it the name Governors

---

3 Sugar cone, to be specific.

Island after taking charge of the colony in 1664, as the royal governors of the New York colony would indeed live here.

The island would be less hospitable to the British a century later, when in 1776 the Continental Army constructed earthen forts here to ward off British war vessels during the early years of the Revolutionary War. While its guns did scare off two British ships on July 12, 1776, the British succeeded in driving the Continental Army out of New York during the Battle of Long Island. They would occupy Governors Island—and all of New York—throughout the conflict.

In 1783, at the end of the war, the new Americans ushered the British out of the harbor with gusto.[4] But fears of their return continued for decades afterward, presenting the young government with the alarming thought of New York being recaptured. And so, with tensions mounting in the run-up to the War of 1812, two very different fortresses were constructed here. Fort Jay, sitting on the site of the original Revolutionary War defense, was designed like a five-pointed star fort surrounded by a dry moat. Castle Williams, sitting on the shoreline,

The strange silhouette of Castle Williams, 1890 (photo: Langill & Darling).

was given an almost completely circular shape, punctured with openings for dozens of cannons. Both fortifications have survived and can be visited today, most likely because neither ever saw an actual battle.

Aware of the island's strategic location for defending the nation's most important city and harbor, the U.S. Army moved out to Governors Island in the 1830s, and would remain stationed there until 1965. During the Civil War, the forts were reworked into holding cells for Confederate soldiers, Union deserters, and criminals. Captured Confederate officers were held in relatively posh quarters at Fort Jay,[5] while regular soldiers were thrown into the much less comfortable prison at Castle Williams.

As Lower Manhattan developed skyward in the late nineteenth century, the close proximity of two military forts to the nation's largest city was a bit, well,

---

4   Evacuation Day! See Chapter 2.
5   During the nineteenth century, Fort Jay was renamed Fort Columbus due to the souring reputation of its previous namesake, John Jay. Fortunately his reputation—and the fort's name— were restored by the twentieth century.

surreal. Meanwhile a sort of small-town life developed here on the island, and by the 1880s, rows of elegant Victorian brick houses were constructed for Army officers and their families. A genteel life among the cannons!

In the first years of the twentieth century, the island more than doubled in size — the "cone" was added to the ice-cream scoop — with landfill mostly taken from excavations of New York's subway system, which opened in 1904. This

new flat expanse, located so close to lower Manhattan, was an ideal spot for the city's first airstrip. In 1909 Wilbur Wright lifted off here in his flying machine, coasting around the Statue of Liberty and later up the West Side as far as Grant's Tomb. It seemed like such a logical base for air transport that in the 1930s Mayor Fiorello La Guardia tried to build the city's first permanent airport there.[6]

Admit it, it looks like an ice cream cone. Governors Island from overhead, 1920s (photo: Ewing Galloway).

The gigantic Building 400 (later renamed Liggett Hall) was the largest military building in the world when it was completed in 1930. The structure separates the original section of the island from its twentieth-century addition and lends the island something of a college campus feel. You can easily imagine how charming it must have been in the 1940s — there's even a playhouse where Irving Berlin debuted a revue in 1942 called *This Is the Army*. Of course, charming revues couldn't mask a more harrowing reality: The island's residents were fully engaged in fighting World War II.

In 1966, the island changed administrative hands, as the Coast Guard moved in and increased the population by nearly 4,000 people. The leafy lanes became ever more bucolic, as small-town amenities were added, including a bowling alley and a supermarket. And, almost three centuries after the British left, another royal was installed here — His Highness, the Burger King.[7] By 1996, the Coast Guard had departed for roomier shores, leaving the island and its royal burger palace desolate.

---

6   If Governors Island had become New York's first municipal airport, most likely it would have been swiftly expanded or even abandoned due to the growing size of airplanes. Of course, LaGuardia Airport is hardly what anybody would call adequate!

7   This Burger King also sold beer, making it the most raucous bar on Governors Island.

Governors Island had been the property of the federal government since the early nineteenth century. When in 2003[8] the island was sold to New York City, many wondered what could possibly become of the now-abandoned settlement. That same year the island opened its shores on weekends to visitors — they were free to explore, often with great astonishment, some of the empty structures, as if they were wandering ancient ruins. Today, after more than a decade of thoughtful preservation and promotion, thousands of New Yorkers enjoy the island during the summer, visiting the officers' homes (now home to arts and music groups), newly landscaped parks (in the landfilled "cone" section), and weekend arts and food festivals.

And after all this time, Fort Jay and Castle Williams, now maintained by the National Park Service, still stand watch over the harbor. Oh, the things they've seen.

Liberty Island/Ellis Island

POINTS OF INTEREST

1 CAPTAIN KIDD'S BURIED TREASURE Long before the installation of the gigantic green Lady, the tiny piece of land now called Liberty Island had a quiet, if rather dark, history. During New York's British years (1664–1783) it was named for owner Isaac Bedloe and later hosted a pesthouse (a forced quarantine for those carrying dreaded diseases). But here at the water's edge played out one of the great urban legends of New York City history: the tale of Captain Kidd's treasure and the ghost of Bedloe's Island.

As the tale would have it, famed pirate Captain William Kidd (1645–1701)[9] was believed to have buried some of his stolen booty on a coastline somewhere in the harbor.

One moonlit night, over a hundred years later, two treasure-seekers snuck outside and

---

8 For the grand sum of one dollar.
9 Kidd was also a prominent New York citizen. See Chapter 4.

began digging along the northern shore. They reportedly hit upon a treasure…and a phantom. To their horror, they had released the ghost of one of Kidd's pirates, a poor soul murdered by Kidd to forever guard his treasure!

This spooky story has haunted the island since the mid-nineteenth century, well before Lady Liberty made her grand appearance. Today, no visitors are allowed on the island after dark. Are they afraid we'll find something? (*Standing on the north side of the island, with Ellis to your left, the pier to the right*)

2 THE SMALLEST STATUE OF LIBERTY OF ALL Five slender sentries stand in the shadow of the Statue of Liberty, five individuals who contributed to her construction and lasting legacy. They include Édouard René de Laboulaye, the French intellectual who initially conceived the project; Frédéric Auguste Bartholdi, the master sculptor who designed it; Alexandre Gustave Eiffel (yes, *that* Eiffel), the engineer who essentially got her to stand; Joseph Pulitzer, the American publisher who tirelessly raised funds for her pedestal; and Emma Lazarus, whose poem "The New Colossus" gave Liberty her voice. (See page xx for the full poem.)

There are two amusing details to these modern statues. Next to li'l Eiffel is a mini-me version of his famous Parisian tower, essentially a younger brother to the Statue of Liberty, erected in 1889, less than three years after Liberty's completion in New York. And look closely at Bartholdi—he's standing in front of a small replica of the Statue of Liberty, perhaps the only miniature Lady Liberty on the island that's not for sale. (*Northern path closest to the statue*)

3 LADY'S GOT BACK Standing on Liberty Island, the Statue's magnificent, even awesome size becomes obvious. She's so massive that it can be

challenging to take her all in—most views on the island, in fact, are of her backside! But this is where you can appreciate the mastery of Bartholdi's achievement, observing some surprising details that you may not have already seen a million times before: the folds of her classical drapery, the intricate details in her hair, the late-afternoon sunlight upon her green patina, the results of her oxidizing copper skin. For better full-on views, you might want to wait until you get back on board your boat (or

The Wondrous Journey of the Statue of Liberty's Right Arm

The Statue of Liberty arrived in New York Harbor on June 19, 1885, making the journey across the Atlantic aboard the French Navy vessel *Isère*. She didn't arrive fully assembled and standing, of course (although *that* would have been a sight!). Rather, Lady Liberty traveled in 214 crates, ready to be welded together stateside. However, there was a problem: Funding for the pedestal, left to the Americans to finance, had not yet been completed, so she literally didn't have any place to stand. Thus, this beacon of liberty sat around in crates on Bedloe's Island for several months.

Give her a hand: Lady Liberty's arm and torch turns heads in Madison Square.

However, not all of her was making the journey for the first time. One of her body parts had already been on a tour of the United States. In fact, it had even enjoyed a lengthy residence in one of New York's most beautiful parks.

You see, to stir up American enthusiasm for his statue, sculptor Frédéric Auguste Bartholdi decided to first complete the statue's right arm and torch, and send it off to America in 1876 on a grand fundraising tour, well in advance of the rest of the body.

Nearly a decade before the rest of her would be shipped over, craftsmen in Paris scrambled to complete the 37-foot appendage in time to be displayed at Philadelphia's 1876 Centennial Exposition. (They didn't quite make the opening ceremony: The Lady's arm arrived fashionably late three months after the fair opened.) Visitors paid fifty cents for the opportunity to climb a ladder inside the arm to the torch's balcony, from where they could observe the fairground and all of its assembled marvels, including such wondrous inventions as the typewriter and the telephone.

A few months later, the arm and torch made their way to New York, where they were planted in the northwest corner of Madison Square Park. "[O]ne of the arms of the Bartholdi statue, with its accompanying hand, has been placed on a pedestal in Madison Square, where it has excited the warm admiration of the infants who infest the place," the *New York Times* dryly noted.

The torch stood watch over the park from 1876 to 1882. It was then shipped back to France, only to make the return voyage—with the rest of her body in crates—three years later.

board the Staten Island Ferry for free from Battery Park for a passing view). *(Standing at the flagpole, before approaching security to enter the pedestal)*

4 TRIBUTE TO THE FORTY STATES The Statue's pedestal provides magical views of the surrounding area—even the industrial areas of New Jersey seem enchanting. But spend a few moments observing just the details of the pedestal itself, designed by Richard Morris Hunt, New York's premier architect of the 1880s, with an unusual nod to both Egyptian[10] and Aztec temples. No going low-key here!

Instrumental to the power of these ancient-world flourishes are the 40 discs that surround the pedestal. Hunt's intention was to put the coat of arms of the 40 American states that existed at the time of its dedication—rather, 38 states and a couple of key territories—on the discs. But flash forward to 1890, just four years after the Statue's dedication, and America had six additional states (North Dakota, South Dakota, Montana, Washington, Wyoming, and Idaho). Thankfully this idea was scrapped

Before tourists: The statue's pedestal was built upon old Fort Wood (1885, W. P. Snyder).

before it was carried out too far. Hastily nailing on a couple of extra discs to the side would have looked a bit awkward. *(Base of the pedestal, from any angle)*

5 THE FORT BENEATH HER FEET There's an intriguing symbolism to placing the Statue of Liberty atop an old army post. Fort Wood, completed in 1811, must have seemed especially impressive in its day, a star-shaped fort with eleven bastions topped with cannons and weaponry aimed into the harbor. What an honor, then, to rest Lady Liberty, the embodiment of so many American values, atop the old fort. Even still, the U.S. Army held barracks on other parts of the island, where military families were housed well into the mid-twentieth century.

You can fully explore the top of the fort at the very end of your trip to the Statue. Don't rush past this part to the exit; stop at the individual bastions and imagine what a young soldier would have seen from this vantage point 200

---

10 People were going nuts for Egyptian architecture by this time. See Chapter 22 on Central Park and the article on Cleopatra's Needle.

years ago, the harbor busy with ships, periaugers (early ferries), and sailboats. Near the exit, you can see a trace of the fort's old face — the original brickwork on an exposed wall. (*Statue of Liberty, rampart level*)

ELLIS ISLAND

6 STAND HERE: Anywhere near the front of the Main Building on Ellis Island. Turn and look past the ferry slip to the buildings standing on the other side, those closed to the public (*on "Island 2"*). *Why?* Everything to the south sits on landfill. In fact, 90 percent of the island is landfill!

The climb up the Statue of Liberty affords a few striking views of New York Harbor. From the pedestal, even the container ships look good!

This area vividly illustrates how urgently America needed to expand and expedite the processing of immigrants a century ago. For most of the nineteenth century, this responsibility belonged to the state of New York, which ran its processing center at Castle Garden off the tip of Battery Park.[11]

However, by the 1880s Castle Garden was swamped by arrivals and deemed woefully inadequate. The federal government took over in 1890 and promptly moved these services to Ellis Island in 1892.

The numbers are astounding, and the task daunting. In that first year alone, more than 450,000 immigrants passed through Ellis Island. The Main Building

---

11   Today's Castle Clinton. See Chapter 2.

struggled to keep up with the crowds and the services needed to process them: physical inspections, interviews, medical examinations, legal review. Millions more would arrive in the coming years; over 1 million immigrants were processed in 1907. It was during this period that the island was enlarged (as with Governors Island, mostly with landfill from subway excavations) and most of the buildings lining the south side were constructed.

Imagine arriving at this gorgeous building on Ellis Island after weeks at sea—in steerage, no less.

At the top of the slip is the glorious — and seemingly anachronistic — 1930s art deco ferry terminal. Then, going right to left, you see a cluster of buildings built to help process the shiploads of arriving immigrants, including a laundry facility, psychiatric ward, main hospital, administration building, and hospital annex. Behind these buildings are a great many other structures, now abandoned, including various isolation wards (for contagious diseases), a powerhouse, a recreational shelter, and a mortuary.

One final intriguing detail of this landfilled creation: For a time, the island was shaped like an "E," with two ferry slips essentially parceling the island into three parts. The southern slip was later filled in.

7 THE SOUND EXPERIENCE OF ELLIS ISLAND Most of the points of interest in this book are feasts for the eyes. But to appreciate the profound burden that was placed upon the Ellis Island Immigration Station, you'll need to close your eyes and let your ears imagine the story.

The Great Hall served as the central processing area for arriving immigrants. After leaving their possessions downstairs, the exhausted passengers climbed a central staircase (now gone) to this impressively mighty[12] hall, which feels as capable of handling crowds as a train terminal. It was here that officials ushered immigrants into tight lines before registering, interviewing, and inspecting them for contagious diseases.

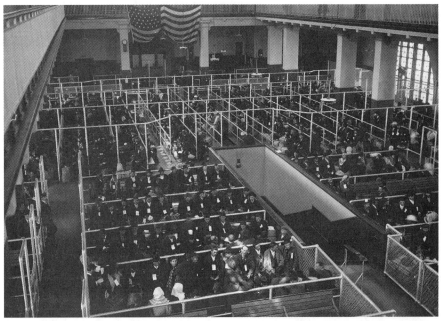

The Great Hall served as the central processing area for arriving immigrants (photo: Edwin Levick).

Close your eyes and imagine the cacophony—the nervous mix of Italian, Polish, Yiddish, German, and Russian, the cries of frightened children, the anger and confusion as "processing" didn't go the way some expected— all of it clashing and bouncing in this vaulted hall. Over 12 million people passed through this room, their fates determined here. For many, turned away because of ailments, this is the closest they ever got to New York, and the most they ever saw of it was through these windows. (*The Great Hall, Ellis Island*)

8 THE EXPLOSIVE ISLAND Ellis Island took various names in its early days, most notably Gibbet Island, named for the convicted criminals and pirates executed here.[13] Sometime around 1785 it was finally affixed with the

---

12 The ceiling is covered in the tilework of Rafael Guastavino. You'll see examples of his work at many sites in this book, especially in Chapter 18.
13 "Gibbet" sounds like a cute little word—perhaps a nice name for a pet frog—but it means gallows. So this was essentially Gallows Island.

name of one of its owners—Samuel Ellis—and commissioned with a small defense called Fort Gibson. No serious military actions ever took place here, and Fort Gibson ended up being an ammunition dump. Thousands of pounds of explosive material were stored here before the island was completely redeveloped in the 1890s. Oh, but all of that explosive power is still here! Kinda. Although it's now buried beneath significant landfill, an excavated portion of its walls can be seen behind the Main Building. (*Behind the Main Building, Ellis Island*)

You might stumble upon the once-explosive ruins of Fort Gibson on Ellis Island.

9 THE WRITING ON THE WALL Newly arriving immigrants were carefully checked for "conditions" that might prevent them from becoming productive members of American society. In the rooms surrounding the Great Hall, people were physically scrutinized, and if deemed "risky" they were marked as such, often with a chalk letter. Today exhibits within these inspection rooms recount these traumatic procedures.

Those who were deemed physical risks were ushered into dormitories where they'd nervously await their hearings before the Board of Special Inquiry, who determined whether they'd stay or be shipped back home. On the walls of a former waiting room, you can still make out the graffiti left by those who were soon to be informed of their destiny. Signatures are scrawled. Even the childlike drawings of a horse and quail can be seen. Did they stay in the United States? Were they separated from their families? Their stories are lost, but these markings survived, discovered during restoration work in the early 1990s. (*Northeast room on the second floor, Ellis Island*)

10 **THE VIP BRIDGE TO NEW JERSEY** Believe it or not, you can actually walk to Ellis Island if you know the right people. A footbridge linking Ellis to Liberty State Park in Jersey City, New Jersey,[14] was constructed in 1985 to transport materials during the island's renovation. Protests from New York officials and the ferry company have kept the bridge strictly "employees only" to this day. Boo! (*North path, behind the Main Building, Ellis Island*)

---

14 And here's where we must confess—Liberty Island isn't entirely owned by New York. It's not even *mostly* owned by New York. Ninety percent of the island—essentially anything created from landfill—is controlled by the state of New Jersey, which won jurisdiction rights in a 1998 Supreme Court case. Joint custody, baby! It's like a state-sized version of *Kramer vs. Kramer*.

Where Dutchmen once, in ages past,
Huge walls and ramparts round them cast
New fabrics raise, on new design,
Gay streets and palaces shall shine.

Another George shall here reside,
While Hudson's bold, unfettered tide
Well pleased to see his chief so nigh,
With livelier aspect passes by.

Along his margin, fresh and clean,
Ere long shall belles and beaux be seen,
Through moon-light shades, delighted, stray
To view the islands and the bay.

~ Excerpt, "On the Demolition of Fort George 1790" by Philip Freneau, 1917

Chapter 2//
Battery Park

Trendy neighborhood: New Amsterdam, around 1650, probably the last time the rent was pretty affordable.

SITUATE THE READER
-Battery Park-

The story of New York City begins here in Battery Park. By the 1620s the Dutch West India Company had declared this region their own—New Netherland—and sent company ships to set up small colonies in today's New York state, New Jersey, and surrounding areas. By 1625 work began on a fort at the southern tip of the island that would anchor a new settlement to be called New Amsterdam. That fort was here.

You can visualize where it once sat, just north of the modern Battery Park at almost the precise spot where Alexander Hamilton's U.S. Custom House would be built nearly 275 years later. Just erase all the gorgeous Gilded Age finery that hangs around here today and replace it with a rugged military redoubt of questionable security. (In 1641 a passing Jesuit priest noted, with a touch of snark, that the "ramparts of earth had crumbled away—the fort could be entered at all sides.")

Still, it was the anchor of the original Dutch community, a collection of homes, meetinghouses, taverns, and even a few windmills that hugged the water's edge.

Locating the original shoreline can be a bit tricky today. Most of the Battery Park you see now is, in fact, landfill, built up in the nineteenth century to extend the island around the former fort, once connected to land only by a bridge. The original shoreline of New Amsterdam ran, approximately, along Water Street to the east, State Street to the south, and Greenwich Street to the west.

The history of early New York is underneath you as well. Early New Yorkers used anything they could grab for landfill—not just excavated earth from building projects, but garbage, detritus, even the hulls of old ships. It's like a Colonial thrift store down there.

It's this unusual composition that brought a serious crisis to Battery Park when Hurricane Sandy struck in 2012, wreaking havoc upon the park and the nearby subway stations. Some effects of this terrible storm remain, but the park has returned.

POINTS OF INTEREST

1 Long Battery Life

2 Read This Quote

3 House of the Saint

4 The Birthplace of Moby-Dick's Dad

5 The New Pantheon

6 The Cute Little Subway House

7 On the Fence

8 Echoes of Steamship Row

9 The President Moves In

10 The Solar Secret of the Korean War Memorial

11 Stand Here

12 The Pier with No Peers (Literally)

13 Strange Symbolism

MA Castle Clinton

Castle Clinton

Tourists looking to purchase tickets to the Statue of Liberty and Ellis Island enter an old circular stone structure in Battery Park called Castle Clinton. Ticket selling is by far the least exciting job in the fort's history, a rather banal function for a building that traces its origins to the founding of the United States.

Back in 1783, fresh from the victories of the Revolutionary War, New Yorkers gathered around the docks on November 25 to forever wave off the British from New York Harbor. When it was soon discovered that one last British flag remained hanging from a greased flagpole—a final goodbye prank, as it were—jaunty patriots shimmied up to remove it. This event would soon become the driving force of New York's annual Evacuation Day celebrations, a symbolic marker of the end of British rule. (If we could come up with a method to safely secure drunk revelers as they climbed greased flagpoles today, then we'd say let's bring it back!)

Battery Park in 1902, when Castle Clinton was the New York Aquarium.

But the threat of an unwelcome British return lingered on. In 1790, the city dismantled Fort George (the dilapidated fort built by the Dutch), and the cannons that gave the Battery its name were removed and replaced with a strolling promenade. But less than two decades later, new saber rattling by British forces so unnerved New Yorkers that they built new, stronger forts at locations scattered throughout the harbor. Some of them—like Fort Wadsworth on Staten Island and Castle Williams on Governors Island (see Chapter 1)—still stand today.

But none has had the inconceivable adventures of West Battery, completed in 1811 as an island fort, located 300 feet from shore and connected to the mainland by a long bridge. Its thick stone walls could withstand a vicious attack, and its 28 guns aimed into the harbor would surely beat back any aggressors. It was later renamed Castle Clinton, after New York's governor (and former mayor) DeWitt Clinton, a hopeful name, given Clinton's own political tenacity and endurance.

But while the War of 1812 would come to American shores, it never arrived in New York Harbor. After serving some minor military purposes, Castle Clinton was eventually sold by the federal government to the city in 1823. And it was then that things got decidedly more festive for the old fort.

First it was transformed into an entertainment palace, rechristened Castle Garden, and greatly expanded, with a spacious second floor and an ornate fountain at its center. Still accessed by a narrow bridge, the experience was magical and otherworldly for visitors, its gaslight illuminations dancing above the waves.

Castle Garden was a ballroom, concert venue, lecture space, and even beer hall. In 1824, the Marquis de Lafayette, the most exotic still-living embodiment of the Revolutionary era, was feted here by grateful New Yorkers. In 1842 Samuel Morse demonstrated a new gadget that would change the world—the telegraph. (A line was strung between here and Castle Williams; its first message was, rather dramatically, "What hath God wrought?" And they hadn't even seen their phone bill yet!) For

Care for a stroll? A lovely day at Castle Garden in the mid-nineteenth century.

a short time, you could even enjoy luxurious saltwater baths out on the Battery promenade.

But the most famous evenings at Castle Garden belonged to the Swedish opera singer Jenny Lind. Extensively hyped by impresario P. T. Barnum, the so-called Swedish nightingale brought New York music lovers to tears here on September 11 and 13, 1850, perhaps the most legendary concert nights in American history (pre–stadium seating, that is). "Jenny Lind has already won a hold on the sympathies of the American public, such as no other vocalist ever obtained," cooed the *New York Daily Tribune*. "The audience for which she sang was the greatest ever assembled at a concert in this city."

Just five years later, in 1855, Castle Garden would see thousands more foreign imports, albeit less enthusiastically proclaimed. For it was then that the old fort-turned-amusement venue became New York's first immigration depot, a desperately needed transformation, coming as a tidal wave of European immigrants vexed the ports. Newly arrived Irish and German immigrants during the 1840s and early '50s had been taken advantage of by greedy "runners," unscrupulous characters who led them into scams or false promises of housing and employment, often leaving them with neither (and empty pockets). Castle Garden, as an immigration depot, registered the new arrivals and provided vital connections with immigrant aid societies. It would be a proto–Ellis Island, processing more than 8 million people upon their arrival to America. Most likely some of you reading this have ancestors who passed through the halls of Castle Garden.

Castle Garden as an immigration station, 1861, the former battery swarming with activity. Millions of immigrants arriving in New York passed through this depot.

By 1890 the federal government finally got involved with immigration processing and built a new processing center upon a little island in New York Harbor, long ago owned by Samuel Ellis. This switch freed Castle Garden to occupy itself with some other residents — this time of the underwater variety.

After a redesign by the renowned architectural firm of McKim, Mead, and White, the New York Aquarium would open here in 1896, its former concert hall and processing desks replaced with the latest aquatic technology of the day. By this time, of course, landfill had joined the structure to the mainland. Families could now gallivant through Battery Park and into the front gates to explore a maze of open pools and glass exhibition tanks, filled with a variety of creatures that (more often than not) did not survive the changing of seasons.

They were a surprising yet appropriate pairing, the old fort and a bunch of tropical fish, replete with harbor waves crashing nearby. Unfortunately, Parks Commissioner Robert Moses was not a fan and decreed that the retrofitted old fort had finally performed her last number. In 1941, Moses used the construction of the Brooklyn–Battery Tunnel as an excuse to move the popular aquarium to Coney Island, snarling that "the Aquarium is an ugly wart on the main axis leading straight to the Statue of Liberty." The fort should be destroyed entirely, he explained, for "its guns never fired a shot against an enemy."

His destructive urges were only partially rebuffed by the community. Most of the frill and finery — almost everything that had been added since 1823 — was removed, leaving only the barren stone form of the original fort intact. And that's exactly how it has remained ever since. Castle Clinton received National Monument status in 1975.

Today the old fort quietly allows New York's showier landmarks their day in the sun. But we challenge you, Mr. Moses. There may never have been a shot fired from Castle Clinton, but these walls have seen more drama and have been more important to the American experience than almost any other American fort standing today.

Battery Park

POINTS OF INTEREST

1 LONG BATTERY LIFE Despite being completed just two years after the U.S. Custom House, the robustly green Battery Maritime Building has been one of the most mistreated buildings in all of downtown Manhattan since its construction in 1909. Its primary function, as a ferry terminal for vessels to and from 39th Street in Brooklyn, was eliminated in 1938, and the building was loaned out to private ferry operators, who trashed the place. Its most glamorous feature, a sparkling stained glass ceiling, was brazenly torn out at some point. Next door, its twin sister, the Whitehall Street Ferry Terminal, was gutted in a fire in 1991 and replaced with the high-tech Staten Island Ferry Terminal you see today.

Fortunately the Maritime Building is getting a fancy upgrade and even a couple of new glass floors. You can catch the Governors Island Ferry from here too. (*4 South Street*)

2 THE QUOTE INSIDE THE STATEN ISLAND FERRY TERMINAL Inside the Staten Island Ferry waiting room, emblazoned like a banner, is a line from the poem "Recuerdo" by Edna St. Vincent Millay, written in 1919. "We were very tired / We were very merry / We had gone back and forth all night on the ferry." Fun fact: Edna gets her middle name from St. Vincent's Hospital, once located in the West Village. Her uncle was a sailor who almost perished at sea in 1892, his life saved by the good doctors at St. Vincent's.

3 HOUSE OF THE SAINT Progress has swept away almost all the Colonial era structures from downtown Manhattan. However, the James Watson House, built in 1793, better known today as the Shrine of St. Elizabeth

Ann Bayley Seton, remains standing. Viewing it from across the street, sandwiched between cold, slender office towers, the house and adjoining parish seem like an apparition from another world.

Seton, the first American to be canonized by the Catholic Church, lived here only as a young woman from 1801 to 1803. Had she stayed another couple of decades, she could have been Herman Melville's babysitter. (*7 State Street*)

Praise be! A glorious relic of old New York on State Street.

4 THE BIRTHPLACE OF MOBY-DICK'S DAD (Vanished) No house survives, but you can find a plaque and a strange little bust of Herman Melville (1819–1891). He wrote about the Battery in his classic *Moby-Dick*:

> *There now is your insular city of the Manhattoes, belted round by wharves as Indian isles by coral reefs — commerce surrounds it with her surf. Right and left, the streets take you waterward. Its extreme downtown is the battery, where that noble mole is washed by waves, and*

cooled by breezes, which a few hours previous were out of sight of land. Look at the crowds of water-gazers there.

(*6 Pearl Street*)

5 THE NEW PANTHEON This area was the heart of the Gilded Age travel business, so it's no surprise to find the Alexander Hamilton U.S. Custom House here, once used to monitor and regulate the country's imports and exports. Its extravagant Beaux-Arts architecture was designed by Cass Gilbert and constructed between 1902 and 1907. European-style adornment drips from every surface like an overfrosted cake.

This is America! Well, America as depicted in Daniel Chester French's *Four Continents* outside the Custom House.

The building's exterior is loaded with wacky symbolism, locking in the imperial impressions and prejudices of the day in glorious marble. Daniel Chester French, best known for his Lincoln Memorial in Washington, D.C., was responsible for the four ornate depictions of "the four continents" at ground level—Asia, the Americas, Europe, and Africa. Look for the little Buddha sitting on Asia's lap, a cluster of marble cacti to the back of America, and the creepy robed figure at the back of Lady Europe.

But the real treasures are along the top: sculptural representations of the twelve countries considered to be the principal seafaring authorities. They stand here like a new pantheon of powers—or the cast of a great new superhero movie. Take note of statue #10. This fine armored woman used to represent Germany, but protests made during World War I required her transformation into a representation of Belgium.

Today this structure is home to Smithsonian's National Museum of the American Indian and offers a far more culturally sensitive tribute to Native American cultures inside than you'll find over some of its doorways. (*Bowling Green*)

6 THE CUTE LITTLE SUBWAY HOUSE The subway entrance in Battery Park is one of the loveliest in all of New York. Its history traces back to the beginnings of the subway itself when, in 1905, it was built by the subway's first operator: the Interborough Rapid Transit Company. Contrast the beauty of its limestone and granite exterior with the, er, grittier reality of the tracks and station below. (*Entrance to Battery Park*)

7 ON THE FENCE The oldest thing near Battery Park is not a tree, believe it or not, but the iron fence around Bowling Green, first erected in

A fine crest: A bit of Australia at 1 Broadway, the former home of the International Mercantile Marine Company.

1771. Certainly a Founding Father or two probably touched this fence, so go ahead and rub it for good luck! (*Whitehall Street*)

8 ECHOES OF STEAMSHIP ROW More than 100 years ago you'd head to Bowling Green to buy tickets for transatlantic ocean liners. The ornate buildings that held the offices of the two major lines are still here: 11 Broadway for the White Star Line and 25 Broadway for the Cunard Line.

In 1912 hundreds of panicked New Yorkers filled the streets in front of the White Star building after hearing rumors that its prestigious *RMS Titanic* had sunk. Less than three years later, the scene was grimly repeated in front of the Cunard Building after news of the destruction of the *RMS Lusitania*.

At 1 Broadway, the former home of the International Mercantile Marine Company, observe the spectacular depictions of the great ports of the world (added during the building's remodeling in the early 1920s). At the corner, next to each other, you'll find Southampton (the *Titanic*'s port of departure) and Liverpool (the *Lusitania*'s intended destination). (*1 Broadway*)

9 THE PRESIDENT MOVES IN (Vanished) New York was the heart of the fledgling United States federal government from 1789 to 1891 and was George Washington's first home as president. He first lived in a home on Cherry Street (we'll get to that later) that was not to his liking, so he moved into a home at 39–41 Broadway. Also living with him inside the house: many of Washington's slaves from his home in Mount Vernon.[1] (*39–41 Broadway*)

---

1   The Washingtons had seven slaves with them, including a fifteen-year-old girl named Ona, who served as Martha's personal assistant.

The Day They Tore Down Poor King George

Bowling Green is New York City's oldest park, tracing its creation to the era of British New York. In 1733 wealthy landlords leased the property from the royal Crown to lay out a charming lawn, surrounded by an iron fence, its grasses occasionally tended to by grazing sheep. And yes, on sunny afternoons, local residents really would bowl here.

But affairs of a more violent nature would shake the park more than four decades later. In 1770, as a not-so-subtle reminder to the increasingly independence-minded locals of who was boss around here, a stark, imposing equestrian statue of King George was installed in the center of the park. Paired with the nearby fort (also renamed for George), it was hard to shake the feeling that a certain someone was making a royal point.

The Sons of Liberty yank down the statue of King George III and make a mess of Bowling Green.

In 1776, revolutionary rebels had their own point to make. On July 2, the Continental Congress in Philadelphia adopted a resolution to declare independence from the oppression of Great Britain. Two days later, on July 4, they issue their Declaration of Independence, a de facto declaration of war.

Meanwhile, General George Washington had amassed his Continental Army in New York. One week later, on July 9, he received his copy of the Declaration and boldly read it aloud to his troops in the city's common grounds (the area of today's City Hall Park). New Yorkers and troops alike quickly became so whipped up with patriotic fervor that they marched down to Bowling Green to deface the most obnoxious symbol of British despotism.

Soon the little old park was packed with angry patriots. They attacked King George's statue with clubs, axes, and knives, intending to melt the whole thing down into bullets and shoot it back with deadly force toward the British troops heading for New York Harbor. However, only a small amount would ever be used for this purpose.

Today an amusing bit of that ill-fated monument still hangs around in New York City: The horse's tail resides at the New-York Historical Society.

10 THE SOLAR SECRET OF THE KOREAN WAR MEMORIAL

Perhaps the most eye-catching of Battery Park's many war memorials is actually a sort of "nonstatue": the New York Korean War Veterans Memorial

by Mac Adams, which was dedicated in 1991 and depicts the silhouette of a soldier cut into a granite obelisk. The memorial was specifically angled to create a startling annual occurrence. On July 27th, at around 10 a.m., the sun streaks through the head of the silhouette, throwing a spotlight upon a plaque on the sidewalk. It's the exact moment that the two sides in the Korean War agreed to an armistice, ending the war (1950–1953).

(Side Note: Every time you see an obelisk in Manhattan, take note. There's always a weird story, as we shall see....)

The haunting Korean War Memorial in Battery Park.

11 STAND HERE: The corner of Battery Place and West Street, looking north. *Why?* Obviously you've been taken with the views of New York Harbor and all the fun things that surround Battery Park. But standing

here at the foot of West Street— which is actually continuing underneath you, via the Battery Park Underpass—affords you an unencumbered view of the most beautiful skyscrapers in downtown Manhattan. Look at them, all lined up in a picture-perfect row: the Whitehall Building (17 Battery Place, 1902–1904) and its extension, Greater Whitehall (the largest office building in New York when it was completed in 1910 at 26 Washington

Building blocks: Impressive old skyscrapers viewed from the tip of Manhattan.

Street); the Downtown Athletic Club Building (20 West Street, 1930); and glamorous 21 West Street (1931), which is as art deco as it gets. And One World Trade Center, of course. (*Corner of Battery Place and West Street*)

12 THE PIER WITH NO PEERS (LITERALLY) Manhattan's shoreline was for much of its history crowded with piers of various lengths and structural integrities. The western side of the island had the largest, most elaborate piers to serve enormous steamships and shipping vessels, large sheds that could accommodate thousands of people and tons of freight. Pier A, originally built for use by the docks department, is the last surviving example of this grand tradition and is a striking one. It was built between 1884 and 1886 with the

Pier A, looking very dapper in 1935 (photo: Berenice Abbott).

Statue of Liberty in mind; not only are there clear views of Lady Liberty from here, but its tower roof is painted green to emulate her oxidized body.

But it's the bling on top—an elegant 1919 clock—that's the most eye-catching. It was installed as a World War I memorial, the first such commemoration here or anywhere in the United States. (*22 Battery Place*)

13 STRANGE SYMBOLISM The award for the neighborhood's most unusual architecture goes to the Museum of Jewish Heritage, completed in 1997. Almost every brick and glass pane in this poignant museum works toward its symbolism, beginning with its curious, six-sided pyramidal roof—a nod to the Star of David, each side representing 1 million Jews who died in the Holocaust. Now you may be asking, "Why did they build a Holocaust museum here?" The answer becomes obvious as you emerge from the galleries into the upstairs sky-lit room, where bay windows neatly frame both the Statue of Liberty and Ellis Island in the harbor. During many years of persecution in Europe, millions of Jews fled to America for the promise of a better life.

Even its original address was symbolic: 18 First Place. The number 18 is written as the Hebrew "chai," meaning "life." Later it was renumbered. (*36 Battery Place*)

Before Times Square became the epicenter of New York's New Year's Eve celebrations, people gathered in the streets around Trinity Church to greet the arrival of a new year. From a report in the *New York Sun*, January 1, 1887:

> The staid and respectable Knickerbockers who were put under the crumbling tablets in Trinity graveyard many years ago did not arise at midnight last night under the mistaken but perfectly justifiable impression that Gabriel had arrived, but an infinite variety of terrestrial beings, with horns of many tones, much volume and no harmony, put the whole power of their lungs and the enthusiasm of their souls into an effort to let everybody downtown and, if possible, even the peaceful buried Knickerbockers, understand that the new year had really come at last.

> The immediate neighborhood of old Trinity was like a magnet from 10 o'clock until midnight to the hundreds of unoccupied men and boys looking for something to do in honor of the change in the calendar.

> At 11½ o'clock, Broadway in front of and near the tall spired church seemed to be about as full of people as it could be. The chimes [of Trinity's church bells] kept up their pealing intermittently until midnight, or at least it is generally so believed. No bells could be distinguished however in the awful medley of tin horns which sounded with renewed force at the very moment of midnight.

Chapter 3//

West Financial District

Just another day on Wall Street in 1903, with Washington
and the Sub-Treasury Building (today's Federal Hall)
to the right and Trinity Church in the distance.

SITUATE THE READER
-West Financial District-

This district—containing Trinity Church, the skyscrapers to the church's west, the World Trade Center site, and Battery Park City—holds the secrets of two great eras in New York City's history, eras more than two hundred years apart.

Trinity Church is a religious vestige of the British Empire's rule over New York City, which lasted from 1664 to 1783. In 1705, the Crown deeded a large portion of land to Trinity that extended up the west side of the island from Fulton Street to the area of today's West Village. Unlike the busy center of town east of here,[1] the west side of the city was only sparsely developed with farms and small docks. In 1754, the church received a royal charter to establish the city's first institution of higher learning: King's College. This would later become Columbia University.

Trinity profited from their grant and, like any good real estate pro, invested in other potentially valuable lots of land. Long after the Revolutionary War and British evacuation, Trinity still wielded extraordinary civic power in its holdings. During the nineteenth century, they were the second-largest landowner in Manhattan (after John Jacob Astor). To this day, Trinity is one of the wealthiest parishes in the world, thanks to the power and glory of Manhattan real estate.

When the land grant was issued in 1705, Trinity was referred to as "the Church Farm," owing to the then-undeveloped nature of its surroundings. Flash forward to the 1960s and a city in desperate need of jumpstarting its business district. The World Trade Center, built partially on the old royal grant, was one of New York's great engineering undertakings of the mid-twentieth century, a controversial project by the Port Authority of New York and New Jersey that took more than a decade to complete. So much ground was excavated during its construction—well over 1 million cubic yards—that the neighborhood of Battery Park City was created from the removed land.

---

1   That would be the area described in Chapter 4.

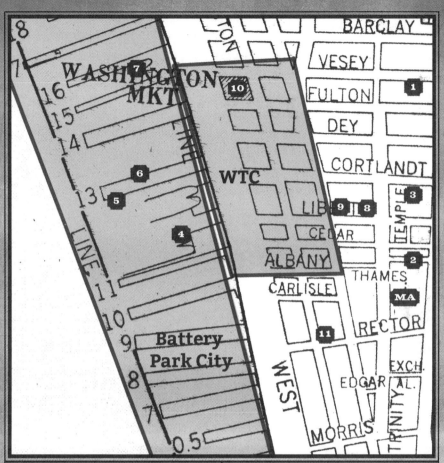

POINTS OF INTEREST

1 The Mysterious Stones

2 Stand Here

3 A Building in Stitches

4 The First Officer to Die in the Line of Duty

5 Read This Quote

6 Put on a Happy Face!

7 The Secret of the Irish Cottage

8 A Shelter in Time of Need

9 Two Sides of a Fire Station

10 The Magic Elevator

11 St. George and the Dragon

MA Burial Ground of Trinity Church

The Burial Ground of Trinity Church

Trinity Church is the greatest living embodiment of the days of British New York, both an instrument and a defender of royal reach over the colony. It stood front and center in the decisions that would unite many (but not all of) the people against the Crown.

But we're not talking about the structure we call Trinity Church today.

The first Trinity Church, built on the site of today's church in 1698, was reduced to ashes by the Great Fire of 1776. Its replacement, constructed after the British fled town, was torn down in 1839 due to another natural force: fierce snowstorms that weakened the roof. The stunning brownstone structure that today calls itself Trinity Church was designed by the renowned architect Richard Upjohn (1802–1878), the man who more or less designed every mid-nineteenth century church in America (either literally or, more often, indirectly through imitation). When it opened in 1846, this third Trinity Church became the tallest building in New York City, a record it would hold for an impressive forty-four years.

But only the church building is new. That earlier history that unfolded during the dawning days of the British American empire can still be found here. But it's mostly underground....

The burial ground of Trinity Church (and that of St. Paul's Chapel, located six blocks up the street from here) make for some of downtown Manhattan's most

The strange fate of Trinity Church, an elder statesman amid the skyscrapers.

striking visual juxtapositions, as haunting slabs of stone, tilted and broken, contrast with the expanse of steel and concrete towering around them. If placed upon a desolate hill on a dark and stormy evening, Trinity's churchyard would fit naturally into a creepy Bela Lugosi movie. But here, gazing down Wall Street, it sits rather incongruously, a captive inside a constructed canyon.

Its star-studded burial ground speaks to New Yorkers' continued reverence for Trinity. As the city became wealthier, the church became an acceptable arena for flaunting one's status, character, and even style. Pews were sold or rented to the city's most prominent families, and space was reserved in their burial ground for the final resting places of its most affluent congregants.

The Trinity Church burial ground became such an esteemed place that exceptions were made for it when, in 1851, the rapidly expanding city passed an ordinance forbidding further burials south of 86th Street. Eventually, Trinity would acquire another burial ground far uptown at 550 West 155th Street (at Broadway), which today hosts an equally impressive lineup of mayors, artists, and socialites.[2]

A very grave view: Trinity Place behind Trinity Church, 1861.

Back downtown, however, the star of this posthumous production is Alexander Hamilton (1755–1804), the first treasury secretary, the most rascally and passionate of the Founding Fathers, and arguably the greatest genius of the Revolutionary era. On July 11, 1804, Hamilton was mortally wounded in a duel by Aaron Burr, his political nemesis and the sitting vice president of the

2   See Chapter 25.

United States at the time. Even with Trinity's British association still smarting, there was little question as to the final resting place for this graduate of King's College, a place where Hamilton had, as Ron Chernow would write, "studied and lived, practiced law and served his country."Rather offputtingly, the stone bearing the name of Hamilton's wife, Eliza Schuyler (1757–1854), is placed less honorably in front of his like a welcome mat. This kind and especially patient woman would live another 50 years after her husband's passing.[3] During that time, Trinity would be rebuilt and the churchyard vaults vastly overcrowded. She earned her place, connected to yet independent of her husband.

Nearby sits the engineer Robert Fulton (1765–1815), the man largely responsible for perfecting steam power and for crafting the first commercial

Fierceness: The statesman John Watts in all his monumental glory, standing proud in Trinity Church Cemetery.

steamship, the steam generator, and even the submarine. He died suddenly in the winter of 1815 after rescuing a friend from drowning in the icy Hudson River.

But wait, who's that bewigged gentleman with his own life-size statue, the only such bronze personage anywhere in the churchyard? This is John Watts (1749–1836), a New York congressman and judge who left a remarkable legacy. Watts's close friend Robert Leake had willed the politician a fortune to open a home for orphaned children. That organization, Leake and Watts Services, is a social services agency that operates to this day.[4]

Among the tombstones situated in the northern grounds, you'll find the final resting place of Albert Gallatin (1761–1849), also a former secretary of the treasury and a visionary ethnologist who studied America's native people. Gallatin was a true Founding Father, like

---

3   Remarkably, she also lived for a time in the area of today's East Village. See Chapter 10.
4   There is an astonishing secret related to Mr. Watts that sits behind the Cathedral of St. John the Divine. See Chapter 24.

Hamilton. But consider this rather academic historical quirk: Gallatin was the founder of the University of the City of New York, today's New York University. And here he resides for all time, at Trinity—the former home of King's College, today's Columbia University. Having it both ways, Al?

The centuries-old tombstones of Trinity Church Cemetery have seen it all.

Rich ties to education and heritage abound along the pathways and in the vaults below. Early New York icons of free speech John Peter Zenger (1697–1746) and William Bradford (1663–1752) are here, as are Revolutionary War figures like Marinus Willett (1740–1830) and Horatio Gates (1727–1806).

But the real intrigue in Trinity Churchyard comes from those less familiar to us today, the regular, undecorated folk. Here lie some of the great mysteries of old New York—love and ambition and loss and death, all contained under stones that have watched the city grow up.

What sort of man was young David Ogden, who died, according to his stone, "on the 27th of September 1798, in the 29th year of his age, fell a victim, to the then prevailing epidemic"? (That epidemic was yellow fever.)

What were the dire circumstances surrounding the deaths of two siblings in the summer of 1762 that inspired their tombstone lamentation: "Sleep lovely babes since God hath calld thee hence, we must submit to his blefst [blessed] will and providence"?

And then there's little Richard Churcher, who died when he was five years old in 1681. The New York that his young eyes saw, ever so briefly, is completely different from ours today. He lived to see the wall on Wall Street. His life predated Trinity Church itself, not chartered until 1697. More than 330 years of history have played out since five-year-old Richard Churcher died. His is the oldest gravestone presently standing in all of New York City. RIP, little guy.

West Financial District

POINTS OF INTEREST

1 THE MYSTERIOUS STONES St. Paul's Chapel is the oldest building in lower Manhattan. It became the tallest building in the city when finished in 1766. (The same distinction was bestowed upon Trinity when it was completed in 1846.) St. Paul's nobly survived the Great Fire of 1776 to see the inauguration of President George Washington, who worshipped here during New York's tenure as the nation's capital from 1789 to 1790. It was also a focal

Irish revolutionary Thomas Addis Emmet is not buried here, and it freaks us out.

point for grief in the days after September 11, 2001, its gate adorned with pictures and mementos of those killed in the attacks that occurred just outside its western fence.

St. Paul's burial ground is a nice companion to that of Trinity Church, and is filled with the tombstones of old families and prominent citizens of the eighteenth and nineteenth centuries.

But it's what is *not* buried here that might send a chill up your spine. Near the front of the cemetery is an obelisk-shaped tribute to Thomas Addis Emmet (1764–1827), an Irish revolutionary. The only catch: He's not buried here. Nobody is. Etched upon the stone you'll find a list of coordinates for which there is no known explanation. (Cue: Chill!)

(*Remember the obelisks*. They will come into play throughout this book.)

The second stone of some mystery is that belonging to George Frederick Cooke (1756–1812), an acclaimed English actor who died in New York. It's believed that some portion of his body is buried in this cemetery. In a (perhaps apocryphal) example of backstage drama, his protégé Edmund Kean is believed to have snatched either a finger or a toe from Cooke's grave as a keepsake. A related, if more practical, rumor has it that Mr. Cooke's skull was also taken and used as a prop in performances of *Hamlet*. (What actor doesn't dream of returning to the stage!)

Truth or fiction, this incident does explain one of New York's most dramatic ghost legends: It's said that in the dead of night, the headless body of the great actor scours the graveyard in search of his missing parts. (*209 Broadway*)

2 STAND HERE: Somewhere in the middle of Thames Street, between Broadway and Trinity Place. *Why?* This isn't the most pleasant spot to stand. In fact, it's almost perpetually in a shadow. The two buildings on either side—the Trinity Building and the U.S. Realty Building—were created at the same time (between 1904 and 1907) and practically, but not quite, match each other. (Peek inside the lobbies later to spot the differences.)

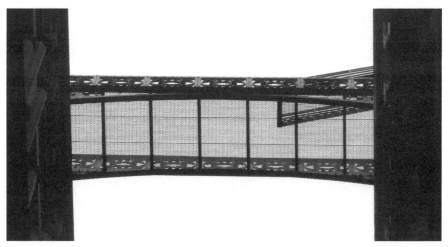

It's a lovely bridge, but we'd prefer to stay on the ground, thank you.

Stand in the middle of the street and look up—to the very top! A very small, very delicate footbridge, the highest building traverse in Manhattan, connects the buildings. It has been a feature of these Gothic structures since 1912. *Who walks on that thing?* (*Thames Street, between Broadway and Trinity Place*)

3 A BUILDING IN STITCHES (Vanished) For a few short months from 1908 to 1909, the building that stood here was the tallest in the world: the forty-seven-story Singer Building, the skyscraper trophy built by the head of the Singer Sewing Machine Company. Its unusual appearance—a

The Singer Building had the title of World's Tallest Building all sewed up in 1908.

narrow red tower shooting up from a chunky base—was among the most glorious on the young New York skyline. Its interior was festooned with bronze medallions engraved with the images of needle, thread, and bobbin. Because we can't have nice things, they ripped it apart at the seams and tore it down in 1967. Prior to 2001, it remained the tallest building in the world ever demolished.

Its replacement, the steel monolith One Liberty Plaza, was constructed, unsurprisingly, for U.S. Steel and was completed in 1973, the same year as the opening of the World Trade Center. (*165 Broadway*)

BATTERY PARK CITY

The neighborhood of Battery Park City didn't exist before 1970. Over two decades, the rickety piers of the western shore were replaced with landfill and sand, upon which gleaming condos and apartment towers were constructed. At times it still has that new neighborhood smell. (Maybe that's just the marina.) The community has had to install relics of history here, dispersed in surprising places alongside its carefully manicured lawns.

4 THE FIRST OFFICER TO DIE IN THE LINE OF DUTY What's especially somber about this memorial to the fallen members of the New York Police Department is that it was dedicated on October 20, 1997, less than four years before the attack on the World Trade Center in 2001.

The first name carved into the monument—the first officer to die in active duty in New York—belongs to a policeman named James Cahill. He was killed while attempting to stop a robbery in the area of today's East Village. He died in 1854, nine years after the force was formed in 1845.

Immediately under the words "IN MEMORIAM," locate the name Joseph Petrosino, who was killed on March 12, 1909. He is perhaps the most famous officer who ever died in the line of duty. Read more about him in Chapter 8. (*Battery Park City, Liberty Street and South End Avenue*)

5 QUOTES AT NORTH COVE MARINA Those quotes running along the barrier at North Cove Marina belong to two great New York–area writers. "City of the world, for all the races are here" is from Walt Whitman's "City of Ships" in *Leaves of Grass*. Next to it runs, "One need never leave the confines of New York to get all the greenery one wishes," from "Meditations in an Emergency" by Frank O'Hara, written in 1957.

Too bad they cut it off there, as that line continues and O'Hara gets a little snarky: "I can't even enjoy a blade of grass unless I know there's a subway handy, or a record store or some other sign that people do not totally *regret* life." Let's put that on a fence somewhere! (*Battery Park City, North Cove Marina*)

A silly face with a serious story stands in Battery Park.

6 PUT ON A HAPPY FACE! Four pieces of the Berlin Wall stand in New York City today.[5] These slabs, boldly painted on one side, were once part of the eighty-seven-mile wall that separated East and West Berlin. The absurd

---

5   Where to find the others: at United Nations Headquarters, at 520 Madison Avenue, and believe it…or not, at Ripley's Believe It or Not! on 42nd Street.

blue face with gigantic red lips faced west. The barren side reflects the severity of the east. (*Battery Park City, between Gateway Plaza and North Cove Marina*)

7 THE SECRET OF THE IRISH COTTAGE The Irish Hunger Memorial, completed in 2002, is a life-size diorama of an ancient Irish countryside, "a fragment torn from Slievemore and transplanted to Manhattan," according to its creator, Brian Tolle. Come here on a gray, windy day, and you'll feel like you've just been dropped into a blustery romance novel. The memorial commemorates the plight of thousands of Irish immigrants who voyaged to America in the mid-nineteenth century to escape the terrible famine of their old country.

Cut them some Slack: This mysterious Irish cottage tells a poignant story.

The memorial contains stones and vegetation from various areas of Ireland, but its most peculiar import are the remnants of a mysterious cottage. This be no fakery. The cottage housed six generations of the Slack family from the parish of Attymass outside Ballina in County Mayo. Attymass was the first parish in Ireland to record human deaths from the dire famine that swept over the country starting in the 1840s. That these broken walls, seemingly timeless, stand in Battery Park City is incongruous and gives you pause. (*Battery Park City, North End Avenue and Vesey Street*)

Return to glory: The spectacular One World Trade Center, at 1,776 feet tall.

When they officially opened in 1973, the World Trade Center towers, designed by Minoru Yamasaki, were considered the apotheosis of postmodern design and the apex of New York City construction. Everything grand and intolerable about the city in the late 1960s and early 1970s was embodied in these two impossibly tall shafts of metal. Today it's impossible to forget them; their memory is knit close into the surrounding area. The two sleek towers that once stood over downtown Manhattan are visible still, their footprints now the shape of plunging fountains next to the National September 11 Memorial and Museum, their height recalled in the powerful sweep of One World Trade Center, their likenesses reproduced on countless cheap souvenirs found along the perimeter of the site.

8 A SHELTER IN TIME OF NEED This would be an otherwise ordinary deli, a rather standard type of snack seller found on thousands of corners throughout the city. This particular deli opened in 1972 to cater to the thousands of employees who worked inside the newly opened World Trade Center. But on September 11, 2001, it served another purpose, functioning as one of four emergency triage centers, its shelves lined with emergency supplies for the National Disaster Medical System (NDMS). Powered only by a generator, the deli became the home base for rescue workers and recovery crew for weeks following the attacks. (*112 Liberty Street*)

9 TWO SIDES OF A FIRE STATION The simple station house for Engine Company 10 is graced with moving and emotional artifacts along its two street-side walls. You can't miss the spectacular bas-relief sculpture on its Greenwich Street side, dedicated to the hundreds of firefighters who perished on September 11, 2001.

The Liberty Street side has a very modest plaque, unveiled at the building's dedication in April 30, 1979, with mayor Ed Koch officiating. Life was much simpler then. (*124 Liberty Street*)

10 THE MAGIC ELEVATOR From the observation decks of One World Trade Center, you may feel that you're inside a spacecraft floating dizzyingly over the city. This vantage point affords a bird's-eye view of many of Manhattan's greatest marvels: the grid plan of streets and avenues, the bursts of skyscraper developments downtown and farther up in Midtown, the higher topology of upper Manhattan. (We'll get to all of these things later.)

Yet the ultimate history-lesson-as-thrill-ride comes from the high-tech (and high-speed!) elevators. As you ascend on your forty-seven-second journey, video screens reveal the rapidly unfolding history of Manhattan, as it evolves from swampland to the modern metropolis. It's so awe-inspiring that you may just want to keep riding it all day. (*One World Trade Center*)

11 ST. GEORGE AND THE DRAGON One hundred years ago, strolling along Washington and Rector Streets, you would have found yourself within the enclave of New York's first Middle Eastern community. Its residents and businessmen were mostly of Syrian or Lebanese descent, first arriving during

We're the Kids in America: The little faces of Little Syria, photo taken 1910–1915.

the late-nineteenth century. Little Syria (or the Syrian Quarter) featured rug shops and restaurants with "exotic" cuisine mentioned frequently by the newspapers of the day. In many ways it resembled the early days of Chinatown—a closed community, rich in history and confounding to many New Yorkers.

Most of the neighborhood was eliminated with the construction of the Brooklyn–Battery Tunnel in 1950, and many residents relocated to communities in Brooklyn and Queens. But one stunning reminder of this forgotten community still exists—the former St. George's Syrian Catholic Church. St. George's is the most playful building on the street, thanks to the wondrous terra-cotta relief over the door depicting St. George slaying a dragon. (You just don't see enough church dragons anymore, do you?) Today it has been transformed into a restaurant and lounge, so you can raise a glass to the old fire-breather. (*103 Washington Street*)

On fire: A little mythical drama at St. George's Syrian Catholic Church.

PETER STUYVESANT'S RULES FOR DRINKING

When Peter Stuyvesant arrived on the shores of rowdy and chaotic New Amsterdam, he put his foot down (or more precisely, his wooden peg down) on some of the settlement's more disreputable practices. In 1647 he laid down the following laws for drinking and selling liquor:

I'm Peter Stuyvesant and I'm no fun.

1. "Henceforth no new taproom, tavern, or inn shall be opened."

2. "The taverns, taprooms, and inns, already established, may continue for at least four consecutive years, but in the meantime the owners shall be obliged to engage in some other honest business at this place."

3. "The tavern-keepers and tapsters shall henceforth not be allowed to sell or give beer, wine, brandy, or strong waters to Indians or provide them with it by intermediaries."

4. "To prevent all fighting and mishaps they shall daily report to the Officer, whether anybody has been hurt or wounded at their houses, under the penalty of forfeiting their business and a fine of one pound Flemish for every hour after the hurt or wound has been inflicted and been concealed by the tapster or tavern-keeper."

5. "The orders, heretofore published against unseasonable night tippling and intemperate drinking on the Sabbath, shall be obeyed by the tavern-keepers and tapsters with close attention."

Needless to say, Stuyvesant's buzzkill regulations neither sobered up the locals nor filled up the church pews on Sunday.

Chapter 4///
East Financial District

A view of bustling street life along Wall Street in the nineteenth century, top hats and all.

SITUATE THE READER
-East Financial District-

This compact little neighborhood comprises most of the original Dutch settlement of New Amsterdam. No really, this was pretty much all of it.

Many of today's streets follow the exact same bends and twists as those first paths laid long ago, and some even trace their names to Dutch origins. Chief among these is one of New York's most famous thoroughfares: Wall Street.

The hodgepodge of skyscrapers and landmarks that line Wall Street today look down over the site where an actual wall once stood. "De Waal Straat" was indeed home to an impressive barrier, constructed in 1653 of earth, rock, and fifteen-foot timber planks sold to the Dutch by a notorious Englishman named Thomas Baxter, who later pirated Dutch fishing boats with his rugged group of "Rhode Island marauders."[1]

When New Amsterdam's increasingly jittery director-general, Peter Stuyvesant, called upon the colony's wealthiest residents to fund the construction of the wall, he hoped to prevent not only attacks from the native Lenape tribes, but also those from those pesky English colonies up north. (Essentially, the wall that gave us Wall Street was built to keep out the crazies from Connecticut and Massachusetts!)

Early in the 1660s, the Dutch enhanced their wall to include brass cannons and two sturdy gates—one at today's intersection of Wall and Broadway (for land), the other at Wall and Pearl Streets near the water's edge. All of this wall building and upgrading was carried out by slave labor, provided by the Dutch West India Company.

When the British took over New Amsterdam in 1664—renaming it New York—they kept the wall intact for a time, although it had become more a relic than a serious defense. It was finally torn down in 1699, and some of the material was salvaged to help construct a new City Hall nearby at the corner of Nassau Street and the newly christened Wall Street. When the British were sent packing in 1783 by the Americans, the City Hall building was renamed Federal Hall and became the first official headquarters of the new American government from 1789 to 1791.

---

1   As described in 1909 by Mariana Griswold Van Rensselaer in *History of the City of New York in the Seventeenth Century*.

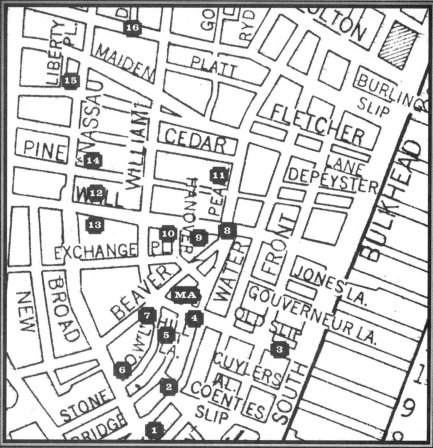

POINTS OF INTEREST

1 The Attacks on Fraunces Tavern

2 The Old City Tavern, Still Open for Business

3 The First Precinct

4 The Home of Captain Kidd

5 The Shortest Street in Manhattan

6 Look at This Awesome Sign

7 The Marble Columns of Pompeii

8 The New York Slave Market

9 Gods and Sea Monsters

10 Proof That the City Was Once Quite Small

11 The Secret of the Pyramids

12 The Book of the Freemasons

13 Pockmarked History

14 Shadows of the Past

15 There Be Alligators!

16 Opening Cries of the Revolutionary War

MA Hanover Square

Hanover Square and the Great Fire of 1835

Stone Street, Pearl Street, and the other curvy, narrow lanes that surround Hanover Square may say more about New York's history than any other area in the city. They're like the rings of an old tree.

Today's streets mimic the original lanes used by the residents of Dutch New Amsterdam, who were themselves following old Lenape Indian paths

The Merchants Exchange ablaze during the Great Fire of 1835 (lithograph: N. Currier).

established long before. Stone Street retains only a portion of its original length (the lobby of the out-of-place 85 Broad Street tower helpfully brings the two sections of the street back together). Pearl Street was the original coastline.

These street names originate from a variety of eras. Pearl Street was a British corruption of the Dutch "Peral-Straat," named for the pearly oysters that bedazzled the riverbed. William Street is named for the Dutch landowner Willem (or Wilhelmus) Beekman; he was such a stand-up guy that you'll see his name all over the city.

And Beaver Street might have the most important name of all. As New York was initially a settlement for fur traders, city fathers named a street for the mammal that traders killed the most. Beaver "wool," as they called it, was exported from the new colony to Europe in the seventeenth century, where it was all the rage.

Hanover Square sounds *rather* British, and it is, named in the 1730s for the English dynastic House of Hanover, of which King George III was a member. His was the equestrian statue ripped down in Bowling Green in 1776 (see Chapter 2). He was also almost certainly mentally ill, but that's for another book.

So you get the picture: Both the physical streets and their names go way back. But with the exception of Fraunces Tavern (which is today mostly a reconstruction anyway), no buildings stand here that are more than 200 years old. Where'd they all go? Almost everything, from Wall Street all the way down to the Battery, was destroyed in a single terrible incident: the Great Fire of 1835.

Stone Street charms today, but it too was engulfed by flames during the 1835 blaze.

By the 1830s the area below Wall Street had become the commercial heart of the island. Hanover Square, its name restored following the understandably anti-British period that swept through New York following the Revolutionary War, was by now surrounded by newspaper offices and book publishers. The streets bustled all day long with residents and merchants (many of whom lived above their shops). The side streets just off the square were lined with dry goods wholesalers and warehouses, each packed with merchandise and supplies that were being bought, traded, and stored — fabrics, housewares, lumber — all of it fueling the city's growth, and all of it quite flammable.

On the windy and exceptionally cold evening of December 16, 1835, a fire broke out at a dry goods wholesaler at the corner of today's Pearl Street and Exchange Place. As the streets were so narrow, flames handily leaped from building to building. Volunteer firemen from around the city raced to the spot, the area of the fire now quickly growing, to try to contain the blaze, but they found themselves direly outmatched. As they frantically pumped water from the East River, the frigid night air froze the water to ice right inside their leather hoses. Their pumps jammed. When, finally, they could get the water to flow again, the frozen spray blew back upon the men, covering their coats in ice.

Soon every bell and alarm in town was sounded, and anxious (and curious) New Yorkers raced down to witness the fire. Afraid that the fire would soon engulf their shops, business owners began tossing their inventory out into the street. Some hauled their property off to seemingly safer buildings outside the path of the blaze, only to see those buildings too succumb as the fire, spreading unpredictably, changed course and engulfed them.

City on fire: The horrific scene from the corner of William and Wall Streets (image: Nicolino Calyo).

"[T]he fierce dragon of flame soon overtook them in these places of fancied security and devoured the edifices with their precious contents," wrote historian Benson John Lossing in 1884. "When the shutters, warped with heat, were unfastened and flew open, the interior of these great stores appeared like huge glowing furnaces. The copper on their roofs were melted and fell like drops of burning sweat to the pavement."

For a time, Hanover Square was giving shelter to valuable goods, but these too were caught aflame by flying embers. Saltpeter began exploding a block away. For several hours, the fire raged on, spreading uncontrollably. By midnight New York's entire East Side was in flames. The fierce night wind blew embers, like fiery bombs, across the East River, catching the rooftops of Brooklyn houses on fire.

Amazingly, those raging bitter winds kept the inferno to the south side of Wall Street. But soon the Tontine Coffee House, by 1835 one of the city's most important financial centers, was endangered, its shingles now flecked in fire. One wealthy bystander, Oliver Hull, announced he would give $100 to the firemen's fund if rescuers could save the building. His offer was accepted—

the unpaid volunteers who made up New York's fire department were able to save the Tontine from the blaze.[2]

Firefighters had no other choice—they had to use dynamite on their own city in order to save it. Only by blowing up the buildings in the blaze's path were they able to stop its terrible progress.

By the time the last flame was extinguished, New York had lost more than 700 buildings, leaving a sizable portion of the city (which, at this time, only extended up to about 14th Street) in smoldering ashes. The city had suffered a financial and emotional wallop, and countless businesses simply vanished or went bankrupt. Incredibly, not a single human life was lost in the disaster.

"That portion of the city which has been destroyed contained more of talent, respectability, generosity, industry, enterprise, and all the qualities that ennoble and dignify our race, than the same space, perhaps in any other city in the world," wrote the *New-York Mirror* two weeks later. The city quickly rebuilt over the so-called burnt district with a patriotic zeal.[3]

Wall Street was nearly reduced to ashes by the Great Fire.

Most of the buildings that today line this portion of Pearl Street, Stone Street, and South William Street were constructed in the years immediately following the fire. Several have experienced radical redesigns, but most retain their original form: three- to four-story Greek Revival buildings, the most popular architectural style of the postfire period. For decades, commercial concerns here sold everything from crockery and umbrellas to an exotic variety of imports. Today's Stone Street is where you go for a pint (or three), perhaps a meal of fish and chips, and a side order of forgotten history.

---

2   Firefighters from several companies later laid claim to the prize, and several witnesses were called to testify before proper credit was given to the intrepid men of Engine Company No. 13.
3   A similar spirit would inspire Americans to rebuild after another disaster, a quarter of a mile west of here and 166 years later, following the attacks of September 11, 2001.

East Financial District

1 THE ATTACKS ON FRAUNCES TAVERN Fraunces Tavern is one of the most important historical buildings in New York City, the site of meetings during the Revolutionary War and the place of George Washington's emotional farewell speech to his Continental Army officers after America had secured its freedom in 1783. In the two brief years that New York served as the new nation's capital, the offices of the Departments of War and Foreign Affairs were located right here in the Tavern. At some point, both Alexander Hamilton and Aaron Burr worked here. Can't you just see them with big stacks of parchment, squeezing past each other in the hallway?

Much of the colonial exterior you see today is a fanciful reconstruction. But Fraunces has always endured as a persistent embodiment of American virtue, even surviving destruction twice by terrorizing forces — 200 years apart.

Fraunces Tavern is one of New York's true historic survivors, a witness to the birth of America.

In the opening chords of the Revolutionary War, Samuel Fraunces was an open supporter of America's fight against the British. During the summer of 1775, when student instigators from nearby King's College — including the aforementioned Hamilton—stole a cannon from the Battery and fired at a British naval ship, the war vessel returned the compliment, sending a cannonball crashing through Fraunces's roof.

A more deadly attack occurred exactly 200 years later and from a truly mysterious source. The tavern was busy with a lunchtime Wall Street crowd on January 24, 1975, when a bomb tore through the dining room, killing four men and nearly blowing out the side of the restaurant. The bomb was planted by FALN (Armed Forces of Puerto Rican National Liberation), a rogue terrorist group that bombed several locations in New York in the 1970s. No one was ever arrested for the attack.

Inside the dining room along the Broad Street side hangs a large mural depicting New York in 1717. It's scarred by a large crack, a lasting reminder of the FALN attack. (*54 Pearl Street*)

2 THE OLD CITY TAVERN, STILL OPEN FOR BUSINESS The office tower at 85 Broad Street might seem ordinary and uninteresting—the former home of Goldman Sachs, natch—but it happens to shield an important piece of New York City's history in its shadow.

On its northeast corner on Pearl Street, you'll find cream-colored bricks in the sidewalk that demark the location of New York's first City Hall building. It was also, no surprise, a tavern.

In 1641, Director-General William Kieft had a costly stone structure built at what is today Coenties Slip and Pearl Street and called it City Tavern. Why "Tavern"? Back then, taverns served more purposes than simply dispensing booze. They served as inns, meeting halls, social networking places, and sometimes even offices. It makes sense then that when the city was incorporated in 1653, City Tavern morphed into what would be New Amsterdam's very first city hall (*Stadt Huys*, or city house).

A 1902 illustration depicting how the New York slave market might have looked along the waterfront in 1730.

When the British took over control of the colony in 1664, the building kept its place of importance. Underscoring its position was the building to its south, erected in 1670 as a tavern and owned by the governor of New York, Colonel Francis Lovelace.

Lovelace's Tavern was conceived as a second-tier administration building and seemed to offer the same services as the larger building. (It's sometimes referred to as the "King's House.") In fact, the tavern connected right into the municipal chambers, making it effectively an annex of City Hall. Lovelace's Tavern was a popular place, its halls crowded until the wee hours with revelers, drinking wine and smoking their pipes.

Lovelace's Tavern burned down in 1706 and the land was reallotted for development in the growing mercantile district. But you can still see remnants underfoot, here in the shadow of 85 Broad Street. (*85 Broad Street*)

3 THE FIRST PRECINCT Imagine all the cop shows and movies you've seen that are based in New York. If they shot on location, they probably took place in some of the city's old Gilded Age police precinct buildings, which popped up optimistically all over town about 100 years ago during a period of massive police reforms. This stalwart at 100 Old Slip, built in 1909, was specifically designed to police the waterfront district. In fact, the street's name references the original water inlet that once ran along here. Today the building is home to the New York City Police Museum, although damages suffered during Hurricane Sandy have kept it shuttered for years. (*100 Old Slip*)

The police station at 100 Old Slip must have seen its share of seafaring scallywags.

4 **THE HOME OF CAPTAIN KIDD (Vanished)** Not only was the legendary seventeenth-century privateer (okay, fine, "pirate") William Kidd (aka Captain Kidd) a New Yorker, he was a wealthy one at that. His home at 119 Pearl Street, at the southern tip of Hanover Square, was situated close to the old wall for which Wall Street was named. It was waterfront property, back before all that landfill got in the way, the better to gaze out over the harbor's many islands where *maybe* he buried a treasure or two. (See Chapter 1.)

Room with a View: The home of Captain William Kidd near the old wall of Wall Street.

The Kidds' lavish home — with "104 ounces of silverware,"[4] a healthy wine cellar, and the biggest Turkish carpet in the city — allowed him to pay for a pew at the newly built Trinity Church in 1698. The captain even donated equipment to aid in the church's construction. No Kidding. (*119 Pearl Street*)

5 **THE SHORTEST STREET IN MANHATTAN** The street is named Mill Lane, stuck like an appendage between South William and Stone Streets, a half block south of Hanover Square. It's approximately thirty feet long, or the length of five or six Wall Street bankers, laid end to end. (*Mill Lane*)

Mill Lane: Home to the city's first Jewish community during the Dutch years.

---

4   From Edward Robb Ellis's *The Epic of New York City.*

6 LOOK AT THIS AWESOME SIGN The tile mosaic above the entrance at the International Telephone and Telegraph Building at 75 Broad Street, constructed in 1928. A brawny nude angel directs electricity into the dual worlds of telecommunication. So subtle! (*75 Broad Street*)

7 THE MARBLE COLUMNS OF POMPEII Delmonico's was New York's first great restaurant, introducing in 1827 the fineries of French cuisine to a city accustomed to gorging on oysters out of a slop bucket. For more than a century their various locations throughout the city became the feasting place of cigar-chomping power brokers and celebrated authors salivating over Lobster Newburg or a flaming Baked Alaska (both of which were first cooked up in Delmonico's kitchens).

Delmonico's still dishes it up in a swanky setting here on South William Street.

Delmonico's original restaurant at 23 William Street was destroyed in the Great Fire of 1835. They quickly rebuilt, and when an enlarged restaurant opened in 1891 here at 2 South William Street, the architect incorporated elements from the original location: a set of columns purportedly plucked from the ruins of Pompeii (back in the days when one could just pluck columns from ancient ruins). Had one of the original Delmonico brothers, John or Peter, visited Greece instead of Italy, maybe we'd see a piece of the Parthenon hoisted over the door. (*2 South William Street*)

8 THE NEW YORK SLAVE MARKET (Vanished) Many secrets lie locked within the street plan of lower Manhattan. One of the most disturbing is the city's relation to slavery, which existed in the city from its earliest days until the early nineteenth century. Many of the structures mentioned in this chapter — including the wall of Wall Street itself — were constructed by slave labor. One of the most notorious landmarks of the slave trade sat here, at the corner of Wall and Water Streets (once the shoreline, back in British New York). The Meal Market was established in 1711 not only for the buying and selling of raw products like grains, but also for the purchase and leasing of "negroes and Indian slaves."[5] (*Wall and Pearl Streets*)

9 GODS AND SEA MONSTERS Float around the Financial District and admire the impressive architecture — and notice that everything seems to be always sitting in the shadows. Because there are so few wide-open public spaces down here in Lower Manhattan, building designers and architects often made the details on these facades extra bold in order to make them "pop" along the dark canyons. Many of these details recall a time when sea transportation and shipping were critical to the financial success of New York City.

The towers at the corner of Wall and Pearl Streets wear the brooches of ocean travel. The Seamen's Bank for Savings was formed in 1829 as a sailors' bank. Onto the exterior of its former headquarters at 74 Wall Street, built in 1926, you will find fantastic carvings of sharks, pelicans, sea monsters, and other living accouterments of the sea.

Across the street, over at 67 Wall Street, more bold mythological drama awaits: the whimsical faces of gods and goddesses, including Athena's owl. (*67 and 74 Wall Street*)

10 PROOF THAT THE CITY WAS ONCE QUITE SMALL (Vanished) We visited Washington's former residence in Chapter 2. Now get this: 1) Thomas Jefferson's former home was at 57 Maiden Lane (there's a plaque in the enchantingly named "Home Insurance Plaza" approximating

---

5   Notes of the City Council, December 13, 1711.

its location); 2) Alexander Hamilton's former home, 57 (then 58) Wall Street, was three blocks away from Jefferson's; 3) Aaron Burr's former home, 3 Wall Street, was just two blocks away from Hamilton's. And as if we need to remind you — Burr would later mortally wound Hamilton in a duel in 1804. (*57 Maiden Lane*)

11 THE SECRET OF THE PYRAMIDS At first glance, 70 Pine Street does not appear to be filled with intrigue. This glamorous 1932 art deco skyscraper, once called (rather blandly) the American International Building, has delightful silvery ornamentation that makes it feel like the Chrysler Building's fancy-pants downtown sister. But hang on, because things get really "reflective" in the entranceways.

The building features a fourteen-foot miniature representation of itself inside the center pillar of the east portal. And inside that mini-me? Another, even tinier version. And this continues, building reflected in building, into the realm of subatomic particles. (Okay, we exaggerate a bit. But it gets seriously small.) Creepy things continue around the doorways, where an unusual pyramidal motif will leave you with more unanswered questions.

Are the Freemasons behind this? Is there a spooky message to decipher? Does this have to do with Mary Magdalene? Alas, no. The building was originally commissioned by Henry L. Doherty as a temple to his Cities Service Company, a utility company. Their logo was a pyramid. Today we know a greatly expanded Cities Service Company by another name: Citgo. Their logo? A pyramid. (Mic drop.) (*70 Pine Street*)

Mystery of the pyramids: Intriguing iconography adorns this skyscraper on Pine Street.

12 **THE BOOK OF THE FREEMASONS** Federal Hall National Memorial, currently administered by the National Park Service, has always been a popular landmark with tourists, thanks to its position on one of the most photographed intersections in New York. Who can resist that noble statue of George Washington silently meditating on the financial juggernaut of the New York Stock Exchange? As he took his presidential oath on April 30, 1789, Washington looked down this very street, Broad Street, packed with residents witnessing the birth of their new nation.

Washington looks somewhat askance at the New York Stock Exchange (built across the street in 1903).

He did not, however, take the oath in the building that stands there today. The original structure was built in 1699 by the British, who used materials from the city's demolished defense wall — the "wall" of Wall Street — to construct it. The building became the center of most governmental functions, from city administration to the meeting place of Congress and the seat of the federal government from 1789 to 1790.

The present building, the Federal Hall National Memorial (originally the U.S. Custom House, opened in 1842), looks more like an ancient Roman temple. Throw a toga over Washington's shoulders and you could call him Caesar. But a curious link to both the original structure and Washington's inauguration can be found inside a dark room within the building: the Freemason's Bible used for the swearing-in of the president. Both Washington and the man administering the oath, Robert Livingston, were loyal Masons. (*Wall and Broad Streets*)

13 **POCKMARKED HISTORY** The Wall Street exterior of the former J. P. Morgan Bank is covered in small cuts, traces of a terrible terrorist attack that occurred on Wall Street on September 16, 1920. That day, as the streets were filling with office workers taking their lunch breaks, an unidentified man parked a horse and carriage near the corner, about 100 feet east of Broad Street. As the Trinity Church bells rang at noon, the man dropped the reins and fled, never to be seen again. One minute later, 100 pounds of dynamite exploded inside the wagon, blasting back everything in its sphere while iron slugs shot through the air, creating a horrific scene of carnage. Thirty-eight people were killed and more than four hundred were injured in the attack, many while sitting inside at their desks.

Morgan famously refused to repair his bank building, preferring to leave the pockmarks on its side in a sign of defiance. With a little morbid imagination and some amateur sleuthing, it's still possible to trace the trajectory of the explosion along the wall to the very spot where the poor horse and wagon stood. The culprits, rumored to be Italian anarchists, were never caught. (*23 Wall Street*)

14 SHADOWS OF THE PAST The Equitable Building (120 Broadway) is a whole lotta skyscraper for such a little space. Its striking, robust form befits its original tenant, the Equitable Life Insurance Society. But many considered it a harbinger of gloom and doom when it was completed in 1915 in the Wild West days of skyscraper construction. As buildings grew taller, residents soon complained that the superstructures cast enormous, dreary shadows along the streets of Lower Manhattan. Due to the controversy surrounding buildings like the Equitable and the Woolworth Building, New York's crucial Zoning Law of 1916 dictated that buildings be constructed with setbacks, in the "wedding cake style," as they called it, to help contain shadows and to allow more sun to reach the sidewalks.

Compare the Equitable Building with 28 Liberty Street (formerly One Chase Manhattan Plaza), one block east, the one with the weird white-tree sculpture (called *Group of Four Trees*). The modern plaza exemplifies the second great zoning change in New York (passed in 1961), which made it easier for skyscrapers to ascend straight up without setbacks when open public spaces were constructed at their bases. (More on that in Chapter 18.) (*Pine and Nassau Streets*)

15 THERE BE ALLIGATORS! Sure, across Nassau Street from 55 Liberty Street stands the hefty Federal Reserve, an imposing *Game of Thrones*–like fortress literally filled with billions of the world's lucre. Who needs it! Let us cast our eyes instead upon the mischievous carved alligators that adorn the doorway of this graceful, slender tower. Why might they be smiling?

One possible clue: It was on this very spot that the American Society for the Prevention of Cruelty to Animals was founded by Henry Bergh[6] in 1866.

For decades this building was the headquarters of Sinclair Oil, instigators of the Teapot Dome scandal in the 1920s that almost brought down Warren G. Harding's presidency. Their famous mascot is a green dinosaur named Sinclair, a distant ancestor of these alligators here. (*55 Liberty Street*)

16 OPENING CRIES OF THE REVOLUTIONARY WAR The sturdy John Street Church, which sits between two hemmed-in, open-air

patios, was built in 1841, six years after the Great Fire. This was the Methodist congregation's third church; the first was constructed on this same spot in 1768. The church's contributions extend beyond religious history. During the Battle of Golden Hill,[7] a conflict in 1770

The view of Golden Hill (sometime in the 1760s) and the original John Street Church.

that took place between British forces and the revolutionary-minded Sons of Liberty, injured soldiers were taken to the first John Street Church for shelter. Today this is an almost embarrassing example of lovely old architecture being unceremoniously dwarfed by new (in this case, the Philip Johnson–designed 33 Maiden Lane, which looks like something out of a frightening science fiction novel). The berobed bust of the English theologian John Wesley (1703–1791) in the courtyard is *so* not amused. (*44 John Street*)

---

6   The roots of Mr. Bergh's other great contribution to American life can be found in Chapter 16.
7   The Battle of Golden Hill took place approximately at the corner of John and William Streets. While a minor skirmish in the revolutionary scheme of things, several New Yorkers were injured and one was killed. Perhaps even more unbelievable: This was an actual hill at one time and, yes, actually golden—with amber stalks of wheat.

Short History of Staten Island

"God might have made a more beautiful place than Staten Island, but He never did."

— George William Curtis

Staten Island—or should we say Richmond, for that was its official name until 1975—is probably the most misunderstood borough of New York, its personality at greatest odds with the frenetic energy of Manhattan. But this lush, isolated place, home to the native Lenape for hundreds of years, gives a great first impression. It's this island, after all, that received the harbor's first Europeans—first Giovanni da Verrazzano in 1524, then Henry Hudson in 1609. (One got a bridge named for him, the other a river.)

The Dutch presence here was small but enduring, Dutch farmers having lined its shores with docks in order to send goods to market. The name Staten Island is a nod to ye olden Dutch days, "Staaten" being a tribute to Staaten-Generaal, the Dutch parliament. The oldest settlement, Oude Dorp (Old Village), was founded along the eastern shore in 1661 and populated by French Huguenots (French Protestants). By the eighteenth century, the British had taken such a fancy to the place—now renamed for the Duke of Richmond—that they headquartered here during the American Revolution.

But it would be one particular Dutch descendant who would bring special prominence and fame to the island. Cornelius Vanderbilt (1794–1877) turned his fleet of swift periaugers into a flotilla of steamship ferries that ruled New York's harbor. By the end of his life, Vanderbilt's railroads would dominate transportation along the East Coast of the United States.

Remoteness was a virtue at times. The island's position in the harbor made it an ideal spot to construct, in 1663, a sturdy fort at the Narrows, later renamed Fort Wadsworth in 1864. And Richmond's pastoral grace appealed to naturalists like Henry David Thoreau, who wrote in 1843, "The sea seems very near from the hills, but it proves a long way over the plain, and yet you may be wet with the spray before you can believe you are there. The far seems near, and the near far." These same sea-breezy attributes made it appealing to the builders of Sailors' Snug Harbor, who built some of the island's finest architecture along its north shore in 1833.[8]

But New York had a pesky habit of exporting its undesirable institutions to the island. This was exactly the case with the much-hated Smallpox Hospital, which angry residents burned to the ground in 1858. Yet by the 1870s its shores had become an appealing getaway for New Yorkers looking to escape their overcrowded city. An elite class of locals with proper Gilded Age trappings soon developed here, fostered by the success of the Vanderbilts and other enterprising natives. On the social register was vanguard photographer Alice Austen (1866–1952), whose fetching home on the island's eastern shore operates today as a museum.

With its absorption into Greater New York in 1898, the new borough was poised for growth, its former farmlands quickly parceled into new suburban-style lots. Immigrants, largely Italian, relocated here, eager to finally possess spacious homes far from the madding crowds. The city struggled for decades with ways to link Staten Island to the rest of the city, which finally led to the construction of the colossal Verrazano–Narrows Bridge from 1959 to 1964. (New Yorkers were actually quite outspoken over the proper spelling of the Italian explorer's name, but Governor Rockefeller preferred the "Americanized" version with one "z." Fewer letters saved money on sign painting too!)

But animosity soon crept into the relationship between the borough and the city, fueled in part by the development of the Fresh Kills Landfill and its 2,200 acres of toxic garbage (thankfully closed in 2001). The Staten Island Ferry, which traces its operations back to the early 1800s, serves as both a lifeline to Lower Manhattan and a symbol of the borough's treasured distance from it. The ferry charged a small fare until it was made free by Mayor Rudolph Giuliani in 1997. Even still, the island's residents voted to secede from New York City in 1993, but the state blocked it. Hurricane Sandy shook its neighborhood community hard in 2012, and residents rebuilt or moved inland to safer shores. But it will take far more than a hurricane to disrupt the city's scrappiest sector.

---

8 Equally impressive is the collection of over 30 notable buildings in Historic Richmond Town, New York's only living history village!

THE STRIKE OF THE NEWSBOYS!

In the late nineteenth century, young men and boys scraped together a living on street corners, hawking papers hot off the presses, fiercely competing for every sale. These "newsies" were one of the chief methods of newspaper distribution in the city, and unsurprisingly, their working conditions were miserable. In 1899, they united against the unfair pricing practices of two of the city's largest dailies, the *New York Journal* and the *New York World*. The *New York Times*, a competitor not plagued by the strikes, relished the opportunity to cover the protracted battle between titans and teens:

THE STRIKE OF THE NEWSBOYS—Continues with Unabated Vigor and Spasmodic Attacks on So-Called Scabs—Women Not Molested

"Please don't buy *The Evening Journal and World*, because the newsboys has striked."

"I ain't a scab."

These and similar notices were pinned on the hats and coats of newsboys all over the city yesterday, for the strike has spread from the Battery to the Bronx, and even across the Brooklyn Bridge. The Harlem newsboys have organized into a union and a number of newsdealers there and in the Bronx have also refused to handle the barred "extries" or "uxtras."

"Dere's t'ree t'ousand of us, and we'll win sure," one of the boys declared.

~ *New York Times*, July 22, 1899

City Hall and South Street Seaport

New York City Hall (completed in 1812) sit on the old Revolutionary War–era Commons.

SITUATE THE READER
—City Hall and South Street Seaport—

City Hall is the symbolic center of New York City's political life. Congested thoroughfares enfold it, while an approach at its front door allows thousands to make the majestic journey high over the East River on the Brooklyn Bridge. The area surrounding the bridge's Manhattan base slopes toward the waterfront to a neighborhood that still holds charming vestiges of New York's port past. Retooled today into the district called South Street Seaport, it's possible to imagine a simpler era here, even as traffic barrels along the elevated FDR Drive high overhead.

The wedge of land comprising City Hall Park was once a communal livestock pen for the Dutch, equipped, naturally, with windmills. Later, in the eighteenth century, the area was transformed into a commons and hosted no shortage of early revolutionary escapades, from spirited rallies to liberty poles.[1] By the beginning of the nineteenth century, this versatile triangle of land had also been home to New York's almshouse, a notorious prison (named Bridewell), the city's first hospital (the forebear of today's Bellevue Hospital), and the city's first historical association (the New-York Historical Society).

As is the case with much of New York's modern shoreline, most of today's South Street Seaport is built atop landfill, the old docks and slips drained and filled in over the centuries as the booming city's land values skyrocketed. Even still, before skyscrapers raced to block its view, City Hall's visitors could look eastward and observe a forest of masts from one end to another.

The Brooklyn Bridge may have been the crowning achievement of this increasingly powerful city when it was completed in 1883, but its luster did not rub off on the shoreline industry located in its shadow. By the early twentieth century, these docks had been made obsolete by the larger ports on the Hudson River side and in Brooklyn and New Jersey. Even today the character of the Seaport neighborhood remains uncertain, the survival of its seafaring identity—even in its present tourist-friendly incarnation—still a struggle. Comparing it to a ship in a bottle seems apt in more ways than one.

---

1   In the years running up to the Revolutionary War, the Sons of Liberty frequently erected liberty poles to protest British rule. Today a liberty pole stands to the west side of City Hall in commemoration of this rebellious act.

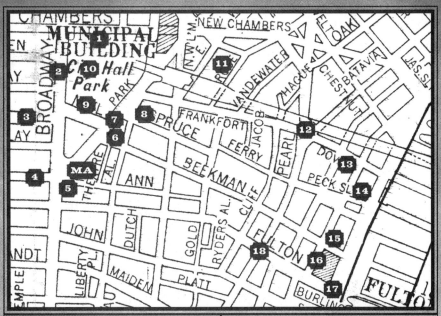

POINTS OF INTEREST

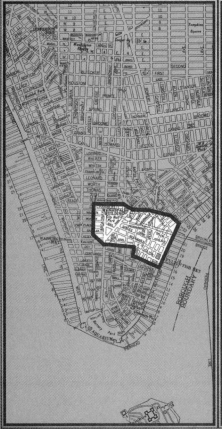

1 Stand Here

2 The Wind Tunnel

3 Firecracker Lane

4 The First Hotel

5 Barnum's Greatest Show in New York

6 The Ancient Alley

7 Dog's College

8 Why Is Benjamin Franklin Standing Here?

9 The World's Worst Post Office

10 The Silent Sentry

11 The Old Jail Window

12 George Washington Slept Here, Nightly

13 Kit Burns Rat Pit

14 Look at This Awesome Sign

15 The Sea Creatures of Beekman Street

16 The Secret Hideaway

17 The Old Hotel on the Wharf

18 The Lonely Lighthouse

MA Park Row and Woolworth Buildings

The Park Row Building and the Woolworth Building

For several decades in the late nineteenth and early twentieth centuries, it seemed that the city's highest (or at least tallest) achievements loomed around New York's relatively delicate City Hall. Completed in 1812, the white, lacy administrative home of the mayor was designed by Joseph François Mangin and John McComb, Jr., and is the oldest operating city hall in the United States today. Yet its loveliness is literally overshadowed by that which towers over and around it, some of it among the city's most beautiful architecture.

Sprightly "newsies" sell their publications on the steps of City Hall, 1896.

The Brooklyn Bridge, completed in 1883 (more than seventy years after City Hall), was designed by John Augustus Roebling as a Gothic urban monument, almost rugged in comparison with New York's other bridges. Meanwhile, buried beneath City Hall is one of the most spectacular stations in the city's subway system, its grand arches lined with Guastavino[2] tiling. (While the station shuttered in 1945, it is occasionally open for tours.)

But equal to these marvels is the array of skyscrapers that stand at the perimeter of the park, gazing down at the triangle of trees. While none of these buildings can still claim to be "the tallest in the world" (three held this title at various times in the twentieth century), they all still dazzle.

Two of these "tallest" skyscrapers are still around today. One of them — the Woolworth Building — is an icon of grace and style. The other — the Park Row Building — is, well, um, we're just happy it's still around.

---

2   The second mention of Guastavino in this book! You might be sick of tiles by the time we're done.

Up until 1890, the tallest building in New York was just down the street: Trinity Church.[3] The notion of building other structures any closer to the heavens would remain an engineering impossibility (not to mention a sacrilege) until the substantial development of two key building features: steel-frame construction to support the weight and improve the economics of a taller building and, of course, the elevator to shuttle people up and down the tall structures.

With the introduction of both of these innovations in the mid- to late nineteenth century, tall buildings soon began shooting up here, in Chicago (New York's chief rival for the skies in the late nineteenth and early twentieth centuries), and in other major cities around the country. The word "skyscraper" would soon be coined to describe these unique rectangular towers.

Skyscrapers first sprouted in the City Hall area along the narrow little street to its east: Park Row. By the 1840s this street was already home to New York's most important newspapers, and the open plaza at the street's northern end became known as Printing House Row. With the rise of sensational, page-turning, scandal-icious "yellow" journalism

The oft-ignored Park Row Building, located across from City Hall Park, topped with its two cupola apartments.

in the late 1800s, newspapers became fabulously lucrative businesses, and their publishers, wealthy braggadocios.

---

3   A temporary structure called the Latting Observatory, built in 1853 for the Exhibition of the Industry of All Nations's main hall, the Crystal Palace, briefly bested Trinity.

The Icons: Wonder of the Brooklyn Bridge

There are bridges and then there's the Brooklyn Bridge. No other landmark embodies the aesthetic of "old New York" quite as well as the first suspension bridge over the East River, the first to link New York with the city of Brooklyn. No other achievement of that era would equal its beauty and seeming simplicity.

And boy, did the people know it! The epic celebration at its opening on May 24, 1883, has rarely been surpassed in American history, with highlights that included U.S. President Chester A. Arthur leading a parade of marching bands, ceremonies linking the two cities, and a huge display of fireworks—*lots* of fireworks! "Forty pyrotechnists superintended the display. There were 6,000 four-pound skyrockets, 400 bombshells, and 125 fountains of colored lights."[4]

Today the Brooklyn Bridge has become a sort of graphical shorthand for New York. It's part of a very select set of city icons (the Big Apple, the Empire State Building, the taxicab, "Start spreading the news..."), any of which represents New York at least as superficially as the Eiffel Tower does Paris.

Perhaps the bridge is still universally revered today because of what its form actually says about New York City. It turns the force, the churn, and the chaos of a metropolis into something graceful and effortless.

The Cost: $15.5 million dollars (adjusted for inflation: over $380,000,000). The bridge was conceived as a way to foster economic brotherhood between the two cities that sometimes competed for resources. But corrupt powerbrokers (including Tammany Hall's Boss Tweed) saw the project as a veritable moneymaking machine, and he and his cronies benefited handsomely. Millions of dollars in public funds would eventually line their pockets.

The Cables: Approximately 3,600 miles (total length of wire spun into each cable). The key to the bridge's design was in its cables made of tightly wound wire. Naturally, the bridge's architect John Roebling was also a wire manufacturer and had successfully used his twisted-wire technique in other spans. He modestly looked forward to building the bridge, calling it "the greatest engineering work of the continent and of the age." (Everybody talked like that back then.) Unfortunately, early in the construction, while surveying construction of the first tower, Roebling's foot was crushed by a docking boat. His toes were amputated, which led to more serious afflictions, and he died on July 22, 1869, 14 years before the bridge was completed.

The Caissons: 78.5 feet deep (New York side), 44.5 feet deep (Brooklyn side). John's son Washington Roebling took over the project in time for the sinking of the tower caissons, which rooted the bridge to the river's

---

4   From the *New York Sun*, May 25, 1883.

floor. Lengthy periods in the pressurized chambers, however, caused the workers (almost all new immigrant laborers) to experience grueling pain and even paralysis due to "caisson disease" (decompression sickness, or "the bends"). Washington Roebling himself became paralyzed from the disease; fortunately, his wife, Emily Warren Roebling, was more than up to the task of managing the project.

The Towers: Both 276.5 feet tall. The bridge's cables would be strung from two massive, breathtaking towers, their double arches shaped like the windows of a great Gothic cathedral. Their effect upon people crossing the bridge has indeed been described as religious. Some probably noticed their austere similarity to New York's tallest building at the time (Trinity Church at 284 feet) and to the forest of church steeples on the Brooklyn side. The future borough was, after all, nicknamed the "City of Churches."

The Anchorages: 60,000 tons per anchorage. In many ways, it was the construction of the anchorages—the massive structures inside which the bridge's cables are secured—that most disrupted the lives of everyday New Yorkers. Building the hulking anchorage on the New York side required the wholesale destruction of hundreds of buildings. (Approaches to the bridge would later wipe out hundreds more.) Incidentally, it wasn't all about cables: Their cavernous interiors proved ideal for storing wine and champagne. On the Brooklyn side, the anchorage even contains a Cold War–era bunker. John Roebling had once imagined the anchorage interiors might be used as marketplaces. Given the relative dankness of these chambers, that idea was never fully explored.

The Pedestrian Walkway: Between 8 and 16 feet wide (varies). The link between New York and Brooklyn finally became tangible for residents with the opening of the bridge's promenade. With trolleys and horse-drawn cars streaming below them, pedestrians could now walk between two great cities. The union was later reinforced in 1910, with Brooklyn now a borough of Greater New York, when Mayor William Jay Gaynor walked from his Brooklyn home over the bridge to City Hall on his first day on the job.

Tourists cram onto the bridge's promenade today with little trepidation. But when the bridge first opened in the spring of 1883, people were unsure of its safety. And it's that uncertainty which sparked a tragedy on May 30, a mere six days after its opening. A woman fell on the stairs leading to the New York–side promenade, and rumors quickly shot through the crowded walkway that the bridge was collapsing. Panic ensued as terrified pedestrians stampeded, frantically attempting every means possible to escape from the bridge. According to the *Brooklyn Daily Eagle*, "Two men tried to raise the prostrate woman and were instantly trampled and paid forfeit with their lives. In a few seconds human beings were piled four deep at the foot of the steps, and the crowd was hurried over them." Twelve people died in this terrible tragedy.

In 1890, Joseph Pulitzer built a new headquarters for his *New York World* at 99 Park Row, the building nearest the entrance to the Brooklyn Bridge, which had opened just seven years before. (It was located so near, in fact, that the building would be torn down in 1955 to accommodate a new bridge on-ramp.)

Frank W. Woolworth didn't nickel and dime the construction of his new building. (He paid for it in cash.)

The *World's* height—308 feet tall, 40 feet taller if you counted the antenna—was chosen to spite his rivals at the *New York Times*, which had just constructed their new headquarters a block away at 41 Park Row. Pulitzer even employed George Post, the same architect that the *New York Times* had hired for his newspaper's palace, but not before bribing him with a $10,000 bonus to make the World Building taller. The architect later said of his challenge, "It would be an interesting problem to construct two buildings in sight of each other for rival papers, and to make the buildings as different as the politics of the papers."

Naturally, the amoral idea of a commercial building reaching closer to the heavens than a house of worship left many New Yorkers appalled. Any momentary spiritual outcry, however, was quickly muffled as an all-out skyscraper race consumed the attention and resources of major American cities for decades to come.

In 1899 another building on Park Row grabbed the tallest-building trophy. The Park Row Building, still standing today at 15 Park Row, came in at 391 feet, thanks in part to two striking cupolas, clad in copper and reminiscent of a Portuguese cathedral.

Unlike many of the showier skyscrapers of the day, the Park Row Building was funded and built by a syndicate of businessmen, including August Belmont, Jr., future benefactor of the New York subway system and chairman of the Interborough Rapid Transit Company (the "IRT"). With its matching cupolas, the skyscraper was considered downtown's original "Twin Towers." But while the building was indeed filled with hundreds of offices, the cupolas were actually home to apartments, including that of the city's most powerful political figure, Tammany Hall's Boss Croker.

The Park Row Building has managed to survive despite some nasty critiques when it opened. One critic bellowed, "New York is the only city in which such a monster would be allowed to rear itself."[5] Another nickname lobbed at it was the "horned monster," not the sort of reaction that usually greets a classic.

The Park Row Building's importance fizzles when compared with the gem that would rise just a few hundred feet from its front door less than fifteen years later. While midtown Manhattan soon attracted the city's new crop of skyscrapers, one final grand gesture awaited the streets surrounding City Hall. It would take three years to complete, but by its opening in April 1913, the Woolworth Building (at 792 feet) would become an icon of American

capitalism, and a symbol of the power and wealth of New York's real estate. Its technical achievements, impossible to imagine a decade prior, only reinforced the themes of the day—money could indeed defy gravity.

Designed by Cass Gilbert for the "five-and-dime" retail king Frank Woolworth, the Woolworth Building was a glowing candle of a skyscraper next to dainty little City Hall. The Woolworth's intricate facade was adorned with many of the "international races" echoed down at Gilbert's other big Manhattan building, the U.S. Custom House (1 Bowling Green).[6]

Because the Woolworth was built before zoning "setback" laws were passed, its main tower shoots straight up from the sidewalk.

Built three years before the city enacted stricter zoning laws (which, among other things, forced the construction of setbacks that would result in tiered

5   From *The Real Estate Record and Guide*, 1898.
6   See Chapter 2.

wedding cake–shaped structures), the Woolworth simply zooms straight up into the sky.

Advertisements to fill the office space in the Woolworth Building made use of its unique place in American commerce. Said one ad, "Customers will never overlook your store if it is in the Woolworth Building. The sight and thought of the world's greatest structure will remind them of you and your store."

The Woolworth Building is in both every tome on great urban architecture and every tourist's guidebook to New York. The Park Row, meanwhile, is almost always overlooked. It's like a burnished spinster compared with the Woolworth, but both, it should be remembered, held the same glorious title for a time. We'll take an apartment in the Park Row cupola over the Woolworth any day. (Who are we kidding? We'll take both!)

City Hall/Brooklyn Bridge

POINTS OF INTEREST

1 STAND HERE: On the top step of the Tweed Courthouse. *Why?* Today the Courthouse is officially named after Boss Tweed, the notoriously corrupt and wildly powerful leader of Tammany Hall from 1858 to 1877. The building's construction (and budget) dragged on for more than a decade before it finally opened in 1872. Its costs were almost laughably inflated by Tweed & Co.'s graft, kickbacks, and shameless shenanigans. As interesting as all of this is, however, turn your back to the building and gaze upon the three fantastic structures that line the northern side of Chambers Street.

At the far right is the Surrogate's Courthouse, completed in 1907 with as much Gilded Age giddiness as could be conjured from stone. Its exterior is festooned with statues of individuals from New York's past. (See if you can locate Peter Stuyvesant and his wooden leg.) In the middle of the block is the Emigrant Industrial Savings Bank, the tallest bank building in the world when it opened in 1912. Finally, at the corner of Broadway and Chambers can be found the oldest and most famous of the three — the former A. T. Stewart department store, built in 1848 and nicknamed the "Marble Palace." Stewart's is considered the first department store in America.[7] (*52 Chambers Street*)

---

7   He would top this achievement with another architectural marvel described in Chapter 11.

2 THE WIND TUNNEL (Vanished) In one of the ballsiest moves ever in the history of New York City, Alfred Ely Beach, a man truly afflicted with "tunnel vision," dug the city's first subway tunnel in 1870 less than a block from City Hall...without the city's permission.[8] The short tunnel operated on pneumatic power and consisted of a train car propelled by wind produced by large fans. Intended only as a demonstration, Beach's subway line was a choice novelty for a couple of years before closing in 1873. All traces of this glorious pneumatic system are today sadly gone. To approximate its very short journey today, start on Warren Street and Broadway, walk

This ride sucks! Waiting to board Alfred Ely Beach's windy pneumatic ride in 1872.

south on Broadway one block, and turn again on Murray Street. What a ride! (*Broadway, between Warren and Murray Streets*)

3 FIRECRACKER LANE Mere steps from City Hall, New Yorkers could once buy all the fireworks they desired! From the late nineteenth century until the 1930s, Park Place was New York's official "fireworks mart," even while its ornate new neighbor, the Woolworth Building, towered over its shelves of fanciful explosives (or "celebration goods," as they called them back then). Fireworks wholesalers were many, and included Pain's Fireworks, famous for their ravishing nightly displays out on Coney Island. In perhaps the least surprising plot development in city history, residents eventually started avoiding Park Place, getting to nearby elevated train stations by taking the long way around, avoiding the boxes of potentially combustible merchandise stacked atop the sidewalks. You could still find fireworks wholesalers here as late as the 1930s, but state laws soon snuffed them out. (*Park Place, between Broadway and Church Street*)

---

8   Well, technically he did have the city's permission—to build a pneumatic *mail* tube. He just interpreted that as meaning a tunnel that could comfortably accommodate a mailman as well.

4 THE FIRST HOTEL (Vanished) On this corner once sat the mighty Astor House, considered to be the first luxury hotel in New York. Opened in 1836 (notably the year after the Great Fire), the Astor House soon offered the

The Astor House: New York's first trendy hotel, undoubtedly with overpriced artisanal cocktails.

most elegant accommodations in town and typified the graceful modernity of New York in the mid-nineteenth century. "The simple, square, unornamented architecture of the Astor House makes, to my notion, the best appearance of any building in New York," wrote Walt Whitman. When it was demolished in 1913, old-timers mourned the loss of a more refined, genteel, and "real" New York (in much the same way that old-timers whine about the good ol' days on Facebook today). It was replaced with the office building that still stands on the corner today, respectfully named the Astor House Building. (*Broadway and Vesey Street*)

5 BARNUM'S GREATEST SHOW IN NEW YORK (Vanished)
Perhaps the most exciting place that has ever existed in Lower Manhattan was

Barnum's museum burned down in 1865. It moved to another location...and burned down again in 1868.

P. T. Barnum's American Museum, which delighted and fascinated millions of museumgoers from 1841 to 1865, well before his traveling circus hit the road. An earlier museum[9] was housed in a building just north of City Hall; Barnum moved it to this corner and infused it with his trademark showmanship and razzle-dazzle. The museum attempted to be all things for all audiences—educational, debauched, exotic, and scintillating. He crammed the building with interesting objects, animals, and people—in a rather un-nuanced way that would horrify anyone concerned with human and animal rights today. Among the most disturbing displays: two Beluga whales held in

---

9   Scudder's American Museum operated from 1810 to 1841, which was when Barnum bought up most of the interesting parts of the collection.

poorly ventilated tanks in the basement. The institution went out with a bang on July 13, 1865, as a spectacular blaze destroyed it, releasing animals into the sky and streets, as melting wax figures tumbled from windows. (*Broadway and Ann Street*)

6 THE ANCIENT ALLEY The narrow passage called Theatre Alley commemorates one of the first great theaters in New York, the Park Theatre, which once stood at today's 21–25 Park Row. The Park opened in 1798 and was the Lincoln Center and Carnegie Hall of its day. It burned down in 1848, but the alley which for half a century was lined with the waiting carriages of wealthy theatergoers has somehow retained its name to this day. (*Beekman Street, between Park Row and Nassau Street*)

7 DOG'S COLLEGE Currently part of Pace University, this building

The Puppy Plaque: Pace University's mascot is quite fetching.

was the headquarters of the *New York Times* from 1889 to 1903. The university expanded here in 1951, and two years later a curious plaque was placed at the entranceway that includes the profile of a dog. It's a wonderful pun—their sports teams are the Pace Setters. (Get it?) The official mascot of Pace University is named T-Bone. Good dog. (*41 Park Row*)

8 WHY IS BENJAMIN FRANKLIN STANDING HERE?

Benjamin Franklin, one of America's first great printers and publishers, strikes a pose.

Philadelphia-based printer-turned-author, inventor, and diplomat Ben Franklin never lived in New York, although he visited on many occasions during his long, illustrious life. So why then is there a prominent statue of Franklin in front of today's Pace University? The clue is in his hand: a copy of his newspaper, the *Pennsylvania Gazette*. The statue was placed here to commemorate both Franklin's long career as a printer, and this spot, "Printing-House Square," the center of New York's newspaper industry in the late nineteenth century. And guess who unveiled the statue in 1872? None other than Samuel Morse, who would become known for revolutionizing another form of communication—the telegraph. (*1 Pace Plaza*)

9 **THE WORLD'S WORST POST OFFICE (Vanished)** This was the prevailing opinion regarding the poorly designed, awkwardly dolled-up building that once occupied the southern tip of today's City Hall Park, a five-

It's all just a bit...much. The dowdy old City Hall post office, 1935 (photo: Berenice Abbott).

story post office and courthouse built in 1869. The flagrant nature of this structure was notable even in those good old corrupt days of outlandish and wildly expensive building construction. Charmingly nicknamed "Mullett's Monstrosity" after its architect, Alfred B. Mullett, the post office looked even sadder with the arrival of the beautiful Woolworth Building across the street in 1913. The "unsightly and unsanitary old structure" was finally stamped "return to sender" and torn down in 1939. (*Southern tip of City Hall Park*)

10 **THE SILENT SENTRY** A man stands forever facing New York City Hall, a man who did not live to see it built or even to see the independence of the United States. Nathan Hale was a spy for George Washington's Continental Army who was captured by the British in the early fall of 1776 and hung, but not before uttering a version of the immortal line, "I only regret that I have but one life to lose for my country."

But in sculpture he lives on, forever standing within spitting distance of City Hall. This is primarily due to the former purpose of this piece of land. This was the former common area during the Colonial era and the site of several dramatic protests by the Sons of Liberty against the British. Indeed, it is perhaps one of the most important pre-1776 sites related to American independence, and debonair Mr. Hale here, sculpted by Gilded Age–favorite

Frederick MacMonnies, embodies the passion and vitality of the patriots. He became a permanent fixture of the park in 1893, and was occasionally moved over the decades before finally planting himself in front of City Hall in 1999. Unlike the hundreds of city employees passing by him daily, Hale doesn't look the least bit stressed out. (*Front of City Hall*)

New York City Hall, still the seat of city government today, features dozens of rare paintings along its hallways.

11 THE OLD JAIL WINDOW Those British, they ruined everything— even New Yorkers' taste for sugar. During the years of the Revolutionary

War (1775–1783), they turned the old Rhinelander's Sugar House, originally at the corner of Duane Street (which still exists) and Rose Street (long gone), into a make-shift prison. This jailhouse window, tucked behind the Manhattan Municipal Building near the subway entrance, is a surprising surviving remnant of that structure.

From this cell window, prisoners could look out to streets filled with British soldiers, rampaging fires, and

general mayhem. The prison held those early New Yorkers "suffering under the stigma of patriotism," including publishers of rebellious newssheets, and sometimes even their readers too!

Today 1 Police Plaza, the concrete cubic headquarters of the New York Police Department, stands approximately at the spot of the old sugar house. So these ancient bars now take on an additional relevance. (*1 Police Plaza, behind the Manhattan Municipal Building*)

12 GEORGE WASHINGTON SLEPT HERE, NIGHTLY (Vanished) Looking at the chaotic underbelly of the Brooklyn Bridge today, you'd never guess that this was the site of the nation's first presidential mansion. George Washington and his family lived here, at the base of Cherry Street, from April 1789 to February 23, 1790, just a short carriage ride to Federal Hall on Wall Street.[10]

As was customary back in the pre-preservation era, city planners unceremoniously tore down Washington's home in the 1850s to widen the street. It was a mercy killing of sorts. Just 60 years after the nation's first president resided here, the neighborhood had devolved into New York's notorious Fourth Ward, lined with saloons and brothels, and once-glorious mansions had turned into dingy boardinghouses. A couple of decades later, much of the neighborhood (including several blocks of Cherry Street) would be wiped away to make way for the Brooklyn Bridge entrance. (*Pearl and Dover Streets*)

13 KIT BURNS RAT PIT A smattering of structures from the scandalous Fourth Ward days can still be found south of the Brooklyn Bridge, including this charming home at 273 Water Street, once the location of a popular saloon owned by the ruthless and imaginative Kit Burns. Opened in 1863, its centerpiece was a backroom pit where dog fighting and, if you were lucky, rat baiting entertained gamblers (and drinkers, we imagine) for hours on end. Soon social crusaders waged a clean-up campaign against this sort of grisly entertainment and general depravity. This building, beautifully restored, is not alone in its possession of dirty secrets. Most of the old buildings surrounding it were nineteenth-century watering holes, brothels, and boardinghouses and

---

10 He then moved to the mansion mentioned in Chapter 2, which is also, unsurprisingly, no longer there.

catered to the neighborhood's thirsty, randy, and tired sailor population. (*273 Water Street*)

14 LOOK AT THIS AWESOME SIGN Actually, it's a trompe l'oeil, a curiously lifelike painting meant to evoke the area's rustic history…and distract from the fact that it's painted onto an otherwise nondescript brick Con Ed electrical substation. Part of the piece, painted in 1977 by Richard Haas, is actually indicative of the architecture surrounding the area. The faux arcade—complete with a view of the bridge—is corny but lovable. (*Peck Slip*)

Richard Haas's classical-inspired tribute to the Brooklyn Bridge is a powerhouse.

15 THE SEA CREATURES OF BEEKMAN STREET Portside architecture is rarely fun. These old buildings held counting houses, warehouses, and workshops; nobody came here for whimsy. But that didn't stop the prolific architect George Post from having a little maritime merriment, bestowing the details of sea life to its redbrick exterior in 1885. Look for a community of starfish and cockleshells up and along its walls. (*142–144 Beekman Street*)

16 THE SECRET HIDEAWAY The cloistered alley known as Cannon's Walk, tucked behind a building on 206 Front Street, feels forgotten and even off-limits. Although it was created in 1983, it commemorates something quite a bit older — the location of an eighteenth-century wharf owned by John Cannon, back before landfill created much of the Seaport area today. It helps that you get to peek into the back entrance of Bowne Printers, a 1975 reboot of an eighteenth-century print shop. (*206 Front Street*)

Cannon's Walk: A secret spot tucked behind the old structures of South Street Seaport.

17 THE OLD HOTEL ON THE WHARF When Schermerhorn Row was constructed between 1810 and 1812, the refined lineup of brick counting houses were among the tallest buildings in the city and served as an essential part of the port's daily business operations. But things got a little saucy here as the area deteriorated in the mid-nineteenth century. Saloons took over the bottom floors of many of these buildings, and in 1868 the building at the corner of Fulton and South Streets was renovated into a glitzy hotel. Of course, this being the waterfront district, all manner of sleaze and lawlessness were carried on here. (Case in point: In 1875, the hotel's deceitful proprietor was arrested for hiding thousands of dollars in diamonds from his creditors. You get the idea.) Yet it remained a hotel — the Fulton Ferry Hotel — well into the 1930s. The place fascinated *New Yorker* writer Joseph Mitchell, who explored the abandoned property with wonder, making it the subject of a famous story, later titled "Up in the Old Hotel." (*Fulton Street between Front and South Streets*)

18 **THE LONELY LIGHTHOUSE** The stubby lighthouse standing at the entrance to South Street Seaport might look merely decorative today, but it was once fully operational. Designed as a memorial to the *Titanic* disaster of April 15, 1912 (which killed more than 1,500 people, including a great many New Yorkers), the lighthouse was originally installed in 1913 atop the Seamen's Church Institute at 25 South Street. The lighthouse includes a time ball that was lowered at noon to help distant sailors adjust their equipment—similar to the one that rings in the New Year in Times Square. (*Fulton and Pearl Streets*)

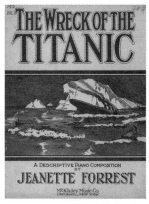

Where's Celine Dion when you need her?

REGARDING COLLECT POND

In aboriginal times the Manhatoes lived on its banks; and from their excursions to the oyster beds in the adjacent waters the Indians brought vast quantities of oysters—coming in through the stream which connected the pond with the East River, or through the larger stream from the North River [Hudson River]. The women, we are told, dried the oysters for future use and cast the shells on the shore, so that in time there came to be great heaps of oyster shells on the west bank, and when the Dutch gave the place a name they called it Kalch Hoek, which meant Shell Point. When the English succeeded the Dutch, the name Kalch Hoek was easily corrupted into Collect, and thenceforth the water was known as the Collect Pond, or the Fresh Water.

~ From *Forest and Stream*, published 1902,
by Charles Hallock and William A. Bruette

Chapter 6//

Tribeca and Foley Square

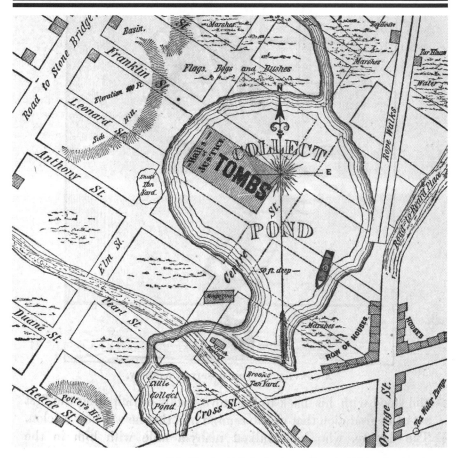

Collect Pond, an idyllic freshwater pond turned putrid dumping ground, once
filled the area of today's Foley Square and lower Chinatown.

SITUATE THE READER
~Tribeca and Foley Square~

Foley Square, the heart of modern New York's legal universe, where law and order are steadfastly enforced, sits partially upon the site of the long-gone Collect Pond and its marshy surroundings, a once serene and picturesque freshwater source that quickly became fetid and polluted as the young colony's industry expanded in the late eighteenth century. Soon slaughterhouses drained into the pond, releasing their blood, offal, and animal carcasses—but, of course, even that didn't stop brewers from sometimes using the Collect Pond as a water source. (Thirsty?)

New Yorkers eventually drained the polluted mess through a canal built just for the occasion in the 1810s—the canal of Canal Street fame. But little built upon this not-quite-solid ground would ever be very desirable or structurally sound, and as buildings leaned and "respectable" tenants fled, seeking more stable ground, the neighborhood descended into one of the city's most dangerous districts. (See Chapter 7.) In the early twentieth century the city finally cleaned house, rezoning the entire area for government use and building new structures with extra deep, dry, and solid foundations.

The scene west of here was a bit more amenable to human habitation—at first. Trinity Church, which owned most of the land, turned it into New York's swankiest post–Revolutionary War residential neighborhood. The city's finest families lived in townhouses surrounding St. John's Park, a leafy green haven that had become the center of elite society by the 1820s.

In the mid-nineteenth century, however, as the same families moved into even finer residences near Washington Square and later Union Square and Gramercy Park (they were a restless lot, their eyes always gazing farther north), this once-tony district lost its luster. The demise of St. John's Park was further hastened by industrial development along the Hudson River shoreline. By the 1860s Cornelius Vanderbilt had snatched up the entire area and redeveloped it into St. John's Freight Terminal for his thriving Hudson River Railroad.

Today, unsightly Holland Tunnel access roads twist around the lonely vestige of St. John's Park, strangling it with a constant parade of traffic. But beauty of a sort has returned in the restoration of the surrounding Tribeca neighborhood (TRIangle BElow CAnal—a portmanteau it gained in the 1970s). Today the district features some of the most architecturally striking warehouses (and equally striking rents) in the city.

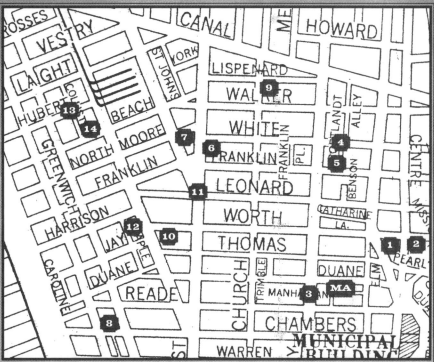

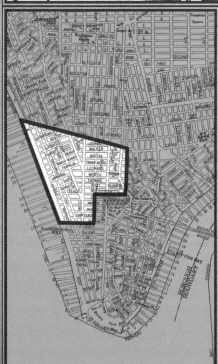

African Burial Ground

And then there were those backs upon which the early city was built....

The African Burial Ground, tucked right into the heart of Lower Manhattan, two blocks north of City Hall, represents one of the greatest archaeological finds and saddest stories in New York's history. The somber new monument, opened in 2007, gives long overdue respect and honor to the remains buried here of New York's first African and West Indian communities.

Contrast this with the other notable burial ground previously mentioned — Trinity Church (Chapter 3) — with its carefully preserved marble tombstones and prestigious roster of permanent residents. Whereas Trinity's cemetery has a fence to preserve the peace, this burial ground has no such border to keep the city at bay.

By Jacob Radcliff Mayor, and Richard Riker Recorder, of the City of New-York,

It is hereby Certified, That pursuant to the statute in such case made and provided, we have this day examined ___ certain ___ Negro Slave named ___ the property of ___

which slave ___ about to be manumitted, and ___ appearing to us to be under forty-five years of age, and of sufficient ability to provide ___ we have granted this Certificate, this ___ day of ___ in the year of our Lord, one thousand eight hundred and ___

Register's Office Lib. n° 2 of Manumissions page 62

A manumission certificate for a slave named George, signed by Mayor Jacob Radcliff on April 24, 1817.

In fact, the African Burial Ground is far larger than the site of today's monument. Its true size is unknown, although it is believed to cover about seven acres, stretching out under many of the surrounding buildings, including those in Foley Square and along Chambers Street.

The burial ground dates back to the seventeenth century, when New Amsterdam was a company town for the thriving Dutch West India Company, and the town's early settlers were primarily traders, not builders or town planners. In their eyes, they didn't sail all the way across the Atlantic from Holland to do menial work.

And so in 1626, to stimulate and facilitate the colony's growth, the Dutch imported the New World's first African slaves, a group of eleven people. Early records show that they were assigned names associated with their homelands or original captors: Antony Congo, Dorothe Angola, Jan Negro. Slave labor would be used to build many of New Amsterdam's major structures, including the large wall that lined the northern edge of town.

It's interesting to note that under the Dutch, enslaved men and women *could* earn their freedom and eventually own property. But those who did gain independence were not permitted to reside within the city's walls. Instead, they were forced out beyond the borders to settle in the "free Negro lots" found around the southern edge of Collect Pond.[1]

Things got worse for the colony's slave population in 1664, when the British took control and renamed the colony New York. They brought with them their own stricter slavery traditions and stripped away those meager legal protections that had been afforded by the Dutch. New York was not a plantation town; many families owned one or two slaves and they were usually kept in or near their homes. By the 1740s thousands of enslaved men and women from Africa and the Caribbean lived in New York, more than one-fifth of the city's population.

While a diverse number of religions were practiced under English rule, most black New Yorkers eventually converted to the Anglican Church. But Trinity Church did not allow the remains of black people, slave or free, to be buried in its churchyard. And so this population was forced outside the city walls again, this time claiming some land south of Collect Pond as their own private burial ground.

In their burial ceremonies and mourning practices, the city's African and Caribbean residents were able to display their original religious beliefs, and could come here and bury friends and loved ones according to traditional burial customs. In the early years, at dusk, New Yorkers would hear the foreign-sounding music, drum beats, and the sounds of exotic ceremonies drifting down from the burial yard. Well, that was simply too frightening for some white New Yorkers, and so, starting in 1722, it became illegal for blacks to congregate at night, and a 1731 law prohibited more than twelve people from gathering during the day at the burial ground.[2]

---

1 Today, Foley Square and the southern portions of Chinatown and Little Italy sit on the location of Collect Pond.
2 These draconian laws against black New Yorkers were instigated due to the events of April 1712, when a group of slaves conspired to burn the city. Twenty-one enslaved and freedmen were put to death in retaliation.

While these laws put a damper on many religious ceremonies, it was still possible to show some freedom of expression in the burials themselves. The dead were buried in wooden boxes, most facing east, as was customary for some African religions, and trinkets of religious or personal value (cowrie shells, pipes, buttons, and pieces of coral and crystal) were placed inside the coffins with the deceased.

The site of the African Burial Ground Monument is graced with profound symbolism throughout.

With the departure of the British in 1783 and the beginning of the city's great march northward, this land quickly became much more valuable. By the early 1810s, Collect Pond and its now-spoiled natural surroundings were simply filled in, the marshes drained, the hills leveled. The graves of many of New York's early slave and free black population, the resting place of approximately 15,000 bodies here, were covered over in landfill, in some places 16 to 25 feet deep.

The early structures built atop the burial ground were not very tall, none more than a few stories high. As a result, the depths of their foundations were no deeper than 20 feet or so. In some places, the burial ground lay below the newly erected buildings, completely preserved by the landfill that had been hastily thrown over it.

Flash forward — way forward — to 1991, when New York City was home to hundreds of skyscrapers, but unbelievably this small seven-acre area still only held structures of modest height. When work began on a nearby government building at 290 Broadway, excavators happened upon the first evidence of human remains. Throughout the next year, excavations would uncover a total of 419 bodies, along with a wide assortment of artifacts.

The monument to this discovery, completed in 2007 and operated by the National Park Service, returns a bit of grace and reverence to this site, and focuses on the spiritual beliefs of those who were interred here centuries ago. Immediately to your right is a set of seven evenly and elevated spaced beds of grass, where the bodies of the 419 have once again been buried, collected in hand-carved wooden sarcophagi. The following words are inscribed upon the monument (*Duane Street, between Broadway and Lafayette Street. Visitors' center at 290 Broadway*):

> *For all those who were lost*
> *For all those who were stolen*
> *For all those who were left behind*
> *For all those who are not forgotten*

Tribeca and Foley Square

POINTS OF INTEREST

1 WHAT THE HECK IS GOING ON IN FOLEY SQUARE? A whorl of government buildings surrounds Foley Square, which is rather ironic as this area is named for "Big Tom" Foley, a turn-of-the-twentieth-century political boss who had deep ties to organized crime. But Tom was a *complicated* man. He was especially beloved for his beneficence, and became a positive influence on a young Al Smith, who would become New York's progressive governor in 1918. Still, his reputation makes him an odd choice to share space with Thomas Paine Park, the attached leafy square just steps to the north that's named for a Founding Father.

The sculpture *Triumph of the Human Spirit* at Foley Square marks a sacred spot.

Reflecting the complex history of the neighborhood is the object at the center of Foley Square, a mysterious sculpture named *Triumph of the Human Spirit* by the Brooklyn artist Lorenzo Pace, which was unveiled in 2000. It speaks to that which lies underground here—a portion of the African Burial Ground. It takes its form from a West African headdress, called a Chi Wara, that features a male and female antelope. (*Center of Foley Square*)

2 THAT QUOTE ALONG THE TOP OF THE NEW YORK COUNTY COURTHOUSE IS ATTRIBUTED TO GEORGE WASHINGTON "The True Administration of Justice Is the Firmest Pillar of Good Government." Except he actually didn't say that! The quote is from a letter written by Washington on September 28, 1789: "Impressed with the conviction that the DUE administration of justice is the firmest pillar of good Government." This might very well be the truest typo in the history of government buildings. (*Foley Square, east side*)

You've seen it on TV! Now marvel at the slight misquote that tops it.

3 **REVOLUTIONARY CONVENIENCE (Vanished)** New York's ubiquitous drugstore chain Duane Reade is in fact named for the chain's first original shop that opened in 1960 on this block. But indirectly, of course, the shop is named for two prominent men from Revolutionary-era New York. James Duane (1733–1797) was a delegate for the Continental Congress who became New York's first post–Revolutionary War mayor. Joseph Reade (1694–1771) was a prominent merchant and a vestryman for Trinity Church. (And ironically, they both reportedly shopped at Target.) (*Broadway between Duane and Reade Streets*)

4 **ITS NAME WAS MUDD** The stark and shadowy alleys and industrial architecture of this neighborhood made it a natural fit for nightlife in the swingin' 1970s and '80s, and this address was home to one of the most glamorous spaces of them all: the Mudd Club,[3] a multilevel playground for the avant-garde and strictly fabulous. One of the most innovative clubs of the '70s, the Mudd Club played more to the burgeoning new wave and punk scene than to the disco beats echoing through other halls in town. The place became known as much for its Jean-Michel Basquiat exhibitions as it did for its groundbreaking performances by Fab Five Freddy and Bow Wow Wow. David Byrne and the Talking Heads immortalized the club in their song "Life During Wartime": "This ain't the Mudd Club or CBGB, I ain't got time for that now…" The club closed in 1983. (*77 White Street, near Cortlandt Alley*)

5 **THE FANCY ALLEY** The Van Cortlandts were among the wealthiest and most respected Dutch families to remain in New York after the British took charge of the colony in 1765. Today the family's name still graces an impressive variety of lanes, avenues, and parks throughout the city. This particular alleyway feels like a movie set (perhaps because it has costarred in so many TV shows and films?) and contains two notable curiosities.

The first is the bold industrial building (54 Franklin Street) at the corner of Cortlandt Alley and Franklin Street, with its medieval-style stone doorways and dramatic green shutters. Built in the 1890s for dry goods merchants, its severity still makes us, um, shutter. The second is New York's tiniest museum, called the Mmuseumm (4 Cortlandt Alley), with its petite displays

---

3   The club has a curious connection to the nineteenth century: It's named for Samuel Mudd, the doctor who treated an injured John Wilkes Booth after he assassinated Abraham Lincoln. He was accused of being a conspirator alongside Booth.

of weirdness and stuttering m's. Their slogan: "As is the macrocosm, so is the microcosm." (*Cortlandt Alley, between White and Franklin Streets*)

We shutter to think of all the secrets held along moody old Cortlandt Alley.

6 LOOK AT THAT AWESOME SIGN There are ghost signs all around Tribeca, traces of the industrial firms and warehouses that once called the district home. The sign for the Goodall Rubber Co. is in gorgeous shape, tracing back to a New York facility that opened in 1912. The company remained in this location until relocating to New Jersey in the 1970s. (*White Street and West Broadway*)

7 THE GHOSTBUSTERS FIREHOUSE The most photographed building in Tribeca is undoubtedly the Hook and Ladder Company No. 8 fire station, an oddly shaped structure that gained silver screen immortality in the 1980s as the headquarters of a group of likable Ghostbusters (in both the 1984 and 1989 films). Until the 1910s the firehouse was twice as large as the present building, but was cut in half to accommodate the widening of Varick Street during that decade.

By the way, you might have noticed that this neighborhood, with its trendy bars and restaurants, is the first we've visited that could rightly be called "très chic." But in *Ghostbusters*, Spengler (Harold Ramis) says of the firehouse, "I think this building should be condemned.... The neighborhood is like a demilitarized zone." Perhaps an exaggeration, as the converted lofts and warehouses of Tribeca—the neighborhood's name was hardly a decade old in 1984—were already a haven for artists, designers, and musicians by this time. But still, it would have certainly been deemed "gritty" by a majority of American filmgoers in the 1980s. (*North Moore and Varick Streets*)

8 THE FIRST CHRISTMAS TREE STAND Today's cute little Washington Market Park sits on the spot of New York's most important outdoor market of the nineteenth century. In the days before mass refrigeration and chain grocery stores, Washington Market was the place where New Yorkers came to buy their meats and fresh produce. First opened in 1812, the market offered many residents their first encounter with exotic food items from across the country and around the world. (Today a Whole Foods one block away provides much the same function, albeit with higher prices and gluten-free options.)

The hustle and bustle of old Washington Park, pictured here in 1868.

Deck the halls: By the 1910s, a sizable Christmas tree market had developed along West Street.

But this market wasn't just for edibles. In 1851 a woodsman named Mark Carr, living in the Catskill Mountains, chopped down a selection of fir and spruce trees, shoved them into two ox sleds, carted them over to Manhattan on a ferry, and set up shop in the market, paying one dollar for the privilege of selling his

Frederick Douglass, one of America's most famous abolitionists.

rather prickly merchandise. Holiday revelers were thrilled to be spared the journey out of town, and Carr's entire stock of evergreens sold out within the day. No surprise then that other farmers jumped on this evergreen opportunity, and within a few years the open-air Christmas tree market was born. (*Chambers and Greenwich Streets*)

9 **THE LIFESAVER OF LISPENARD (Vanished)** In the early and mid-nineteenth century, the Underground Railroad secretly escorted tens of thousands of Southern slaves to Northern destinations, where slavery was illegal. The African American publisher David Ruggles was born a freeman in Connecticut and moved to New York to energize the emerging abolitionist movement. And thank goodness he did. For at his home at 36 Lispenard, Ruggles sheltered an estimated 600 fugitive slaves, including in 1838 a man named Frederick Washington Bailey, who had escaped a life of slavery in Maryland.

That's no Brooklyn hipster! That's a Western Union delivery boy.

Under a new name, the abolitionist Frederick Douglass later wrote about how he felt arriving in New York: "Anguish and grief, like darkness and rain, may be depicted; but gladness and joy, like the rainbow, defy the skill of pen or pencil." (*36 Lispenard Street*)

10 **THE INTERNET BUILDING** From afar, 60 Hudson Street looks rather plain and brown, especially in comparison with the lively cast-iron architecture around it. But it may be one of the most important buildings in New York City, as it's densely wired in fiber-optic cable and serves the needs of more than 100 telecommunication companies. This has great poetic symmetry with the building's original purpose, as the headquarters of telegraph giant Western Union, built in the late 1920s. And the structure's initial hum-drum architecture becomes more interesting as you take in the art deco touches and the top floors' dramatic setbacks. The building's facade features nineteen shades of brown building materials that play tricks upon the eye. How many can you spot? (*60 Hudson Street*)

11 STAND HERE: Intersection of West Broadway, Varick, and Leonard Streets. Look north toward the two great antennas in the sky. *Why?* If 60 Hudson contains a bulk of New York's Web infrastructure, the building before you with the antennas, the AT&T Long Distance Building (*32 Avenue of the Americas*), holds the East Coast's critical telecommunication skeleton. Many of the major cellular companies lease space within this classic art deco building. Those "communication masts" were built here after September 11, 2001. From this distance, they look so part-and-parcel of the building's severe profile that one could imagine Batman standing between them and waving down at you. Peek inside the lobby for some rich allegorical depictions of the continents, courtesy of muralist Hildreth Meière. (*Intersection of West Broadway, Varick Street, and Leonard Street*)

A touch of old Victorian England on tiny Staple Street.

12 STABLES ON STAPLE Tribeca has perhaps the greatest collection of alleyways in all of New York City. But the most striking of them all is Staple Street, a tiny little thing that really only pretends to be an alley, its carriage-width dimensions still charmingly preserved. The star of this show is the glorious traverse, or skybridge, which links together two buildings that once held a common purpose. The structure at 67 Hudson Street was formerly New York Hospital's Hudson Street House of Relief and was linked to the hospital's ambulance annex — in essence, a stable — by this skybridge, built in 1907. At night you can hear the ghostly echoes of hooves (or maybe that's just the gutter gurgling). (*Staple Street, between Jay and Harrison Streets*)

13 THE AMERICAN EXPRESS CARRIAGE HOUSE Built in 1866, this structure was a home for horses, three floors of them, and served the equine needs of the original American Express office around the corner (55–61 Hudson Street). As the company was originally in the express mail business, the horses' rest and readiness was key to its success. Note the grotesque bulldog — the original American Express mascot — emerging out of the logo at the top. (*Hubert and Collister Streets*)

14 IF ONLY ALL STREET SIGNS WERE THIS BEAUTIFUL The

The fancy-pants sign at the corner of Beach and Hudson is tricked out, nineteenth-century style.

building on the northwest corner of Beach and Hudson Streets features one of the most surprising architectural features in the entire neighborhood — a flamboyant corner carving presenting the names of the streets. Built in 1886–1887, this fortress-like structure bears almost no other architectural feature of note. It's literally like they went mad on this one corner, giving us something to muse over today, as traffic spills out of the Holland Tunnel across the street. (*135 Hudson Street*)

Execution at the Tombs

The Tombs, New York's most infamous prison, was constructed in 1839 near the heart of the overcrowded Five Points slum. The imposing,

Many found the imposing Egyptian-style architecture of the Tombs quite arresting.

ornate structure took design inspiration from ancient Egyptian mausoleums and boasted a fittingly frightful facade, given its reputation as a vile, sweltering house of horror.

It was a place some prisoners went to die. The notoriously dank and foul-smelling complex was the scene of a great many public executions, but one particular execution that took place here on February 21, 1862, was especially notable. It was the only execution of an American convicted of being a slave trader.[4]

The import and export of slaves into the United States was technically banned with the U.S. Piracy Act of 1820, which included "human cargo" in its definition of international piracy. But this did not deter Nathaniel Gordon,

The Tombs' legendary "bridge of sighs" connected the prison to the criminal court.

who sailed to North Africa in 1860 and loaded a boat with nearly 900 people, intending to return home and sell them off to Southern plantation owners.

Gordon was caught just 50 miles offshore from port and brought to the United States for trial. He would have received a stern sentence even before the Civil War, but with the conflict in full swing by the time of his trial in late 1861, Gordon's defense team never stood a chance. Despite pleas from wealthy supporters, Gordon was sentenced to die on February 7, 1862. President Abraham Lincoln gave him a two-week stay of execution, and Gordon's supporters might have even convinced him to commute it further had Lincoln's young son Willie not died of typhoid on February 20.

One interesting note: The Tombs was a city prison, but Gordon's crime was a federal offense. This was the only federal execution to take place here.

The present Manhattan Detention Complex (still ominously nicknamed "the Tombs"), built in the 1980s, sits at White and Centre Streets on the site of the original prison.

---

4   Violating the 1820 piracy law that outlawed international slave trading.

REGARDING FIVE POINTS,
FROM A COMFORTABLE DISTANCE

Five Points, America's first slum, belongs to the past. Go slumming in Madison Square—there the trees throw shadows and make mystery. Go slumming under the arch of the Municipal Building—someone "interesting" or "picturesque" may lurk there. Slum anywhere, in fact, in preference to Five Points, for only the points are left. Five Points from now on will be simply the place where Baxter, Park, and Worth streets cross. City improvements are completing what Mulberry Bend Park [Columbus Park] began. Five Points has "a place in the sun." Surface cars pass in full sight of it, subways shed their crowds within a stone's throw, the New Yorker of the present, to-and-froing on Centre Street looks indifferent at areas newly opened toward Chatham Square, and would just as soon walk there as not. But the old New Yorker still looks over his shoulder when you say Five Points, and in his day there was a reason.

~ From the *New York Tribune,* April 9, 1916

Chapter 7 //

Chinatown
and Little Italy

Don't let this charming illustration of Five Points in 1859 fool you. The neighborhood had a notorious reputation for squalor and vice (and, apparently, playful dogs).

SITUATE THE READER
~Chinatown and Little Italy~

The infamous and dangerous Five Points neighborhood, site of much nineteenth-century gang warfare, never stood a chance. The entire area, its streets, homes, and stores, was built upon sinking foundations caused by the incomplete drainage of putrid old Collect Pond (as discussed in Chapter 6). It wasn't supposed to turn out this way. After it was drained, the new land was given the upbeat name Paradise Square. Respectable types built homes here, but then the ground began to shift and give way, and by the 1840s the housing market started to collapse—literally. All of this came just as Irish immigrants were arriving in New York Harbor in droves, seeking out a better life—and the cheapest dwellings in town. As buildings here packed in the city's poorest residents, the neighborhood became known as "Five Points," named for the intersection of four streets: Orange (now Baxter), Cross (now Mosco), Anthony (now Worth), and Little Water (which was entirely wiped off the map).

Its old tenements, its sorry squalor, its brothels and gambling dens were nefarious in ways New York had never known. And, incredibly, by the end of the nineteenth century, they'd be cleared away in a wave of social reforms and new city regulations.

The city's most notorious intersection once sat roughly on the site of today's Columbus Park, a busy square that is now home to cheerless concrete playground structures shaded by a small forest of trees. But the ghosts of Five Points still haunt these old streets, which today belong to the neighborhoods of Chinatown and Little Italy.

Mulberry Street, with its broken bend that hugs the eastern side of the park, was the center of Italian life in the 1890s. Over on Mott Street sat the city's first Chinese-owned businesses, some aboveboard and many, well, very, very below-board. As Chinatown has grown with the surge of Asian immigration in the twentieth century, the old Italian quarter has shrunk and is today mostly contained to Mulberry Street for a few blocks north of Canal Street. Meanwhile, "Little Italy" has become a charming tourist cove, its festive eateries and cafes smothered in tasty, red-sauce kitsch.

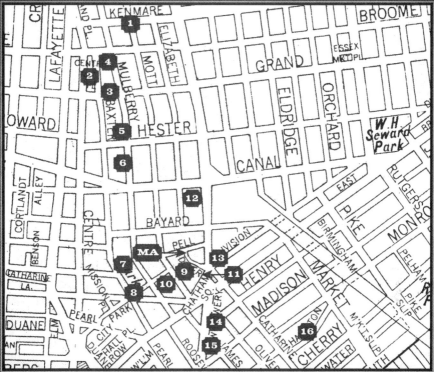

Doyers Street—the Bloody Angle

There are a handful of streets in New York that feel imaginary, too perfectly worn, as if sets from film noir, needing only a fog machine and a Max Steiner soundtrack to reach their atmospheric potential. Doyers Street, hardly 70 yards long, is one such place, marked by one subtle bend as it leaves Chatham Square, then breaks to the right like a broken arm, and then bends again to Pell Street. Doyers is an impractical little street, named for a brewer who long ago sold his wares here.

Doyers Street in 1909 presented a world that felt exotic and mysterious to many outsiders.

The history of Doyers Street is marked with violence and obscured in mystery. But nobody could say that it hasn't earned its nickname: the Bloody Angle. Many men have died along these 70 yards, both on the street and below it.

The first Chinese immigrants to arrive in New York in the 1870s were sailors and former employees of the First Transcontinental Railroad. These were men who had faced great hardships making their journey to the West, and then, once there, great discrimination while toiling away on the tracks. Mott Street became the locus of activity for the Chinese who continued on to New York, and once here they opened cigar shops, grocery stores, and laundromats. The more enterprising of them—with support from political machines and street gangs—turned to operating opium dens and brothels.

The nearby Five Points slums, which had somehow managed to get even more despicable in the decades following the Civil War, didn't survive the reform movements cleaning house throughout the city's poorest neighborhoods in the 1890s. The neighborhood was completely erased by the end of the century, dispersing many of these ethnic enclaves out into the city.

But the Chinese stayed.[1] By the 1890s about 2,500 Chinese immigrants called the neighborhood home, which now spread up Mott Street, over to Pell, and finally to Doyers.

Given the combination of physical hardships that they faced—the rugged voyage from their homeland, their spike-slamming manual labor out West,

menial jobs in New York, and the Chinese Exclusion Act of 1882 that put a stop to further immigration from China—the Chinese presence in New York remained almost exclusively male for some time. This so-called "bachelor society" tried to keep any homesickness at bay by forming social clubs, establishing shrines, and opening gambling

The Cafe Mandarin at 11–13 Doyers Street.

dens. They cooked up New York's first Chinese restaurants on Mott Street and, by 1893, opened a modest opera house at 5–7 Doyers Street devoted to Chinese music and performance.

As with other new arrivals who found solidarity and protection in street gangs, so too did the Chinese gang up, but with a twist. Nineteenth-century gangs such as the Bowery Boys or the Whyos often had tenuous connections to political leaders who sometimes employed these ruffians to do their nefarious deeds. In Chinatown, secret fraternal organizations called tongs served several

---

1 As did the Italians, confined over to Mulberry Street. Over the years, the Italian presence moved north and expanded greatly.

purposes. While they publicly protected the needs of the community, they also violently guarded the commercial interests of Chinatown's most illicit affairs.

Rival tongs frequently met to duke it out in bloody skirmishes, street thugs fighting for gambling cuts or to revenge a territorial encroachment. Their favorite arena? Crooked old Doyers Street. Already suited for street warfare — that bend could shield a gang or hide a surprise attack — Doyers also concealed tunnels below that came in handy when you were fleeing the cops or losing your enemy. It's believed that some tong members fought with hatchets — allegedly inspiring the phrase "hatchet man" — although by this time revolvers were more plentiful and much more effective.

You can see why the ravenous press of the day pounced upon Doyers Street as a gloriously gory setting for tales to delight their readers. Pulp detective novels burnished Chinatown's criminal reputation, exposing Doyers Street, in particular, as a nest of exotic vice in such titles as *Dark Doings on Doyers Street* and *The Plot to Burn Chinatown*, both published in 1906.

A view of Doyers Street in 1935, taken from under the elevated railroad tracks that ran up Bowery.

For a while, the Chinese Opera House was considered a neutral zone and off-limits to fighting. The *New York Sun*,[2] dropping a somewhat tasteless pun,

---

2   Another curious detail from that *Sun* article, which ran August 7, 1905: "Oddly enough there weren't any white people in the theater, although it was Sunday night, when the rubbernecks usually go to the theater in droves."

noted, "No matter how many fights and gunplays there were in the rest of Chinatown, it was always safe for all Tong men to go to the theater and bury the hatchet while watching the show."

However, one night in August 1905, members of two rival tongs—the On Leong Tong and the Hip Sing Tong—were taking in an evening of theater, hatchets temporarily buried, when Hip Sing gunmen arose from their front-row seats, turned, and brutally mowed down their On Leong adversaries sitting right behind them.

As shocking, nay "operatic," as this violence might seem to us today, it wasn't terribly surprising at the time, and outrageous acts of terror defined Doyers Street well into the 1930s. Unsurprisingly, it also lured adventurous uptown residents who yearned for a taste of something exotic. They often "slummed it" down to the Chatham Club (8 Doyers Street), operated by the enterprising Chuck Connors, who happily welcomed bohemian sightseers into his music hall, only to allow them to be quickly set upon by pickpockets. But hey, at least they'd get to enjoy the show, which usually featured toe-tapping Tin Pan Alley tunes performed by singing waiters (including a young Irving Berlin in 1906). Today at that address you'll find a hideously ugly post office (with singing clerks—sigh … we wish).

Walking along such a bruised little street, you probably wouldn't expect to happen upon fine cuisine. However, the celebrated (and fancy-sounding) Chinese Tuxedo restaurant was located at 2 Doyers Street above a trunk store. Opened in 1897, the eatery offered balcony seating so close to Chatham Square's elevated train that the waiters could have practically handed steamed buns to the passengers.

The still-surviving (and still-thriving) Nom Wah Tea Parlor arrived at Doyers Street in 1920. When it opened nearly a century ago, it sold almond cookies and moon cakes just like all the other Chinese bakeries in the neighborhood. But today, Nom Wah remains something of a miracle, gussied up, perhaps, for a gentrified New York, but still holding some of the mysteries of old Chinatown.[3]

---

3   And still a fine place to get dim sum today.

Chinatown and Little Italy

1 OUTDOOR PROHIBITION LIQUOR MARKET, YEE HAW! The early years of Prohibition in New York were characterized by some joyfully audacious behavior. In 1921, the intersection of Kenmare and Mott Streets functioned as a *very* unofficial "curb exchange" for liquor wholesalers to peddle their illegal wares to speakeasy owners. Nearby buildings served as warehouses and were overloaded with booze that awaited delivery to the thousands of illegal bars operating in the city. Controlled in part by mobster Joe Masseria, things got messy at the exchange when people began shooting each other, and by 1922, it ceased to exist here. (*Corner of Kenmare and Mott Streets*)

2 THOSE "OTHER" LIONS That entire boozy episode is even more egregious when you consider that the city's Beaux-Arts police headquarters was located just two blocks away at the time. This ornate Gilded Age confection, with its intricate facade, was designed by architects Hoppin and Koen, who took inspiration from City Hall's frilly flourishes. The intent was "to impress both officer and prisoner...with the majesty of the law." We're neither, but we're still impressed.

The lions in front of the old police headquarters look positively stressed out.

Today the old HQ has been divvied up into swanky apartments, but for most of the twentieth century (from 1909 to 1973) it served the New York Police Department. Two lions sit outside the building's front doors that are just as old as their uptown cat companions in front of the New York Public Library on 42nd Street, but these are not nearly as popular with selfie-snapping tourists. Come on, give 'em some love. (*240 Centre Street*)

3 THE MARVELOUS LABORATORY OF NICOLA TESLA (Vanished) Everybody's favorite underappreciated inventor, Nikola Tesla (1856–1943), moved to New York in 1884 to work for Thomas Edison. When the two geniuses got in a tizzy over his salary, Tesla struck out on his own. Their rivalry would spark the great "war of the currents" (AC vs. DC) and rev up public interest in electrical power. Tesla maintained a few laboratories throughout the city, including one on Grand Street in 1889. It's believed that the Tesla coil—that cool thing that sprays electricity from a central transformer—was perfected at this spot. (*175 Grand Street*)

4 THE TENOR IN THE BASEMENT Grotta Azzurra, named for the sea cave on the Isle of Capri, has a whole lotta stories embedded within its brick walls. It's one of Little Italy's oldest eateries, tracing its lineage to a restaurant that opened here in 1908. During the 1950s Frank Sinatra and the Rat Pack frequented the eatery (although the same might be said of many of the restaurants lining Mulberry Street). However, it was another frequent diner a half century before them that gave Grotta Azzurra its basement secret.

Caruso, legendary tenor, sang the praises of Little Italy's restaurants.

Enrico Caruso, one of America's most popular singers in the early 1900s, dined here often, sometimes with his entire opera troupe. One can just imagine the big personalities and hand gestures! In tribute, the restaurant opened a mini-museum in the basement, now christened the Enrico Caruso Room. We'd give a cannoli for every rendition of "O Sole Mio" that's been sung here. (*177 Mulberry Street*)

5 LIFE IMITATING ART IMITATING LIFE The restaurants of Little Italy are filled with wondrous and dangerous tales. Pop into any of the vintage eateries here, and the proprietors and waiters will be armed with interesting stories of days gone by, of famous movie stars, crooners, and mobsters (and perhaps, in the latter case, assassinations).

Today the restaurant Da Gennaro sits on the site of the infamous Umberto's Clam House. On April 7, 1972, the mobster Joe Gallo was brutally gunned down here while celebrating his forty-third birthday with his family. The gruesome hit reads something like a scene out of *The Godfather*, which, incidentally, was released just three weeks before Gallo's death. Should you wish to experience Umberto's today, it's located just across the street at 132 Mulberry. *Buon appetito!* (*129 Mulberry Street*)

Life Is Beautiful: A 1910s street scene in the area of today's Little Italy.

6 THERE WILL BE BLOOD Love it or hate it for its inescapable rowdiness and sizzling street food, the annual San Gennaro festival along Mulberry Street in mid-September is one of New York's oldest outdoor traditions, and dates back to 1926. Italian immigrants imported the Italian festival, which honors the martyrdom of San Gennaro (called Januarius by the Christian Romans). It's believed that during the celebration each year, dried blood contained in a relic back in Naples liquefies in its ampoules. While they might not have that miracle blood at the Church of the Most Precious Blood on Mulberry Street, they do have an extraordinary collection of statuary and artwork that manages to feel like both a rural Neapolitan church and an urban sanctuary. From this church a statue of San Gennaro is paraded up Mulberry Street at the climax of the festival each year. (*109 Mulberry Street, enter on Baxter Street*)

The Church of the Most Precious Blood offers a sacred escape from Mulberry Street.

7 THAT QUOTE IN COLUMBUS PARK Below the statue of Dr. Sun Yat-sen, the quote reads, "All under heaven are equal." This is a version of the motto he used when he formed the Republic of China in 1912 and is based on the far older saying, "Everything under heaven belongs to all." The word *tianxia,* "under heaven," has profound meaning in Chinese culture, ascribed first to the spiritual world, then the political one. (*Columbus Park, north end*)

The statue of Dr. Sun Yat-sen is surrounded by residents of all ages daily in Columbus Park.

8 STAND HERE: The southwest corner of Columbus Park, near the park's entrance at the corner of Baxter and Worth Streets. *Why?* You're standing at the former intersection that gave "Five Points" its name. It was perhaps the most written-about and notorious neighborhood in New York during the nineteenth century, legendary even then for being a miserable mess.[4] In reality, while crime was certainly rampant, it was also the home to thousands of hardworking and newly arrived immigrants, who struggled every day to get by and get out.

You're probably wondering why you won't find any historical marker today that pinpoints the dastardly spot. Reform-minded New Yorkers, it turns out,

The rowdy and ramshackle street life of Five Points in 1873 (artist, C. A. Keetels).

worked vigorously for decades to scrub away its memory. Its reputation was so bad that simply changing the street names couldn't wash away the stain. And so they razed it—all Five Points of it—and planted a park to soothe the soul. Columbus Park, opened in 1897, was designed by Calvert Vaux (of Central Park fame) and was initially so formal that visitors weren't allowed onto the grass. As you can see from the frenzied park scene today, they've loosened up quite a bit. (*Southwest corner of Columbus Park*)

9 THE WORLD FAMOUS DANCING AND TIC-TAC-TOE CHICKEN Mott Street is famous for many unusual things, one of which is

Why did the chicken cross the road? To escape from that blasted arcade!

tap-dancing poultry. Unlike the plucked candied ducks hanging in restaurant windows elsewhere in Chinatown, the birds at Chinatown Fair kept their coats on while performing amazing feats in this noisy, hole-in-the-wall arcade. The game room featured chicken-powered "games" starting in the 1960s, most of them with chickens either dancing on command or playing tic-tac-toe against their human "competitor." The first chick was named Clarabelle, and the last Lillie (who died in 2001). The whole thing was a foul endeavor, which probably explains

---

4   A bit of the blame can be attributed to Charles Dickens, who wrote of Five Points: "This is the place; these narrow ways diverging to the right and left, and reeking everywhere with dirt and filth"; and to Herbert Asbury, who romanticized the area in his 1927 book, *The Gangs of New York*.

why the arcade today is a chicken-free zone. (Although the sign outside is still the clucking best.) (*8 Mott Street*)

10 WHAT'S NEW YORK WITHOUT CHINESE FOOD?
(Vanished) The first Chinese permanent resident of New York City is believed to be a man named Ah Ken, who arrived in town in 1858 and eventually opened a boardinghouse here on Mott Street. Other Chinese men came too, boarded here, and soon more followed. And they needed to eat. And so it was on this street that New York met its first Chinese restaurant.

The Port Arthur Restaurant, the city's most famous Chinese eatery a century ago, opened on the second and third floors here in 1897 and dished up noodles for nearly 85 years. It was also the city's first Chinese restaurant to have a liquor license, which made it extra popular with thirsty bohemians and adventurous uptown residents who were "slumming it" down in the exotic neighborhood.[5] (*7–9 Mott Street*)

Port Arthur Restaurant's all decked out for the Chinese New Year in the early 1910s.

11 THE SOLDIERS' TATTOO PARLOR (Vanished) Charlie Wagner's tattoo parlor is the kind of place that really should have a plaque. Wagner was New York's most skilled and revolutionary tattoo artist of

---

5 "Slumming it" was a term coined in the late nineteenth century.

his day. He got started in 1904 and by the 1940s was inking up customers behind a partition of a five-chair barber shop here, located in the rumbles and shadows of the elevated train that ran up Bowery. During World War II, his most popular design featured a dagger with the phrase "Remember Pearl Harbor, Dec. 7, 1941."

Wagner held the patent for an early version of an electric "tattoo machine" still used by tattoo artists today. And he didn't decorate just soldiers: He covered many of Coney Island's early sideshow stars and is credited with being among the first to apply "permanent lip liner" for women. (*11 Chatham Square*)

12 WHAT BULL IS THIS? (Vanished) This address was once the location of the Colonial-era Bull's Head Tavern, which served as a gathering-place for farmers, drovers, and merchants in the eighteenth century. As the area surrounding the nearby Collect Pond became overrun with tanneries and slaughterhouses, it was soon the center of Manhattan's meat selling and rendering industry.

'Til the cows come home: It was always a cattle call at the Bull's Head Tavern (pictured here c. 1801).

On November 25, 1783, as the British pulled out of town on Evacuation Day, George Washington and his entourage met at the Bull's Head to prep themselves for their triumphant reentry into New York. Governor George Clinton and more than 800 uniformed troops and jubilant townsfolk gathered outside the tavern, preparing for the procession, a victory parade for the general who had won the war. (*50 Bowery*)

13 THE SECRETS OF CONFUCIUS PLAZA The very tall and very brick Confucius Plaza Apartments was completed in 1975, and a likeness of the ancient philosopher was placed here as its kindest ornament. He is a calming force along a section of the Bowery that holds both violent and incomplete histories. Beneath his feet sits a 700-foot section of the Second Avenue Subway, an underground train line that was abandoned mid-construction in 1974 at a particularly bleak moment in the city's financial crisis. Meanwhile, just to the north of Confucius once sat one of the most lawless bars to ever pour drinks in the city. The cheerfully named Morgue (25 Bowery) was the preferred hangout of the deadly Whyos gang in the 1890s. The Whyos, an enterprising gang of hit men, actually offered their clients a menu of violent services — something to cater to every budget (from your simple nose-breaking to a full-on hit).

Confucius may have had a few choice words to say about his perch in Confucius Plaza.

Confucius said, "When anger rises, think of the consequences." Alas, he showed up too late. (*Intersection of Bowery and Division Street*)

14 THE OLD CEMETERY A surprise awaits just south of the traffic-clogged intersection of Chatham Square: the second-oldest cemetery in New York City. Although today it's permanently locked behind gates, a cursory glance inside from the street reveals gravestones in English, Spanish, and Hebrew. This is the First Shearith Israel Graveyard, built in 1682 when this land was located far outside the town limits. (*55–57 St. James Place*)

The tucked-away First Shearith Israel Graveyard is one of America's oldest burial grounds.

15 THE ANCIENT ORDER OF HIBERNIANS On Mott, Pell, and Doyers Streets, you'll find traces of Chinese fraternal orders that kept the community empowered during the 1880s and '90s. But just a few blocks away is the location of an organization valued by those of an earlier immigration wave: the Irish.

Thousands of Irish immigrants had already arrived in New York by the time the Irish potato famine brought millions more in the 1840s.[6] In 1836, embattled Irish immigrants, facing a growing anti-Catholic nativist sentiment in the city, formed the Ancient Order at St. James Church. (Hibernia was the Roman name for Ireland, so they took their ancient stuff seriously!) This group was critical to the survival and well-being of Irish New Yorkers. The Order came to the church's rescue in 1986, saving it from a slated demolition, and still remains active today. (*32 James Street*)

16 THE DEADLY LUNG BLOCK (Vanished) This entire block is dominated by one massive complex of nearly 1,600 apartments quaintly named Knickerbocker Village, built in the 1930s. Like many of the area's

6   Just over 4.2 million Irish immigrants would arrive in America between 1830 and 1900.

housing projects, the Knickerbocker replaced a dense and squalid collection of deteriorating tenements from the nineteenth century.

Once called Cherry Hill, the neighborhood developed an especially bad reputation because of its most lawless slum, Gotham Court (social reformer and photographer Jacob Riis crowned it one of the worst tenements in the city). Soon it was called something more foreboding—the "Lung Block,"[7] due to the high rate of deaths from tuberculosis among its residents.

Also found on this ghastly block was a tenement nicknamed the "Ink Pot." In 1906 Ralph Waldo Trine wrote of this wretched building, "Here the plague lives in darkness and filth—filth in halls, over walls and floors, in sinks and closet.

Jacob Riis documented the plight—and changed the fate—of New York's poorest neighborhood.

Here in nine years alone twenty-six cases have been reported." (*The entire block, framed by Monroe, Catherine, Cherry, and Market Streets*)

---

7 It was Riis himself who coined the phrase in his iconic 1890 social commentary *How the Other Half Lives: Studies among the Tenements of New York.*

Tastes of History: Little Italy's Restaurants

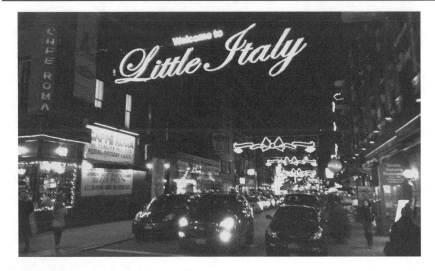

Little Italy, the city's most famous Italian enclave, developed in the second half of the nineteenth century, first at the base of Mulberry Street before moving north. Food shops opened almost immediately to cater to the new arrivals from Italy, most of them men who had left their mothers and wives back home.

Specialty grocery stores imported or produced Old World cheeses, pastas, and sauces, and some restaurants, particularly along Mulberry, satisfied the neighborhood's cravings. In the 1950s and '60s, the rise of Chinatown and allure of the suburbs would slice back Little Italy's borders dramatically.

Today tourists still flock to the impressive lineup of "red sauce" restaurants along Mulberry and Hester, along with the neighborhood's fine bakeries and food markets:

ANGELO'S OF MULBERRY STREET

Angelo's is the elder statesman of the Mulberry Street restaurants; it's been serving plates of fresh pasta since 1902, making it one of the oldest establishments in Little Italy. A Naples transplant, Angelo Tulimieri sold his restaurant to the current owners in 1960. Countless celebrities have dined under these soft lights, including President Ronald Reagan in 1981. (*146 Mulberry Street*)

FORLINI'S

"Big Joe," "Little Joe," and Derek run the show at Forlini's, a vintage Italian American restaurant opened in 1943 by their grandfather. Located half a block south of Canal on Baxter, the place is just off the main tourist drag and offers a throwback dining experience inside, where patrons are seated under chandeliers and beside now-retro oil paintings. (*93 Baxter Street*)

THE ORIGINAL VINCENT'S
Opened at the corner of Mott and Hester Streets in 1904 as Vincent's Clam Bar, Vincent's still packs 'em in with fresh seafood and pasta dishes, along with their "internationally celebrated Vincent's Sauce." (*119 Mott Street*)

PUGLIA RESTAURANT
Located just across the street from Vincent's, this rather rambunctious southern Italian restaurant was opened by Puglia native Gregorio Garofalo in 1919 and is today run by his grandson Joe. Forget about a quiet candlelit dinner; Puglia is all about long, communal tables and lively "nightly entertainment." Move over! (*189 Hester Street*)

UMBERTO'S CLAM HOUSE
See page 112. (*129 Mulberry Street*)

FERRARA BAKERY AND CAFE
A Little Italy institution deserving of its flashy, Broadway-style marquee, Ferrara's has been serving cakes, cannoli, and gelato to anyone in search of a sugar rush since it opened here on Grand Street in 1892. Still operated by the Ferrara family, the cafe claims to be the nation's first espresso bar. Get it to go or have a seat in the somewhat hectic mirror-lined dining room. (*195 Grand Street*)

ALLEVA DAIRY
Head inside the self-proclaimed "oldest cheese store in America" on Grand Street to pick up some mozzarella or ricotta made fresh every morning. The Alleva family has been cutting the cheese here since 1892, and the store supplies many of the pizzerias in the neighborhood. (*188 Grand Street*)

PIEMONTE RAVIOLI
Located just next to Alleva Dairy, Piemonte started cranking out fresh pasta for hungry families and restaurants in 1920. Today their production is split between the small kitchen here and a larger facility in Queens. Eager to sample the ravioli but forgot to bring a pot? The cashier can point you to nearby restaurants that serve each of their noodles. (*190 Grand Street*)

DI PALO FINE FOOD
Opened in 1925, Di Palo is today the busiest retailer of Italian food on this stretch of Grand Street. Push your way in past the hanging salamis and cheese wheels, and grab a number. Wait your turn to discuss (and sample!) freshly made cheeses, sliced prosciutto, and even antipasti. (*200 Grand Street*)

An advertisement for the show *The Black Crook*—considered by some to be the first Broadway musical—which made its debut on September 12, 1866, at Niblo's Garden (Broadway and Prince Street)

NIBLO'S GARDEN

Doors open at 7. Commences at 7½.

EVERY NIGHT AND SATURDAY AFTERNOON,

BRILLIANT SUCCESS

of the

GORGEOUS SPECTACULAR DRAMA

THE BLACK CROOK

Introducing Jarret and Palmer's

GREAT PARISIENNE BALLET TROUPE

MARIE BONFANTI, RITA SANGALLI

And FIFTY DANSEUSES from principal European Theaters

MAGNIFICENT SCENERY,

SUPERB COSTUMES,

DAZZLING ARMORS,

STARTLING EFFECTS.

And the bewildering TRANSFORMATION SCENE

Admission 75 cents. Secured seats in Dress Circle $1,
Reserved seats in Parquet and Parquet Circle $1.50, Family Circle
(entrance on Crosby Street) 50 cents. Private Boxes $5 and $10

Chapter 8///

SoHo and Nolita

A boxy view greets you along Spring and Varick Streets, 1935 (photo: Berenice Abbott).

SITUATE THE READER
–SoHo and Nolita–

South of Houston (SoHo), North of Little Italy (Nolita)—their names are trendy mash-ups, devised by modern residents and real estate developers.[1]

In the 1960s and '70s, artists and urban activists fell in love with the lofts below Houston Street, clad in beautiful cast iron but virtually abandoned by industry. By the 1970s, the neighborhood had been given its portmanteau and historic designation by the city. Gentrification arrived at the streets around Old St. Patrick's more than a decade later, with most of Manhattan's Italian population having already fled to other neighborhoods. Unlike touristy Little Italy to its south, Nolita is glam and ready-to-wear.

But these new developments hide very rich histories behind their catchy names. Acts of violence against Catholics by so-called nativists rocked the neighborhood in the 1830s and '40s, causing the city's first Irish immigrants to seek refuge inside Old St. Pat's, the second Catholic church in New York. A few decades later, it would be Italian-born Catholics who would work and live here, and the neighborhood's tenements were as overcrowded as the ones down on Mulberry Bend (see Chapter 7).

The first theaters located on Broadway proper were situated on the stretch between Canal and Houston—pleasure gardens, vaudeville houses, and even minstrel theaters. The most sinful of venues, the dance hall, also debuted along this span of Broadway in the 1850s. As proper society gradually moved uptown over the next few decades, these streets were taken over by warehouses. But the boardinghouses and brothels that had been mainstays along the waterfront many blocks away soon relocated to these desolate streets, and the cast-iron district, long before it was called SoHo, sank for decades into a depressed funk.

---

1   The area to the far west of this neighborhood is called Hudson Square, which sounds more authentic but is actually a newer name than SoHo.

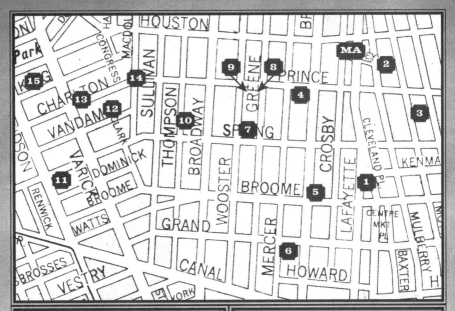

POINTS OF INTEREST

1 Petrosino!

2 The Catacombs of St. Patrick's

3 Gods and Monsters of Elizabeth Street

4 The Little Singer Building

5 The Magical Emporium of E. V. Haughwout

6 The World Sits High on a Shelf

7 The Haunted Well

8 The Cast-Iron Faker

9 Awesome Sign Alert

10 The Playground Named for a Bakery

11 Chief the Dead Fire Dog

12 Hail to the Huron

13 The Vice Presidential Mansion

14 Stand Here

15 Let the Music Play

MA The Puck Building

The Puck Building

Of all the fashionistas who have exposed themselves along Houston Street over the past century, none has been as smug and self-absorbed as Puck.

Gold, pudgy Puck, barely clothed, with a tilted top hat, poses high above the corner of Houston and Mulberry on a golden nugget, clutching an oversize pen and a hand mirror. For decades, this little sprite has perched overhead,

Call him Mr. Vain? Perhaps—but Puck holds some surprising secrets.

with nary a concern for those passing by. Perhaps he hopes you'll rush past without noticing his little secret.

The building on which Puck stands is a Romanesque Revival number nearly as bold and rascally as he is. Its myriad arches and rich red brick are indicative of one of the coolest-named architectural styles in history—*Rundbogenstil*, hailing from Germany. A fitting choice, as the building was once home to one of the greatest German-language publications in America.

Puck magazine was the wonderfully twisted product of Austrian immigrant Joseph Keppler, an illustrator with a fine pen and a wry sensibility. He first debuted a humor weekly called *Puck* while living in St. Louis in 1871, but it wasn't until he moved to New York that the magazine's unique satirical style found a readership. Restarted in New York in 1876 with the help of printer Adolph Schwartzman, *Puck* became the rage, and its English-language edition outsold its German version.

Puck was a precursor to *Mad* magazine, *The Onion*, and *The Daily Show*. A highly skeptical and thought-provoking survey of politics and current affairs, it was infected with poignant wit that directed its aim at the most powerful men of the day. It achieved this with illustrations, many done by Keppler himself, including three full-page color images with many smaller ones throughout.

Although Keppler considered himself a Democrat, his targets were frequently the fat cats of the Tammany Hall Democratic machine. The weekly came into prominence after the fall of William "Boss" Tweed in the 1870s, and readers were open to Keppler's adroit observations paired with sumptuous illustrations that are considered the hallmarks of early political cartoons. And all of it ran under the banner of the weekly's telling slogan, "What Fools These Mortals Be!"

By the mid-1880s, publishers vied to outdo each other, constructing lavish headquarters that very publicly demonstrated their newspaper's or magazine's popularity and influence. In 1890 Joseph Pulitzer's office for his *New York World* would become the tallest building in the

Puck magazine was the most prominent illustrated satirical magazine during the Gilded Age.

world. Keppler aimed for a different area of town, but planned for a building no less sensational.

Designed by Albert Wagner, the massive Puck Building was completed in 1886, then expanded southward in 1893 to accommodate both the publication's offices and its printing presses in the basement. It was one of the largest buildings in the neighborhood, and straddled by tenements to the south and cast-iron constructions to the west.

But here's the catch: When originally constructed, the Puck Building was actually much larger than it is today. Five mighty arches, 120 feet across, once ran along the Houston Street side. (Today there are only three.) Across from the Puck was a very small street called Lafayette Place, which didn't stretch down past Houston Street. In 1897, the city, having cleared away the old Five Points neighborhood and started construction on Civic Center's government buildings, wanted to extend what would become Lafayette Street down to greet it.

The Puck Building (pictured in 1893) was once much larger until Lafayette Street lopped off a western chunk.

Puck, however, stood in its way. The city's plan would have wiped the office building off the map, and, many buildings farther south were in fact bulldozed. But instead of demolishing Puck, he was simply whittled down—an entire third of the building's western side was sliced off and a new entrance was created on Lafayette. On that side of the building you'll find a second little Puck figure leering down at the disruptive new street beneath it.

Puck magazine would thrive in the 1890s and early 1900s. But with the rise of printed photographs in magazines, illustrated weeklies started to look antiquated. What had seemed so ribald and edgy in the Gilded Age had lost its sting by the 1910s.

In a fitting and ironic punchline to the story, the magazine would be killed off by one of its chief targets: the extravagant publisher and politico William Randolph Hearst, who bought it in 1917 and stopped its presses a year later. For Hearst, who later inspired the title character in Orson Welles's 1941 film, *Citizen Kane* after multiple failed attempts to be elected to public office, silencing one of his chief critics must have been a sweet revenge.

By the end of the 1910s, the center of the printing trade had moved west—far west—to the area of today's Hudson Square. But publishers would still make the Puck Building home for decades after the magazine's closure. In the 1980s, satire returned to the building in the form of *Spy*, a beloved magazine more trenchant in its aim at celebrities like Donald Trump and John F. Kennedy, Jr.

Today the building's ground floor retail tenant is the rugged outdoors and fitness chain REI. They've preserved many original elements of old *Puck* magazine, including the massive steam engine flywheels in the basement and a collection of lithographic stones from Puck's golden age.

Speaking of the actual Puck, still standing there, gazing into that mirror—things are not what they seem. What appears to be a bronze statue is made, in fact, of zinc. While it wasn't an uncommon material for sculpture in the nineteenth century, it's still not quite as glamorous as you might think. Then there's the figure of Puck himself. Or rather, *herself*. Keppler modeled the original image of Puck on drawings of his young daughter. So many secrets—no wonder he's, or rather *she's*, smirking.

SoHo and Nolita

POINTS OF INTEREST

1 PETROSINO! This tiny wedge of a park commemorates the life of Joseph Petrosino, the intrepid police officer and the first Italian speaker to be recruited into the NYPD. He devoted his dramatic career to cracking down on organized crime, especially the secretive "Black Hand" blackmailers, who terrorized Italian immigrants in the early 1900s. Petrosino was celebrated as a scrappy and relentless investigator, but he might have become too well known for his own good. When he traveled to Sicily on a top-secret mission, an informant ratted him out, and he was assassinated on March 12, 1909, in Palermo.

Petrosino continues to keep watch on this busy intersection.

This park sits about halfway between Petrosino's former apartment at 233 Lafayette Street and the police department's elaborate Centre Street headquarters (discussed in Chapter 7), which would open the year he was murdered. One can only imagine how Joe might have handled the mob during Prohibition. (*Petrosino Square*)

2 THE CATACOMBS OF ST. PATRICK'S This fantastic old cathedral—make that *basilica*, an august appointment made by the Vatican in 2010—is one of New York's great original landmarks, the touchstone of the city's Catholic (and specifically Irish-Catholic) community since it was dedicated in 1815. More than two decades later, angered by the swelling population of

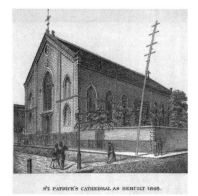

ST. PATRICK'S CATHEDRAL AS REBUILT 1868.

St. Patrick's Old Cathedral holds secrets of the neighborhood's history in its burial ground.

Irish-born Catholics in the city, nativists (who considered themselves to be "real" Americans) nearly destroyed the church multiple times in violent street riots.

Peeking into the church's picturesque cemetery is a thrill, although you're only seeing half the story. Hundreds more permanently reside here in the network of catacombs buried beneath the church. Its most famous interment for many years was the Venerable Pierre Toussaint (1766–1853), the Haitian hairdresser and slave-turned-philanthropist who assisted in funding the construction of St. Patrick's Cathedral uptown. Due to his veneration, he was removed from Old St. Pat's and is now interred at the midtown cathedral (see Chapter 19).

These grounds, however, are now taking reservations! A new columbarium in the crypt opened in 2013, making it Manhattan's only Catholic cemetery. (*263 Mulberry Street*)

3 GODS AND MONSTERS OF ELIZABETH STREET There is a strange lot between Elizabeth and Mott Streets where aging mythological artifacts silently rule. It is an ever-changing population of sphinxes, griffins, lions, and dragons. Stone reliefs, fountain remnants, and iron beams with rusted pilasters sit around a fecund garden, which by all by all appearances seems to be the ruins of an abandoned estate.

The Elizabeth Street Gallery has owned this unique showroom since 1991, and it's become a park of sorts. And yes, these items are for sale (in case you happen to be in the market for a marble sphinx). Otherwise, simply ponder the mysteries of the sphinx from one of the garden's many benches. (*209 Elizabeth Street*)

4 THE LITTLE SINGER BUILDING The tallest building in the world from 1908 to 1909 was the goofy-looking Singer Building at 149 Broadway, mentioned in Chapter 3. But that was the *second* home of the Singer Sewing Machine Company. The first remains with us

There goes the neighborhood! Stone lions and mythical behemoths for sale on Elizabeth Street.

today, an unusual L-shaped building with two entrances, one on Broadway and one on Prince Street. Loaded up with wrought iron tracery and New Orleans–style flair, the 1904 "Little Singer Building," as it's nicknamed, was designed by Ernest Flagg, the same architect who would build Singer's second skyscraper four years later. In a district of cast iron, this makes for a striking, flamboyant interloper. (*561 Broadway, also on the Prince Street side*)

The Prince Street entrance of the L-shaped Singer Building cuts an elegant profile.

5 **THE MAGICAL EMPORIUM OF E. V. HAUGHWOUT** Cast-iron construction, pioneered in America by architect James Bogardus in the 1850s, became the preferred method of building large dry goods shops and department stores in the mid- and late nineteenth century, thanks to the speed

with which these enormous buildings could go up and the savings they presented over heavier, more cumbersome construction methods. Today SoHo contains the largest surviving collection of cast-iron buildings in the world. Wandering through these streets in the late afternoon, sun ignites their white- and cream-colored exteriors. It's magical — and the stuff of a million postcards, album covers, and selfies.

Cast-iron architecture defines Soho architecture, including here at Broadway and Broome Street, 1935 (photo: Berenice Abbott).

But one of these buildings is perhaps more famous than the rest: the former emporium of E. V. Haughwout, at Broadway and Broome Street, which sold fine china and glassware. The corner building's two-sided cast-iron construction and facade was the first of its kind when it was completed in 1857, and soon inspired blocks lined with similar construction throughout SoHo. But its most important contribution was placed inside — the very first passenger elevator, which lifted and lowered its wealthy clients (such as First

Lady Mary Todd Lincoln) to its various exotic departments.

Haughwout's Emporium was famed for its French champagne and for the fine flutes that it was drunk from. Surprised? While the neighborhood today still pops more than its share of bubbly, SoHo was never more glamorous than during the Haughwout years. (*488 Broadway*)

6 **THE WORLD SITS HIGH ON A SHELF** No, really, cross the street and look at the top of this building. There's an imprint of the world affixed

Globe-Wernicke: You'll never look at bookshelves the same.

to this otherwise average structure, the former home of Globe-Wernicke office furniture, dating from 1916. The company was best known for their patented "elastic bookshelf," the flexible (and stackable!) modular shelving design that is the basis for most of the affordable bookshelves you can buy today. (IKEA tips its hat to them.) Their slogan for this marvelous device was "It grows with your business and your business grows with it."

Now look at this building again, and tell us it doesn't look a little bit like an old-timey bookshelf. (*451–453 Broadway*)

7 THE HAUNTED WELL Tucked away today in the basement of a European clothing chain on Spring Street sits the remains of the Manhattan Well, a centuries-old well that was the source of one of the city's most famous ghost stories. In the winter of 1800, the body of young Gulielma Sands was found strangled at the bottom of this well, then located in Lispenard Meadows. Her groom-to-be, Levi Weeks, was tried in court for her murder but eventually acquitted. It helped that he had excellent representation—no less than Alexander Hamilton *and* Aaron Burr, fighting together for him (before they'd fight each other). The

Well dressed: A grim story lurks in the basement of this Spring Street boutique.

Manhattan Well was eventually covered up, but stories of a haunting specter have vexed the buildings that have stood over it ever since. Today you can gawk at this historic structure while strolling between racks of clothing. But what's that over there? Did you see something move? (*129 Spring Street*)

8 THE CAST-IRON FAKER With all this incredible cast-iron architecture and ornamental ironwork surrounding you, why search out the fake stuff? Because it gives us an excuse to use the phrase "trompe l'oeil" again. In 1975 Richard Haas was commissioned to paint this replica of a cast-iron facade on the boring brick side of an ornate cast-iron structure, and he attacked it with mind-bending gusto. Three year later, he would paint a more impressive trompe l'oeil at Peck Slip in the South Street Seaport (which includes an impressive, and fake, view of the Brooklyn Bridge, see page 83). This one on Prince Street has been systematically topped off with graffiti over the years. (*112 Prince Street*)

9 AWESOME SIGN ALERT The heart of New York's printing business

would drift from the area north of the Puck Building to the district west of SoHo, today called Hudson Square. This signage remnant above the storefronts at 120–126 Prince Street seem stuck in the transition, its rusted advertisements promise a range of printed products — "Stationery, Office Supplies, Paper, and Twine" and "Manifold Books, Special Forms, Engraving." (*120–126 Prince Street*)

10 THE PLAYGROUND NAMED FOR A BAKERY At first blush, you might think the Vesuvio Playground is named for Mount Vesuvius, the volcano in southern Italy that famously destroyed the city of Pompeii, and that's actually true — indirectly. This is the first and only public playground — possibly in the world — named for a bakery. Vesuvio Bakery, at 160 Prince Street, opened in 1920, a rare remaining outlier of the Italian community that made the southern part of Greenwich Village home in the early twentieth century. You can visit the bakery today, sort of; the storefront still says Vesuvio, but the establishment inside is the Birdbath Bakery. Alas, Vesuvio baked their last batch in 2009. (*86 Thompson Street*)

11 CHIEF THE DEAD FIRE DOG Among the incredible delights on display at the New York City Fire Museum, one of our favorite museums in the city, is something that will certainly give you *paws*.

In 1929 a little dog named Chief pranced into the firehouse of Red Hook, Brooklyn's Company 203. The canine fearlessly fought blazes alongside the firefighters, saving countless lives on late-night calls by charging into burning buildings and barking to wake tenants. Chief served for ten years and won several badges of honor before being struck by a car in 1939. This tail is not over, however, as his body was preserved (thanks to taxidermy) and now stands guard over one of America's finest displays of fire equipment and vehicles, as well as a moving memorial to the firefighters lost in the attacks of September 11, 2001. (*278 Spring Street*)

12 **HAIL TO THE HURON** The Charlton-King-Vandam Historic District is a small bundle of charming early nineteenth-century Federal-style homes that make a quaint contrast to the mighty cast-iron district to its east. Today the SoHo Playhouse makes good use of the decadent little space that was once the Huron Club, ostensibly a Tammany Hall social club, but really a speakeasy of the most glamorous sort. (Its name still adorns the front of the building.) During the dry Prohibition days of the 1920s, it was Mayor Jimmy Walker's neighborhood watering hole. He was known to get so blitzed that he would regularly pass out in the bedroom upstairs. (*15 Vandam Street*)

13 **THE VICE PRESIDENTIAL MANSION (Vanished)** Though hard to imagine today, a great mansion once sat on this spot called Richmond Hill,

Richmond Hill, home of two American vice presidents, was something of a mobile home.

an expansive 26-acre estate located on what was, in the seventeenth century, the outskirts of town. The estate served as a headquarters for General George Washington during the Revolutionary War, and soon after was home to the new nation's first Vice President, John Adams, for those months[2] that the nation's capital was based in New York. A decade later, Richmond Hill became the home of America's second vice president, Aaron Burr. It was to here that he retreated on that fateful day, July 11, 1804, after shooting Alexander Hamilton in a duel.

The house was sold in 1807 to John Jacob Astor, who promptly sliced and diced the property for development. As for the mansion, in 1820 it was rolled atop logs to this newly carved street corner and reopened as a theater and opera house. Today at the same space, WNYC radio's live broadcasting studio, the Greene Space, keeps the performance tradition alive. (*44 Charlton Street*)

14 **STAND HERE: The northwest corner of Charlton Street and Sixth Avenue, looking north.** *Why?* This is a subtle example of how street expansion in an ever-growing city like New York can create some awkward little spaces. Congress Street — yes, actually named for the U.S.

---

2 New York was the seat of federal government from March 4, 1789, until the summer of 1790.

Congress—once ran through this very spot in the nineteenth century. It was a wee, angled little street in keeping with the wily roads of the West Village. But when Sixth Avenue was slated to be extended south, from Carmine Street to Franklin Street, Congress Street (acting like its namesake) stood in the way, blocking its passage. Alas, Congress Street was bulldozed, and its demolition left several buildings on the west side of the street with blank sides hovering over an unusually shaped green space. Newer constructions mask the destruction today, but the remaining Federalist-style houses, most dating from the 1820s, still remember when Congress was in session.

Old Maids: Impressive Federalist-style homes in the Charlton-King-Vandam Historic District.

15 LET THE MUSIC PLAY This unusual-looking parking garage was once one of the city's most influential music venues—which is saying a lot in New York. The Paradise Garage operated from 1977 to the late 1980s as a discotheque and a late-night haven for music lovers. Its leading star was DJ Larry Levan, a well-regarded patron saint of the dance music scene who would smoothly shuffle disco into the '80s, while popularizing a new style of dance music called "house"—electronic infusions into soul, funk, and disco. In fact, "garage music" is a specific type of house music that has a raw, "big room," urban quality. And named, of course, after the Paradise Garage. (*84 King Street*)

The Drunken Ghost of the Ear Inn

Once upon a time there was a sailor named Mickey. Well, probably. Assuming that he did exist, he, like so many sailors, would have enjoyed his time off from the busy docks by tippling at one of New York's many fine waterfront saloons. On one particular evening—again, most likely—Mickey had a bit too much to drink at the Green Door, a weathered old pub on the far western reaches of Spring Street. He stumbled out into the street after too much fun and—purely speculation, but let's say, most *certainly*—got killed in a traffic accident.

We hear the Ear Inn (326 Spring Street) is a great place to go for spirits.

This was no mere drinking hole of little consequence. The Green Door was housed inside a modest but important Federalist-style structure that was built in 1817 by James Brown, an African American tobacconist who had served in the Revolutionary War. Of this we are entirely certain.

It was a tavern for many decades. Before landfill would extend the island west of here, the waterfront was much closer to the tavern's front door, and most of its clientele were most likely seafaring men. During Prohibition, the building served a long list of vices, giving home to a speakeasy, a smuggler's hideout, and even a brothel.

It later took the name the Green Door, and was a favorite of the area's longshoremen and, we believe, that included Mickey, who died one night in the mid-twentieth century and has haunted the building ever since.

In the 1970s, some clever bohemians bought the now-landmarked structure and renamed it the Ear Inn, after a music publication they produced upstairs. To this day, it remains one of New York's most gnarled, irascible treasures of old, decorated in historical photographs and nautical gear.

They say that Mickey floats through the building, disrupting drinkers, stealing full mugs of beer, and even touching patrons in inappropriate places. But this is absolutely true: If you spend a few evenings at the Ear Inn, we guarantee that you'll eventually misplace your drink. Or was it snatched by the thirsty ghost of a drunken sailor (who absolutely, probably, really existed)? (*326 Spring Street*)

An excerpt from Jacob Riis's landmark social profile *How the Other Half Lives* (first published in 1890), surveying life in New York's poorest neighborhoods:

We have reached Broome Street. The hum of industry in this six-story tenement on the corner leaves no doubt of the aspect Sunday wears within it. One flight up, we knock at the nearest door. The grocer, who keeps the store, lives on the 'stoop,' the first floor in East Side parlance. In this room a suspender-maker sleeps and works with his family of wife and four children. For a wonder there are no boarders. His wife and eighteen-year-old daughter share in the work, but the girl's eyes are giving out from the strain. Three months in the year, when work is very brisk, the family makes by united efforts as high as fourteen and fifteen dollars a week. The other nine months it averages from three to four dollars. The oldest boy, a young man, earns from four to six dollars in an Orchard Street factory, when he has work. The rent is ten dollars a month for the room and a miserable little coop of a bedroom where the old folks sleep. The girl makes her bed on the lounge in the front room; the big boys and the children sleep on the floor.

Chapter 9///
Lower East Side

The tenement-lined streets are filled with pushcart sellers and customers at the corner of Orchard and Rivington Streets on the Lower East Side, mid-1910s.

SITUATE THE READER
–Lower East Side–

This now-trendy neighborhood wasn't always the Lower East Side. For much of the city's history, this was simply the East Side—that is, of course, until New York's wealthy residents moved north of 23rd Street in the second half of the nineteenth century.

By then this "lower" district had become one of the most densely populated areas in the United States, first with Irish and German immigrants in the mid-nineteenth century, followed by Jewish immigrants from Russia and Eastern Europe decades later. But it was on these streets, inside the claustrophobic tenements and among the overflowing pushcarts, that the modern American Jewish identity would develop in the late nineteenth and early twentieth centuries. Most Jewish Americans can trace their family stories to ancestors who once lived and worked here.

Today the neighborhood continues to knit together some of the city's newest arrivals, making it a vibrant amalgamation of Chinese, Puerto Rican, Hasidic, and hipster.

The streets of the Lower East Side are set off from the Manhattan grid that begins just north of it, above Houston Street. Yet the Lower East Side has its own street grid— one that was laid out in the 1760s by the family of James Delancey, a wealthy businessman and a powerful British loyalist. Then came the Revolutionary War (1775–1783), and those loyalist Delanceys wisely relocated to England, leaving their property behind. However, the city holds no grudges; one of the neighborhood's largest thoroughfares, after all, bears the family name today. Delancey Street intersects with Orchard Street, named for Mr. Delancey's fruit trees. These days, that intersection, often clogged with automobiles, is hardly as peaceful as the names might suggest.

Meanwhile, down by the waterfront lies what's left of Corlears Hook, a part of Manhattan that juts out into the East River. Its tenements were eliminated in the late 1930s and replaced with housing projects. The whole neighborhood, churning with activity at all hours of the day and night, hums along thanks to two giant structures that keep the traffic flowing along its edges: the Williamsburg Bridge (finished in 1903) and the Manhattan Bridge (opened in 1909).

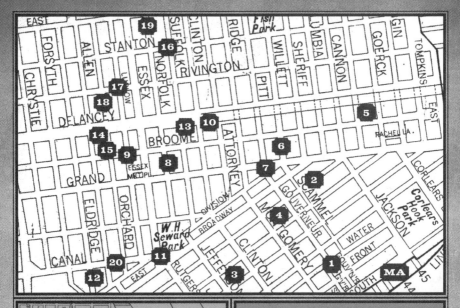

POINTS OF INTEREST

1 The Curves Were the Cure

2 The Slave Galleries

3 Ancient Secret of the "Little Flower"

4 The Magic Garden

5 The Owls Are Not What They Seem

6 The Slimmest Building

7 The St. Patrick's Day Riot

8 The Abandoned Synagogue

9 The Prison of Boss Tweed

10 What the H?

11 Stand Here

12 Stranger in a Strange Land

13 Hollywood on Delancey

14 View from the Top

15 The Finest Outhouse

16 Awesome Sign Alert

17 Heaven in Hell Square

18 The Apple of Orchard Street

19 And Now for the Oldest (and Coolest) Synagogue

20 The Woolworth Building of the Lower East Side

MA The Amphitheater of Corlears Hook

The Amphitheater of Corlears Hook

The Corlears Hook of old—the ships, the scum, the pirates—has been efficiently washed away by housing developments, the East River Drive (FDR Drive), and the lovely East River Park. There's a good reason for that: For much of the city's history, life along this old, rotting waterfront was bleak and depraved.

Girls Just Wanna Have Fun: Corlears Hook Park, circa 1910s.

Its history stays alive, in name at least, thanks to Corlears Hook Park, which when it opened in 1905 was one of New York's first municipal parks and probably the most serene thing to have happen to it in 400 years. Cross the pedestrian bridge that spans the congested FDR Drive, and you'll find a peculiar sight—the East River amphitheater, its rows of cement seating tumbling downhill toward a wacky-looking stage. It kind of looks like a childish drawing of Saturn crashed down upon the East River, its orbiting ring waving from the water.

Constructed in 1941, this incongruous nod to ancient Greece is actually a tribute, of sorts, to the neighborhood's most famous former resident at the time, governor of New York Al Smith, who had pursued acting in his youth. It's one of the most interesting features of East River Park and seems a bit out of place among the ball fields, playgrounds, and paved picnic areas.

Had, by some wizardry, this amphitheater existed almost 400 years ago, with its seats turned around to view the island instead of the river, what might its audience have witnessed? What is this forgotten neighborhood that it traipses upon today?

As improbable as it seems, Corlears Hook was once a sandy beach, surrounded by marshy wetland and rising westward in a series of slopes. Its incline made it perfect for the native Lenapes to launch or dock canoes, and its shape—a pointed protrusion into the East River—made it a natural navigational guide.

When the Dutch came to the island of Mannahatta in the seventeenth century, Director-General Wouter van Twiller granted this area to his friend Jacobus van Corlaer. The area, of course, would take his name (or almost—they'd decide along the way that flipping the vowels would make life easier for everyone).

In 1643, New Amsterdam's next bully of a leader, William Kieft, ruthlessly authorized the wholesale slaughter of a Lenape village, who sought refuge here. More than 100 Lenape were cruelly murdered and, in some cases, their heads brought back down from the island to

According to legend, New Amsterdam trumpeter Anthony van Corlaer (Corlear), a relative of Jacobus, alerted the colony to attackers by blowing his trumpet.

New Amsterdam in a sign of victory. This violent display sparked a battle with the region's angry Lenape tribes that would last for years and would eventually force the Dutch to replace Kieft with Peter Stuyvesant in 1647.

The British, when they dropped anchor in New York in 1664, had more industrious plans for the neighborhood. Having rechristened it Crown Point, they turned it into a Colonial center for shipbuilding. Soon, its shoreline teemed with piers and its waterfront was packed with sail makers, rope makers, coopers, and other handy types.

This was the business of the neighborhood—this *was* the neighborhood. By 1815, Corlears Hook had the greatest concentration of shipbuilding businesses in the nation, and the shoreline was completely obscured with piers, ships, and vessels of all sorts. It would gain literary immortality

It's ships for days at the East Side docks, from South Street to Corlears Hook, circa 1876.

in 1851 when Herman Melville would set the first scene of *Moby-Dick; or The Whale* right here, in a shipyard at Corlears Hook.

But who wants to live near a sprawling, smelly shipyard? No one, really. But those who couldn't afford to live anywhere else didn't really have much of a choice, did they?

By the 1830s, one in ten people living in the area were receiving some sort of charity from the city—and this was long before charity was readily available. The world's very first tenement—the cheapest form of multifamily housing in the nineteenth century—went up in 1833 on a section of Water Street that

is today contained within Corlears Hook Park.

So if it's New York, and you've got a bunch of sailors and shipbuilders hanging around day and night, you're naturally going to attract some other *industrious* types. Sure enough, by the 1830s Corlears Hook had become a notorious red-light district, with "ladies of the night" setting up shop in the neighborhood's saloons and cellars.

And in this chaotic neighborhood they didn't even pretend to hide it.

History is always center stage at the Corlears Hook amphitheater.

Prostitutes were such a part of the waterfront district, in fact, that, as popular legend would have it, the ladies of the Hook would give the oldest profession a new name: hookers.

But wait, it gets better! Waterfront gangs added the threat of violence to this foamy mix of chaos and carnality, claiming the entire East River shoreline as their territory. In 1850 a police report estimated that up to 500 such "river pirates" terrorized the waterfront district. It was easy pickings along the East River, where ships were smaller and lightly guarded.

Among the colorfully named gangs were the Swamp Angels, an especially foul collection of hoodlums famous for navigating the neighborhood's sewers to emerge, unsuspected, at water's edge. There these ruffians would spring aboard clueless vessels and quickly relieve them of their possessions before vanishing again down the drain. Their efficiency was impressive—they'd sell their stolen booty before their victims even realized they'd had been robbed. (Hopefully, they'd clean off the merchandise first.)

But certainly, one needed to drink too. For that you'd head inside any number of dingy waterfront saloons with foreboding names like the Lava Beds, Cat Alley, and Swain's Castle. One of the worst dives was called the Tub of Blood; many of its clientele were members of the colorfully named Tub of Blood Bunch, a group who specialized in the murder of sailors. They were also apparently raging alcoholics. One member, Brian Boru, got so plastered that he passed out and was promptly devoured by rats.

And let's not forget the Hook Gang, a group of thieves who began as pickpockets but diversified by the 1870s to include a bit of theatrical piracy. One of their signature techniques was to completely block off a wharf's loading area and, disguised as construction workers, loot everything in sight. Amazingly, this little charade worked very well for them.

They might still be going at it had New York's shipping industry not set sail for the west side of the island. The arrival of giant luxury liners in the early twentieth century required larger docks and more space, something that only the West Side could accommodate. But these new facilities brought greater security and less opportunity for petty crime.

In the 1890s, thanks to newfound concern for the plight of the city's poorest residents (brought about by city reformers and journalists, such as Jacob Riis), the city government passed stricter housing laws, and in certain neighborhoods demolished unsanitary slums. By the 1940s, the city was constructing thousands of units of middle- and lower-income housing throughout the city. The saloons, prostitutes, slums, and pirates of Corlears Hook were soon lost to sea, replaced by Robert Moses's projects in the 1950s and, down by the water in 1941, the East River amphitheater.

But the show's not over. The amphitheater itself played a part in New York City's theater history as the first stage for Joseph Papp's Shakespeare in the Park festival in 1956. During the 1990s, the whole amphitheater was fenced up and closed down, and, with the help of neighborhood vandals, descended into a ruin worthy of its ancient brethren. It was finally renovated in December 2001, curiously enough, as part of a reality television show called *Challenge*

America, hosted by Erin Brockovich. Yes, Julia Roberts's Erin Brockovich. Fact is sometimes stranger than fiction.

Lower East Side

1 THE CURVES WERE THE CURE It's worth a trip to the waterfront to check out the striking former Gouverneur Hospital building from 1901, a lovely redbrick structure that's notable for its triple-decker curved verandas. For nearly half a century those verandas, located on the south side of the building, would have looked over the waterfront and Corlears Hook, as the East River Drive wasn't built until the 1940s.

Healing architecture: The Gouverneur Hospital building (1901).

There's a rather grim story behind those curved bays. On hot summer days, hospital patients could rest out on the balconies, taking in the fresh air. It was believed that tuberculosis lurked in "dark, dirty corners," so eliminating corners altogether seemed like a good idea. But placing an elevated highway next to them? Hmmm. The institution lives on in name over at Gouverneur Health on nearby Madison Street, which opened in 1972. (*621 Water Street*)

2 THE SLAVE GALLERIES Of the many great old houses of worship that have miraculously survived on the Lower East Side, St. Augustine's just might be the most intriguing. (But not the oldest; that honor goes to St. Mary's Church at 438–440 Grand Street, built in 1826.) This was once a house of worship called All Saints Free Church, because in 1829, when it was completed, worshippers didn't have to pay for a pew like they did in other churches. Oh yes, pews went for top dollar in New York's finer churches like Trinity and, later, Grace Church. Not so at All Saints Free Church.

Except that "free" didn't mean "freedom." Up in the organ loft are two galleries where slaves would sit during services. Although slavery had been completely abolished in New York in 1827 (the year before the church opened), chapels throughout the city would continue to feature this upstairs/downstairs divide.[1] (*290 Henry Street*)

3 ANCIENT SECRET OF THE LITTLE FLOWER "Little Flower" was the nickname of Fiorello La Guardia, New York's short but forceful mayor, who during his tenure (1934–1945) introduced many vital housing reforms. The sprawling thirteen-building housing development known as LaGuardia Houses was completed in 1957, ten years after his death. A bust of La Guardia sits in the adjoining park—Little Flower Playground.

A splash of Rome: An abandoned public bathhouse on the Lower East Side.

---

1 African American parishioners would continue to sit in the galleries, separated from white worshippers, for decades afterward.

But the treasure here is the extraordinary relic located next to it. This is the former public bathhouse, called the Whitehouse, which opened on December 23, 1909, and was one of thirteen public bath facilities in New York. It was built for the poor residents of Corlears Hook who lacked adequate water facilities, a function reminiscent of the ancient bathhouses of Rome. By the 1940s indoor plumbing had rendered the public bath obsolete, and so it was converted into a public swimming pool and gymnasium. Today it sits unused, a ruin from another time. (*Madison Street between Clinton and Rutgers Streets*)

4 THE MAGIC GARDEN The idea of a public playground seems so obvious to us today—outdoor play is an essential part of a healthy childhood. But, for the most part, public recreation spaces did not exist in the nineteenth century. Children on the Lower East Side played in the dirty courtyards behind tenements, on the sidewalks, or, worse, out in the street.

Looking down Pike and Henry Streets toward the majestic Manhattan Bridge, 1935 (photo: Berenice Abbott).

Henry Street Settlement, a lifesaving organization founded by Lillian Wald that had already brought health care and social services to the crowded Lower East Side, came to the rescue. In the 1890s she turned the backyard of the Settlement's townhouses into a public playground. It was a hit—children lined up to get in. Today you can get a look at this playground when touring the marvelous Henry Street facilities, although you can also see the walls of the playground from inside the adjacent Martin Luther King Community Park. (*265 Henry Street*)

5 THE OWLS ARE NOT WHAT THEY SEEM Find the remnant of little Cannon Street and you'll find a building most fowl—or rather, most *owl*. PS 110, Florence Nightingale School, is festooned with owl carvings, perched everywhere from the doorways to the rooftops, making an impressive lineup of stoned birds. The building was constructed in 1903 and named for Nightingale (1820–1910), the English social reformer who was a pioneer of modern nursing. She *loved* owls, and even kept a pet owl named Athena. It's nice to see the city's school planners actually gave a hoot.[2] (*285 Delancey Street at Cannon Street*)

6 THE SLIMMEST BUILDING One of the most curious buildings in the neighborhood actually adjoins one of its most famous, the Bialystoker Synagogue. Built as an Episcopal church in 1826, it converted to Judaism in 1905, reflecting the neighborhood's changing demographics, and has been active ever since. Most of the founding members of the synagogue were immigrants from Bialystok, Poland—thus the name. (And thus the name of the bialy, a traditional Jewish roll.) The beautiful but shockingly slender building in the synagogue's side courtyard, now called the Daniel Potkorony Building, was constructed in 1920 as a Hebrew school. For very, very small children, it seems. (*7 Willett Street*)

The beautiful old Bialystoker Synagogue holds a slender secret behind it.

7 THE ST. PATRICK'S DAY RIOT (Vanished) Those New Yorkers, they just loved to riot! Well, newspapers usually used the phrase "riot" to mean any altercation instigated by an ethnic group. In the case of the tumult that erupted on St. Patrick's Day in 1867 at the intersection of East Broadway, Grand, and Pitt Streets, it was the Irish at battle with the police.

During the St. Patrick's Day parade on March 17, a wagon driver blocking the parade route was immediately set upon by angry marchers. When a police

---

2   These are but the first of many owls that you'll see in this book. See Chapter 17 for the most striking examples.

officer intervened to protect the driver, he too was assaulted, "knocked down and severely injured by being trampled upon."[3] Soon Grand and Pitt was the scene of senseless violence. "The Hibernians broke their staves of office and used the fragments as shillelaghs and clubs, with such effect, that the officers were the recipients of several ugly scalp wounds and bruises." Another report

lists the unique weaponry as "sword canes, society emblems, and other missiles."

The *New York Times*, a fairly anti-Democrat, anti-Irish paper in the mid-nineteenth century, was outraged: "We trust there is no Irishman or Irish American, outside of a small lawless minority, that does not feel keenly the disgrace brought upon such celebrations as that of yesterday, by the wanton and

Panic in the streets: East Broadway erupts in St. Patrick's Day violence, as depicted in this 1867 Thomas Nast illustration.

brutal assaults upon the Police." (*Intersection of East Broadway, Grand Street, and Pitt Street*)

8 THE ABANDONED SYNAGOGUE Beth Hamedrash Hagodol, a nineteenth-century synagogue, sits in a sad, abandoned state today, as though everyone's afraid to go near it. Built as a Baptist church in 1850, it too

was converted into a synagogue in 1885. It played an important role in Jewish American history, as it was connected to the oldest Eastern European Jewish congregation in America (Beth Hamedrash, formed in 1853), and yet today it sits eerily unused. Hopefully somebody will come to its rescue before further deterioration—or the forces of gentrification—cause it permanent harm. (*60–64 Norfolk Street*)

The abandoned Beth Hamedrash Hagodol synagogue on Norfolk Street.

---

3   *Frank Leslie's Illustrated Newspaper*, April 6, 1867.

9 **THE PRISON OF BOSS TWEED (Vanished)** The Ludlow Street Jail, formerly located at the southeast corner of Ludlow and Broome Streets, opened in 1862 and sat for many years smack in the middle of a stretch of tenements. Originally a debtors' prison, the redbrick jail complex had eighty-seven cells and an open courtyard. It later kept

Ludlow Street Jail (left) and its reading room (right).

county detainees, some of whom could pay a little extra to receive perks, like comfier accommodations, tastier food, and other upgrades. One of these VIP inmates was the notoriously corrupt leader of the Tammany Hall political machine, William "Boss" Tweed, who died inside a prison cell here on April 12, 1878.[4] The location where he was born — on Cherry Street — was only a short walk away. (*Ludlow and Broome Streets*)

10 **WHAT THE H?** Back when Williamsburg, Brooklyn, was an independent municipality of Kings County, it was called Williamsburgh. Although the borough's name had already been truncated by the time the Williamsburg Bridge

No road ahead: Williamsburg(h) Bridge before its 1903 completion.

was completed in 1903, that old "h" still clings for dear life to the dedication plaque, heavily obscured under layers of colorful graffiti. C'mon, hipsters, why haven't you brought this spelling back into vogue? (*At the fork of the pedestrian path on the Manhattan side of the Williamsburgh, er, Williamsburg Bridge*)

11 **STAND HERE: Straus Square, the plaza at the intersection of East Broadway, Canal Street, and Essex Street.** *Why?* All that is vibrant and progressive about the Lower East Side emanates from here. Here is the handsome New York Forward building (built in 1912), home to America's most influential Yiddish-language newspaper until it moved in

---

4   But not before escaping from his cell in 1875. He fled to Spain but was hastily recaptured.

1972. It towers over East Broadway, lined up as you head eastward with several addresses important to Jewish American history, including the Educational Alliance, which opened in 1889 (*197 East Broadway*). Across the street, Seward Park was the first municipally built playground in the United States when it opened in 1903, and was named for New York Governor (and

Abraham Lincoln's Secretary of State) William Seward.

Next to the park sits a matronly Beaux-Arts jewel, the Seward Park Library, built in 1909 with funding from the Carnegie Foundation. On the other side of Essex Street, meanwhile, sits the old Loew's Canal Street Theatre (31 Canal Street), built in 1926, with more than

Check this out: Sumptuous Seward Park Library, opened in 1909.

2,000 seats still inside. A marquee once hung over the sidewalk, touting film premieres that starred, among others, local-boy-done-good Eddie Cantor.

Put it all together, and it's one of New York's most wonderful plazas. (Go back to our introduction for some more fascinating — and personal — tales of Straus Square.) (*Intersection of East Broadway, Canal Street, and Essex Street*)

12 STRANGER IN A STRANGE LAND Of the great variety of synagogues in the neighborhood, the Eldridge Street Synagogue stands out as the most architecturally profound. It opened in 1887, right at the time that

Russian and Eastern European Jewish culture was dominating life here. Able to accommodate up to 750 worshippers, the sanctuary was one of the largest on the Lower East Side — a distinction that nearly led to its demise. By the 1950s, with increasing numbers of Jewish residents taking off for the comforts of the suburbs, the synagogue became too expensive to maintain.

Eldridge Street Synagogue.

While a core group of faithful continued to worship in the synagogue's smaller house of study, the huge sanctuary was eventually closed. It gleams today thanks to preservation efforts that saw it reopen in 2007. But, now in its second life, its neighbors have changed. The street's dominant culture today is Chinese, with food shops and street signs in Mandarin changing the flavor of this old street. The juxtaposition of the neighborhood's immigrant past and present is striking. (*12 Eldridge Street*)

13 HOLLYWOOD ON DELANCEY Considering the radical changes that sped along Delancey Street during the twentieth century, it's a genuine wonder that this cavernous old building still exists—the former Loew's Delancey Street Theatre, which opened in 1912 and sat a whopping 1,700 people. In the early days of silent movies, many films were shot in New York and New Jersey, and at first were shown as just one part of a variety program that often also included singers, dancers, and comedy acts. In the 1930s and '40s, the Delancey brought Hollywood classics to the neighborhood. The theater closed in 1976. Today you can order a Whopper from the Burger King that's located near the spot where you once paid for popcorn. (*Delancey and Suffolk Streets*)

14 VIEW FROM THE TOP The brawny colonnade facing Delancey Street is a distinguishing feature of this building constructed in 1913 for the Bank of United States, a commercial bank that would not survive the Great Depression. For one, it had no ties to an *actual* bank of the United States, so there's that. It did, however, have one surprising feature: a rooftop garden for the blind.

Open-air fun and games (circa 1915) atop the Bank of United States garden for the blind.

A century ago, most Lower East Siders spent a lot of time hanging out (and even sleeping) on rooftops, believing that the neighborhood's freshest and coolest air could be found there. (This wasn't illogical, given the stifling and unsanitary tenement conditions and the city's lack of public parks at the time.) But this building offered something additional up on its rooftop to the city's blind community: safety. "[T]he roof is floored with tile and surrounded with a high wall so that the blind may move about in safety," wrote the *New York Times* about the garden's opening in 1915. "This is said to be the only place on the Lower East Side where the blind can be sure of safety from pickpockets."

Blind residents of the Lower East Side were brought to the roof garden with the help of "light bringers," a group of 150 child volunteers from nearby public schools. (*77 Delancey Street*)

15 THE FINEST OUTHOUSE In 1988, two historians were startled to find an Orchard Street tenement with upper floors that had been sealed off since the 1930s. They did more than document their findings—they preserved the entire building, turning it into the main feature of today's Tenement Museum. Today, the popular Lower East Side museum shuffles several tour groups a day along the same wooden floors that housed an estimated 7,000 immigrants over the seventy years that it functioned as a tenement building. Visitors don't just get to observe how these people lived and worked, they even get to see how the bathrooms operated.

The tenement at 97 Orchard Street was built in 1863 and was not originally furnished with indoor plumbing. So an outdoor privy has been reconstructed in the courtyard behind the building that shows exactly how primitive tenement living was for millions of New Yorkers. (You can also see it from the sidewalk on the Allen Street side.) You'll never complain about a gross Starbucks bathroom again. (*97 Orchard Street*)

16 AWESOME SIGN ALERT: Louis Zuflacht Smart clothes, smarter sign. Men's haberdasher Louis Zuflacht died in 1986, but the sign to his clothing shop has kept his name alive to the residents of the Lower East Side. Subsequent building owners have kept the fetching sign intact. There might just be a (highly justifiable, if minor) riot if anybody ever attempted to take it down. (*154 Stanton Street*)

17 HEAVEN IN HELL SQUARE The grid of blocks bordered by Houston, Essex, Delancey, and Allen Streets have become crowded — overrun — nay, "infested" — with bars and boisterous restaurants that have recently lured a new demographic group to the Lower East Side, at least at night. As darkness falls these sidewalks fill up with young merrymakers, hopping from bar to small-plates eatery to rooftop dance club. At the stroke

of midnight, however, the scene takes an ugly turn as this festive group transforms into a motley crew of rabble-rousers, fumbling on the sidewalks and stumbling upon broken high heels, forcing passersby to dodge their puddles of … well, you get the point.

Talmud Torah: A reminder of a rich Jewish past at 96 Rivington Street.

You've arrived in "Hell Square," a nightlife boom that followed the gentrification that picked up steam in the early 2000s. Entire blocks of historic buildings (including rows of tenements and synagogues) were demolished to make way for swanky hotels and luxury condos, many of which appropriate the neighborhood's colorful history to attract high-paying tenants. (But maybe we're just getting old and cranky?)

However, you will still find a fascinating trace of the past at the southwest corner of Ludlow and Rivington Streets. Above the door of 95 Rivington is the sign for a Talmud Torah, a Hebrew religious school for Jews of Romanian heritage. Its next-door neighbor for more than 100 years was an associated synagogue called the "Cantor's Carnegie Hall" for its popularity as a performance space for Jewish music. In 2006 its roof collapsed, and sadly the synagogue was demolished.

By the way, next door at 99 Rivington Street is the building used on the cover of the Beastie Boys' iconic 1989 album *Paul's Boutique*. And to think it was right next to all this history. (*95 Rivington Street*)

18 THE APPLE OF ORCHARD STREET This street was best known in the twentieth century for its clothing, fabrics, and luggage retail shops, especially after Jewish shop owners nimbly skipped New York's closed-on-Sunday laws to create an exclusive weekend destination for shoppers.[5] It borrowed from generations of pushcart salesmen who lined these same streets a century before, and from the area's legacy as a once-thriving garment district.

The Beckenstein name lives on along Orchard Street, even when the shop moved to Midtown.

This sign at 130 Orchard Street says it all, screaming "WOOLENS RAYONS SILKS DRAPERIES" in bright colors, defiant of its age. Samuel Beckenstein ran a pushcart rag business in 1919 and worked from a retail store here for generations. His family kept the Beckenstein name in fashion when they moved the business up to the midtown Garment District in the 1990s. But like any good fashion brand, the tags of his empire still mark the place where he began. (*130 Orchard Street*)

---

5   The so-called blue laws were abolished in 1976, taking away the neighborhood's exclusive Sunday-shopping advantage.

19 AND NOW FOR THE OLDEST (AND COOLEST) SYNAGOGUE
We always love seeing an older person sporting incredibly youthful style. That's New York for you! But it's not limited to people. Even the oldest places of worship reinvent themselves, as is the case with the oldest surviving synagogue in New York—Anshe Slonim Synagogue, built in 1849 for a German Jewish congregation. During much of the 1970s and '80s, it sat abandoned until it was rescued in 1986 by Spanish sculptor Angel Orensanz, who resuscitated it by wiping away years of vandalism and converting it into a performance space. Today it hosts avant-garde theater, MTV concerts, and wedding ceremonies, including—hold on to your hat!—the wedding of Sarah Jessica Parker and Matthew Broderick in 1997. (*172 Norfolk Street*)

20 THE WOOLWORTH BUILDING OF THE LOWER EAST SIDE The Jarmulowsky Bank Building was literally designed to be the fanciest and tallest building on the Lower East Side. The banker Sender Jarmulowsky, who had founded a bank for Jewish immigrants in the neighborhood in 1873, wanted an elegant skyscraper similar to those giant structures near City Hall. His extraordinary plan actually inspired the *Jewish Daily Forward* to construct their own skyscraper two blocks away in Straus Square. It was an unofficial competition; the *Forward*, a socialist-leaning newspaper, "did not relish the idea of a capitalist symbol rising so high on the East Side," according to author Melech Epstein.

But Jarmulowsky thwarted the *Forward* builders by slapping on an ornate cupola to the top of his building, making it, in fact, the tallest in the neighborhood when it opened in 1912. The cupola was removed in the 1990s, but a replica might have taken its place. As of press time, the Ace Hotel plans to re-create that original feature.

As for Jarmulowsky, however, he barely lived to see his building's completion, dying just weeks after it opened. His bank fared poorly without him. With the outbreak of World War I, so many German immigrants withdrew their money to send home to relatives that it resulted in a bank run and the collapse of the bank in 1914. (*54 Canal Street*)

Tastes of History: The Delicatessen

Delicatessens, from the German *Delikatessen*, meaning "delicacy," originally referred to shops, often department stores, where shoppers could pick up fancy prepared foods, meats, and cheeses. (Many upscale European department stores still offer these gourmet food sections today.) In New York, new arrivals from Poland, Russia, German territories, and other eastern European countries in the late nineteenth century brought with them their appetite for cured meats and smoked fish, as well as their bagel-making and pickling skills. Soon, the streets of the Lower East Side offered kosher delis, which served meats, and "appetizing stores," which sold mostly smoked fish, spreads, and cheeses.

Delis and appetizing stores multiplied throughout the city as their specialties—pastrami, corned beef, bagels and lox, matzo ball soup—were too good to keep to any one neighborhood. Today, the term "deli" is used broadly to refer to almost any corner sandwich shop. But there are still a few old-fashioned New York delicatessens that serve a throwback meal, pickle and all.

KATZ'S DELICATESSEN

Don't eat here because Meg Ryan's really, really, really fond of it in the movie *When Harry Met Sally....* Eat here because it's a vestige of Lower East Side life gone by. Founded by the Iceland brothers in 1888, this nonkosher deli changed its name 15 years later when Willy Katz joined the business. The boisterous deli specializes in pastrami and corned beef, but during World War II, soldiers got their fill of another favorite thanks to the restaurant's wartime slogan: "Send a Salami to Your Boy in the Army." Katz's has moved location only once, to permit for the construction of the subway. So today, even though its neighbors have completely changed, Katz's is still there, grilling up your favorite high-cholesterol delights. (*205 East Houston Street at Ludlow Street*)

RUSS AND DAUGHTERS

This Lower East Side appetizing store, known for its impeccably well-stocked shelves, was founded by Joel Russ, who, upon immigrating to New York from today's Poland in 1907 sold mushrooms along the streets of the Lower East Side. He set up his first store in 1914 on Orchard Street, focusing on salt-cured herring and salmon, and moved the shop to its present Houston Street location in 1920. Within a few years, Russ started running the business with his three daughters. And it's still in the family to this day! (*179 East Houston Street*)

BARNEY GREENGRASS

No, this is not a classic 1960s Hanna-Barbera cartoon character! This Upper West Side staple has been satisfying the neighborhood's smoked fish needs since 1908. (It's been at its present location since 1929.) Proclaiming itself The Sturgeon King—and no one's contesting that royal declaration—the shop sticks to the appetizing tradition of offering breakfast- and brunch-style hits, including whitefish, lox, sturgeon, and a list of fishy spreads. The store remains in the Greengrass family to this day and boasts a vintage interior that makes the experience deliciously retro. (*541 Amsterdam Avenue, between 86th and 87th Streets*)

ZABAR'S

Another Upper West Side institution, Zabar's traces its history back to a Brooklyn food market stall operated by Louis Zabar, who immigrated to the United States in the 1920s from the Ukraine. In 1934, Zabar opened his first modest food shop along Broadway, but over the decades, it has grown to encompass much of the block. Known for its dizzying array of bagels, spreads, and prepared foods, and for its deli counter, Zabar's remains a family enterprise and a neighborhood staple. (*2245 Broadway at 80th Street*)

CARNEGIE DELI

Midtown diners have been snapping photos and writing home about the Carnegie Deli's overstuffed pastrami sandwiches since the Parker family started carving them here in 1937. (We're not joking: Each sandwich is packed with an artery-busting pound of meat.) Its proximity to Carnegie Hall—it's named for the hall and, indirectly at least, Andrew Carnegie (who almost certainly never ate a pastrami sandwich in his life)—has made the deli popular with a roster of celebrities, many of whom are enshrined in photographs on the walls today. And the crusty waiter routine gives tourists a dose of "big city" shtick. The deli and its flamboyant signage remain in the Parker family, now in its third generation as owners. (*854 Seventh Avenue at 55th Street*)

PETER STUYVESANT'S OTHER NICKNAME

After the departure of Kieft the most picturesque figure of the period of Dutch rule in America appeared at New Amsterdam, Petrus or Pieter Stuyvesant. We

Hi, I'm still Peter Stuyvesant, and I'm still a grouch.

have an authentic portrait in which the whole personality of the man is writ large. The dominant nose, the small, obstinate eyes, the close-set, autocratic mouth, tell the character of the man who was come to be the new and the last Director-General of New Netherland. As Director of the West India Company's colony at Curacao, Stuyvesant had undertaken the task of reducing the Portuguese island of St. Martin and had lost a leg in the fight. This loss he repaired with a wooden leg, of which he professed himself prouder than of all his other limbs together and which he had decorated with silver bands and nails, thus earning for him the sobriquet of "Old Silver Nails." Still, so the legend runs, Peter Stuyvesant's ghost at night "stumps to and fro with a shadowy wooden leg through the aisles of St. Mark's Church near the spot where his bones lie buried."

~ *The Chronicles of America Series*, **volume 7, published 1919**

East Village

The original East Villager. This 1902 *Collier's* magazine cover gives
Stuyvesant a most impressive peg leg (artist: Edward Penfield).

SITUATE THE READER
-East Village-

In September of 1664 Peter Stuyvesant (1612–1672) was abruptly fired from his job as Director-General of New Amsterdam. It wasn't a big surprise. He was fired, after all, by the new British authorities, who had just captured the former Dutch colony and turned it over to the English crown. (They also quickly renamed the place after King Charles II's brother, the Duke of York.) He made his home on the Dutch company's old farm, a sprawling tract of land he'd purchased between today's Bowery and the marshy coastline of the East River. This land would become home to generations of Stuyvesants, and the family would become one of New York's most important dynasties, the jewel of the so-called Knickerbocker aristocracy.[1]

More than a century later, in the late 1780s, Peter's great-grandson, Petrus Stuyvesant, carved out a street grid upon a section of the old family farm, although not much is left of it today except Stuyvesant Street (the location still today of St.-Mark's-on-the-Bowery, their family church and the burial site of Old Peg-Leg Pete). With the introduction in 1811 of the much more ambitious Commissioners' Plan, Stuyvesant's flimsy old street grid was almost entirely tossed aside.

In the 1830s, a portion of swampy land near the East River was gifted to the city by yet another Peter—Peter Gerard Stuyvesant, the son of Petrus and great-great-grandson of the big P. (There'll be a pop quiz later.) This old swamp would be filled in and eventually developed into Tompkins Square Park in 1850. The lots around the park soon filled with tenements, which received waves of new immigrants—first Germans, and later Polish and Eastern European Jews.

This district, stretching north to 14th Street east of the Bowery, was called the Lower East Side—well, at least until the 1960s, when artists and bohemians rechristened the section of it north of Houston Street the East Village in order to better align it with the counterculture happenings of Greenwich Village just to its west. Meanwhile, all the way to the east, nestled into the shoreline, the tight grid of streets located east of First Avenue took on the name Alphabet City, as it's only in the East Village that lettered avenues (A, B, C, and D) exist in Manhattan.

---

1   The phrase was invented by Washington Irving for his satirical *A History of New York*. Irving made up a few stories about Peter and described him as having "a countenance sufficient to petrify a millstone." (We imagine they would not have been friends.)

Map labels (upper map):

17

14

16 15

13

12

E. E. E. E. E. E.

PL. STUYVESANT HALL PL.

E. E. E.

11

E.

10 9

FIRST EAST 1

EXTRA PL.

SECOND

A. AVE. AVE.

MA 8

Tompkins 7 Square

6

5

4

3

HOUSTON

2

13
12
11 C. D.
10
9
8
7
6
5
4
3

DRY DOCK

AVE. AVE.

B.

Hamilton Fish Park

CLIN RID SUFF

POINTS OF INTEREST

1 This Is the Beginning

2 What's the Time in Mother Russia?

3 El Jardin del Paraiso

4 Miracle Garden

5 6th and B Garden

6 Awesome Sign Alert

7 The Dry Fountain

8 The Church of Jazz

9 A Most Sacred Tenement

10 Dueling Cemeteries

11 The Most Glamorous Fire Escape Ever

12 The Layers of St. Mark's Place

13 Can You Name These Faces?
(No, Probably Not.)

14 The Stage of Superstars

15 The Stars Underfoot

16 Stand Here

17 The Parting of a Pear Tree

MA General Slocum Memorial Fountain

General Slocum Memorial Fountain

The General Slocum Memorial Fountain is not a very awe-inspiring memorial.

This is no dig at the custodians of Tompkins Square Park, where the memorial has been on display since 1906, nor at Bruno Louis Zimm, the fountain's sculptor whose creation presents two children in idyllic profile, next to an engraving: "They were Earth's purest children, young and fair." Its left side unveils its more tragic context: "In memory of those who lost their lives in the disaster to the steamer *General Slocum*, June XV MCMIV."

The understated and oft-overlooked General Slocum Memorial Fountain in Tompkins Square Park.

The fountain, while charming and tranquil, is inadequate in expressing the grief and horror that filled New Yorkers on June 15, 1904, when, during a church-sponsored day trip headed for the Long Island Sound, the *General Slocum* steamboat caught fire and sank in the East River, killing more than a thousand passengers, mostly women and children. This tragedy was the single deadliest event in New York City history until September 11, 2001.

This disaster virtually wiped out the German presence on the Lower East Side—entire families perished, many of whom had just gotten a foothold in New York a generation before. In a single morning the lights of Kleindeutschland, New York's Little Germany, permanently faded.

The boat had been chartered by St. Mark's Evangelical Lutheran Church[2] for their yearly day trip excursion to the Long Island Sound. It was a chance for the congregation to briefly break out of the crowded Lower East Side to enjoy a day in the sun. Among the passengers was the Liebenow family, the parents and their three daughters, Anna, Helen, and Adella, along with several aunts and cousins.

The *Slocum* submerged.

The *Slocum* left the pier shortly before 9 a.m. and began its slow crawl up the East River. Captain William Van Schaick had been principally concerned that morning with one turbulent spot up the East River, a dangerous confluence of waters known as the Hell Gate. It had already sunk hundreds of vessels as far back as the seventeenth century. By 1904 it was still a dangerous pass, but on this day, the Hell Gate would not be the problem.

About 30 minutes into the voyage, a child noticed that a small fire had started in the lamp room below the main deck. A crewman tried to stamp it out, throwing charcoal on it in an effort to contain it. But the flames only grew larger. Crewmembers grabbed a firehose—only to find it rotten to the point that it burst wide open. These were not men trained for emergency situations; once they realized the hoses were useless, they simply gave up.

Civilized behavior soon gave way to panic as the flames quickly spread through the lower levels of the steamer, fire jumping from passengers' clothing to hair. Families moved away from the flames only to find themselves pressed up against the boat's railings as panicked crowds pushed forward in search of fresh air. Children lost hold of their parents, never to see them again.

Crowds surged toward the *Slocum*'s six lifeboats and attempted to hoist them down. But they wouldn't budge—somebody had wired them to the wall. The life preservers, never properly inspected, were filled with rotten cork, and several exploded into dust. They were not only useless—they were actually dangerous. Panicked parents strapped preservers to their children and tossed them overboard, only to watch in horror as they sank from sight.

---

2 St. Mark's is located on East 6th Street, between First and Second Avenues, in the heart of New York's first and largest German neighborhood. A plaque honoring the victims hangs in front.

Below deck, passengers were burned to death—huddled in groups and trapped in corners. Smoke choked many, causing unconsciousness; many were trampled underfoot.

Some jumped into the violent waves. "There was little hope that any of the children who jumped overboard could be saved," reported the *New York Evening World*.

Bodies washed up upon the shore of North Brother Island.

"The current all along the course taken is on a section of the river where not even a strong swimmer can breast the currents. Scores of little ones were sucked in by the whirlpools in Hell Gate."

Crowds formed along the shores, their attention drawn by the billowing smoke, fire, and horrifying spectacle before them. The captain managed to steer the boat toward North Brother Island, where nurses, doctors, and even patients from the smallpox hospital ran to the water to rescue and attempt to revive those who had washed ashore. The *Slocum* eventually floated out into the Long Island Sound, puffing clouds of cork dust into the air, while leaving a trail of tragedy in its wake.

Just after noon, the burning vessel sank, a single paddle box and a smokestack jutting out of the water.

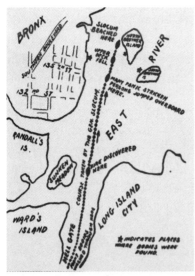
A map tracing the *General Slocum* disaster, printed in the *Brooklyn Daily Eagle*.

By the final count, 1,021 people perished in the *General Slocum* disaster that day, making it the deadliest single event in the city's history up to that date. In the weeks following the disaster, the streets of Kleindeutschland—today's East Village—were filled with mourners, as the community attended funerals in the homes of those who had perished and held solemn processions through the streets.

The Liebenow family was hit particularly hard. The entire Liebenow family died in the disaster—all except baby Adella, just six months old at the time of the tragedy.

Two years later, now only two-and-a-half years old, Adella was hoisted to a podium here in Tompkins Square Park. She stood before a community that hadn't yet fully recovered—would they ever?—as she tugged at a cloth to unveil the General Slocum Memorial Fountain.

No, the fountain is not perfect. How could it be?

But why hasn't this tragedy been better memorialized? It's such an important event in the city's history, and yet so many don't know its whole story. There are a few theories about this, many having to do with the anti-German sentiment that cropped up a decade later at the beginning of World War I.

Or was it the social class of the victims that caused it to recede from memory? Adella, who died in 2004, 100 years after the disaster, believed that this might be the case. To a crowd at a 1999 commemoration of the tragedy, she said, "The *Titanic* had a great many famous people on it. This was just a family picnic."

East Village

POINTS OF INTEREST

1 THIS IS THE BEGINNING Most of Manhattan, at least above Houston Street, is a breeze to navigate today, thanks to the tidy grid system imposed upon this part of the island by the Commissioners' Plan of 1811. In the first years of the nineteenth century, New York City didn't stretch much farther than today's SoHo, and it was getting more crowded by the day. City planners recognized that New York needed to expand, and as it was geographically confined to an island, it could move in only one direction: north. This was a rare opportunity to mold a modern city that was more orderly, more sophisticated, and even (they thought at the time) more sanitary than the old one. A neat grid of numbered avenues (running north and south) and streets (stretching east and west) was imposed upon the terrain regardless of the hills, streams, or even existing property that lay in its way!

The grid's southern border was initially called (somewhat ironically today) North Street, for it was truly north of the city at the time. Today's Houston Street is actually the combination of two roads, North Street and an old path that cut through the property of Nicholas Bayard (a property that included much of today's SoHo). Bayard renamed the path for his new son-in-law, the esteemed Georgian patriot William Houstoun. Later, Houstoun's street was linked to North Street and the entire stretch renamed Houston Street (sacrificing a "u" in the process).

The modest little park here is named First Park (opened in 1935), its name celebrating its distinction as the little triangle upon which the world's most famous grid rests. (*The park at First Street and First Avenue*)

It's always random o'clock atop the Red Square Apartments.

2 WHAT'S THE TIME IN MOTHER RUSSIA? Don't even try to set your watch to the peculiar clock atop the Red Square Apartments. Its numbers are in random order, a bit of kooky late-'80s-ness that's part of the apartment complex. And that man next to the clock isn't hailing a cab; that is actually an 18-foot statue of Vladimir Lenin, installed here in 1994. (*250 Houston Street*)

THE GARDEN DISTRICT

East Village residents a century ago would never have said to themselves, "What a grand place to plant flowers!" But it would be their very tenements that would later indirectly lead to the sprouting of so many East Village neighborhood gardens. At the bleakest moments of the 1980s, when burned-out buildings and empty lots defined the neighborhood, community leaders took beautification efforts into their own hands, clearing abandoned lots and planting leafy, magical, and art-filled oases.

Once a mere curiosity of the East Village, the gardens have now become one of its defining features. There are about 40 gardens today in the neighborhood. One could spend an afternoon with a good book, tiptoeing from garden to garden, each with its own flora and fecundity. Plan your adventure around these three:

3 El Jardin del Paraiso Most of the East Village was once high salt marshes and tidal meadows (called Stuyvesant's Meadow), which gradually mixed with trees and plants at the shore. It's not a stretch to imagine those verdant old days at this garden, created in 1981, which also includes a fabulously imaginative willow treehouse. (*Spans 4th and 5th Streets, between Avenues C and D*)

4 Miracle Garden The name of this peaceful respite recalls the garden's opening in 1983, when a batch of toxic soil killed off all of the first plantings. It might have spelled doom for the entire lot if not for the diligence of neighborhood gardener Penny Evans. But the name may also hint at the fact that this flourishing spot sits on the site of a former crack house. (*194–296 East 3rd Street*)

5 6th and B Garden While there might be fuller and lusher gardens in the East Village, this corner spot, which frequently hosts musical events on its central stage, was famous for its astonishing 65-foot tower of toys. Artist Eddie Boros constructed the playful structure in 1988 out of found toys. Sadly, the structure was torn down by the city in 2008, a year after Boros died. (*6th Street and Avenue B*)

6 AWESOME SIGN ALERT "For over 60 years Peter Jarema Funeral Home; Air Conditioned Chapels" is a terrifically large and faded sign that still hovers over the bar at 7th Street and Avenue B. Jarema opened his funeral concern in 1906 and most likely added this old classic sometime in the 1960s. Not only is the sign still here, so is the funeral home (at 129 East 7th Street). The establishment beneath the sign has been in the livelier business of serving alcohol since 1935, when it was first known as Vazac Hall. (*Avenue B and 7th Street*)

A ghostly advertisement for the hereafter.

7 THE DRY FOUNTAIN When it opened in 1850, Tompkins Square Park was considered a "people's park," the people in question being poor and middle-class German immigrants who had recently arrived in the neighborhood. To encourage the locals to resist the lure of the bottle, anti-drinking advocate Henry D. Cogswell planted a "temperance fountain" in the park, topped with the goddess Hebe. He so believed that encouraging people to drink water would keep them from the evil devil juice that, during the 1880s and 1890s, he installed fifty temperance fountains throughout the country. As you can tell from the dozen or so bars and taverns surrounding the park today, this particular temperance fountain failed to completely make the case for teetotaling. (*Tompkins Square Park, near Avenue A entrance*).

8 THE CHURCH OF JAZZ This unique 1849 Gothic Revival townhouse — slightly churchlike in its appearance — was home to a long list of lodgers

during its first hundred years. And then, in 1950, a superstar moved in — Charlie Parker, the jazz saxophonist who took music (and listeners) to new places with his alto saxophone. Because he was already famous when he lived here, the house too became legendary. The stretch of Avenue B in front of the building is called Charlie Parker Place and entered the National Register of Historic Places in 1994. Don't you wish that all music legends lived in historic old homes? Just makes sightseeing more convenient — you get two for one! (*151 Avenue B*)

The Bird's Nest: The classy nineteenth-century home of a jazz legend.

9 A MOST SACRED TENEMENT Oh sure, the Hare Krishna movement remains beholden to its Eastern religious roots, but its birthplace is the East Village. Hindu teacher A. C. Bhaktivedanta Swami Prabhupada arrived in New York in 1966 and gravitated toward the East Village, the nucleus of counterculture at the time. The guru and his young followers could frequently be heard chanting their ubiquitous mantra around a tree in Tompkins Square Park called the Hare Krishna Tree. But their home was this former curio shop. They kept the old Matchless Gifts sign over the shop window, while followers decorated the interior with handmade tapestries. This became their central New York temple and remains vital to worshippers to this day. (*26 Second Avenue, between First and Second Streets*)

10 **DUELING CEMETERIES** There are two terrific — and confusing — 1830s cemeteries in the East Village, and they're located less than a block from each other. Confusing because one (the older, dating from 1830) is called the New York Marble Cemetery, the other (opened in 1831) the New York *City* Marble Cemetery. You can see the former if you peek through the old iron gate next to 43 Second Avenue (fittingly, a funeral home). The larger, 1831 burial ground is also located behind an iron gate, but it's in clear view of the sidewalk. Both are vestiges of a time when burials were permitted in lower Manhattan. That would change — after all, just think about the real estate! They're also both early surviving examples of burial grounds independent of any particular church congregation, a concept that would gain popularity

New York Marble Cemetery (top) and the more dramatic New York City Marble Cemetery (bottom).

with larger rural cemeteries, including Brooklyn's Green-Wood Cemetery, which opened in 1838. (*41½ Second Avenue and 52–74 East 2nd Street*)

11 **THE MOST GLAMOROUS FIRE ESCAPE EVER** This block of 4th Street contains two stages that have changed the face of modern American theater. On the south side, La Mama Experimental Theatre Club (at 74 East 4th Street) was one of the earliest venues for off-off-Broadway theater (a catchall phrase for New York's many microstages and experimental theaters) when it was founded by fashion designer–turned–theatrical producer Ellen Stewart in 1961. Just across the street, the New York Theatre Workshop (at 79 East 4th Street) brought the ultimate East Village musical, *Rent*, to New York audiences (and once-in-a-lifetime reviews) in 1996 before moving to Broadway for its epic twelve-year run. (Most of the musical's scenes took place in East Village lofts, Tompkins Square Park, and the former Life Café, on the northeast corner of the park.)

But an oft-overlooked star on the block, if you ask us, is the weird structure at 62 East 4th Street, built in 1899 and notable for the spiral staircase attached to its exterior. This is actually the building's fire escape. One can easily imagine a silent film star standing there in the open loggia, perhaps melodramatically descending the spiral stairs to escape an inferno. (*62 East 4th Street*)

12 THE LAYERS OF ST. MARK'S PLACE This street, named for the church where Peter Stuyvesant is buried, is today a slightly more sober version of its former self. During the 1980s and '90s, St. Mark's was a grungy street of bars and nightclubs that catered to the city's alternative punk scene. But this street has led several lives, and bits of each period still exist today, like layers of paint on an old wall. During the 1960s, counterculture icons lived

Eliza's Punk Salon: A Hamilton home–turned–alternative clothier on St. Mark's Place.

and partied in its deteriorating tenements. At the turn of the twentieth century it housed the German working-class families of the Kleindeutschland community. (Evidence of this period appears on the theatrical facade at 12 St. Mark's Place.)

But before that, in the 1830s, it was an elegant block of Federalist-style homes. It was in 1831 that Alexander Hamilton's son (also named Alexander) and his family moved into 4 St. Mark's Place, including the Founding Father's widow, Eliza Schuyler Hamilton. For decades, the longtime punk clothier Trash and Vaudeville inhabited the same rooms that the Hamiltons once called home. (*4 St. Mark's Place*)

13 CAN YOU NAME THESE FACES? (NO, PROBABLY NOT.) One of the few remaining vestiges of the neighborhood's German community is this redbrick German Dispensary (health clinic), built in 1883–1834. Similar in design to the nearby Puck Building, we think it's one of the most beautiful structures in the East Village today. Look toward the rooftop—notice any faces staring down at you as you walk by? Don't worry, they're all respectable guys, including botanist Carl Linnaeus (father of modern ecology), Wilhelm von Humboldt (father of linguistic studies), and Antoine Lavoisier (yet another father, this one of chemistry), among others. (*137 Second Avenue*)

What are you looking at? Stony faces on Second Avenue.

14 THE STAGE OF SUPERSTARS Second Avenue was once known as the Jewish Rialto, the world capital of Yiddish theater during the early twentieth century. This Second Avenue theater opened in 1926 to mount elaborate productions by Ukrainian-born theater star Maurice Schwartz. Even though the theater today has been subdivided into the Village East Cinemas, many details still exist that showcase its Jewish heritage, including a Star of David in the auditorium and carvings in Yiddish in the lobby.

But that's not all! The stage had a renaissance as a home to a few off-Broadway productions. Both the scandalous *Oh! Calcutta* and high school musical staple *Grease* made their New York stage debuts here (in 1969 and 1972, respectively). Billie Holiday gave her final performance at the theater in 1959. And Meryl Streep gave one of her first New York performances here in 1976 in the obscure Tennessee Williams play *27 Wagons Full of Cotton*. (*181–189 Second Avenue*)

15 **THE STARS UNDERFOOT** A relative latecomer to the kosher deli scene, the Second Avenue Deli opened in 1954 in the heart of today's East Village. Known for serving up classic dishes, the deli also celebrated the Yiddish theater scene that had thrived near its Second Avenue and 10th Street location just decades before. While the old deli closed in 2006 and moved to Murray Hill,[3] you can still find a trace of the old place — and a reminder of that old Jewish Rialto — on the sidewalk. Owner Abe Lebewohl created a "Yiddish Walk of Fame" in the cement, celebrating the work of Paul Muni, Zvee Scooler, and other Jewish theater greats. (*Southeast corner of Second Avenue and East 10th Street*)

16 **STAND HERE: Short little Stuyvesant Street, facing directly into St. Marks-in-the-Bowery.** *Why?* You're standing upon a peculiar

St. Mark's Church in-the-Bowery has provided the neighborhood with real direction since its completion in 1799.

artifact, a street that predates the 1811 grid plan. As the Stuyvesants developed their land in the seventeenth and eighteenth centuries, they formed their own grid of streets, named for various family members. This street connected their gracious manor home and church with the farm road (today's Bowery).

How did this vestige of an earlier grid survive the Commissioners' Plan of 1811, you ask? It didn't hurt that it had been laid by one of New York's most important families (although the same could be said of their other streets, some of which were unceremoniously buried). More important, Stuyvesant Street was home to this stately church, built in 1799, and situated — still today — along the angles of the family's since-vanished grid.

This street holds a spectacular distinction — it's one of the few streets in New York that truly runs east to west. No, really, pull out your compass (or even

---

3   Now located at 162 East 33rd Street. An Upper East Side location also opened in 2011 in the area of old Yorkville.

your smartphone)! The Commissioners' Plan, on the other hand, would orient itself relative to the island, à la *On the Town* — "the Bronx is up, but the Battery's down." While that's a handy reference (and a catchy tune), it fudges the true north and south points by about 29 degrees.

Cool, right? After you pick yourself up off the ground, go into the church courtyard and say thanks to Peter himself. The Dutch director-general is interred beneath the church, and his stern visage greets you as you enter. (Legend has it that he can also be heard thumping around at night....) (*Stuyvesant Street and Second Avenue*)

17 **THE PARTING OF A PEAR TREE (Vanished)** Before 1867 New Yorkers enjoyed the company of a very living reminder of the days of Peter Stuyvesant — his old pear tree, which once sat at the corner of 13th Street and Third Avenue. Planted either in 1647 (when Stuyvesant was director-general) or 1667 (when he returned to Manhattan under British rule), the tree was a stoic and sturdy reminder of Peg-Leg Pete, unbending even as the old Stuyvesant farmland gave way to the grid plan. Perhaps it might still be standing to this day[4] if not for an unfortunate horse-drawn truck accident in late February 1867. "The destruction of this old landmark is stated to have resulted from a collision of vehicles," reported the *New York Times*, "one of which was thrown against the tree with sufficient force to break it down." A witness to this tragic tree takedown still sits on this corner — the skin care retailer Kiehl's, which began as a pharmacy here in 1851. The build-

Ode to a Pear Tree: Stuyvesant's famous fruit tree before it was unfortunately trampled down.

ing wears a plaque in honor of the tree, and in 2003 Kiehl's planted a new pear tree in front of their shop. Their popular lip balm is also pear-scented, just as Stuyvesant would have liked. (*109 Third Avenue*)

---

4   The Hangman's Elm, which you'll meet in Chapter 12, is nearly as old.

A Short History of Brooklyn

To remember Brooklyn is to be wistful.

When the independent city of Brooklyn became a borough of the city of greater New York in 1898, Brooklynites lamented their loss of identity. One hundred years later, when that borough, now the most populous in the city, became the hottest area for gentrification, lifelong Brooklynites mourned their borough's loss of character (and affordable rents).

What is the real Brooklyn? Its namesake was founded in 1646 by the Dutch as the port town of Breukelen, named for a municipality back in the Netherlands. But just as important were the five other independent settlements in western Long Island, settlements whose names still live on today as neighborhoods: Gravesend, Flatlands, Flatbush, New Utrecht, and Bushwick.

Gravesend was populated with nothing more than pleasant farms and estates in 1776 when British troops landed here to rout the Continental Army from their makeshift perches during the early days of the Revolutionary War. During this conflict, the Battle of Long Island (or "Battle of Brooklyn"),

Before gentrification: An idyllic view of the Brooklyn waterfront in the early nineteenth century.

General George Washington met one of his worst defeats near the banks of the Gowanus River, and his troops later escaped from the town of Brooklyn under cover of night.

In the early nineteenth century, Brooklyn became the nation's first commuter town, a residential suburb for wealthy New Yorkers that, thanks to the Fulton Ferry, was now close to downtown Manhattan's business district. In the 1820s, Brooklyn's city planners created a grid plan of tree-lined streets radiating from the old town, giving birth to an elite society that rivaled New York's, within the elegant brownstones of today's Brooklyn Heights.

Similar development happened slightly north in the nearby settlements of Bushwick and, more specifically, its western extension, Williamsburgh,[5] for a short time a city of its own, which benefited from the mass industry along

---

5   The "h" would fall off at some point in the late nineteenth century.

its East River shoreline. All of this would eventually be absorbed by a growing city of Brooklyn in 1854 and rechristened its Eastern District. Brooklyn's brownstone life extended farther south toward Green-Wood Cemetery (founded in 1838 and still acclaimed for its solitude). When the spectacular Prospect Park opened to the public in the 1860s, it attracted well-to-do residents to its surroundings; they constructed mansions and handsome brownstones in today's Park Slope and Prospect Heights neighborhoods.

Brooklyn's appeal also lay in recreation, as the beach properties of Coney Island and Rockaway Beach drew thousands by the late nineteenth century to their delirious delights. With the construction of elevated railways, trolleys, and (eventually) subways, residents raced from all corners of the growing city to these recreational areas, spending days on their beaches and amusement parks, and evenings in their ballrooms and grand hotels.

Brooklyn was booming. By the 1880s it was the third largest city in America, benefiting by 1883 from the Brooklyn Bridge's link to New York. But the cries for unification by New York's city planners won out over fierce opposition mounted by the proudest of Brooklynites (and, to be fair, a few corrupt politicians). In 1898, the city of Brooklyn became the borough of Brooklyn.

Industry thrived in Brooklyn in the early twentieth century—the docks of Red Hook, the Brooklyn Navy Yard, the Coney Island amusements—but, sadly, most withered by century's end. Meanwhile, the vast highways constructed by Robert Moses midcentury facilitated movement through the borough, even as they sliced up and sometimes isolated neighborhoods. New housing developments in the 1940s through the 1960s opened the borough up to extraordinary diversity—the historic African American neighborhood of Bedford-Stuyvesant, the Russian American enclave of Brighton Beach, the Italian Americans of Bensonhurst. In 1964, the borough finally linked up to Staten Island via the Verrazano-Narrows Bridge, the longest suspension bridge at the time of its construction.

New York's financial downturn in the 1960s and '70s hit Brooklyn especially hard, but a rather unexpected twist in the early 1990s brought young artists to Williamsburg, kicking off an escalation of gentrification throughout most of the borough that seems only to be picking up steam at press time.

This, in turn, has given rise to a new sense of wistfulness (and sardonic disbelief) every time a local hears of moneyed Manhattanites "discovering" the borough today. They're only about 200 years late.

THE BOWERY'S MOST NOTORIOUS DIVES 1903

The following list of the Bowery's most "evil resorts" was published in an article in the *New York Tribune*, on April 12, 1903, that touted the city's reform efforts. Quotations are from the article. (Note: To locate some of the spots of these charming former establishments, you'll need to backtrack to Chapter 7, "Chinatown and Little Italy.")

15 Bowery "Known to the criminal 'under world' as Spanish Mamie's. Took its name from the presence of a Spanish girl, the associate of many crooks. This was a dive of the lowest sort."

19 Bowery "A back room 'ginmill,' the headquarters of 'Boston Charlie,' a well known character, and his even more notorious woman pal 'Boston Clara.'"

25 Bowery "The New-York Tavern. A low order of 'crooks' made this their 'hang out.'"

115 Bowery "Little Jumbo. Criminals and 'panhandlers' made it their headquarters, and sailors were the victims of all sorts of crime, from robbery to murder."

119 Bowery "'Eat 'Em Up Jack' McManus's Rapid Transit House. McManus was known to his 'pals' as a 'strong arm' man, one who garrotes victims he is about to rob with his crooked arm."

287 Bowery "The Tivoli — A concert hall where women in indecent costumes sang indecent songs on the stage."

291 Bowery "The Volks Garden — The most notorious concert hall in the Bowery, a resort for prostitutes. As many as fifty women were attached to this place, and the business was carried on brazenly, numbers of 'barkers' and 'pullers in' being stationed at the door to drag people in by main force."

Chapter 11 //
The Bowery and
Astor Place

It's a helluva town: The Bowery, looking south from the roof of Cooper Union, 1864.

SITUATE THE READER
–The Bowery and Astor Place–

Broadway and the Bowery represent a tale of two cities, the two iconic streets of New York City's high and low society in the nineteenth century. The old farm road *bouwerij* (Dutch for "farm") once led past the many gracious estates dotting the bucolic countryside north of the city, including those of the Stuyvesants' (see Chapter 10), the Bayards', and the Brevoorts'. The grid plan carved up most of those farms into city block–sized parcels in the nineteenth century; however, blocks south of Bleecker Street[1] rebelled against the plan.

The Bowery itself was briefly fashionable in the early nineteenth century, its lower portion home to the city's finest theaters. But these would soon relocate as the Bowery made room for more "popular" houses of entertainment. This was especially the case as immigration picked up steam in the 1830s, and the new, significantly poorer, arrivals started packing into rooming houses and tenements in the blocks surrounding the Bowery. The wealthiest New Yorkers, meanwhile, moved to lavish new residences built upon land sold to them by a new breed of entrepreneur, the real estate developer, most prominent among them John Jacob Astor (1763–1848). The intersection that took his name, Astor Place, links Broadway and the Bowery in just two short blocks.

But the class friction between the Bowery and Broadway was a ticking time bomb. After the deadly Astor Place Riot in 1849, the city's wealthy residents packed up their trunks and moved to quieter new developments farther north. Cooper Union, built in 1859 on Astor Place, brought a revolutionary concept to the neighborhood: free education for working-class New Yorkers.

The Bowery, meanwhile, became defined in the late nineteenth century by its rowdy saloons, notorious brothels, and dangerous street gangs. During the Depression in the 1930s and for decades following it, the street was New York's skid row, its very name synonymous with being on the outside, down on your luck, forgotten. Today, much of the lower Bowery acts as a main Chinatown artery, jammed with intercity bus depots and restaurant supply stores, while the section north of Delancey Street has turned a trendy corner.

---

1 Bleecker is also named for a family who owned an old farm here. Anthony Lispenard Bleecker was known as an infamous New York joker. William Cullen Bryant later claimed that one woman had "gone to the country to take refuge from Anthony Bleecker's puns." A man after our own hearts.

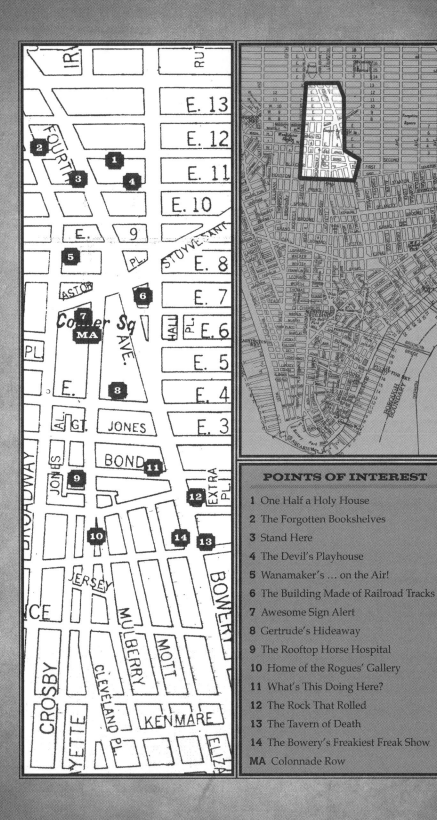

POINTS OF INTEREST

1 One Half a Holy House

2 The Forgotten Bookshelves

3 Stand Here

4 The Devil's Playhouse

5 Wanamaker's … on the Air!

6 The Building Made of Railroad Tracks

7 Awesome Sign Alert

8 Gertrude's Hideaway

9 The Rooftop Horse Hospital

10 Home of the Rogues' Gallery

11 What's This Doing Here?

12 The Rock That Rolled

13 The Tavern of Death

14 The Bowery's Freakiest Freak Show

MA Colonnade Row

Colonnade Row and the Astor Place Riot

On May 10, 1849, Astor Place erupted into bloody violence as crowds took to the streets and battled it out over ... a Shakespearean actor. It was the first time in American history that a state militia trained its muskets upon the very population it had been sworn to protect.

Yet of the many structures today surrounding Astor Place, only Colonnade Row (at 428–434 Lafayette Place) still remains from that dreadful day. From between its columns that May night, residents observed the horrifying violence firsthand. These old buildings, distinctive for their Corinthian columns, seem especially weathered when compared with the dazzling Astor Library across the street, home to the Public Theater since 1967. (Colonnade Row, it should be noted, is also something of an off-Broadway landmark. The Astor Place Theatre, located in the basement, has been home to the flamboyant

Pillars of Astor Place: La Grange Terrace in its full, original majesty.

Blue Man Group spectacle for so long that the original performers have since turned gray.)

In 1805 this area was home to Vauxhall Gardens, an outdoor recreational venue that functioned something like a privately run park. But the city was expanding north, and wealthy fur trader–turned–real estate tycoon John Jacob Astor understood high society's desire for more refined residential quarters. In 1826 Astor sliced a street right through Vauxhall Gardens and named it after the Marquis de Lafayette.[2] Upon the western side of Lafayette Place (now Lafayette Street) he commissioned an upscale housing complex originally called La Grange Terrace, named for the marquis's estate back in France.

---

2   Lafayette, commemorating France's contributions to the American Revolution, made a highly celebrated tour of the United States in 1824–1825. Many places in America were named for the revered officer at that time.

As historian Alvin F. Harlow later observed, Astor "was ridiculed for his folly in building such mansions on the very outskirts of town, but he was right."[3] Completed in 1833, La Grange Terrace was quite a large and lavish address, boasting nine residences (today's Colonnade Row contains only four of these original houses) that attracted notable members of high society — a relation of Washington Irving, the father-in-law of President John Tyler, even Astor's own grandson. They were among the toasts of the town, hosting dinner parties in their twenty-six-room(!) mansions, and enjoying such state-of-the-art luxuries as central heating and indoor plumbing.

Some residents of La Grange Terrace were home on the evening of May 10, 1849, the night that all hell broke loose.

Located just up the block between Astor Place and 8th Street, the Astor Place Opera House had opened two years before as a place for the city's elite to gather, flaunt their good fortune, and take in an evening of (often imported) culture. Indeed, this was the case on the night of May 10, when they gathered to witness a highly antici-pated performance of *Macbeth*, starring William Charles Macready, England's most famous tragedian.

Astor Place Opera House, depicted here in 1850.

For years Macready had been engaged in high-profile thespian warfare with New York's most celebrated hometown actor, Edwin Forrest, a charismatic star whose rugged, brawny performances endeared him to working-class audiences. At first, the publicity surrounding their rivalry was a boon to both actors and to ticket sales wherever they performed. Both Macready and Forrest toured the United States in separate productions, many times visiting cities just days apart from each other. Audiences would attend both shows and argue for days about the superiority of one performance over the other.

Soon, however, it seemed these boisterous theatrical arguments were about something larger than the delivery of a Shakespearean soliloquy. Tensions were simmering about something deeper than any actor or performance, but

---

3 From *Old Bowery Days: The Chronicles of a Famous Street*, 1931.

rather that which they represented. Forrest's popularity among the Bowery crowd, especially the new Irish immigrants seeking to survive on the lowest

The dashing and very British William Macready in 1838, more than a decade before the Astor Place fiasco.

rung of New York life, emboldened them against Macready. Macready's fans, meanwhile, were eager to associate themselves with the fineries of English society. To Macready's rarified audiences, Forrest represented the growing dangers of the impoverished immigrant class in the rapidly expanding city.

As the actors' public feud grew more heated, so too did the ire of their respective audiences. And here, in May of 1849, both actors were performing in the same city at the same time. Tensions were high.

On May 7, Forrest supporters had disrupted a performance of *Macbeth* at the Opera House, pelting the stage with wilted vegetables and rotten eggs. Scorned and embarrassed, the English actor vowed never again to perform in New York and packed his bags to head back to London. Prominent city leaders (including Washington Irving, a frequent guest at La Grange Terrace) convinced him to stick around for his final, highly anticipated performance three days later. Macready begrudgingly acquiesced.

That night, May 10, thousands of anti-Macready rioters packed into Astor Place, pushing up against the police forces gathered around the theater. Tensions mounted as the crowds swelled, raising their voices—and then the stones started flying. Protestors pulled cobblestones from the street, pelting the police officers while screaming to burn the theater to the ground. Inside, the audience tried to keep its focus on Macready, who gave a fine performance, given the circumstances, the drama of the

When the militia arrived, they discharged their weapons indiscriminately into the crowd.

evening enhanced by the growing sense of danger in the air. Once the show was over, Macready wisely disguised himself and made a quick exit through the back of the theater, never to perform in America again.

As darkness fell, the police struggled to contain the crowd and needed backup. The state militia marched from Washington Square and gathered inside the stables of La Grange Terrace, ready to disperse the agitated crowd that filled the square. The soldiers fired shots into the crowd, seemingly without a distinct target. Anger turned to panic as thousands pushed and shoved, pulling in and trampling innocent bystanders in their path. By the time the crowd finally dispersed, at least twenty-five people had been shot and killed, some from stray bullets that hit them inside their homes.

Night fell upon a street scene in chaos – rioters, police, and militia at each other's throats.

This violent episode signaled the beginning of the end for Astor Place as an elite destination. Soon, ritzy developments opened farther north near Union Square, Gramercy Park, and later, Madison Square, and the old Opera House was torn down.[4] In the 1850s Astor Place saw the opening of two institutions that would give it a new educational purpose: the private lending library owned by the Astor family (opened in 1853) and the Cooper Union institution of higher learning (in 1859).

Unsurprisingly, La Grange Terrace experienced a spectacular fall from grace. It played various roles over the next several decades, functioning as various hotels and boardinghouses, before five of the nine houses were demolished in 1902. The other four continued into the twentieth century as curious relics of a bygone era. In 1965 they were among the inaugural structures to be saved by the newly formed Landmarks Preservation Commission. Even with battered old columns, this landmark tells a marvelous story of New York—from blue bloods to Blue Men.

---

4   It survived many decades as a home for the New York Mercantile Library until it was finally demolished in 1890.

Astor Place and the Bowery

1 ONE HALF A HOLY HOUSE Old churches that are no longer active suffer unusual fates in New York City. While some are unceremoniously

torn down, others are converted into condominiums or transformed into infamous nightclubs. (See the Limelight on page 266.) But none seems as peculiar as that of old St. Ann's Church. Originally constructed in 1847 as a Baptist church, it briefly served as a synagogue before a new Catholic congregation bought the building in 1870, kept the facade and tower, and erected a new sanctuary behind it. More than 135 years later, the church was slated to be demolished to make way for NYU housing. After public protest, the university agreed to

Saving face: Part of St. Ann's Church
still stands on East 12th Street.

keep the original facade, but cleared away everything behind it, including St. Ann's later additions. Today it stands like a defiant ruin—like something you might see in post-war Europe—fronting a truly snooze-worthy dorm. (*120 East 12th Street*)

2 THE FORGOTTEN BOOKSHELVES The Strand Bookstore, at East 12th Street and Broadway, is one of New York's most legendary booksellers, boasting "18 miles of books," but half the magic can be experienced perusing the carts of discounted books outside on the sidewalk. Now imagine that same experience replicated up and down Fourth Avenue, from Union Square to Astor Place. This stretch was New York's old "Book Row," a place where literary types could get lost for hours. It's said that the stuffy, dusty, and often chaotic booksellers lining these five blocks offered more than 1 million books for sale—imagine the treasures! While most of these small shops were killed off by big book chains in the 1990s, a few remain, including the Strand, which opened in 1927. (*828 Broadway*)

3 STAND HERE: Grace Church, but on the Fourth Avenue side, where it meets East 11th Street. *Why?* Of course, check out Grace Church's gorgeous facade, facing Broadway, to take in the ornate design of masterful architect James Renwick, Jr. (1818–1895). One of the city's leading church architects of the nineteenth century, Renwick was only in his twenties at the time of this commission. Step inside the Episcopal church to find one of New York's most ravishing interiors, completed in 1846, and the private pews for which the city's most notable families would pay dearly. (You can still see the names of some of these families affixed to the fronts of their pews.)

How can Grace Church block East 11th Street from passing through? Ask Henry Brevoort!

But one of the most interesting stories can actually be found behind the church, along the row of Gothic Revival church houses out back. New York's grid plan of 1811 divvied up Manhattan into numbered streets and avenues and made very few exceptions along the way. Why, you might ask, doesn't East 11th Street cut through this block from Fourth Avenue to Broadway?

The answer stems from the land's previous owner: the wealthy and powerful Henry Brevoort. You see, at the time the grid plan was adopted, this was the site of his prized apple orchard, and he simply couldn't *bear* to see the fruits of his labor chopped down. It was only after he died in 1841 that his son sold the lot to Grace Church, located at the time down at Broadway and Rector.

Renwick, by the way, was Brevoort's nephew. Because it always goes back to who you know in the Big Apple! (*East 11th Street and Fourth Avenue*)

4 THE DEVIL'S PLAYHOUSE Webster Hall is one of the most decadent sites in all of New York City. But the deejays and punk rockers who play here

today can only dream of shocking their contemporaries in the same way that partygoers were shocked a century ago. Opened in 1886, the hall hosted the annual Greenwich Village Ball from the 1910s to the 1930s, a bacchanalia where artists, bohemians, drag queens, and general reprobates of the best kind came to drink, dance, and seriously make merry until early morning. It worked hard to earn its nickname "the devil's playhouse." Author Allan Church wrote, "So many dances-till-dawn and fancy dress balls were held there that one Villager said of himself and his wife: 'We've sold our bed. Why sleep when there's a dance every night at Webster Hall?'" (*119–125 East 11th Street*)

5 WANAMAKER'S … ON THE AIR! Two great department stores inhabited Astor Place at different times. On Fourth Avenue between 9th and 10th Streets sat A. T. Stewart's grand "Iron Palace" department store, so nicknamed for being the largest cast-iron building of its day when it was constructed in 1868. In 1896, Stewart's was purchased by its chief rival, Wanamaker's, which took up shop inside the Iron Palace before expanding into a massive new "annex" next door to the south.

This addition, constructed in 1902 and designed by Daniel Burnham,[5] was linked to its iron sister by a fanciful skybridge, or traverse, which hovered over 9th Street.

Although the Iron Palace burned down in the 1950s (and was replaced by a boring white apartment building), a K-Mart store keeps the retail tradition alive in the bottom floors of the old annex, while offices upstairs house dot-com powerhouses Facebook, AOL, and the Huffington Post. But the

---

5 He's better known today for the Flatiron Building.

building has another unique distinction worth noting—as one of New York's first television studios. The DuMont Network,[6] an early player in network television, had TV studios in the store's auditorium as early as 1946. (*770 Broadway at East 9th Street/Wanamaker Place*)

The "Iron Palace" of Astor Place: The old Wanamaker's Department Store, 1935 (photo: Berenice Abbott).

6 THE BUILDING MADE OF RAILROAD TRACKS Peter Cooper (1791–1883) was one of New York's most famous inventors, a fanciful and bearded genius with a rags-to-riches tale, who constructed, among other things, one of America's first steam engines. When he decided to build an educational institution that was "open and free to all," he also borrowed heavily from the invention he had helped create. The building was one of the first to use steel I-beam construction, a common feature of most buildings

Cooper Union, opened to students in 1859, was originally "open and free to all."

---

6 DuMont is known as the network that debuted Jackie Gleason and *The Honeymooners* in 1951 (although that was filmed in a studio uptown).

today. The beams his building employed were actually modified railroad ties from the same ironworks that Cooper used for regular track production. Cooper Union's unwavering construction would symbolically match the many important speeches given in its central auditorium, including one in 1860 by a young presidential candidate named Abraham Lincoln. Since then, it's become almost a requirement for both presidents and candidates to speak here — from Ulysses S. Grant to Barack Obama (in March 2008, eight months before his first election). All aboard! (*30 Cooper Square*)

7 AWESOME SIGN ALERT Many of the latest constructions to go up around Astor Plaza seem planted by aliens without regard for the surrounding neighborhood. You'll find a particular example of this at Astor Place Condominiums, located on the south side of the plaza, which throws a sun glare upon a gigantic musical note affixed to a wall behind it. Carl Fischer Music opened on East 4th Street in 1872 as a retailer of musical instruments, but would become world renowned as sheet music publishers. The company moved to Cooper Square[7] in the mid-1920s, occupying a vast retail space where musicians could find literally *scores* of music. After the publisher moved out in 1999, the building became a condo, and today an exercise club occupies the spot where stacks of sheet music used to be. While a clock has graced this wall since 1929, it was transformed into a large musical note only in 1994. Let the music play. (*62 Cooper Square*)

The Merchant's House Museum, a time capsule where somebody is always home.

8 GERTRUDE'S HIDEAWAY The Merchant's House Museum, housed in a lovingly preserved 1830s townhouse, is both beautiful and unsettling. Beautiful, for it's still stocked with the original fineries and furniture of its long-time resident Gertrude Tredwell, born in the home in 1840. And disturbing, well, for the same reasons. Gertrude, an eccentric and broken-hearted spinster, lived in the house her entire long life (she died at age 93 in 1933), and furnished it with objects

---

7 The plaza south of Cooper Union is actually named Cooper Square, while north of East 8th Street it's Astor Place. A similar configuration exists between Greeley Square and Herald Square (see Chapter 17).

from the Victorian Era. Magnificent decoration meets you on every floor, as do hints of a New York that is at once civilized and very private. Lady Tredwell may still be around — the Merchant House is reportedly haunted, if you believe in those kinds of things. (*29 East 4th Street*)

9 THE ROOFTOP HORSE HOSPITAL In 1866, philanthropist Henry Bergh formed the American Society for the Prevention of Cruelty to Animals (ASPCA), partially to serve the needs of horses, the principal pullers of Gilded Age New York's street transportation. By 1914, however, it had also become fashionable to keep pets at home. It was then that the ASPCA opened the Free Hospital and Dispensary for Animals, the first full-service animal hospital in the United States, which could accommodate more than four dozen horses at one time, in addition to many more domesticated creatures.

Horses were mostly quartered and operated upon on the second floor. But a rooftop garden catered to the sickest horses who were in need of fresh air and sunshine, and they were lifted there by a state-of-the-art (heavy-duty) elevator. Autopsies were also conducted on the roof, and dead animals were disposed of in a basement incinerator.

Perhaps most curious of all, an entire floor served as an apartment for the hospital's lead veterinarian, Dr. Bruce Blair, and his wife. Because, again, it's who you know in this city! (*350 Lafayette Street*)

The first dog patient (and his physician, Bruce Blair) served by the Free Hospital and Dispensary for Animals, 1914.

10 HOME OF THE ROGUES' GALLERY (Vanished) There is nothing extraordinary about 300 Mulberry Street anymore—just a standard six-floor apartment complex and a parking garage. But for much of the Gilded Age,

Criminal Minds: The New York Police Department's infamous Rogues' Gallery, 1899.

from 1862 to 1909,[8] this address was the grand headquarters and center of crime fighting for the New York Police Department. "No other building in the city, probably, is richer in memories than 300 Mulberry Street," wrote the *New York Times* in 1909. "It is famous the world over." Notable among its many rooms was the famed "Rogues' Gallery," a collection of photographs of the city's most notorious criminals. (Some criminals considered it a badge of honor to be included here.) However, many social reformers thought it should rather be a row of mirrors, as the building embodied the corruption of the New York police force in the late nineteenth century. (*300 Mulberry Street*)

Cast-iron cutie: 54 Bond Street has seen great changes on the Bowery.

11 WHAT'S THIS DOING HERE? This five-story ivory-colored cast-iron beauty seems like it belongs in SoHo, not along the Bowery.[9] Since its construction in 1874, the structure has played several roles: It was a bank for many decades, and later home to an off-Broadway theater (the Bouwerie Lane Theatre) from 1963 to 2006, before being converted into private, ultra-ritzy apartments. Rewind several decades, however, to a Bowery district that was decidedly down on its luck, and imagine how

---

8 In 1909 it moved to the police headquarters we mentioned in Chapter 7.
9 In fact, it's part of the NoHo (North of Houston) Historic District, which includes structures along the cobblestoned streets of Great Jones and Bond Streets to the west.

this Italianate beauty must have stood out. It was made a New York City landmark in 1967. (*54 Bond Street*)

12 THE ROCK THAT ROLLED When the old punk rock club CBGB[10] finally closed for good with a Patti Smith concert in 2006, many felt that the soul of New York City had shuttered along with it. The dingy, often claustrophobic space saw performances by many rock legends in their infancy, including the Talking Heads, the Ramones, and Blondie. What began in 1969 as just a regular bar owned by Hilly Kristal, transformed into a rock club by 1973. Kristal was an innovator, but hardly the first bar owner to occupy the space, as saloons had been serving drinks here off and on since the building's construction in 1878. (If these walls could talk … most likely they'd throw up on you.) The club closed in 2006, and Kristal died a year later. A John Varvatos shoe store moved in a year after that. (Sigh.) (*315 Bowery*)

13 THE TAVERN OF DEATH (Vanished) It's difficult to imagine a more loathsome drinking establishment than McGurk's Suicide Hall, a standout a century ago even among the most debauched dives on the Bowery. One had to have fallen pretty low to even enter John McGurk's establishment. Opened in 1895, within four years it had gained notoriety as the location of a great number of suicides, almost all of them female prostitutes who had either ingested carbolic acid or taken a fatal leap from the building's fifth-story window.

John McGurk, a morbid showman who made P. T. Barnum seem like a class act by comparison, actually renamed his place Suicide Hall as a macabre marketing ploy. And the dive's reputation did draw its share of curiosity seekers, often from the upper class, who were looking for a bit of macabre excitement after a night at the theater. "This is Suicide Hall, gents," proclaimed the barker who stood outside. "This is the real original place. Step in and look it over." The building was demolished in 2005 and replaced with a glass condo. (*295 Bowery*)

14 THE BOWERY'S FREAKIEST FREAK SHOW (Vanished) Many structures along the Bowery share a versatility with 298 Bowery, today one of many restaurant supply stores on the block. The original structure, built in 1879, was a knockoff of Barnum's American Museum called, unoriginally,

---

10 Its full name, CBGB & OMFUG, stands for Country Bluegrass, Blues, and Other Music for Uplifting Gormandizers.

The Bowery was dominated by an elevated railroad line, which cast shadows onto the street.

the New American Museum. Unfortunately, it also imitated the demise of the original when it burned to the ground within the year. Rebuilt as the Globe Dime Museum, it featured such sideshow attractions as the India Rubber Twins, the Elastic-Skinned Man, the Turtle Boy, McClane's Enchanted Closet, a trio of semitrained wolves, and a popular "contest of handsome women and homely men." Things must have gone awry in 1883, as it was briefly closed due to charges of prostitution and child labor. (*298 Bowery*)

Who Are the Bowery Boys *Really?*

The Bowery Boys are about as close as New York City gets to homegrown outlaws, its own Butch Cassidy and the Wild Bunch. Their legend inspired street gangs well before New Yorkers had ever heard of the Mafia. Their reputation has been burnished in *Gangs of New York* (both the 1928 Herbert Asbury book and the 2002 film it inspired). Heck, a couple of Lower East Side podcasters even appropriated their name in 2007!

Dandies or derelicts? These "Bowery b'hoys" (drawn in 1846) were dapper dressers, while the Bowery Boys ganged up on immigrants.

But who were they? Notably they were *not* from the rising swell of young Irish immigrants who came to America starting in the late 1830s, called "Bowery b'hoys" (and "g'hals") in the press for their accents and rugged slang. With their particular, even dapper style of dress and swagger, the b'hoys dominated life on the Bowery, ushering along the avenue's transformation into a working-class district of amusement and vice.

By contrast, the Bowery Boys gang were nativists, aggressively anti-Irish and anti-Catholic, and were often dolled up in top hats and soap locks (hair tightly stuck to the temple). They patrolled the streets, often at the behest of local politicians. Their crimes, while often vicious, would pale in comparison with those of later gangs. While we might chuckle at the thought of highly coiffed, dandily dressed thugs in top hats, their violent exploits became legendary, especially their bloody altercations with their nemesis gang, the Dead Rabbits. Both the Rabbits and the Bowery Boys were gone by the late 1860s, replaced by more nefarious gangs.

In the 1930s, an acting troupe would take the name The Bowery Boys, producing plays and a series of slapstick films in the 1940s and 1950s. With all due respect to Huntz Hall, Leo Gorcey, and Bobby Jordan, neither they (nor we!) would have lasted long against the ferocity and ruthlessness of the original gang.

WASHINGTON SQUARE: A RHAPSODY IN A-FLAT

O! You Greenwich Village!
Land of love and passion's
tillage,
I hail.
Sweet vale,
Your type diverting;
Your feverish flirting;
Your Guido-Brunos,
And goodness-who-knows;
Who, over countless demi-
tasses
Kiss their lassies; read *The
Masses*,
And roast the lordly upper-
classes.
I admire your habits!
You live like rabbits,
Or old cave-dwellers,
In holes and cellars;
Garrets or stables,
Or under tables;
Anyway but normal,
It's so informal!
There's De Veer—the great
seer—
Such a hairy old dear,
They say that he writes all
his sonnets in beer.
And Hashish—the Swami—
Deliciously "balmy,"
You know what I mean,
Has a highly strung bean.
And—but one can't keep
count of 'em,
Such an amount of 'em
Grave men and brave men.

~ George S. Chappell, published in *Vanity Fair*
and in the *New York Tribune*, August 5, 1917

Chapter 12 ///
Greenwich Village

MacDougal Alley in Greenwich Village was the home to many great artists, including Jackson Pollock at 9 MacDougal Alley (photo: Berenice Abbott).

SITUATE THE READER
–Greenwich Village–

Greenwich Village has been the heart of New York's countercultural identity for more than 150 years. It's the birthplace of the city's bohemian scene, where classes collided, the iconic outsider neighborhood between midtown's office blocks and the cast-iron palaces of SoHo.

In the seventeenth century, New Amsterdam's director-general Wouter Van Twiller planted a vast tobacco plantation in the area of today's West Village, while his home sat around today's intersection of West 8th and MacDougal Streets. He'd name his plantation Sapokanikan after an old Native American village, and it was oft referred to as "Bossen Bouwerie" (farm in the woods). Other Dutch company men settled around here, becoming *co-patroons* of an area that would be known as Noortwyck (simply north of the city).

But the real godfather of the Village may be the superbly named Yellis De Mandeville, who purchased a farm here in the seventeenth century and named it for an old Long Island Dutch settlement: Greenwijck, meaning "Pine District." Once the British took charge and their wealthiest moved into mansions here, it must have been tempting to just simplify the name to the more familiar Greenwich—as in the tony district in southeast London, with all the upper-class implications that came with it.

This new Greenwich wasn't a village in the traditional medieval England sense, but rather a cluster of establishments that served the area's countryside estates. It was truly tranquil. For a time.

POINTS OF INTEREST

1 Stand Here

2 Something About the Row

3 Muse of the Mews

4 The Triangle Lives On

5 Evidence of an Unquiet Riot

6 From Cable to the Big Screen

7 The Mighty, Mighty (Short) Mayor

8 Rent Just Twenty Cents a Day!

9 Good Times at the Slide

10 Music by Gaslight

11 What's Behind the Wall?

12 No Ordinary Church

13 All Hail the Hellhole!

14 Awesome Sign Alert

15 The House of Death

16 The Tilting Townhouse

17 Oh, To Be a Fly on the Wall Here!

MA Washington Square Park

The Hanging Tree and the Birth of Washington Square Park

Manhattan's oldest living resident is an English elm that watches over the northwest corner of Washington Square Park. It is believed to have sprouted sometime around 1679, well before there was a park here or a Greenwich Village or, for that matter, a United States of America.

For centuries the tree has been the subject of mystery and urban legend: Its branches were used for public hangings, its roots run thick with blood. Given its nickname—the "Hangman's Tree" or "Hangman's Elm"—you'd be excused for assuming that city officials regularly disposed of criminals from its mighty limbs. Unfortunately for those drama seekers out there, there are no documented hangings from this particular tree. Not that the area hasn't seen its share of trauma, bloodshed, and death.

The handsome, well-manicured Washington Square Park contains disturbing secrets—both inside the park and underneath it!

When this elm was but a small sapling, the Minetta Creek—home to fish of all sorts—ambled by just south of it, twisting its way through these fields, flowing up the island to the area around today's Union Square.

In 1797, the elm, now all grown up, looked down upon the stream—and upon New York's largest potter's field that surrounded it. While New York was still situated much farther south, the city's overcrowding made it susceptible to disease and epidemics. That year, the city was struggling with an outbreak of yellow fever. The city's existing cemeteries had filled to capacity, and city leaders looked north to bury their dead. By November, this land had been transformed into a burial ground. Over the next 28 years, the field would see the burial of more than 20,000 bodies.

A guidebook[1] would later declare, "Where now are asphalt walks, flowers, fountains, the Washington arch, and aristocratic homes, the poor were once buried by the thousands in nameless graves."

Being an undesirable parcel of land, it naturally attracted more than its share of mischief (including duels between angry men) and even public executions. The tree was more than a century old by the early 1800s, and already rather robust and distinguished. At some point, legends began to cling to its branches and rumors of its notorious past begun to surround it.

But still, there was at least one documented hanging near the potter's field: the 1819 execution of a young black woman named Rose Butler, who had been convicted of arson. But there isn't any proof that the execution occurred at the tree. In a way, its very nickname is a sort of slander. There are already enough potential ghosts in permanent residence in Washington Square Park. We don't need to conjure up new ones.

A landowner who lived just north of the tree (in the area of today's Washington Mews) nearly bestowed a more pleasing fate upon the tree. Upon his death in 1801, Robert Richard Randall willed his estate to be used as a home for retired sailors. But his relatives contested the will, blocking the home's construction. The entire project was later moved to Staten Island, where the peaceful Sailors' Snug Harbor (built in 1831) still sits at its northern shore. Had it remained

---

1   *King's Handbook of New York City: An Outline History and Description of the American Metropolis* (1892).

back in the Village, retired sailors might still be enjoying the shade of the old Hangman's Tree.

By the 1820s the growing city south of it saw Greenwich Village as an ideal candidate for new development.[2] In 1826, the potter's field was turned into a

Passing through: Washington Square Arch was constructed between 1890 and 1892.

military parade ground and named for George Washington in commemoration of the fiftieth anniversary of the Declaration of Independence. Public burials for the city's poorest residents were now held farther uptown,[3] but most of the 20,000 bodies that had already been interred here were left untouched.

It was also at this time that Minetta Creek was covered over and channeled into sewer tunnels. But just like the undisturbed graves, the creek may also still lurk underfoot. Residents of the neighborhood sometime experience flooded or leaky basements that many believe come from the underground stream, now searching for direction.

As for the elm — the not-really-a-hangman's elm — it continued to grow. As it stretched taller, it witnessed the paving over of the surrounding dirt paths and the construction of extravagant Federal-style homes along the north side of the park in the 1830s. In less than ten years, the elm saw its neighbors go from the city's most impoverished deceased to its wealthiest living. This was the ultimate gentrification.

By the late 1840s the tree was officially fenced off and designated the oldest original component of Washington Square, which by now had become a strolling ground for the city's elite. A decade later came the first water fountain at the center of the park. Why put a fountain there, the elm probably thought. There are people buried under there!

---

2   Of course, a significant African American population in New York lived in the area, sometimes called "Little Africa," but as you'll see in this book, the creation of Old New York often meant the displacement of its most vulnerable citizens.

3   The area of today's Bryant Park.

Those who believe tales of executions at the Hangman's Elm are barking up the wrong tree.

The elm was already more than fifty years old when George Washington was born in Virginia in 1732. By 1895, it had lived to see the dedication of the park's most dramatic landmark—the (second, and permanent) Washington Square Arch. The Arch stands about 100 feet east of the elm and serves as a base for Fifth Avenue, which shoots north from its foundation. But during its construction in 1892, workers dug up human bones, coffins, and even gravestones.

Deep roots: The tree at the northwest corner of the park has watched New York grow up around it.

Think of the Hangman's Elm not as an ominous bark-covered monument, but as a silent witness to the city's growth over the past 300 years. It observed the protests of preservationists who battled against Park Commissioner Robert Moses' plans to plow roads through the park in the 1950s. It certainly took part in the bohemian renaissance of the 1950s and '60s, and listened to the music and poetry of thousands of young artists performing under its branches. It witnessed the drug dealing, the shady deals, and the arrests.

The elm survived the rough times, and sits today like a prized living legend, a symbol of the park's latest revival. The only thing hanging from this tree is more than 300 years of history.

But, seriously, we really need to change that name.

Greenwich Village

POINTS OF INTEREST

1 STAND HERE: Top of the Washington Square Fountain, looking north through the Arch. *Why?* Take a look up Fifth Avenue, as it stretches north as far as the eye can see. This street was the backbone of New York society during the Gilded Age of the late nineteenth century. And

The Washington Square Park fountain, installed in 1852.

the foundations of Fifth Avenue's haughty reputation are laid right here with the townhouses on the north side of Washington Square.

But even the Arch itself is a piece of Gilded Age largesse, created more than a century ago by the city's best-known architect of the day, Stanford White, to evoke nothing less than the triumphal arches of ancient Rome. But not to disappoint you—the Arch you see today is actually a copy.

The original, built in 1889 for the 100th anniversary of George Washington's inauguration (which occurred down on Wall Street), was made of wood and stucco and placed on the other side of Washington Square North, hovering over the bottom of Fifth Avenue. New Yorkers were so enamored of White's first beautiful arch—which was garnished with flowers, bunting, flags, and strings of electric lights—that it was rebuilt here in marble and was officially dedicated in 1895. (*Center of Washington Square Park*)

2 SOMETHING ABOUT THE ROW The line of identical homes facing the park on the north side are referred to as "the Row." These genteel residences were built here in the 1830s, back when they overlooked a military parade ground, not a fashionable park. These were the most luxurious homes in the city at the time, and still today they represent one of the best remaining lineups of Greek Revival housing in the United States. As wealthy New Yorkers kept movin' on up the island in the mid-nineteenth century, this stretch of homes became a relic of "old money," a bygone age, as depicted by Henry James in his 1880 novel *Washington Square*.[4] When the old families finally moved away, artists moved in. Edward Hopper lived and painted at #3 from 1913 until he died in his studio—comfortably in his chair—in 1967. (*3 Washington Square North*)

Trendy living: The Greek Revival rowhouses of Washington Square North were hot property in the 1830s.

3 MUSE OF THE MEWS You could easily forget that you're in the center of a metropolis when ambling along the quiet cobblestoned street behind the Row. This is the Washington Mews. These structures once served as the stables and servants quarters for nearby wealthy residents, including many of the families who lived along Washington Square. In the twentieth century, many of these charming little homes were refitted as artists' studios.

---

4   As a young boy, James would frequent 18 Washington Square North, the home of his wealthy widowed grandmother, Elizabeth Walsh.

Of note, number 58–60 became the studio of Gertrude Vanderbilt Whitney (1875–1942) in the years after she founded the Whitney Museum in 1931.[5] Her niece and official ward, Gloria Vanderbilt, lived with her for a time. Too bad Gloria's son, CNN anchor Anderson Cooper, didn't hold onto the lease. (*58–60 Washington Mews*)

4 THE TRIANGLE LIVES ON It's strange today to look at the Asch Building, at the corner of Greene Street and Washington Place, knowing its tragic history. It seems so solid, so respectably quiet. Students and park-goers rush right past without looking. But this building is central to one of the darkest sagas in the city's history.

In 1911, its top three floors were occupied by the Triangle Shirtwaist Factory, which employed mostly women and girls in the manufacture of shirtwaists, which were fashionable women's blouses of the days, with long sleeves and high collars. On March 25, a fire started on the eighth floor and within

moments overtook the floors above it, all of them packed with workers. Nearby residents and those passing through the park spotted the smoke and the fire and flocked to the street to witness the blaze.

What they saw was a macabre and horrifying display; many initially thought they were watching bundles of clothes being tossed

The devastating scene on the ninth floor of the Asch Building, following the Triangle Shirtwaist Factory fire on March 25, 1911.

from the factory's windows. It wasn't until they moved closer that they realized those "bundles" were, in fact, people. These poor victims had tried to escape down the stairway, only to find that factory bosses had locked them in. Trapped, suffocated, and blinded by the flames and smoke, they threw themselves toward fresh air, hoping to survive the fall.

One hundred forty-six workers perished that day—almost all of them poor immigrant women. You'll find a plaque honoring the victims on the south side of the building. The tragedy led to stricter fire safety codes for residences

---

5   The first incarnation of the Whitney Museum is just a short walk from here at 8–12 West 8th Street. Gertrude really must have loved the Village life, as she lived above the gallery.

and businesses throughout the city. Those same top floors today hold NYU chemistry and biology laboratories. The school's Center for Developmental Genetics today occupies the ninth floor. (*23–29 Washington Place*)

5 EVIDENCE OF AN UNQUIET RIOT The University of the City of New York was founded near City Hall in 1831 by Albert Gallatin, Thomas Jefferson's Secretary of the Treasury. He didn't stay involved long enough to see the school relocate in 1835 to a cathedral-like administration building that was located on the northeast corner of Washington Square Park. (The Silver Center sits on that spot today.) This ostentatious structure was built using prison labor to save money. Needless to say, this cheap labor supply didn't thrill local stone-cutters, who promptly rioted in the streets. (Honestly, what were school administrators thinking?)[6]

Class is dismissed: The Old University Building, with its haughty Gothic architecture, proved a bit much for the fledgling school.

Today we call this school New York University, and its campus comprises many of the buildings surrounding Washington Square Park and others throughout the Village. That massive Gothic structure—Henry James called it "the gray and more or less hallowed University Building"—was demolished in 1894. But a piece of the old tower, called the Founders Memorial, still stands tall in Schwartz Plaza like a bishop's hat, well out of reach of any future riots by stonecutters or stoned students. (*Schwartz Plaza, at the corner of West 4th Street and Washington Square East*)

Washington Square Park with the original campus of the University of the City of New York (later New York University) to its east.

---

6   Neighborhood residents and preservationists still frequently ask this question.

6 **FROM CABLE TO THE BIG SCREEN** Stanford White (1853–1906) designed several of the Village's most impressive structures. Here's another, the so-called Cable Building, completed in 1894 during the brief, marvelous period when cable cars ran along Broadway.[7] Engineers installed an impressive series of winding wheels deep in the building's basement, which constantly turned, keeping the cables embedded in Broadway moving along. When the cars were ready to move, they'd simply grab onto the cable and off they'd go. The system, however, soon proved unwieldy, and the city switched completely to electrical operation by 1901. The underground rooms where the gigantic wheels once turned have been home to the Angelika Film Center, one of New York's premier art house cinemas, since 1989.[8] However, some of the old cable turbines reportedly still exist in the building's basement. (*611 Broadway*)

Turbines in the basement of the Cable Building kept New York cable cars tugging along Broadway.

---

7   The city's first cable car operated on the Brooklyn Bridge in 1883. The last cable car was taken off the New York roads in 1909, a victim of improved transportation by electricity-run trolleys.
8   We were going to write, "Where once the wheels of cable operation turned now spin the reels of art house cinema," but the Angelika projects are in digital format now. Alas.

7 THE MIGHTY, MIGHTY (SHORT) MAYOR Judging by the statue of Fiorello La Guardia that stands in an active pose facing LaGuardia Place, the former mayor was a very, very short man—5'2", more than a foot shorter than Mayor Bill de Blasio. But considering his many accomplishments during his eleven years in office (1934–1945) — stamping out corruption, keeping New York afloat during the Depression years and during World War II—he stands taller than almost anyone who's ever held the office. The statue was placed *here* to celebrate his Greenwich Village birth in 1882, despite the fact that he was actually born a short distance away on Sullivan Street. But have you *seen* the rents on Sullivan Street? (*Plaza at LaGuardia Place between West 3rd and Bleecker Streets*)

A man of great stature: A dynamic statue of Mayor Fiorello La Guardia keeps Greenwich Village in check.

8 RENT JUST TWENTY CENTS A DAY! Feast your eyes on the glorious sign at the corner of Bleecker and Thompson that still advertises the legendary jazz club the Village Gate. The club operated from 1958 to 1994 and spotlighted a long list of performers, including Nina Simone and Aretha Franklin. Indeed, it was instrumental to Greenwich Village's development as a performance mecca. But the grand building that housed it also has an interesting story. Halfway along Bleecker, over an ornate doorway, you'll see a sign for "Mills House No. 1," the name of the building. This was constructed in the 1890s as a socially progressive men's hotel, equipped with unconventional amenities like a smoking room and a library, the better to keep men away from the saloons. And all this for just twenty cents a day! One catch—the entire building was locked up from 9 a.m. to 5 p.m. to encourage men to go find work. (*160 Bleecker Street*)

9 GOOD TIMES AT THE SLIDE Bleecker Street had its share of wily and debauched basement dives in the late nineteenth century that appealed to less mainstream tastes. In the early 1890s, 157 Bleecker was home to the Slide, one of the first recorded bars that catered to a gay clientele. The basement was packed nightly with men who fancied "male degenerates" (in the words of the unsurprisingly unsupportive newspapers of the time), along with the occasional female customer looking for something outrageous. Music, drinking, and laughter prevailed until the early morning; female prostitutes mingled with the boys. The air was filled with cheap booze, wild sex ("orgies beyond description"[9]), and tunes banged out on an old piano. If you visit the restaurant that calls this building home today, you can visit the basement bathrooms to take in the aura of "degeneracies" gone by. (*157 Bleecker Street*)

The *Evening World* ran exposés in the 1890s that decried the presence of "fairy resorts" like the Slide.

10 MUSIC BY GASLIGHT MacDougal Street should be high on any music and poetry lover's list of historical streets to visit. In the 1960s and '70s, it was the Broadway of folk music, its cafes and bars packed with performers attending to hipster (in the midcentury sense of the term) audiences. Young singers who would later change the sound of American music sang for tips alongside future comic legends and writers.

Of the many smoke-filled venues that lined the street, perhaps none was as important as the basement of 116 MacDougal: the Gaslight Cafe. Opened in 1958, this tiny club saw early performances by Bob Dylan, Richie Havens, Jimi Hendrix, and Bruce Springsteen. The hepcat cliché of snapping your fingers instead of applauding was allegedly started here, and was instituted following noise complaints made by neighbors. The Gaslight closed in 1971. (*116 MacDougal Street*)

11 WHAT'S BEHIND THE WALL? It's believed that Edgar Allan Poe wrote "The Cask of Amontillado" at a modest house at 85 West 3rd Street, where he lived from 1845 to 1846. The house is no longer there, but an "interpretive reconstruction" of the facade strangely is, half a block away from where it was built and stuck to the side of a modern structure, like historical appliqué. Horrors! (*85 West 3rd Street*)

---

9   *The New York Herald*, January 5, 1892.

12 NO ORDINARY CHURCH The venerable and graceful Judson Memorial Church was designed by an architect whose creations we've already visited a few times in this chapter, Stanford White, and completed in 1893 for minister Edward Judson, who saw the church as a tribute to his Baptist missionary father. The church's campanile, its distinctive bell tower, originally doubled as an apartment building, which was intended to partially fund the church. Almost immediately, Judson took on the needs of the neighborhood. The pioneering doctor Eleanor Campbell (1878–1959) opened a community health center in the basement here in 1921. By the '50s, the health center had moved out, and the congregation took on a rather radical and nonconformist tone, inviting experimental artists, beatnik poets, and avant-garde dancers to perform. Believe it or not, Judson is also considered to be one of the city's first stages for off-off-Broadway theater, a form of intimate, edgy theater that began in the 1960s. (*55 Washington Square South*)

Judson Memorial Church has become a towering presence for many Greenwich Village residents.

13 ALL HAIL THE HELLHOLE! The Golden Swan Garden is a pleasant little corner park, isn't it? It's hard to imagine that this was once the spot of a devilish tavern. The Golden Swan was one of Greenwich Village's seediest *and* most influential hangouts, the inspiration for artists, thinkers, and playwrights. As with any place overrun with creative types, the Golden Swan Cafe was given a whole slew of nicknames, most notably the "Hell Hole," although there are few signs that anything truly hellish happened here. Its most famous regular was playwright Eugene O'Neill. He wrote to his wife in 1919, "Last night I made a voyage to the Hell Hole to see how it had survived the dry spell.[10] There was no whiskey in the house … and it had to be stolen by some of the gang out of a storehouse. All hands were drinking sherry and I joined this comparatively harmless and cheap debauch right willingly." (*Southeast corner, Sixth Avenue and West 4th Street*)

14 AWESOME SIGN ALERT: Bigelow Drugs Neon Sign Clarence Otis Bigelow opened his drugstore here all the way back in 1838. Since then the chemists have filled the orders of a wide range of clients from Thomas Edison to film director John Waters (who loved its soda fountain). This beautiful vintage neon sign is actually one of the store's newest design features, constructed almost exactly 100 years after Bigelow first opened his doors. (*414 Sixth Avenue*)

10 Prohibition was around the corner, but by 1919, wartime actions had already greatly limited the sale of strong spirits.

15 **THE HOUSE OF DEATH** This perfectly lovely townhouse also happens to be one of the most haunted places in all of New York. Mark Twain lived here in 1900 and clearly had a fondness for it, as he's still reportedly hanging around. His apparition has been seen walking along the hallways, along with more than twenty other ghosts. (They're busy hallways.) Ghost sightings have vexed residents since the 1930s. Of course, rents being as high as they are, many of these longtime specters have reportedly moved to Brooklyn. (*14 West 10th Street*)

A long way from Hannibal, Missouri: Mark Twain lived in this West 10th Street brownstone.

16 **THE TILTING TOWN-HOUSE** The handsome town-houses along West 11th Street, once known as Brevoort Row, harken back to the days of horse-drawn carriages and men in boiler hats, and today offer an almost uninterrupted visual of nineteenth-century domesticity. That is, until you get to the unusual townhouse at 16 West 11th Street, which crookedly juts into the street as though hastily wedged into the lot. There once sat a fine Federal-style townhouse here until March 6, 1970, when an explosion tore the building apart. This violent accident introduced New Yorkers to the Weather Underground, a radical organization focused on overthrowing the US government. Three bodies were pulled from the debris that day, all members of the counterculture organization. Their bombs were intended for other sites in New York, starting with Columbia University. The current building here was designed by Hugh Hardy. Now situated in the spot where the explosives went off is a laundry room. (*16 West 11th Street*)

17 **OH, TO BE A FLY ON THE WALL HERE!** Many people identify the Chelsea Hotel as *the* hotel for musicians, artists, and writers, but the Hotel Albert, which opened in 1882, can lay claim to some of that cultural lineage as well. The original structure—it would eventually comprise four buildings—

was built in 1882 and designed by Henry J. Hardenbergh (more famous today for his Plaza Hotel and Dakota Apartments). Writers Robert Louis Stevenson, Walt Whitman, and Hart Crane all stayed here at some point. But the fun really began in the 1960s when the deteriorating hotel became a favorite hangout for rock musicians. The song "California Dreamin'" was written here by John and Michelle Phillips of The Mamas and the Papas; the group released their version of the song in 1965. (*University Place and 11th Street*)

California Dreamin' on University Place.

The Arch Conspirators

There's a spiral staircase inside the western half of the Washington Square Arch, which grants access to the rooftop and fabulous views straight up Fifth Avenue. Public entrance is prohibited, of course, although that didn't stop six fearless malcontents (including the artists Marcel Duchamp and John Sloan) from breaking in to declare a bohemian revolution late in the evening of January 23, 1917.

The escapade was organized by Gertrude Drick, a poet mostly forgotten today but known at the time by the name Woe (as in "Woe is me"). Once atop the Arch, the group decorated the outdoor space with lanterns and balloons, and spent the entire night around a fire, drinking wine and tea (the beverage of revolution). They shot off cap pistols into the wintry night air.

A radical shift in the art scene had already begun in New York, emanating from the streets around Washington Square. Gertrude Vanderbilt Whitney's

Does this 1896 picture of the Washington Square Arch look a bit barren? The two statues of George Washington would not flank the Arch until 1918.

Studio Club was nearby, as were the apartments of many artists associated with the Ashcan School, including Sloan himself.

Greenwich Village, long a magnet for the unconventional, energized this new wave of painters and playwrights as they bonded in nearby cafes and studios. It was in this spirit that the so-called Arch Conspirators, shielding their candles from the wind, unfurled an unusual parchment late that night that declared "a Free and Independent Republic of Greenwich Village."

The only evidence of this grand proclamation the following morning was the balloons that still clung to the Arch's violated rooftop. But the Village did become free and independent to an extent, a pocket universe of creativity for the rebellious musicians, artists, and writers of the twentieth century.

A GLIMPSE OF THE OLD WEST VILLAGE

The Historical Guide to the City of New York, similar in theme to the book you're reading now, was compiled by Frank Bergen Kelley in 1909 from the observations of members of the City History Club of New York. Its objective was to "direct attention to the yet visible traces of earlier times which lie hidden within and are fast disappearing from the city of to-day."

The following is an excerpt of their quick tour through the West Village. Incredibly, very little has changed since the history club's members first documented these streets:

Go west on Bleecker to Christopher Street.

Bleecker Street was originally called Herring Street for the farm of the Herring family. Pass several rows of old dwellings on Bleecker and Carmine Streets.

28. Home of Tom Paine at 309 (some say 293) Bleecker Street, where he lived with Mme. Bonneville. He died at the site of 59 Grove Street....

30. St. John's Lutheran Church, 81 Christopher Street, was built in 1821 as the Eighth Presbyterian Church....

...[C]ontinue east on Christopher Street.

32. Christopher Street Square; the meeting point of eight streets, in the center of what Hemstreet calls "The Mouse Trap." See at the end of the Square the Northern Dispensary instituted in 1827, present building erected in 1831; note the tablet.

33. The houses at 11 Christopher Street, opposite Gay Street, were occupied a century ago by Scotch weavers. The gardens extended down to Greenwich Avenue.

34. Jefferson Market (New Greenwich Market): market, court, prison, the site originally a pond. The building is the home of the Exempt Fireman's Organization, in whose rooms may be seen an interesting exhibit of old fire apparatus, pictures, etc. (visitors welcome).

See the old houses at 129–131 West 10th Street, covered in wisteria vines.

Chapter 13 ///

West Village

Charles Lane, between West and Washington Streets, 1935.

SITUATE THE READER
—West Village—

The West Village is the most wonderful place in the world to get lost. Fortunately, it happens every time we pass through.

When the Commissioners' Plan of 1811 parceled out much of Manhattan into a large grid, it locked in and squared off the flow of almost every neighborhood above Houston Street—except for an exceptionally tangled set of paths in the western reaches of Greenwich Village.

Many of these paths, which would become today's West Village streets, followed the original courses laid by the Lenape Indians, who referred to the area as Sapokanikan.[1] Other trails were blazed by the owners of early farms and estates, who over the course of two centuries of settlement followed the whims of their own street plans. When the Commissioners' Plan was adopted, residents here protested the vulgar imposition of the grid upon their gentle, bucolic land and successfully forced the grid, with its rigid and unforgiving avenues and streets, to start north of the West Village, up at 14th Street.[2]

This is the spirit of the West Village today—the resplendent townhouses and the elegant apartment buildings, the ornate homes embraced by ivy, the streets lined with shade trees, the corner cafes and the tucked-away taverns. It has a palpable and almost literary charm.

You can then imagine how unwelcome was the neighborhood's reception to the news that Seventh Avenue, busy, grimy, and charmless Seventh Avenue, which had been biding its time above 14th Street, was to be plowed through the neighborhood in the 1910s to link up with Varick Street below Houston. The avenue's march south through the neighborhood was merciless, and dozens of buildings in its way were demolished. Today, curious and surprising architectural relics from the event can be found by strolling that wide avenue. Look for buildings sliced up and lopped off, and imagine how violent and odd that must have looked to residents a century ago.

---

1 See Chapter 12's Situate the Reader.
2 This is the first of a great number of preservation victories for the neighborhood, which would later be the home to Jane Jacobs, a crusader who tirelessly fought the city's attempts to modernize (with bulldozers) in the mid-twentieth century.

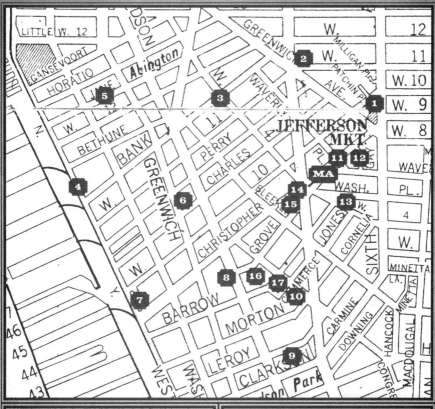

Stonewall Inn and the Legacy of Christopher Street

What would Charles Christopher Amos have made of the events that took place during the early morning hours of June 28, 1969, in front of the Stonewall Inn? What could he have thought of the late-night riots and arrests that led to outrage and protests, then pride and organization, then parades and eventual modern triumphs of the lesbian, gay, bisexual, and transgender (LGBT)?

Riots by vagabonds and degenerates — on my property?

Giving you shade: Historic Stonewall Inn sits upon the former property of a British general.

The path that would one day become Christopher Street passed along the edge of the estate of British Admiral Sir Peter Warren, an Irish derring-do from the early eighteenth century whose fervid support of imperial England belied an equal love for the town of New York. Warren's wife reigned over the manor[3] while Warren was off on his wartime adventures. Their daughter

---

3   The Warrens also owned slaves, as did many of the landholders of Greenwich Village during the eighteenth century.

Susannah married Colonel William Skinner, and the Warrens honored the engagement by naming the old Indian path that bordered their property Skinner Road.

In 1799 the property that included Skinner Road fell into the eager hands of Richard Amos, a trustee of the Warren estate. Ready to capitalize on New York's northward expansion, Amos was quick to lop off parcels of the property to sell to others. But he kept a sizable portion for himself and passed it along to his heir, Charles Christopher Amos, who apparently couldn't resist naming the surrounding roads for various members of the family: Amos Street (today's 10th Street), Charles Street (still exists today), and the former Skinner Road, now called Christopher Street. Very quickly, by the 1820s, this former farmland was unrecognizable; it had been absorbed into the city's expanding urban landscape. Christopher Street was now lined with businesses and functioned as the Village's commercial center.

In the nineteenth century, there were virtually no visible—in modern parlance, "out"—gay or lesbian New Yorkers, at least according to documents of the day, excepting references to those criminally charged with sodomy or "indecency." Meeting other gay individuals often occurred only by happenstance, whether it be in the comfort of a high-society parlor or, more commonly, the shade of a city park.

The rise of bohemian life in Greenwich Village in the mid-nineteenth century did allow for some increased openness among the boldest gays and lesbians. In the late 1850s, Walt Whitman caroused at Pfaff's Beer Cellar (near the corner of Broadway and Bleecker), and had experiences with men that may have later inspired passages in his classic "Leaves of Grass."[4] More commonly, however, gay New Yorkers would have encountered an underground world of homosexuality in the brothels along Bleecker and farther north in the Tenderloin District.

Prohibition was both a blessing and a curse for gays and lesbians of the 1920s. A legion of illegal underground bars created a certain laissez-faire attitude, which, among other things, ushered in an era of fabulous men in drag, some of whom would inspire entertainers like Mae West. But Prohibition also empowered a new criminal underworld that would one day shackle the

---

4 "[A] youth who loves me, and whom I love, silently approaching, and seating himself near, that he may hold me by the hand."

gay-friendly meeting places (under the guise of "protection," of course) after liquor was again made legal in 1933.

By the 1960s the mob had a veritable monopoly on the Greenwich Village gay scene. No bar could stay open without paying bribes (to both the mob and the police), and complaining bar owners had a funny way of finding themselves arrested—or worse. Indeed, police detectives sometimes posed as gay men to corner alleged "homophiles."

In the 1960s, one of these dank and unappealing bars on Christopher Street—the street of Charles Christopher Amos—was the Stonewall Inn. Its history was long and colorful: A former stable, it became a notorious "teahouse" in 1930, then a somewhat respectable restaurant, then was gutted in a fire *before* becoming a darkened-window dive bar catering to homosexuals in 1967.

There was nothing especially notable about the Stonewall, with its watered-down drinks and its hat-and-coat check. There was dancing and a jukebox

and a good mix of white, African American, and Hispanic patrons just looking to have fun. Wouldn't *you* be upset if they kept shutting you down for no good reason?

This is precisely what the police attempted just after 1 a.m. on June 28, 1969, when uniformed and undercover cops raided the packed bar and prepared to arrest the patrons. But people were not having it. A crowd outside the bar began heckling

Warren's long-gone eighteenth-century estate.

the officers as they started their arrests, pulling patrons from the bar and loading them into wagons. One woman in handcuffs fought fiercely, inspiring an extraordinary coalition of street youths and drag queens to push back against restraint. The crowds swelled as patrons from other bars joined the fracas, filling Christopher Street and pushing back against police harassment until well after four in the morning.

What began as proper "rioting"—or aimless anger in the streets—grew more focused over the next several days, as hundreds of marginalized New Yorkers returned to the street in front of the Stonewall with a newfound sense of solidarity. Their example inspired people throughout the city—and around the country. One year after the raid, activists would gather in front of the Stonewall and march up to Central Park, an event that would become the city's annual LGBT Pride March.

Today gay pride celebrations and parades in many European countries are referred to as "Christopher Street Day" celebrations. Although Stonewall Inn has gained national importance today—President Barack Obama mentioned it in his 2012 inaugural speech—it is Christopher Street itself that retains the symbolism for many.

There are four white sculptures in Christopher Park, across from the Stonewall, designed by George Segal and installed in 1992, which feature two gay male figures standing next to two seated lesbians.[5] Nearby is a dandy statue of General Philip Henry Sheridan (1831–1888), the great Civil War commander. Yet despite his name, nowhere is there a statue of Charles Christopher Amos, the unintentional daddy of gay New York.[6]

West Village

POINTS OF INTEREST

1 ORANGE IS THE NEW GREEN The triangle created by the intersections of Sixth Avenue, West 10th Street, and Greenwich Avenue is dominated by one of New York City's most striking structures, the Jefferson Market Library, completed in 1877 and given its dramatic Victorian Gothic design by Frederick Clarke Withers of the architectural firm Vaux and Withers.[7] Built upon the site of a former outdoor market, the structure first served as a courthouse that was home to one of America's first night courts. Needless to say, it was busy at all hours of the night during the vice-corroded Gilded Age. The handsome brick building, replete with stained glass windows, arches, and tower, was slated to be demolished in the 1950s, but

---

5 All figures depicted by Segal appear to be Caucasian, hardly an accurate reflection of the participants of the Stonewall riots.

6 It doesn't appear that any surviving likeness exists of Mr. Amos. But we *are* in the Village. We might be able to find an artist.

7 Yes, *that* Calvert Vaux, the codesigner of Central Park along with Frederick Law Olmstead. Withers may have designed the Jefferson Market Library, but the structure looks quite like two of Vaux's other works—the original Metropolitan Museum of Art and the American Museum of Natural History.

Village preservationists saved it from the wrecking ball. The New York Public Library has operated an award-winning neighborhood branch here since 1967.

Its moody Gothic interior holds a few secrets, although the greatest one may lie under the beautiful community garden outside. Not one, but two, jails resided here at different times. The first, the Jefferson Market Prison, detained those guilty of petty crimes and remained open until it was demolished in 1927, replaced by the Women's House of Detention four years later. Many prominent women were held here, including Angela Davis and Dorothy Day. The prison was torn down in 1973–1974 and replaced by a flowering garden a year later. (*425 Sixth Avenue*)

2 THE GRACE OF SAINT VINCENT'S (Vanished) Bellevue Hospital may be New York's most famous health care facility, but St. Vincent's

The first St. Vincent's Hospital.

was certainly one of its most important. In 1849, four nuns from the Daughters of Charity of Saint Vincent de Paul opened a clinic in a small house on West 13th Street before moving to this corner a few years later. It served the community's health needs for more than a century and a half, caring for those affected by major events and emergencies, from the sinking of the *RMS Titanic* in 1912 to the attacks of September 11, 2001. In the 1980s it contained New York's first AIDS ward, and was the site of much trauma and frustration. The hospital closed in 2010, and today you can buy a luxury condo on this very spot. The park across the street honors the legacy of St. Vincent's with an AIDS memorial slated to open in 2016. (*Southeast corner of Seventh Avenue and West 11th Street*)

3 THE 4TH STREET SPACE-TIME CONTINUUM The West Village's street plan had mostly been laid by the time New York adopted the straitlaced Commissioners' Plan in 1811. Looking at a map today, you'll see that the neighborhood distorts the rigid reality of the rest of Manhattan, especially where streets from the West Village's old neighborhood plan hook up with the rest of the city's new grid, and naming conventions go wildly awry. Take the case of good old 4th Street. Starting on the East Side of Manhattan at Avenue D, it crosses the island westward without interruption, serving for a classy second as Washington Square South. At Sixth Avenue, however, it throws on the brakes, slams into the West Village's alternative street plan, and drunkenly veers north, crossing West 10th through 13th Streets in a mad distortion of space and time. How crazy is this? So crazy that the original name of West 4th Street was Asylum Street, named not for a mental institution but an orphanage founded in 1806 at today's intersection of West 4th and West 12th. Its name was

changed in 1833 so that its eastern route could conform to the grid. But would the western end conform? Never! (*Corner of West 4th and West 12th Street*)

4 INVENTIONS OF GRANDEUR The Far West Village doesn't seem like an obvious home to groundbreaking scientific discovery, does it? Alexander Graham Bell, however, thought otherwise! The structures that comprised Bell Laboratories on West Street were, at one point, the largest research facility in the United States, operating from the late 1890s to 1966. The list of devices either invented or improved upon here is stunning: long-distance phone service, movies with sound, radar, television, long-playing records, condenser microphones ... and the list goes on. (Twenty-first-century podcasters give their thanks for that last one.) The most unusual building in the complex, facing West Street, was once part of the West Side Elevated Railroad (today the High Line). The Westbeth Artists Communities have occupied the Bell Laboratories building since 1970, and provide studio and living space for artists. (*445–465 West Street*)

THE BAYARD MANSION, WHERE HAMILTON DIED.

5 ALEXANDER HAMILTON DIED HERE (MAYBE) "There is a prevalent error in regard to the house in which

Hamilton died, which is worth correcting if only to show how little tradition is to be trusted." – *Gay's Popular History of the United States, vol. 4 (1876–1881)*

"What's Your Name, Man?" "Alexander Hamilton!"

On July 11, 1804, Vice President Aaron Burr shot former Treasury Secretary Alexander Hamilton just across the Hudson River in Weehawken, New Jersey. The gravely injured Hamilton was rowed back across the river and taken to the home of friend and banker William Bayard, Jr. Hamilton died of his injuries the following day. Bayard had a rather sumptuous estate, now long gone, and pinpointing the exact spot of the house, much less the bedroom where Hamilton spent his last day, is virtually impossible. A plaque at 82 Jane Street claims the sad honor. Most historians now believe it would have probably been across the street at 83 Jane Street. (*82 and 83 Jane Street*)

6 THE WEST VILLAGE'S UPPER EAST SIDE HOUSE Occasion-

ally while walking in the West Village, you come across a building that makes you stop in your tracks and ask, What? Such is the case with the unusual, two-story, slightly suburban (look, it even has a driveway!) 121 Charles Street. In fact, this is actually a farmhouse that's nearly 200 years old. It's a quirky and quiet place. You'd be excused for assuming that its unusual wedge shape was caused by some crazy grid-related shenanigans of commissioners past. But in fact, the story is even weirder: The entire house was moved here in 1967 from the Upper East Side. It was literally placed upon a flatbed truck and transported to this odd little lot. It's a private residence, so let it be; after all, it's been through a lot. (Actually two lots.) (*121 Charles Street*)

7 THE OMINOUS ORIGIN OF WEEHAWKEN STREET (Vanished) You may not be aware of the Weehawken Historic District, a collection of fourteen buildings of unique architectural character located in the Far West Village, and the wee little street that those buildings call home: the 63-foot-long Weehawken Street. In the 1800s there was a ferry to Weehawken,

New Jersey, at the nearby waterfront, so yes, it is indeed named for a New Jersey city. But this location has a bit of a darker history. This was the site of Newgate Prison (built 1796–1797), the first New York state prison that was named (or rather nicknamed) for the larger, more infamous prison in London. But New York's Newgate was still ominous, with high stone walls mirroring the shape of forts along the waterfront. Overcrowding and prison riots (and the desirability of Greenwich Village real estate) closed the prison in the mid-1820s. (*Corner of Weehawken and Christopher Streets*)

Greenwich Village's Newgate State Prison in 1801, near the water's edge.

8 A POCKETFUL OF PEACEFULNESS St. Luke's of the Field still thinks it's in a field. The several buildings within the church property — bounded by Christopher, Greenwich, Barrow, and Hudson — sit about happily removed from the city rumbling about them. At the time of its construction in 1821, pretty much all the land surrounding it was undeveloped. Like so much else in this area, the land was owned by Trinity Church, who opened the original Episcopal chapel here to accommodate the growing Village population. Throughout its history, the church's mission has

St. Luke's Chapel in 1935 (photo: Berenice Abbott).

reflected the neighborhood's changing demographics.[8] The charmingly simple church at its center has had some serious work done. After a devastating fire in 1981, the building was meticulously reconstructed by architect Hugh Hardy.[9] (*487 Hudson Street*)

9 **THE FIREMAN'S MEMORIAL STONE** Apologies if you've tired of reading that "this public park used to be a cemetery," but here we go again: James J. Walker Park, a popular location for neighborhood baseball and soccer games, was once the site of a cemetery. In this case, it was the St. John's Burial Ground, which was associated with St. John's Church, farther south on Varick Street.[10] Edgar Allan Poe reportedly wandered among the stones here, certainly woeful and possibly finding inspiration. In 1834, two young firemen, killed on their first day on the job, were buried here under a poignant marble monument, graced with the carving of a fireman's cap and trumpet. By the late 1890s, the cemetery had been turned into a public park. It was later named for Mayor Jimmy Walker, who lived at 110 Leroy Street, facing the park. The firemen's tombstone is all that remains aboveground to mark the park's somber origins.

The Fireman's Memorial is the only reminder of James J. Walker Park's grave past.

---

8   One example: The AIDS Project of St. Luke's has paid special attention to those living with HIV/AIDS since 1987.

9   This seems to be a specialty of Mr. Hardy. He was the architect responsible for designing the Weather Underground townhouse mentioned in Chapter 12.

10   See Chapter 6 for more information on the fate of Trinity-owned St. John's Park.

Oh, and one more thing—the bodies are still buried there. When the park was developed, the city simply removed the gravestones. (*Hudson Street and St. Luke's Place*)

10 HARRY POTTER'S WEST VILLAGE FLAT Manhattan townhouses often seem stacked up next to each other like great books, piled high with stories. In that regard, the house at 75½ Bedford Street is but a pamphlet, although one brimming with colorful words. This almost disturbingly slender townhouse is the leanest in all of New York, at least as tradition has it; it's less than 10 feet across and precisely 30 feet deep. It was constructed in 1873 and first used for commerce (a cobbler, then a candy store). When bohemia seeped into the nooks of the West Village, so came some of 75½'s most famous residents, including poet Edna St. Vincent Millay[11] and anthropologist Margaret Mead. It's like a set piece from a Harry Potter movie. Perhaps Daniel Radcliffe should take a turn here? (*75½ Bedford Street*)

11 AWESOME SIGN ALERT: Northern Dispensary, Instituted 1827, Built 1831, Heal The Sick Thousands of people stream past the triangular brick Northern Dispensary daily, at the confusing mash-up of an

intersection near Sheridan Square and the Stonewall Inn. Built in 1831, the dispensary was a health clinic serving the needs of the neighborhood's sizable poor population. One of those residents, in 1837, was Edgar Allan Poe, who visited the clinic complaining of a terrible cold.

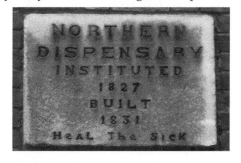

(Perhaps he caught it while wandering around a cemetery!) Dispensary services came to an ugly end here in 1989 when it chose to close rather than provide dental services to people suffering from AIDS. Since that unfortunate decision, it has remained vacant—for nearly three decades. And, as of press time, it still is. (*Christopher and Waverly Streets*)

12 THE PHANTOM OF GAY STREET One of the tiniest, most crooked, and all-around most intriguing streets in New York, Gay Street is named for an obscure former merchant—and not, sorry to say, for gay people. Its

---

11 We first came in contact with Edna in the Battery Park chapter, as her verses line the Staten Island Ferry.

coincidental position in the heart of the gay-friendly West Village, of course, has simply been too much for souvenir sellers to resist: They've made a small

fortune hawking photos of its street sign. But Gay Street's history is indeed rich. It was built in the eighteenth century, not as a place for homes, but for the horse stables of nearby elegant houses on Waverly Place and other pricey addresses. Later, African American residents lived on the street, and it became home to many artisans and tradesmen by the late nineteenth

The homes of haunted Gay Street in 1935.

century. Given the general artistic bent of Greenwich Village and the charming bend of Gay Street, it's no surprise that the one-block stretch developed into a mini-haven for artists and writers by the turn of the twentieth century.

Of Gay Street's many gorgeous townhouses, the one at number 12 is perhaps the most mysterious. The place was hopping during the 1920s; it was both a speakeasy and the home to Mayor Jimmy Walker's mistress, the actress Betty Compton. In the 1950s, resident Frank Paris, the creator of the early children's TV blockbuster *Howdy Doody*, built his famous freckled puppet in the basement. Paris reported seeing ghosts in the house, including one in a theatrical cape that has come to be known as the Gay Street Phantom. Yes, in the West Village, even the phantoms are fabulous! (*12 Gay Street*)

13 WHERE A STAR WAS BORN (Vanished) In the 1930s Billie Holiday became a star in the basement nightclub Cafe Society. Opened on December 18, 1938, Cafe Society was festooned with wacky caricatures of music stars, comedians, and personalities of the time. The club doorman played with the notion of deconstructed glamour, and wore tattered top hats and white gloves with the fingertips ripped off. Holiday, a twenty-four-year-old singer from Harlem, worked here for nine months and debuted the political classic "Strange Fruit" to an enraptured (and racially mixed) audience. Her performances at the club helped catapult her to stardom. (*1 Sheridan Square*)

14 STAND HERE: On top of the mosaic triangle on the southwest corner of Seventh Avenue and Christopher Street. *Why?* In front of the Village Cigars shop, at the most bustling intersection of the West Village, sits a much-contested piece of property, marked with a tile plaque that states "Property of the Hess estate which has never been dedicated for public purposes." When the city decided to unceremoniously plow Seventh Avenue through the West Village in the 1910s, they used the power of eminent domain to acquire all properties that stood in the way. Property owner David Hess, suddenly richer, but nonetheless irked by the imposition, discovered that a tiny smidge of his old land had been

missed by the surveyor's map. Hess refused to donate this minuscule bit of property to the city, and instead planted this plaque here in 1922 in stubborn, and smirking, defiance.

15 THAT QUOTE ON THE THOMAS PAINE PLAQUE: "The world is my country / All mankind are my brethren / To do good is my religion / I believe in one God and no more" — *Rights of Man*

Thomas Paine, the revolutionary who penned *Common Sense* and other eighteenth-century hot-button pamphlets, was born in 1737 in Great Britain and died in 1809 in a house that once stood on this spot. The present occupant, favorite sing-along show tune piano bar Marie's Crisis, recalls in name an early proprietor, Romany Marie, and Paine's work *The Crisis*. The

Marie's Crisis, where the sing-along show tunes are Paine-less.

weathered plaque in honor of Paine was installed here in 1923. (*59 Grove Street*)

16 THE PEACEFUL CHARM OF MIXED ALE ALLEY The West Village has an abundance of secret enclaves, hidden courtyards surrounded by beautiful old residences, insulated from the ugly sounds of traffic. Pure quietude. Grove Court is one of these places and features a jaunty overgrown fountain of greenery and a row of lovely redbrick homes built in 1854. Despite their obvious charms today, these structures were built for poorer residents

and were called "backhouses." (Keep in mind that the outdoor plumbing realities of the day meant that outhouses, vibrant aromas and all, would have also been placed nearby in the courtyard.) Perhaps this explains why the original residents famously drank copious amounts of liquor; so much, in fact, that this courtyard was nicknamed "Mixed Ale Alley." While Grove Court is closed to nonresidents today, you can peek in through the

Tucked away from the street, Grove Court is a charming little escape in the West Village.

gate—and then partake in some mixed ales just around the corner. (*Grove Court, near the corner of Grove and Bedford Streets*)

17 THE FEUDING SISTERS The twin houses at the fork of Commerce and Barrow Streets have their own spectacular New York folk legend. The

story has it that there were once two sisters who so detested each other that their father built them their own separate structures, connected only by a shared garden. The stuff of Hollywood costume dramas— calling Jessica Chastain and Emma Stone!

Unfortunately, that drama appears to be no more than a folktale; however, the street doesn't suffer from any shortage of real drama. Steps away from the "twins" is the off-

The twins of Commerce Street in 1935 (photo: Berenice Abbott).

Broadway Cherry Lane Theatre, one of the most important theatrical stages in the city, a staple of the bohemian and off-Broadway scenes since it opened in 1924. (*39 and 41 Commerce Street*)

There Once Was a Raisin Street

As of the next chapter, the street names get much less interesting.

As we've discussed, most of the streets and avenues above Houston Street were created by the Commissioners' Plan of 1811 and thus conform to the grid's orderly but uninspired series of (mostly) numbers and letters. Although this has made Manhattan a fairly easy place to navigate, the grid wiped away the surprising twists, turns, and dead ends that made things interesting.[12] An old street can help illustrate a city's history unlike most other urban features; it allows you to walk an ancient path whose turns were dictated centuries ago and confirmed by millions of feet that have passed since. It's that mystery, preserved in the West Village's streets that escaped the grid, that gives the neighborhood some of its romance.

Thomas Paine by John Henry Bufford, 1850.

Take the example of Raisin Street, or rather, Barrow Street. It's a quiet hooked lane that heads southwest from the southern side of Sheridan Square, bending west three blocks later when it collides with odd little Commerce Street before continuing westward to the water's edge.

In the heady post-Revolution period, this path was originally named Reason Street, after Thomas Paine's sensational anticlerical pamphlet *The Age of Reason* (published in parts, from 1794 to 1807). Paine lived in a couple of nearby locations, at 309 Bleecker Street and 59 Grove Street (see page 231).

As legend has it, however, residents soon took to calling it "Raisin Street," both as an accented corruption of the original name and, perhaps, as an insult to Paine (whose fortunes had turned by the time of his death in 1809).

While many streets in New York City are named for ripe fruits—Brooklyn Heights offers up Pineapple, Orange, and Cranberry Streets, for example— few are named for shriveled ones. In 1807, after Paine had published his final installment of *The Age of Reason*, Trinity Church, the principal landowner of the street, had officially had enough of his blasphemous publications and had the street renamed for Thomas Barrow, a vestryman and agent for the church. The end of *raison*?

---

12 Several north-south avenues were named with a bit more creativity within the grid, as evidenced by Park, Madison, Lexington, York, and Amsterdam Avenues, along with a few others.

THE ORIGIN OF CHELSEA

Chelsea...was originally the home of Captain Thomas Clarke, an English officer, a veteran of the French and Indian wars, who, on retiring, purchased a large tract of land which formed the district now lying between Eighth Avenue and the Hudson River and Nineteenth and Twenty-Fourth Streets. He called the place Chelsea, as a home for a retired officer.

After the death of Captain Clarke, his widow willed the property to her son-in-law, Bishop [Benjamin] Moore,[1] and in 1813 Bishop Moore and his wife deeded Chelsea to their son, Clement Clarke Moore, and there, in a house where he was born, Dr. Moore wrote "A Visit from St. Nicholas."

Some time before, he had donated to the General Theological Seminary a large tract of land, a field and orchard of Chelsea, what is now the entire block lying between Twentieth and Twenty-first Streets and Ninth and Tenth Avenues, upon which the buildings of the Seminary stand. It is a quiet, peace-inspiring spot, where the vines climb over towered walls and the green grass and the trees high above the noisy streets make an oasis for city-tired eyes. In the refectory at the far end of this green quadrangle hangs the portrait of Dr. Moore, and about it on Christmas Eve the students twine a rope of holly.

~ From *The Delineator*, vol. 80, 1912

---

1   This Benjamin Moore was the second Episcopal bishop of New York and is in no way related to the Benjamin Moore paint company, founded in 1883 in Brooklyn.

Chelsea and the Meatpacking District

New York's hottest club was Chelsea Mansion. Opened in 1750, it had everything—
books, cantankerous professors, famous Christmas carols.

SITUATE THE READER
–Chelsea and the Meatpacking District–

Given its name, the Meatpacking District's history would seem to be self-explanatory. But that's just the beginning of this *bovine* story.

It was indeed to this neighborhood—along with abattoirs scattered farther up the shore—that millions of heads of cattle were brought in aboard the Hudson River Railroad and slaughtered, cut up, sold, and shipped to hungry customers near and far. In the early twentieth century, the meat industries stayed on, even as the luxury ocean liners docking at the nearby Chelsea Piers brought millions of passengers to the neighborhood.

These were busy and bloody streets. Factories and processing plants sat alongside open-air markets, the cobblestone streets sometimes slick with blood and viscera. These days only a very few butchers and food processors remain in the neighborhood, as most have been pushed out by the glamorous boutiques and upscale restaurants drawn here beginning in the late 1990s. Ironically, it was these same quaint cobblestones and distinctive metal awnings, originally meant to shield slabs of freshly cut meat, that lured in their pricey replacements.

A bit farther north, Chelsea has a less bloody history—it started as a planned community carved from the nineteenth-century estate of author and scholar Clement Clarke Moore. High society never planted themselves very far into the neighborhood, and by 1900 a once-elegant apartment house, the Hotel Chelsea, was attracting a more ragged, bohemian set of residents. In the following decades, Chelsea became a middle-class neighborhood, home to many who worked in the nearby docks and factories.

Gentrification in the 1990s, led by the West Village's gay scene moving northward, brought a rotating roster of "straight-friendly" bars and restaurants to Eighth Avenue. (Much of the gay scene has since relocated north to Hell's Kitchen.) Today the neighborhood's trendiest stretches can be found farther west, along Ninth and Tenth Avenues, where a thriving gallery scene has benefited from the opening of the High Line in 2009 and the Whitney Museum in 2015.

POINTS OF INTEREST

1 Fortress of Art

2 The Unsinkable Gate

3 A Real Meaty Magazine

4 The Cookie Skybridges

5 Stand Here

6 Big Wheels Keep On Turnin'

7 Awesome Sign Alert

8 The Center of Chelsea

9 The Curve of Cushman Row

10 Best Brunch Place Ever

11 Why Not Both?

12 Read This Quote

13 Tillie Hart, the Holdout of 23rd Street

14 The Radical Spirit of the Chelsea Hotel

15 Barbecue with a Side of the Macabre

MA The High Line

The High Line and the Legend of Death Avenue

The linear park-on-stilts known as the High Line, one of New York's newest and most popular attractions, sits upon a set of abandoned elevated railroad tracks laid in the 1930s. Today, as you stroll the High Line park, snaking your way through city blocks, into and out of buildings like a drunken roller coaster, it's somewhat difficult to imagine its original purpose. The railway was first constructed for the transportation of freight and to prevent New Yorkers from killing themselves along the dangerous thoroughfare nicknamed "Death Avenue."

The Wild West: Trains with cargo led by "cowboys" on horseback ran down 10th and 11th Avenues in the nineteenth and early twentieth centuries.

But let's rewind: By the mid-nineteenth century, factories, warehouses, and docks understood the benefits of locating themselves along the West Side near the Hudson River. With the opening of the Erie Canal in 1825, the city's manufacturers and importers could sail up the Hudson and then float along the Canal, which connected eventually with Lake Erie and consumers in the American Midwest. New York–based exporters too found the location convenient, as manufacturers in the Midwest could float their products back down to New York's West Side, from where they could be sent off to buyers around the world. In this way, the Hudson (and Erie Canal) fueled a boom to the city's economy in the 1830s and '40s.

The city's reach into the heart of the country expanded enormously with the introduction of a West Side railroad line in 1851. While aboveground trains were understandably banned from the most central and populated parts of the city by this time, the West Side line (later owned by Cornelius Vanderbilt and the Hudson River Railroad) could pull south of 34th Street along 11th and 10th Avenues on tracks at street level that used a "dummy engine"—a disguised locomotive engine.

As it turned out, having a train plowing down the middle of a city street in a densely populated neighborhood quickly proved to be unsafe for virtually everyone involved. The situation was only slightly ameliorated by the introduction of so-called cowboys—railroad men on horseback in ten-gallon hats who galloped in front of the trains, trumpeting their imminent arrival, slowly ushering them down the avenues to their final destination, St. John's Terminal.[2]

The *New York Tribune* published terrifying tales of "Death Avenue" in 1911.

Who doesn't like a flag-waving cowboy gallivanting down the street? (It's a sight you still might find in some parts of Chelsea today, in fact.) However, it simply didn't go far enough to ensure safe streets. And the "cowboys" weren't just trying to clear away pedestrians: Imagine a never-ending line of horse-drawn wagons and carriages, mixed in with vendors with pushcarts and curious kids-being-kids bouncing all over the place—all trying to

2   Cornelius Vanderbilt bought up all the old properties in the neighborhood of St. John's Park (see Chapter 6) and turned it into a railroad terminus in 1867. It was topped with a statue of himself, which you'll discover later in this book.

clear the way for a freight train forcing its way down through the jammed streets. The train would make its way south past the Chelsea Piers, slow to a stop, and then inch along amid arriving and departing ship passengers. It crawled farther south, but why did it keep stopping? It had business to do: At warehouses and factories along its way, it halted to drop off deliveries and load shipments. And when it stopped, so too did the traffic jam behind it.

But it wasn't just slow-moving. It was dangerous.

As a result, by 1892,[3] 10th Avenue, the nucleus of this chaos, had earned the ominous nickname "Death Avenue." And the situation only got worse with the start of the twentieth century and the addition of new-fangled automobiles to this treacherous stretch.

In 1905, the *Evening World* declared that "DEATH AVENUE'S HARVEST" had a "ratio of one victim a week" at the time. Regular pedestrians had to watch their backs. More than 400 people had been killed along Death Avenue during the second half of the nineteenth century. And there were plenty of pedestrians—workers heading to factories, locals milling about, people trying to get to the Gansevoort Market and piers. "How much longer are the murderous conditions to be tolerated?"[4]

Meanwhile, a block east on Ninth Avenue the elevated railroad had been chugging along with passengers high over the avenue with relative safety since it opened in 1868. City leaders saw a possible solution here: Why not put trains and automobiles in the sky too?

And so the West Side Elevated Highway (built in sections between 1929 and 1951) was constructed along the river's edge for through traffic,[5] and those deadly street-level railroad tracks were hoisted up in the sky in 1934 when the elevated West Side Freight Railroad opened. Elevating the railcars had another practical advantage: Trains were now free to move along at their own pace, and boxcars could pull directly into factories for loading and unloading.[6]

---

3 First noted in a series of 1892 articles in the *New York World*.
4 *New York Evening World*, December 1, 1905.
5 By the 1970s it had deteriorated so badly that vehicles literally fell through it. It was thankfully torn down in the 1970s and 1980s.
6 This had the added benefit of safeguarding their contents from the hungry grasps of roving street gangs, who made a fortune selling "hot" supplies on the black market.

This might have been a terrific solution…many decades earlier. However, by the mid-twentieth century, advancements in refrigeration, the development of the American interstate highway system, and changes in grocery consumption would bring an end to New York's food production dominance. As one food manufacturer after another closed up shop along the West Side, the elevated freight train found itself a sweet but obsolete relic. By the 1960s, the city ripped down the elevated tracks south of Gansevoort Street, and by the following decade trains had stopped running along the northern portion of the line. The final journey on these tracks was taken by three carloads of frozen turkeys in April 1980.

And there they sat — abandoned rails, high in the sky. They created a desolate, shadowy stripe along the far west side of Chelsea, which added character and grit in the 1970s and '80s, topping off an area that had become known for its underground sex clubs, gay bars, and all-night dance scene. The tracks were soon overgrown with all manner of plant life and vegetation. By the 1990s, club-goers heading into the Roxy or the Tunnel could spot treetops and bushes peeking over its edge. It wasn't the drugs — they were witnessing a very natural progression.[7]

These overgrown and rusty tracks high overhead were an undisturbed pathway connecting to New York's industrial and natural legacies alike. One man, a Chelsea train enthusiast named Peter Obletz, almost single-handedly saved the tracks from demolition in the 1990s. He envisioned an active passenger train line and convinced the line's owner, Conrail, to sell him the tracks — for $10! But ensuing lawsuits by property owners scuttled the plan, and Obletz died in 1996 before his dream could be realized.

The present High Line park is the result of Joshua David and Robert Hammond, who formed the Friends of the High Line in 1999 to protect and realize the rails' parkland potential. The organization tirelessly worked with designers and architects, city officials and deep-pocketed donors for years, and the

Keeping track of history: The High Line incorporates the railroad's original infrastructure in surprising ways.

---

7   Well, maybe it was *also* the drugs.

first section of the park opened in 2009. Today the High Line draws thousands to the now-revitalized neighborhood daily. Its final stretch opened in 2014 and adjoins the massive Hudson Yards Redevelopment Project.

From bloody backwater to *Sex and the City*, boutiques, and bottle service, this neighborhood has experienced a remarkable change of fate. And these elevated tracks may now be responsible for transforming the entire Lower West Side.

Chelsea and the Meatpacking District

POINTS OF INTEREST

1 FORTRESS OF ART The Whitney Museum of American Art might look like a bulky old air conditioner from the outside (appropriate, given the importance of air conditioning to the city's slaughterhouse industry), but its dazzling, light-filled interiors and ample outdoor spaces make it a perfect addition to the "new" Meatpacking District art scene. Perhaps an avant-garde artist could employ some of the remaining slabs of meat still being processed next door. (That would be *very* '90s.)

Fort Gansevoort was built to protect New York, but it never saw a battle.

Both the art museum and the meat coolers sit atop the site of old Fort Gansevoort, built during the nervous days leading up to the War of 1812. The twenty-two-cannon fort, which never saw serious battle, was named in honor of brave Revolutionary War colonel Peter Gansevoort (1749–1812). He's probably best known today for the nearby street now that now bears his name, but he can claim another distinction: Peter was the grandfather of Herman Melville, another New Yorker and the author of the great American novel *Moby-Dick*, published in 1851. In the 1860s, Melville was employed as a New York customs inspector, and, in a poetic coincidence, worked in an office here at the foot of Gansevoort Street.

Note: If you go into the Whitney Museum (and you should), head to the top balcony, from where you can look down onto the meat processing plants next door, where the old fort once stood. (*99 Gansevoort Street*)

2 THE UNSINKABLE GATE Standing like a ruin along the river's edge, this rusty yet delicate gateway once served as the entrance to massive Pier 54.

It stands today as a reminder of the glory days of Chelsea Piers, the busy set of ocean liner berths that opened in 1910 and lined the Hudson River from this spot all the way up to 23rd Street. Each of the great luxury liner companies of the day had berths here. This pier was the original home of the Cunard Line, which named each of their great passenger ships with monikers ending with "ia." This fleet included the *Mauretania* and *Aquitania*.

You may be more familiar with two other ships that are forever

RMS *Carpathia* in dock, 1912.

associated with tragedy. The RMS *Carpathia* docked here on the evening of April 18, 1912, carrying the 705 survivors of the *Titanic*. And the RMS *Lusitania* frequently made this dock home as well. On May 1, 1915, with Europe at war and despite warnings of possible attacks by German U-boats, the *Lusitania* left the port carrying 1,962 passengers from all walks of life. Just six days later, on May 7, the *Lusitania* was torpedoed by a U-boat and sank off the coast of Ireland, killing nearly 1,200 people. *(Pier 54, 11th Avenue at West 13th Street)*

3 A REAL MEATY MAGAZINE Here's an anomaly: a publishing icon hanging out in a warehouse district. But on this spot, smack in the middle of

a district devoted to food production, butchers, refrigeration, storage, and garages, sat a significant American publishing house, P. F. Collier and Son. They were known for publishing *Collier's Weekly*, one of the most insightful political magazines of the early twentieth century. Their handsome offices were constructed in 1901–1902; above the door sits a flamboyant globe topped with a torch. Why here, you ask? It helped that one of the Collier sons married the granddaughter of William Astor, who happened to own the land. By the way, in April 1905, the magazine ran Upton Sinclair's famous "Is Chicago Meat Clean?" article, the basis for his landmark 1906 novel *The Jungle*. *(416–424 West 13th Street)*

4 THE COOKIE SKYBRIDGES The High Line gets really interesting here, with both a railroad ramp and a skybridge, or traverse, hooking into a building across 10th Avenue and a second skybridge connecting two redbrick structures over 15th Street. The letters "N.B.C." are etched into the door above the building at 10th Avenue, but these were not TV or radio studios. Rather more deliciously, it was a dessert wonderland: the National Biscuit Company, known today by its cute, shortened name, Nabisco.[8]

The metal overpasses allowed for the easy transfer of supplies and products between buildings—without the threat of hungry thieves or broken biscuits. From ovens here, millions of Nilla wafers, Fig Newtons, and saltines were manufactured and loaded onto trains for mass ingestion.

Snacking pilgrims, you've arrived: The Oreo, that ubiquitous chocolate-and-cream sandwich cookie sensation, was invented here in 1912. To commemorate

---

8 Obviously, the company was into shortening.

this notable event, this stretch of West 15th Street was soon referred to as "Oreo Way." Thanks to Chelsea Market, the complex of restaurants, bakeries, and stores that has made its home in the old factory since 1997, visitors can still snack their way through the building today. (*15th Street and 10th Avenue*)

A sweet skybridge hangs over ol' Oreo Way.

5 STAND HERE: The southern tip of Chelsea Waterside Park, 11th Avenue and 22nd Street. *Why?* From this spot, you have a terrific view of the entrance of the modern Chelsea Piers, an upscale athletic and entertainment complex built in the 1990s. But a hundred years ago, your carriage and valet would have waited for you here as your luxury ocean liner pulled into dock at the gigantic pier complex, the original Chelsea Piers.

Full steam ahead: The former Chelsea Piers complex in action.

The sporting complex today comprises Piers 59, 60, and 61, while the adjoining Pier 62[9] is today part of the Hudson River Greenway. Pier 59 was once the home of White Star Lines, and it was here that the RMS *Titanic* was scheduled to dock after its maiden voyage in 1912. Unfortunately, that great vessel smashed against an iceberg in the Atlantic Ocean on April 15 and never arrived at Pier 59. The

9   Manhattan pier numbers do not follow street numbering—for instance, Pier 24 does not run concurrent with 24th Street—but rather a sequential order that begins at Battery Park. Piers 1 through 24 were actually eliminated with the construction of Battery Park City.

fact that the IAC building right across 11th Avenue from Pier 59, designed by Frank Gehry and completed in 2007, resembles either an iceberg or a ship is certainly pure coincidence. (*11th Avenue and 22nd Street*)

6 BIG WHEELS KEEP ON TURNIN' By the 1970s, most of the West Side industries had closed up shop, resulting in the shuttering of many of the warehouses that served them. One warehouse that formerly stored trucks, however, screamed "I will survive" and turned the beat around: It strapped on skates and became a roller-disco! The Roxy opened in 1978 and was Studio 54 on skates. But it kept up with the times: During the 1980s, it played a seminal role in the development of early hip-hop music and break dancing. By the '90s, it had become a gay hot spot, as its DJs defined the era's dance music sound with big beats and wailing divas, and club promoters threw epic evenings of glittery debauchery. Sadly, it had its last dance in 2007, but the space remains open today as an art gallery. (*511 West 18th Street*)

7 AWESOME SIGN ALERT: Tower's Warehouses It's shielded by trees today, but near this wooden High Line seating area is a combination "ghost sign" and graffiti tag that illustrates, in its own poetic way, a conversation between two eras. The older of the two advertises "Tower's Warehouses Inc. U.S. Bonded." (Businesses could store imports without paying duties in a bonded warehouse.) Below it lies the jarring phrase "REVS COST," the tag of two renowned graffiti artists of the 1990s. Portions of the REVS COST were removed by the city with heavy-duty anti-graffiti chemicals in 2010, but a bit of it still remains. (*The High Line, between 22nd and 23rd Streets*)

A wall of few words: A collision of history and graffiti along the High Line.

8 THE CENTER OF CHELSEA Locked tightly into the street grid, Chelsea might not feel as if it has a precise center, but it does. Once Clement Clarke Moore accepted that the family's estate would be divided up by the 1811 grid plan, he threw himself behind the development opportunities it presented. Moore wanted to attract residents of a certain esteemed character, and hoped to create a luxurious and reputable enclave of homes like those popping up in London. At its heart, between 20th and 21st Streets, and Ninth and Tenth Avenues, he placed Chelsea Square, built upon the site of Moore's former orchard.[10]

Empire State Building from the High Line.

But rather than plant a commonplace park here, Chelsea Square was home to the esteemed General Theological Seminary. This Episcopal divinity school, founded in 1817, moved here in 1827. Today the seminary's Gothic architecture stands apart from most of the buildings that surround it. The chapel's tower can be seen from the High Line; at a certain spot, the Empire State Building seems to burst forth from it. Unless you're a seminary student, the closest you'll get to the interior of the church is inside the High Line Hotel on the 10th Avenue side.[11] (*440 West 21st Street; better view from 20th Street*)

Holy preserved: The General Theological Seminary remains largely the same today.

9 THE CURVE OF CUSHMAN ROW One of the wealthiest developers to snatch up Moore's divvied-up parcels was Don Alonzo Cushman, a merchant who had Greek Revival homes built along West 20th Street in 1839–1840 to unique specifications, dictated by Moore himself: The buildings would be set back 10 feet from the property line to allow for charming little

---

10 As we saw with the Brevoorts in the Bowery, land containing fruit orchards was deemed the most beloved and almost sacred.

11 The seminary remains open to this day, making it one of New York's oldest continuing homes for education.

gardens out front.[12] The homes along Ninth Avenue, however, did not have such restrictions, which led to some irregular alignments where buildings met. But when 402 West 20th Street was constructed in 1898 (designed by leading architect C. P. H. Gilbert), its curved front allowed for the setback, creating a building not unlike a puzzle piece that's a perfect fit. As a tribute

to Cushman—who had died in 1875—the engraving above the doorway reads "DONAC." Later Cushmans, along with a brother-in-law, Bernard Wakefield, would start the real estate firm Cushman and Wakefield in 1917, which is today among the most powerful in New York. (*402 West 20th Street*)

10 BEST BRUNCH PLACE EVER Who knew that Chelsea had such a profound effect on the history of breakfast foods? First there's the Nabisco factory, and now, the English muffin (without which eggs Benedict, invented across town at Delmonico's, would be just a sad puddle of hollandaise sauce and ham). When baker Samuel Bath Thomas arrived in New York from England in 1874, he brought along an old family recipe for English muffins. In 1880 he set up his own bakery on Ninth Avenue to sell these fork-split nook 'n' crannied creations. At the beginning of the twentieth century, he opened

St. Peter's Church accommodates both parishioners and theater audiences.

12 Today the entire row here is often called Cushman Row. The house at 404 West 20th Street is considered the oldest standing dwelling in Chelsea, no small feat.

another shop at this location on West 20th Street. This building's prominence in the world of breakfast foods was entirely overlooked until 2006, when tenants uncovered an oven behind a wall during renovation work. Today there's a plaque on the wall proclaiming the building "The Muffin House." (*336 West 20th Street*)

11 WHY NOT BOTH? Theaters and churches, often mortal enemies throughout New York's history, actually have quite a few things in common, including stages and audiences. In fact, St. Peter's Church on West 20th Street is both a church and a theater!

Sprechen Sie Deutsch? Look up as you enter St. Paul's on 22nd Street!

Parishioners still worship in the main church, built in 1831–1832, one of the first English Gothic churches ever built in the United States. (Think of the thousands of churches you've seen that have adopted this style.) The Atlantic Theater Company, the 1985 off-Broadway troupe cofounded by William H. Macy[13] and David Mamet, found the holy grail when they moved into St. Peter's parish house in 1991. What they might not have known at the time was that the parish house, completed in 1871, was itself funded by a stage production—a *tableau vivant*[14] of Charles Dickens's novel *The Old Curiosity Shop*. Curious, *indeed*. (*336 West 20th Street*)

12 THAT QUOTE ABOVE THE DOOR AT THE GERMAN EVANGELICAL LUTHERAN CHURCH OF ST. PAUL "Ich bin der Weg die Wahrheit und das Leben" (I Am the Way the Truth and the Life.) Built in 1897, St. Paul's dedicated itself to serving the working-class Germans who lived in Chelsea at the time. Certainly the most unusual day here must have been May 17, 1928, when the Baron Ehrenfried Günther Freiherr von Hünefeld (known as the Crazy Baron) addressed the congregation shortly after failing

---

13 Sorry, he should have won the Oscar for *Fargo*. Just sayin'.
14 The *tableau vivant* (French for "living picture") was a popular entertainment of the mid-nineteenth century, as racy or suggestive scenes could be enacted as "art."

in his attempt to fly from Europe to the United States, a so-called "reverse Lindbergh." (*315 West 22nd Street*)

13 TILLIE HART, THE HOLDOUT OF 23RD STREET In 1845, Clement Clarke Moore constructed thirty-six beautiful brownstones along the block bordered by 23rd and 24th Streets and Ninth and Tenth Avenues, and gave it another name that hearkened back to merry old England: London Terrace.[15] Nearly 80 years later, in 1929, his descendants leased the block to developer Henry Mandel to construct a massive upscale housing complex that would carry the same name (and which still exists today). All of the old brownstones were demolished that year to make way for the development. All, that is, save one: 429 West 23rd, the home of the feisty Mrs. Tillie Hart. She wasn't moving *nowhere* for *nobody*. Tillie fought her eviction in court and, when that failed, barricaded herself inside her brownstone in late October 1929 and refused to leave. Her plight was covered in the press, and crowds gathered in the street daily to watch the drama unfold. She lost her case and was evicted by the end of the month. Mandel, perhaps in spite, authorized the laying of the cornerstone for today's building (laid by Moore's great-great-grandson) on the very spot of her demolished home. *Meow!* (*North side of West 23rd Street between Ninth and Tenth Avenues, middle of the block*)

14 THE RADICAL SPIRIT OF THE CHELSEA HOTEL The Hotel Chelsea—or "Chelsea Hotel," if you choose—was intended to be a cooperative apartment house, one of New York's first when it opened in 1884. It initially drew tenants from the theater world, which at the time was conveniently located a few blocks away, surrounding Madison Square. However, as the Theater District moved up (first to near Herald Square and then to near Times Square), the Hotel Chelsea fell out of fashion. In 1905, it was retooled as a hotel for both short- and long-term stays.

Today, plaques affixed to the hotel's entranceway celebrate the accomplishments of notable tenants, including Thomas Wolfe, Brendan Behan, Arthur C. Clarke, and many others. You could cover the entirety of its Victorian Gothic facade with markers that celebrate the crop of other famous artists, writers, musicians, and creators who have hung their hats in (and maybe still hang around) the Hotel Chelsea. But its muselike reputation has also lured

---

15 Moore's own home was right across the street, at around 422–424 West 23rd Street.

thousands of others whose names we'll never remember, their stories completely forgotten.

Some of the unusual and overlooked tragedies that have occurred here include a distraught woman who cut off her hand and jumped from the roof in 1922, a Hungarian painter who shot himself here after he was robbed,[16] and a lovesick woman who poisoned herself in 1908 after penning a final love letter. And we shouldn't forget the Chelsea's two most famous tragedies: the death of Dylan Thomas by alcohol abuse in 1953, and the murder of Nancy Spungen by her boyfriend, Sid Vicious[17] in 1978. (*222 West 23rd Street*)

The Hotel Chelsea. Or is that the Chelsea Hotel?

15 BARBECUE WITH A SIDE OF THE MACABRE (Vanished)
Diners today at Dallas BBQ, a popular Texas-size eatery at the northwest corner of Eighth Avenue and West 23rd Street, are probably not aware that they're enjoying their ribs and daiquiris on the site of one of the Gilded Age's most outrageous wakes. On this corner once sat the Grand Opera House.

---

16 Frank Kavecky shot himself on October 25, 1909, after $1,200, held for a Hungarian benevolent society where he was the treasurer, was stolen from him in the subway.
17 Vicious would die of an overdose in the hotel a few months later.

Completed in 1868, it was the project of wine importer Samuel N. Pike, who purchased the land directly from Clement Clarke Moore. It was soon sold to infamous industrialists and notorious robber barons James Fisk and Jay Gould, who used the upper floors as offices. In 1872, "Diamond Jim" Fisk was shot and killed by the jealous new boyfriend of his ex-lover Josie Mansfield. He had become so associated with the opera house that his body lay in state here,

Chelsea's now-forgotten Grand Opera House in 1935.

attended by thousands of mourners and perhaps tens of thousands of curiosity seekers.

It must have been a spectacular farewell. "The showy coffin, liberally adorned with gold-plated ornaments, rested on two low stands, and in this, garbed in the gold-laced uniform of the colonel of the Ninth [Regiment], lay Fisk, his mustache carefully waxed, white kid gloves on his hands, and his feet buried in white flowers, in various devices."[18] (*Northwest corner of 23rd Street and Eighth Avenue*)

---

18 From *The Life and Times of Colonel James Fisk, Jr.* by R. W. McAlpine, 1872.

Chelsea—At the Heart of Christmas

According to the legend, on Christmas Eve in 1822 Clement Clarke Moore completed a seasonal poem to read to his young children. He penned the whimsical little tale—a *throwaway*, really, in comparison with his great and respected academic writings on Greek and biblical literature—from a desk at his comfortable, snow-covered mansion, which the family called Chelsea.

The home sat atop an old hill (near today's modern addresses of 422–424 West 23rd Street), which looked out over Moore's vast estate, stretching to the south from here.

According to legend, Moore had been inspired that day during an outing to Washington Market to purchase a Christmas turkey.

The poem, "A Visit from St. Nicholas" and often referred to as "'Twas the Night Before Christmas," would eventually help shape the story of Santa Claus. His verses practically spelled out the jovial North Pole gift-giver's physical appearance, which was then illustrated by New York–based newspaper and magazine illustrators like Thomas Nast and, in the twentieth century, the Coca-Cola advertising of Haddon Sundblom. Moore even named all eight reindeer.

Moore's poem was published anonymously the following year, and he'd only take credit for penning it—at his children's insistence—in 1844.

A cozy 1896 illustration from *The Night Before Christmas or A Visit of St. Nicholas* (top) while Santa goes for the glamour in his 1894 cover feature (bottom).

Given Moore's original hesitation, some scholars have suggested that another New Yorker, Henry Livingston, Jr., may have written the poem. Until proven otherwise, we like to turn our thoughts to Chelsea—from the wild old hotel to the elevated High Line—every time we hear it.

A REVIEW OF THE PARKS

Here's what the *Appleton's Dictionary of Greater New York and Its Neighborhoods*, 1904, says about two New York City parks:

—Madison Square, a public park of about 6 acres. It is now the center of the world of amusement and fashion of the city. Besides theatres, concert-halls, and the Madison Square Garden, there are in its immediate vicinity 8 or 10 first-class hotels, half a dozen clubs, and the best restaurants the city affords. The park itself abounds with fine shade trees, has a fountain, and in summer is a pleasant and favorite place for children and their nurses.

—Union Square, a pretty and noted public park of about 8½ acres. It has a neat fountain and some fine shade-trees and beds of flowers and foliage plants, and is altogether a pleasant resting-place for the tired wayfarer. Statues of Washington and Lincoln face it on the SE and SW corners respectively, and one of Lafayette is almost hidden among the trees opposite Broadway. A paved plaza borders it on the north along 17th Street where on special occasions a row of ornamental colored gas-lamps are lit. It is brilliantly illuminated at night by electric lights. A cottage within the park, facing the plaza, has a balcony for the accommodation of reviewing officers of military parades. The architecture surrounding the square is of a rather heterogeneous character at present, the private residences which formerly fronted on it having been either converted into stores, or else pulled down entirely and huge iron and stone structures erected in their place.

Union Square and the Flatiron District

William Seward, in sculpture form, watches over Madison Square in 1935.

SITUATE THE READER
–Union Square and the Flatiron District–

In 1873, Mark Twain and Charles Dudley Warner published a novel called *The Gilded Age: A Tale of Today*, a cheeky little satire that coined the phrase "the Gilded Age," referring to an era of new wealth and corrupted ambitions. Today we give the term and the period it represents—the 1870s through the early 1900s—a romantic gloss, as if it recalls a simpler era between the Civil War and World War I.

Life in the city was all hansom cabs, vaudeville, and new skyscrapers, right? Yes, but it was also economic disparity, miserable overcrowding, racial segregation, and the flagrant political corruption of Tammany Hall.

The area between Union Square on 14th Street and Madison Square up on 23rd was one of the great centers of the Gilded Age, a cultural fount for upwardly mobile New Yorkers of the second half of the nineteenth century. Fifth Avenue at the time was lined with opulent mansions, and elegant hotels and chic Parisian-style restaurants soon found their way to the streets around them. Fine shops opened to accommodate the wealthy "carriage trade," which rolled along Broadway, while middle-class New Yorkers flocked to a lineup of cavernous, brightly lit department stores along Sixth Avenue, a thoroughfare served by a convenient, if noisy, elevated train.

The finest theaters, music halls, and vaudeville houses in Gilded Age America brought crowds nightly to the streets around Union Square, while Madison Square (once a potter's field) saw an old train depot on its northeast corner transformed into a raucous performance venue for showman P. T. Barnum. But by 1890, architectural giants McKim, Mead, and White[1] would build an opulent new Madison Square Garden here, which would become one of the most famous arenas in the world.

---

1 The firm is so critical to the Gilded Age—and this neighborhood—that their offices were located here, at 160 Fifth Avenue. So was White's infamous nest for chorus girls and the home of his "red velvet swing"—22 West 24th Street.

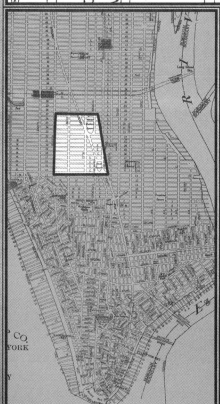

The map labels include: W. 27, W. 26, W. 25, W. 24, W. 23, W. 22, W. 21, W. 20, W. 19, W. 18, W. 17, W. 16, W. 15, W. 14, W. 13, W.

SIXTH, SEVENTH, FIFTH, BROADWAY

MAD. SQ. N., Madison Square, FOURTH, LEXINGTON

E. (repeated), Gramercy Park, GRAM. PK. W., GRAM. PL., GRAM. PK. E., IRVING PL.

Union Square, UNION SQUARE W., UNION SQUARE E., RUTHERFORD PL., Stuy. Sq.

27, 26, 25, 24, 23, 22, 21, 20, 19, 18, 17, SECOND

Point markers: 1, 2, 3, 4, 5, 6, 7, 8, 9, 10, 11, 12, 13, 14, 15, 16, 17, 18, MA

POINTS OF INTEREST

1 Statue of Liberty's Little Brother

2 The Restless Statues

3 Workin' Some Gandhi Mojo

4 Party Animals

5 Scandalous Surprise on Fifth Avenue

6 The Birth of Birth Control

7 This Disco Used to Be a Cute Cathedral

8 The Sacred and the Shopping

9 Roosevelt's Replicated House

10 Stand Here

11 Park of Politicos

12 Lady Liberty Gives a Hand

13 Trading Architectural Icons

14 Read This Quote

15 The Trophy of Madison Avenue

16 Cemetery for One

17 The Lair of the Freemasons

18 No Toying Around in Amen Corner

MA Ladies' Mile

The Glory of Ladies' Mile

Ladies' Mile was not only for ladies and was never a mile long. No race has ever been run along it (unless the finish line was an empty purse or wallet).

New York's premier shopping district of the late nineteenth century, located roughly from 14th to 23rd Streets between Broadway and Sixth Avenue, Ladies' Mile was something to behold, castles of commerce in dizzying procession that provided luxuries in a concentration never before seen in America. Department stores gussied up with glorious cast-iron facades and enormous street-level windows competed to outdo each other with newfangled amenities (escalators!) and all the latest conveniences (one-stop shopping! standardized pricing!).

Union Square Park greeted Ladies' Mile shoppers in 1904.

Broadway, located just a block and a half east, already possessed a vibrant retail marketplace by 1850, although most of its commercial action took place south of Houston Street. Philip Hone wrote in 1850 that "the mania for converting Broadway into a street of shops is greater than ever. There is scarcely a block in the whole extent of this fine street of which some part is not in a state of transmutation."

The birth of Ladies' Mile came twelve years later, in 1862, when dry goods mogul A. T. Stewart, who had revolutionized the shopping experience at his first store near City Hall,[2] decided to dazzle his shoppers with an architectural upgrade at a new location on Astor Place. His so-called Iron Palace, draped in an impressive cast-iron facade, featured almost 30 different departments, a de facto department store by its sheer size alone.[3] Stewart's palace opened during the Civil War—and within praying distance of the nonplussed Grace Church one block up—and proved a template for stores to follow.

---

2   We took a glimpse at the still-existing A. T. Stewart building in Chapter 5.
3   Wanamaker's department store, which still stands in Astor Place today (and seen in Chapter 11), sat across the street from the old Iron Palace.

Competing retailers, however, chose to leapfrog the "Iron Palace" at its 9th Street location and follow the growth of the city north, clustering themselves farther up Broadway. Elegant and powerful Fifth Avenue set the rules for the neighborhood's retail establishments. Lined with the townhouses of the rich and famous, its wealthy residents demanded shopping options close by. Soon Broadway between Union and Madison Squares offered a fine variety of dry goods stores, and developed into a prim and proper "carriage trade," whose customers always (at least in theory) rolled up in style.[4] Arnold Constable & Co.*

Dressed to shop: Lovely ladies shop along Sixth Avenue.

(881–887 Broadway, at 19th Street) opened its "palace of trade" in 1869, and was known for the high-end fabrics and exotic carpets that would entrance the Vanderbilts and Rockefellers. Tiffany & Co. moved its fine emporium, called the "palace of jewels" — you get the point — to its new headquarters at Union Square West and 15th Street in 1870. They even put the French crown jewels on display here in 1887. The Lord & Taylor* store (901 Broadway, at 20th Street), built in 1870, was given a corner tower and mansard roof that still stands today, although passersby are more likely to think it looks like a haunted Gothic mansion than a palace of anything.

Retail establishments targeting less moneyed customers wanted in on the action and chose Sixth Avenue as their main drag, served, as it was, by an elevated train line that opened in 1876. It was specifically called "Fashion Row." Rowland Macy, who had opened a relatively modest store at Sixth Avenue and 14th Street in 1858, expanded by the early 1880s to command much of that block.* Elevated riders marveled at Macy's flamboyant sign, hoisted high above the train line.

The store owned by a Jewish entrepreneur named Benjamin Altman, B. Altman & Co.,* flourished in the Lower East Side before it moved to Sixth Avenue and 19th Street in 1877. It took on competitors in equally formidable cast-iron structures, such as that of Irish mogul Hugh O'Neill* at Sixth Avenue and 20th Street, topped with its golden domes. There were so many stores, in

---

4   * indicates the building is still standing and in fine shape today with different occupants.

fact, that department stores such as Stern Brothers* (at 32–36 23rd Street) spilled over onto the side streets.

Siegel-Cooper advertises fall's hottest fashions (top) and a menu from the store's restaurant (bottom).

But the greatest store on the Ladies' Mile came relatively late to the party and from a surprising place. Chicago retailer Siegel-Cooper catered to a middle-class clientele, but their success permitted them to build a lavish store unlike any other, at 616–632 Sixth Avenue (between 18th and 19th Streets). When it opened in September 1896, so many people arrived to take a look that it disrupted elevated train service and almost caused a riot. Its innovative steel-frame design—the first for a commercial structure in New York—allowed for larger showrooms. Newspapers called it the largest and finest building ever erected, and, at 750,000 square feet, the store touted itself as "a city unto itself."

Its three entrances led into a central chamber, where shoppers were met by a statue of the Republic, sculpted by none other than Daniel Chester French (a couple of decades before his Lincoln Memorial commission). Among its more than seventy departments were a pharmacy, a rooftop photography studio, ample cold storage, a bike shop, a cannery, a florist, a baby nursery, and a free grammar school—reachable, to customers' astonishment, by banks of twenty-two elevators. It was topped with a handsome tower, decked out with a searchlight to beckon additional shoppers.[5]

Alas, it reigned as New York's retail darling for only a few years. Shortly after its 1896 opening, department stores would begin making another migration—

5   The Siegel-Cooper building still stands, but the tower is gone. Current tenants, including Bed Bath & Beyond, use but a fraction of the original space.

this time farther north, to Herald Square. Neighborhood fixtures, like Macy's and Lord & Taylor, soon fled the neighborhood. The area was no longer seen as fashionable mecca. Rather, it was now an "Out-of-Fashion Row." By World War I, almost all of the retail establishments had packed up and left these streets, leaving the old palaces empty, rusting shells of a former age. The fact that you can still walk past many of these iron palaces, most of which are in pristine condition today, is a testament to the tireless work of neighborhood preservationists—and to the palaces' rock-solid construction.

The building, today home to Bed Bath & Beyond, still wears Siegel-Cooper's initials on its facade.

The glittering Sixth Avenue palaces of Ladies' Mile thrive again today.

Union Square
and the Flatiron District

UNION SQUARE

Union Square was the end result of a geographical quandary. Two hundred years ago, Bloomingdale Road, the precursor to Broadway here, intersected

Union Square Park was once oval, 1850s (top); the marquis faces retail, 1935 (bottom).

with the Bowery at a particularly awkward angle. To cover up the curious turn, city planners designed a public space called Union Place — the union of the two roads. By the 1830s it was an elegant oval park, formally developed by Samuel Ruggles (we'll spend more time with him in the next chapter) and surrounded by new townhouses. The fence later came down and the park took a more democratic turn, as the site of early union rallies and parades; in fact, the first Labor Day parade, on September 5, 1882, culminated here. That's a double meaning for Union Square. No, wait, *triple*! At the center of the park is a liberty pole erected in 1924 that pays tribute to the Declaration of Independence — and the *union* of the country's 48 states.[6] (*14th Street between Broadway and Park Avenue*)

1 STATUE OF LIBERTY'S LITTLE BROTHER A bronze man of short stature stands in a heroic pose as traffic whizzes past, indifferent to his presence. For years now, he has suffered the indignity of facing a Babies"R"Us, yet he's passed no judgment. Frédéric Auguste Bartholdi sculpted this statue of the much-celebrated Marquis de Lafayette (1757–1834) and placed it in the

---

6   The pole — often called the "Tammany Pole" in honor of Tammany Hall leader Charles Francis Murphy — was erected from 1924 to 1926. Hawaii and Alaska — shut out again!

park in September 1876. Bartholdi's second gift to New York, the Statue of Liberty, was still very much a work in progress at the time, but one important part of her sat just a few blocks away in Madison Square Park (see page 271). (*Park Avenue South at 15th Street*)

Honest Abe stands silently in the northern section of Union Square.

2 THE RESTLESS STATUES Two of America's greatest presidents are represented here in the park: an equestrian George Washington statue stands at the southern end of the park, and a serene Abraham Lincoln statue stands near the northern end. The two are in direct alignment, with the liberty pole squarely between them.[7] These two statues, however, were in very different spots when they made their Union Square debut. Washington and his horse once stood at the far southeastern corner, nearly in the street, facing west down 14th Street and directly toward Lincoln, who stood at the southwest corner, facing east. Both sculptures are by Henry Kirke Brown[8] (1814–1886),

---

7   This leads us to believe there may be treasure buried beneath the liberty pole, but perhaps we've watched too many Nicolas Cage movies.

8   Washington's statue was beloved by New Yorkers at the time of its original placement; Lincoln's was not. From the *New York Times*: "A frightful object has been placed in Union-Square. It is said to be a statue of a man who deserves to be held in lasting remembrance as a true patriot, a sincere, unselfish, noble-hearted chief in times of great trouble and perplexity — Abraham Lincoln. But it does not resemble Mr. Lincoln."

considered the premier American sculptor of serious men in the mid-nineteenth century. The statues were moved to their current spots during a park reconstruction in 1930. (*North and south ends of Union Square*)

3 WORKIN' SOME GANDHI MOJO Back when Lincoln was off standing in the southwest corner, he presided over some grim affairs indeed. This corner was popularly referred to in the late nineteenth century as "Dead Man's Curve," as it was the scene of several brutal accidents between cable cars (and later streetcars) and pedestrians well into the twentieth century. It would take the removal of streetcar tracks to alleviate the problem. Whatever trauma and bad vibes lingered on were dispersed in 1986, when the city erected this tribute to a great man of peace—Mahatma Gandhi. (*Southwest corner of Union Square*)

4 PARTY ANIMALS Great strides in counterculture were made here, right above the corner pet supply store, PetCo. In this spot in 1848 stood the sumptuous mansion of Quaker dry goods businessman Henry Parish. With the rise of the Ladies' Mile shopping district, Parish's home was unceremoniously knocked down and replaced in 1884 with this six-floor office building, which included a storefront for jewelers and home furnishings. In 1973 the second floor of the building, above today's room of dog collars, was occupied by Andy Warhol and his posse, and was his third New York apartment to go by the moniker "The Factory."[9] Dozens of Warhol's self-made "superstars" climbed the stairs to find their fifteen minutes of fame here. Oh, what additional inspiration might have possessed them all had they climbed those stairs over the meows, chirps, and grunts of today's downstairs tenants! (*860 Broadway*)

5 SCANDALOUS SURPRISE ON FIFTH AVENUE For all its fashion and finery, Ladies' Mile became something downright disrespectful at night (although, to be honest, the name still weirdly fit). With the main thoroughfares and their department stores aglow with electric lights by the 1890s, prostitution thrived along the darker side streets. We're reminded of the neighborhood's less famous sultry side while looking at the top of the Louis Korn 1894 office tower at 91–93 Fifth Avenue. Gracing the top of the building are a set of six topless caryatids, arrayed in rather seductive poses. While

---

9 Warhol's second Factory was just catty-corner to the Parish building at 33 Union Square West. He moved there in 1968 after the building that contained the first Factory—at 231 East 47th Street—was torn down.

Gilded Age New Yorkers found the statue of Diana atop Madison Square Garden to be a scintillating sight, we're certain these that these six ladies must have caused a few stumbles themselves! (*91–93 Fifth Avenue*)

Va-va-voom: This Fifth Avenue architecture is rated Parental Guidance Suggested.

6 THE BIRTH OF BIRTH CONTROL This Greek Revival house, with an interesting curved front bay, is one of the landmarks of the women's health movement. Pioneering activist Margaret Sanger established an ambitious health clinic here in 1930, a greatly expanded version of the one she began on the Lower East Side in the 1910s. Sanger and her physicians advocated for the use of contraceptives to promote women's health and reduce sexually transmitted diseases, and raised awareness of the overcrowding in the city's tenements. Sanger died in 1966, but the clinic thrived well into the following decade. (*17 West 16th Street*)

Margaret Sanger, 1916.

7 **THIS DISCO USED TO BE A CUTE CATHEDRAL** Ranking the most blasphemous places in New York would be challenging, but we'd wager that we've located the number one spot: the Church of the Holy Communion,

also known as the Limelight. It was designed in the 1840s by Richard Upjohn (of Trinity Church fame) for the Reverend William Augustus Muhlenberg, the grandson of America's first Speaker of the House, Frederick Muhlenberg. The first Episcopal convent was soon built as an annex and was overseen by the devout sister Anne Ayers.

Yet a hundred years after Muhlenberg's death (in 1877), the church had been converted into a drug rehabilitation center and had fallen into disrepair. In 1983, eye-patched

Groove is in the Church of the Holy Communion.

Canadian club owner Peter Gatien turned it into the Limelight nightclub, a dazzling disco that nightly concocted a wild mix of legitimate celebrities, fake celebrities (so-called club kids), terrific house and electronic music, and lots and lots of drugs. The club is long gone, and the space is now occupied by an upscale clothing boutique and a branch of Grimaldi's Pizzeria (in the same spot where Sister Ayers once held her daily devotions). "Hold the anchovies, Sister!" (*Sixth Avenue and West 20th Street*)

8 **THE SACRED AND THE SHOPPING** What's more sacrilegious than a disco church? How about a sacred Jewish cemetery in the heart of New York's retail ribbon, namely the third cemetery of Congregation Shearith Israel, which contains Jewish burials from 1829 to 1851. But the city's rapid growth northward thwarted the congregation yet again, and they moved their synagogue but left the cemetery behind.[10] Eventually, the synagogue's property adjacent to the cemetery was purchased by dry goods mogul Hugh O'Neill, who built his store here, the first of many block-long palaces. We

---

10 This was their last Manhattan cemetery. Their present burial ground has been in Ridgewood, Queens, since 1851. Emma Lazarus, author of "Give me your tired, your poor ..." is buried there.

can only wonder if any of his shoppers felt spooked while lugging their purchases by the cemetery's iron gate. Today it feels more of a piece of the area's historical legacy, or maybe we're just telling ourselves that so we can go into the Trader Joe's across the street without feeling creeped out. (*West side of Sixth Avenue and West 21st Street*)

Snowfall upon the stranded cemetery of Ladies' Mile.

9 ROOSEVELT'S REPLICATED HOUSE Theodore Roosevelt is the only US president born in New York City, and just a few feet from Broadway. Young Teddy was born at this site on October 27, 1858, a sickly lad who suffered terrible asthma. But his love of animals and taxidermy were fostered here. These passions would culminate, locally at least, with the creation of the American Museum of Natural History on the Upper West Side, which honors him still today.

Roosevelt's home is no longer here. It was incomprehensibly demolished in 1916, several years after his presidency. This error was quickly understood, because in 1919, the year of his death, a reproduction of his birthplace was planned for this very spot, to be designed by Theodate Pope Riddle, a trailblazing female architect who had survived the sinking of the RMS *Lusitania* just four years before. As an operation of the National Park Service today, Riddle's re-creation serves as both a celebration of Roosevelt's life and as a reminder to keep your damn hands off notable structures in the first place! (*28 East 20th Street*)

President Theodore Roosevelt, one of the greatest New Yorkers of all time, was born just off Broadway in 1858.

10 STAND HERE: The northern tip of the Flatiron Building, 23rd Street at the intersection of Broadway and Fifth Avenue. *Why?* This is the spot where New York's Gilded Age propriety threatened to come tumbling down — or rather, go swirling up.[11]

Flatiron Building.

The twenty-two-floor Flatiron Building was constructed in 1902 by the Fuller Company, which specifically chose this unusual triangular block to present a marvel of architecture. Daniel Burnham's sensational design presents an ornate structure that looks different from every angle, cutting a romantic silhouette at one of the busiest intersections in New York, the confluence of 23rd Street, Fifth Avenue, and Broadway.

---

11 It also happens to be the block where the first electronic billboard debuted in New York, on the side of a hotel that once stood on this plot of land. The sign, which debuted in 1892, advertised properties in Manhattan Beach, Brooklyn, as "Swept By Ocean Breezes."

The building's unusual shape is also credited for creating a great deal of sudden wind gusts, which cut fiercely around the building's sharp corners.

Soon after the Flatiron's opening, the winds were reportedly so strong that they blew out storefront windows in neighboring buildings, and nervous critics predicted that the gusts just might lead to destruction of the building itself!

But the most common wind-related disruptions were experienced by women passing the building, whose skirts had a shocking tendency to suddenly blow up into the air, indelicately revealing a leg or an ankle. Lecherous men would gather at the corner, waiting for a gust to produce such a sinful sight. It got so indecent that for a period in the early 1900s, police could arrest any man loitering at the corner for longer than two minutes. The phrase "23 skidoo" became associated with the Flatiron Building and referred to the shooing away of potential creeps. (*23rd Street and Fifth Avenue*)

MADISON SQUARE PARK

Like so many of the city's parks, Madison Square—named for President James Madison (1751–1836)—started as a potter's field for victims of the city's many epidemics.[12] It was later transformed into a military parade ground, and then opened as a park in 1847. The rather formal park would reflect New York's elegant tastes in the second half of the nineteenth century, when the park was surrounded by swanky restaurants, hotels, and clubs.

Madison Square Park also played a part in the history of baseball. The New York Knickerbockers, one of the first organized baseball teams, played on a lot at East 27th and Madison Avenue back in 1842. The most athletic activity you'll find in the park today can usually be found in the Shake Shack line, where an endless line of ravenous customers will do anything for a ShackBurger. (*23rd Street between Fifth and Madison Avenues*)

---

12 From 1794 to 1797, the ground here was used to inter those who had died at nearby Bellevue Hospital and the local almshouse during a devastating yellow fever epidemic.

Like a dream: Madison Square Garden peeks through the mist.

11 PARK OF POLITICOS Six blocks south of here, Union Square's statuary lineup includes two great presidents and one astounding Revolutionary War figure. The stoned men of Madison Square, however, are a little more complicated. At the park's southeast corner you'll find Roscoe Conkling, New York's ruthless political power broker of the nineteenth century.[13] Near the park's northeastern entrance is a statue of President Chester Arthur (served from 1881 to 1885), a rather ho-hum figure in American history. The two are linked, however: Conkling essentially secured Arthur's position on the presidential ticket with James A. Garfield in a backroom deal at the Fifth Avenue Hotel (across Fifth Avenue, see page 274). In 1881, after the assassination of President Garfield, Vice President Arthur was sworn in as president in a house nearby (see Chapter 16).

On the southwest corner you'll find the accomplished William Henry Seward, former New York governor (from 1839 to 1842) and Lincoln's Secretary of

---

13 During the Great Blizzard of 1888, he attempted to walk back to his room at 25th Street and Madison but contracted pneumonia and died weeks later.

State (serving from 1861 to 1869). Here he's reclining in a state of some concentration. If the seated statue seems a tad off to you, you're not alone. A *New York Times* critic in 1877 wrote, "[T]he gilt Seward which sits at the southern gate [is] in the apparent act of collecting statistics of the number of nurses and children who pass the pedestal." (*Madison Square Park, various spots*)

Seward's monument.

12 LADY LIBERTY GIVES A HAND (Vanished) By the end of 1876, Frédéric Auguste Bartholdi would be able to boast two creations in New York: the Lafayette statue in Union Square and the Statue of Liberty in Madison Square. Yes, here in Madison Square. Okay, just her arm and torch, *but still*! The appendage sat at the northwest corner of the park to whip up enthusiasm about the project. (See Chapter 1 for more information.) (*Northwest corner of Madison Square Park*)

13 TRADING ARCHITECTURAL ICONS (Vanished) Talk about a busy corner! The northeast corner of 26th and Madison was home to not just one but two former Madison Square Gardens. Confusing, we know—keep reading. The site of Vanderbilt's downtown train depot for much of the nineteenth century, the place changed hands in 1871 when the railroad moved up to 42nd Street, and the depot was transformed into an entertainment venue. P. T. Barnum ran his circuses here for five years before bandleader Patrick Gilmore took over the baton, holding concerts and other big-draw events (including the first Westminster Kennel Club Dog Show in New York in 1877). In 1879 it was formally renamed Madison Square Garden. However, it still wasn't sufficiently large, so Stanford White designed an even larger, more sumptuous, venue with the same name in 1890—it could seat a whopping 8,000 people in its main arena. The space boasted a glittering rooftop garden theater topped with a dizzying bell tower modeled after the campanile in Saint Mark's Square in Venice. It was at this rooftop theater where White, a notorious philanderer, was murdered in 1906 by Harry Thaw, the crazed husband of his former paramour, Evelyn Nesbit.

By Prohibition the Garden's Gilded Age luster had dulled, and the once-magnificent structure was demolished in 1925. Fortunately, it was replaced with something beautiful—the New York Life Insurance Building, designed by Cass Gilbert, who had designed the Woolworth Building in 1913. Just as a golden nude statue of Diana once gleamed from the top of the Garden's bell tower, Gilbert's golden cone now illuminates the night sky, worn like a luxurious hat. (*51 Madison Avenue*)

Orphans giddy up to see the horse show at Madison Square Garden, November 1913.

14 THOSE QUOTES ON THE STATUE PEDESTALS OF NEW YORK STATE'S APPELLATE DIVISION COURTHOUSE "Every Law Not Based on Wisdom Is a Menace to the State." "We Must Not Use Force Till Just Laws Are Defied." These are placed below two statues, representing "Wisdom" and "Force." The quotes are supposedly from Solomon's Book of Wisdom, but appear to be liberally interpreted by the sculptor, Frederick Ruckstull, who erected the statues here in 1900. (*25th Street and Madison Avenue*)

15 THE TROPHY OF MADISON AVENUE In 1901 Philadelphia snatched the title of "World's Tallest Building"[14] from New York's Park Row Building with the completion of their mighty City Hall. The rich New Yorkers of the Gilded Age would not tolerate that! And so, for most of the twentieth century, it would be New York skyscrapers that would hold the record: first

---

14 The Eiffel Tower was much taller, but as "novel architecture," it's not often considered in the building height tallies. *Sacré bleu!*

with the Singer Building (see Chapter 3), then in 1909 with the Metropolitan Life Insurance Company Tower, a Venetian-style rocket with a four-faced clock. While the Flatiron Building hogs most of the attention around here, the Met Life Tower, designed by Napoleon LeBrun & Sons, more romantically sets the mood of the square, appearing like an otherworldly mirage at night. Thank God the company's plans to build a daunting 100-story skyscraper across the street were jettisoned after the 1929 stock market crash. (*1 Madison Avenue*)

Metropolitan Life Insurance Company Tower.

16 CEMETERY FOR ONE (OBELISK ALERT #1) Few Americans have had the honor of being buried in the middle of the most famous stretch in the United States.

However, William Jenkins Worth, a military general, can make this claim. Nearly two years after the end of the oft-forgotten Mexican-American War (1846–1848) he died of cholera in Texas, and was transported to Brooklyn and buried in Green-Wood Cemetery (the hot spot for dead celebrities in the nineteenth century). A few years later, he was dug up, brought to Manhattan, and reinterred in this unusual spot under an impressive obelisk designed by James Batterson. Worth's remains were placed here in a solemn ceremony on November 25, 1857, that included nearly 6,500 marching soldiers. Etched upon the monument is a list of Worth's many battles.

Keep in mind that in 1857 this area was relatively tranquil, not a hectic traffic thoroughfare. So why haven't the monument and grave been moved? Perhaps the answer lies in a building one block away.... (*25th Street, between Fifth Avenue and Broadway*)

17 THE LAIR OF THE FREEMASONS (OBELISK ALERT #2) And here we arrive at one of the city's most surprising structures: Masonic Hall, the home of the Grand Lodge of Free and Accepted Masons of the State of New York. Built in 1913 upon the footprint of an earlier lodge, the building astonishes today with its twelve ritual chambers, richly ornamented rooms loaded with mysterious symbolism, and its Grand Lodge Room, which seats more than a thousand people.[15] Obelisks play a key role in early Freemasonry, which is underscored by the ground floor mural that depicts Cleopatra's Needle in Central Park, an object they were chiefly responsible for obtaining!

All human affairs are controlled from this building, with the lodge's most powerful men locked in secret oaths to protect the countless treasures and governmental secrets held by the Freemasons for more than a millennium. Just kidding. They're actually just an old fraternal organization that raises money for a lot of worthy charities. (Or was this statement planted here to confuse you?) (*71 West 23rd Street*)

Broadway and Fifth Avenue, in front of Fifth Avenue Hotel, looking north, past the Worth monument.

18 NO TOYING AROUND IN AMEN CORNER (Vanished) One of most famous hotels in the American hospitality history once dominated the corner of 23rd Street and Fifth Avenue—the logically named Fifth Avenue Hotel. Opened in 1859, it was the venture of wealthy merchant Amos Richards Eno, who accurately predicted that the center of the city's commercial scene would soon settle at 23rd Street. The extravagant Italianate exterior was composed of five stories of imported marble, while austere, carpeted interiors took inspiration from European palaces. Guests enjoyed reading rooms, a luxurious bar, a barber shop, a dedicated telegraph office, and a variety of dining and drawing rooms, not to mention the first hotel elevator ever built

---

15 The Freemasons offer free tours of their headquarters, which we highly recommend.

in the United States, a steam-powered monstrosity that whisked guests to their floors.

During the 1870s, New York politicians became national power brokers and frequently hashed out power deals here. A corridor of the hotel known as the "Amen Corner" was a famous congregation spot for Republican political bosses and reporters. As they frequently powwowed here on Sundays, gatherers would sarcastically proclaim "Amen!" during heated discussions. In 1908 the Fifth Avenue Hotel was demolished and replaced by the sixteen-story Toy Center, which served as the epicenter of toy manufacturing for much of the twentieth century. The street clock remains a F.A.B. detail of the Flatiron District, not merely because it's fabulous, but because of

Classy! This cast-iron street clock in front of the Fifth Avenue Building was fully restored in 2011, paid for by Tiffany & Co.

the toy center's original name: the Fifth Avenue Building. (*200 Fifth Avenue, at 23rd Street*)

A Short History of Queens

The borough of Queens is perhaps the most culturally diverse place in the United States, if not the entire planet.

For much of its existence this area was sparsely populated with small villages—bucolic, rambling, and quiet. But a spirited rebellion filled the citizens of the Dutch-populated town of Vlishing (later Flushing) in 1657 to harangue New Amsterdam's director-general Peter Stuyvesant, for religious intolerance in a document referred to today as the "Flushing Remonstrance."

In 1683 the British formed Queens County from the scattered federation of "Newtowne, Jamaica, Flushing, Hempstead, and Oysterbay, with several outfarms, settlements, and plantacons adjacent."[16] In the early nineteenth century, residents of a town near the East River renamed their town Astoria after Manhattan's most powerful landlord, John Jacob Astor, hoping that he'd help develop it. He gave only a paltry sum (paltry, considering he was one of New York's wealthiest men), but the name stuck.

The John Browne House (built around 1661 and pictured here in the 1820s) still stands in Flushing, Queens.

Queens would become a patchwork of planned communities. By the 1860s, the vast overpopulation and improved financial fortunes of nearby New

---

16 Newtown/Newtowne later became Elmhurst. After consolidation, Hemstead and Oyster Bay voted to exclude themselves from the borders of the new borough.

York and Brooklyn inspired some intrepid developers to sweep into the underpopulated areas of Queens County to develop new towns. Meanwhile, other new communities sprouted up around big factories, like those of piano manufacturer Henry Steinway (the neighborhood with his name is situated today near LaGuardia Airport) and housewares mogul Florian Grosjean, whose company village is the basis of today's Woodhaven.

The consolidation of 1898 folded Queens into the metropolis of New York City, transforming its motley collection of villages and communities into a borough that's nearly coterminous with the borders of Queens County.

The birth of modern Queens kicked off with the completion of the Queensboro Bridge in 1909 and the Dual Contracts agreement of 1913, which brought new subway lines into the borough. By the 1920s the population had nearly doubled as new modern housing developments lured middle-class residents away from the congested old city.

The most radical transformations to Queens in the twentieth century can be credited to Parks Commissioner Robert Moses, who treated the borough as a blank canvas upon which to realize his vision of modern living. A crisscrossing network of highways ensured that Queens would forever be tied to the automobile (to the chagrin of public transit advocates). Moses was key in the development of New York's two major airports, both of which are situated in the borough: LaGuardia Airport (1939) and Idlewild Airport (1948, later JFK International Airport).[17]

But his jewel was an 897-acre park literally created from the remains of an ash dump: Flushing Meadows Corona Park. It was Moses's pet project and never really achieved his lofty expectations, despite the fact that two World's Fairs (1939–1940 and 1964–1965) were held here.[18]

Immigration reforms in the 1960s brought waves of new residents to Queens from a wide range of countries. Today nearly 2.5 million people call the borough home, creating an impressive ethnic mix that lives up to the "melting pot" first proposed from the shores of Ellis Island. It's so vastly developed that some neighborhoods (Astoria and Ridgewood) are now feeling the effects of gentrification, while others (Bayside and College Point) might as well be located in the far reaches of suburbia.

---

17 Moses's domain was out on Randall's Island, connected to Manhattan, Queens, and the Bronx by his proud little baby, the Triborough Bridge.
18 For a short time, from 1946 to 1951, some of the old fair structures hosted the first temporary headquarters for the United Nations.

THOSE DAYS IN GRAMERCY PARK

In 1958, Gladys Brooks, genteel wife of the famed literary critic Van Wyck Brooks, penned a memoir describing her childhood in turn-of-the-century Gramercy Park:

Gramercy Park!

The words were to me almost like those first uttered by an infant, so familiar, so compelling had they been from my life's beginning. There was a picture of me in my baby carriage snapped by some itinerant photographer as I was wheeled to the park by my Irish nurse, Margaret, erect and stern in her tight-fitting bodice and full white apron. Another picture showed us inside the park on a stretch of lawn close to the dogwood tree, and here Margaret, her mood more relaxed, is seen stooping down, arms outstretched, to receive my tottering first steps. Irving Place, in the block between the Park and our house, was the golden place of the Elysian Fields. Indeed, all unconsciously, when first I was told of Paris and the Champs Elysees, I visualized the street on which our house was set. How else could Elysium be described? And, arriving before the benign, sun-baked brick house, wisteria-wrapped, at the corner of Nineteenth Street, with its high welcoming front stoop, the radiance continued.

Inside, the library was the mainland of my childhood life, the room that gave out a human kind of presence. The sofa beside the fireplace, where the logs simmered the long winter through, held a painted scroll along the mantel with the words:

Sit by my side and let the world slip for we shall ne'er be younger.

Chapter 16///

Gramercy Park, Kips Bay, and Murray Hill

The former residence of Mayor James Harper at 3–4 Gramercy Park (photo: Berenice Abbott).

SITUATE THE READER
—Gramercy Park, Kips Bay,—
and Murray Hill

The three East Side residential neighborhoods located between 14th and 42nd Streets all have names that hearken back to a New York of over 200 years ago.

Gramercy Park, surprisingly, has the oldest name. Sure, it has a certain British ring to it,[1] but the name Gramercy is actually a corruption of a Dutch term that described the landscape. The farmland here was once home to a broken, jagged swamp that meandered from the area of Madison Square down to around today's 18th Street and the East River. The Dutch called it Krom Moerasje, a mouthful that means, appropriately, "little, crooked swamp." It was later called Cedar Creek before being filled in by city leaders.

Kips Bay also refers to a long-gone natural feature: an inlet that bent into the area between today's First and Second Avenues. Jacobus Hendrickson Kip (1631–1690) was the first Dutch settler in the area. His father was one of New Amsterdam's most prominent residents— Hendrick Hendrickson Kip or "Kip of the Haughty Lip" for his sassy countenance. Son Jacobus was also married to the daughter of New York's first doctor. With so few people living in New Amsterdam, it was easy to be well connected!

Although greatly smoothed out, one can still feel the slight elevation of the former Murray's Hill, named for the owner of a mansion here in the 1760s named Robert Murray. The gracious manor—which the city folk called Inclenberg—sat here until the early nineteenth century, when the needs of a new railroad system sliced the property asunder.[2]

---

1   According to *Webster's Dictionary*, the archaic "gramercy" means *grand mercy* (or *grand merci*), or great thanks. So when you go to Gramercy Park, you're really going to WOW, THANKS! Park.
2   The home also plays a role in Revolutionary War lore. See Points of Interest for more information.

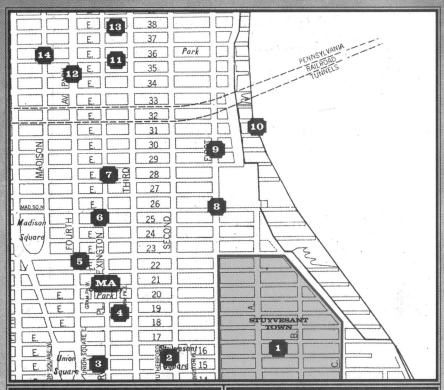

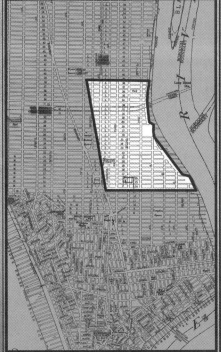

POINTS OF INTEREST

1 The Sweet Smell of the Gashouse District

2 Peg Leg Pete is Watching You

3 A Sleepy, Hollow Lie

4 Rock the Block Beautiful

5 The Marble Children

6 The Ultimate Freak Show

7 Oath for a Mediocre President

8 As Seen on Countless Crime Television Shows

9 The Heart of Madness

10 Stand Here

11 Blink and You'll Miss It Historic District

12 The Charming Hospitality of Mrs. Murray

13 The Miami Vice House

14 Stationary Stone Sisters

MA Gramercy Park

Gramercy Park and the Tragedy of Edwin Booth

Gramercy Park feels like an antique pocket watch that has stopped keeping time. It's tucked into a quiet corner of Manhattan and rarely opened, except by those lucky enough to possess its key. This exclusivity, in fact, has been the park's defining feature since the neighborhood was first formed in the 1830s. And yet, in 1918 they did allow in one resident…permanently – the actor Edwin Booth.

"The new statue of Edwin Booth is the only one of an actor in any of the city parks – unless the Shakespeare statue in Central Park is so defined," remarked

Gramercy Park, 1935.

the *New York Times* on the statue's debut in 1918, underscoring the importance and esteem that New Yorkers placed upon the thespian. How unfortunate that today he's become better known as the brother of an assassin: John Wilkes Booth.

Edwin was born in 1833, the very year that the newly constructed park was lined with the iron fence that incarcerates his likeness today. Land developers during the 1830s were tirelessly luring wealthy residents to their new and luxurious northern developments and away from the crowded city center downtown. Washington Square Park and Astor Place were also developed in the 1830s.

Samuel Ruggles, a well-connected lawyer–turned–property developer, eyed the old farm of New York's first post–Revolutionary War mayor, James Duane, situated near the jagged swamp, as a perfect location upon which to build large homes for wealthy New Yorkers. He concurrently built up Union Place (later Union Square) as a public space where he himself owned a home nearby.

But for Gramercy Park, Ruggles would reinforce for its wealthy homeowners that sense of exclusivity and separation they desired by closing its park off to all but the property owners. To create this tucked-away enclosure, he placed the park in the middle of a block, cutting two small north–south lanes at the park's western and eastern edges between East 20th and East 21st Streets (Gramercy Park West and Gramercy Park East). But he didn't stop there: To give residents an easier carriage ride downtown (to their offices, theaters, shops, and places of worship), he received permission from the city to plow two north–south arteries from the middle of the park's southern and

Always-in-character Edwin Booth.

northern sides. The more important of the two, as far as he was concerned in the 1830s, the street to the south, he named Irving Place for his good friend the beloved American author Washington Irving. He paid tribute to the Revolutionary War, waged more than sixty years before, by naming the other road Lexington Avenue, after the critical battle of Lexington.[3]

The diarist George Templeton Strong lived along the park's northern side (at 55 Gramercy Park North), as did the inventor-philanthropist Peter Cooper (9 Lexington Avenue) and the financier Cyrus West Field (1 Lexington Avenue). On March 10, 1854, Cooper met in Field's mansion with other moneyed gentlemen to conceive the first transatlantic telegraph cable. On that evening, the world began to get a little smaller, more interconnected, and more bonded — and it all started in Gramercy Park.

That statue of Shakespeare mentioned earlier was placed in Central Park in 1864[4] from funds raised by a single performance of *Julius Caesar* on November 25 of that year. The one-night-only production featured the country's most famous actor-brother trio — Edwin Booth, John Wilkes Booth, and Junius

---

3   In a way, this contrivance is actually Ruggles's most valuable gift to New York. As the city grew northward, Lexington Avenue continued traveling up the island — from Gramercy Park to Harlem, where it terminates at the water. With the rise of Midtown Manhattan in the 1920s and '30s, Lexington became a vital anchor for new skyscrapers.

4   We revisit the Shakespeare statue in Chapter 22.

Brutus Booth, Jr. Edwin was a famed theater producer, a beloved tragedian, and a hell of a guy. In 1864, he performed 100 nights of *Hamlet* at his Winter Garden Theater at Broadway and Bond Street.[5] A critic would later comment, "Booth, to many of us, *is* Hamlet." But his fortunes as a stage performer would change forever the next year, when real-life tragedy struck—the assassination of President Abraham Lincoln in April 1865,[6] by Edwin's own brother John.

To be or not to be. While Edwin had already grown estranged from John prior to that tragic night, the assassination weighed heavily upon him for the

Curtain call: Booth's Gramercy Park statue faces south toward Old New York.

remainder of his life. Edwin briefly retired from the stage, only to return gradually, bolstered by the encouragement of his New York fans. In February 1869 he opened the lavish Booth Theatre[7] at 23rd Street and Sixth Avenue, a revolutionary, technological marvel of a theater that featured New York's first theater sprinkler system and hydraulics to move scenery.[8]

In 1888 Booth, now considered the greatest actor in the land, sought to elevate the profession in the eyes of high society by opening a respectable gentlemen's social club. The Players Club, operating out of a posh 1840s mansion at 16 Gramercy Park South, was founded with the lofty aim of promoting the "social intercourse between the representative members of the dramatic profession and of the kindred professions of literature, painting, sculpture, and music." Booth himself lived on the third floor, presiding over late evenings at the club with such luminaries as Mark Twain, Augustus Saint-Gaudens, and Mayor Abram Hewitt. On June 7, 1893, Booth died at his club in

5   Booth actually managed the Winter Garden Theater until it burned down in 1867.
6   John shot Lincoln on April 14 at Ford's Theatre in Washington D.C., and the president died the following morning.
7   Theaters built by the Shuberts called the Winter Garden and the Booth Theater, named in honor of Edwin, still exist in today's Theater District.
8   Perhaps it was too innovative. By 1881, Booth was unable to afford to keep the theater open. The rise of the Ladies' Mile shopping district ensured its fate; it was renovated into a department store. From *Coriolanus* to corsets!

his third-floor bedroom, which to this day remains furnished exactly as he left it. The scenery hasn't changed—it's as if he might make a return appearance.

But he can't because he's standing in Gramercy Park, under lock and key. He faces south, as though acknowledging that his contributions to the stage, although highly revered, are vestiges of the past. The fate of his beloved profession—perhaps its greatest days—would head up the island in the opposite direction.

Gramercy Park, Murray Hill, and Kips Bay

POINTS OF INTEREST

1 THE SWEET SMELL OF THE GASHOUSE DISTRICT Stuyvesant Town–Peter Cooper Village is not a New Amsterdam reenactment park, nor is it a celebration of the many inventions of the great Mr. Cooper. Rather, it's one of New York's largest residential developments, housing more than 25,000

20th Street between First and Second Avenues, 1935.

people in an all-consuming mass of mid-twentieth-century brick apartment blocks that manages to create an almost sheltered, peaceful setting, with its central plazas, playgrounds, and leafy walks.[9]

But in the nineteenth century, this area brought New York to light—literally. As gas lighting grew popular in the 1840s and gas-powered streetlamps were installed throughout the city, massive fuel tanks were built here to hold the city's supply.

Oh, just imagine the pleasing aroma the Gashouse District must have given off! The district, north of the Lower East Side and against the water, was a comfortable distance from the Fifth Avenue parlors basking in its warm glow. But ramshackle tenements sprouted up in the shadow of these massive tanks. So too did gangs of street thugs, like the Gas House Gang, never fearful that law enforcement would chase them too far into their putrid domain.

The district's importance grew with the invention of gas-powered appliances and automobiles. "Have you ever seen this phenomenon of the East Side?" proclaimed the *New York Sun* on March 1, 1914. "It is a weird spectacle. The garnet colored glow stains the entire gashouse district with its ruddy light, and momentarily brightens the great gas tanks, long dismal rows of them, which give the district its name—gloomy metal towers, floating on their unseen water bed, sinking into vague distances."

Construction of the FDR Drive in the 1930s eliminated some of these "dismal" towers, and the need for middle-class housing cleared away the rest by the late 1940s. Today there are flowerbeds sprouting up in various parts of Stuy Town where nobody would have imagined such growth possible just 100 years ago. (*Center plaza of Stuyvesant Town, between East 16th and 17th Streets*)

2 PEG LEG PETE IS WATCHING YOU Stuyvesant Square might have been one of New York's most restful and serene parks had Second Avenue not steamrolled straight through it. True to its name, the park was developed upon the old Stuyvesant family land with the expectation that, like Gramercy Park after it, this patch of green would entice wealthy New Yorkers to construct their homes around it. Today, most people know the square for the

---

9 The development is not, of course, without some controversy. In the late 1940s, Stuy Town was rightly accused of selecting only white tenants for the property. Stunningly, in 1947, the New York Supreme Court sided with the developers and their right to choose people based on their own (in this case, racist) criteria.

religious and medical institutions surrounding it. The beautiful St. George's Church and Friends Meetinghouse were already installed on the western end of the park by the time of the Civil War, and in 1929 the vital community hospital Beth Israel[10] came to the park's eastern end. It expanded over the decades to become Mount Sinai Beth Israel.

A stoic statue of Peter Stuyvesant stands in Stuyvesant Square.

Fortunately, despite the many changes that have occurred around the park, the mighty spirit of Peter Stuyvesant still survives. In 1941 a statue to Stuyvesant was placed in the western half of the park, created by another famous New Yorker: Gertrude Vanderbilt Whitney. She did a spectacular job; Stuyvesant's particular mix of confidence, determination, disgust, and humorlessness shines right through. (*Western side of Stuyvesant Square*)

3 A SLEEPY, HOLLOW LIE Washington Irving (1783–1859), author of *The Legend of Sleepy Hollow* and the man who bestowed the nickname "Gotham" upon New York, never lived on the street which bears his name— Irving Place. Nevertheless, people have stubbornly attempted to place him

here over the years. The street was named for the author in 1833 by his friend the developer Samuel Ruggles. Eleven years later, a corner townhouse at 49 Irving Place was built, and rumors began to swirl that Washington had himself lived there. A spiffy little plaque still celebrates this residency-that-wasn't. It's so pretty no one has ever taken it down. Oddly, there's no such plaque for an actual icon who really *did* live here— Elsie de Wolfe (1865–1950), New York's most famous interior decorator.[11]

---

10 Beth Israel isn't a person, although she would be a lovely one if she were. It's Hebrew for "House of Israel" and owes its creation to the largely Jewish Lower East Side.

11 See Chapter 18 for one of her more magical creations.

For those Irving aficionados disappointed by this unfortunate fact, never fear! The author is here in another form—as a gigantic bust in front of Washington Irving High School across the street (today Washington Irving Campus), built in 1913. (*49 Irving Place*)

4 ROCK THE BLOCK BEAUTIFUL In a way the string of exotic townhouses on East 19th Street, one block south of Gramercy Park, is the least New York–like block in the city. Already in this book, we've passed block after block of homes in similar, if pleasing, styles. How tidy and uniform they seem! But homes along the so-called Block Beautiful are a dazzling and motley lot, intentionally diverse in design with whimsical flourishes—from stepped Dutch gables to brightly colored facades. We have a single architect to thank for this wild mix: Frederick Sterner, who purchased many of the regular old brownstones in the 1900s and made them sparkle. Soon other architects followed his example, each attempting to bring a tasteful, though highly individualistic, design to each home. Stroll up and down the block to find your favorite, then return to 139 East 19th Street, Sterner's first work there. His original backyard here has been described as a "fairytale grotto."[12] The block's creativity has long attracted famous artists and writers, including George Bellows (146 East 19th Street), Lincoln Kirstein (128 East 19th Street), and Ida Tarbell (132 East 19th Street). (*139 East 19th Street*)

Frederick Sterner put his neck out to make Block Beautiful truly unique, including this house at 149 East 19th Street.

5 THE MARBLE CHILDREN Only across the street from 295 Park Avenue South can one fully take in the bizarre set of haunted carvings of scary

12 *Real Estate Record and Builders Guide*, 1910.

little toddlers, their gray faces gazing down at the street, interspersed with dappled wreathes in infinity shapes affixed to its upper floors. The years have given these tots a distinctly possessed quality. However, this structure was actually built in 1892 as a safe space for children. This was the headquarters for the New York Society for the Prevention of Cruelty to Children, founded by Henry Bergh in 1874, several years after he founded the American Society for the Prevention of Cruelty to Animals.[13] The original playroom for abused children was on the third floor.[14] (*295 Park Avenue South*)

A child aloft at 295 Park Avenue South.

6 THE ULTIMATE FREAK SHOW The 69th Regiment Armory was opened in 1906 to house military personnel and equipment. However, it became notorious in the early twentieth century for housing something else, something offensive, blasphemous, morally repugnant, and filthy: modern

The 69th Regiment Armory: Beautiful on the outside and, in 1913, shocking on the inside.

---

13 See Chapter 4.
14 The entire building was turned into apartments in 1982. That former playroom was Greg's first apartment in New York in the early 1990s.

art. The 1913 Armory Show was the first significant display of American and European modern art in the United States. While the show's organizers had hoped to use the event to promote American artists, it was selections from European superstars like Paul Gauguin, Vincent van Gogh, and a young Pablo Picasso that captivated and shocked sell-out crowds. The most notorious piece, "Nude Descending a Staircase, No. 2" by Marcel Duchamp, was a 1912 painting referred to by one critic as "an explosion in a shingle factory." If you could somehow manage to reassemble the original collection that hung in the 1913 Armory Show, its value today would be in the billions of dollars. (*68 Lexington Avenue*)

7 OATH FOR A MEDIOCRE PRESIDENT The home at 123 Lexington Avenue holds a unique distinction in American history: It's the only existing building in New York City that bore witness to the swearing-in of an American president. This was the home of Chester A. Arthur, vice president

Chester A. Arthur.

of the United States, who was quickly given the oath in the early morning of September 20, 1881. President James Garfield had been shot months before, on July 2, and had survived the incident. Although he was expected to make a recovery, he died in the late evening of September 19. Arthur is nobody's favorite president. He served until 1885, a deeply unpopular replacement for Garfield. Following his tenure, he returned to live in this house and died the following year. (*123 Lexington Avenue*)

BELLEVUE HOSPITAL

Here's a little Martha Stewart tip: If you've got an old mansion lying around, consider turning it into a hospital. The more remote the better! The New York Almshouse was looking for just such an opportunity in the late eighteenth century. With yellow fever epidemics raging and endangering the lives of New Yorkers, physicians could no longer lodge sick patients within the almshouse, which was originally located in the spot of today's City Hall. The Belle Vue Farm was located on the old Kips family property; the land was leased to the almshouse, who began moving patients here in 1803, just as another epidemic set upon the city. A larger facility was built in the early 1810s. The Manhattan grid plan, which was being cooked up at the time, took the location of the new structure into consideration when First Avenue was laid out.

The original Bellevue Hospital, admired for its remote location, boasted convenient waterfront access.

8 AS SEEN ON COUNTLESS CRIME TELEVISION SHOWS The official New York City Morgue (today the Office of Chief Medical Examiner) has been on this spot since 1866, although the hospital obviously had a so-called deadhouse for much longer.[15] Bodies required burial after a few days, but for identification and forensic purposes, clothing and other personal articles were kept on display for a month, then put into storage. Behind the original morgue was a "morgue pier," an actual pier used for the grim purpose of identifying bodies during large-scale tragedies, such as the *General Slocum* disaster (1904) and the Triangle Shirtwaist Factory fire (1911).

Bellevue's rich history is evident today just from studying its current layout. Standing in front of the morgue, it seems that the complex of medical buildings fits together like Tetris blocks. In fact, the original entrance to the administration building is today enclosed inside the hospital's modern lobby. (*26th Street and First Avenue*)

9 THE HEART OF MADNESS The barbaric "treatments" that psychiatric patients were subjected to in the late nineteenth and early twentieth centuries have inspired a legion of horror films, much of the Batman/Gotham City

---

15 An earlier incarnation in the 1850s even contained a cabinet of curiosities—Wood Pathological Museum of Bellevue Hospital. It contained "some of the most rare, interesting, and unique specimens of anatomical dissections and pathological specimens to be found anywhere." From *An Account of Bellevue Hospital*, 1893.

mythology, and most likely a few of your nightmares. The Bellevue Psychiatric Ward, which opened in 1931, has been the subject of both fictional and real-life dramas, and called "the Chelsea Hotel of the Mad."[16] Eugene O'Neill, Charles Mingus, and Norman Mailer[17] all spent time here. While Bellevue's own psychiatric practices have thankfully been upgraded to the modern age, its former psychiatric ward retains a rather unsettling appearance, at least from the outside. Stroll around the perimeter and peer through the iron gates to uncover a still-decrepit campus of boarded-up windows and vine-choked walls. Today it serves as a homeless shelter. (*30th Street and First Avenue*)

10 STAND HERE: Between 30th and 34th Streets at the East River waterfront, overlooking the water. *Why?* With the bustling ferries, the active heliport, and the traffic of FDR Drive, it's hard to appreciate the rather lovely view of the East River. It's almost as if New Yorkers want to forget that it was on this very spot that the city lost its freedom during the Revolutionary War.

On September 15, 1776, British forces led by General William Howe landed along this shoreline and easily pushed back the Continental Army's paltry defenses to meet up with George Washington's fleeing battalions. For the next

Kips Bay still retained its bucolic charm in 1830.

seven years, until November 25, 1783, the British would occupy New York and the surrounding areas and make it one of their principal bases for the duration of the war. Although Washington's reasoning for abandoning New York was sound — preserving his army to fight another day was the right tactic — it remains a sad chapter in the city's history, which explains why you won't find any markers or plaques here commemorating Washington's hasty withdrawal. (*Between 30th and 34th Streets at the East River waterfront*)

11 BLINK AND YOU'LL MISS IT HISTORIC DISTRICT Funny how some of the most charming homes in New York were originally built for horses. Sniffen Court, a haunting blind alley on East 36th Street, was once lined with stables for the neighborhood's wealthy homes. As the clip-

---

16 Mark Harris, *New York Magazine*, November 16, 2008.
17 Mailer was admitted after stabbing his wife in 1960.

clopping romance of horse-drawn carriages (and their accompanying animal droppings) gave way to the rumble of the automobile, the old stables found themselves either demolished or transformed into living quarters for people. This court is named for nineteenth-century developer John Sniffen, although there's some dispute as to whether Sniffen even developed anything here at all. But something equine here remains—two fantastic horse reliefs at the far end of the court, designed by sculptor and longtime resident Malvina Hoffman (1887–1966). Unshockingly, this is one of New York's smallest historic districts, granted this status in 1966. (*Sniffen Court, south side of East 36th Street*)

12 THE CHARMING HOSPITALITY OF MRS. MURRAY The farm estate of Robert and Mary Lindley Murray—called Inclenberg—once sat near today's corner of Park Avenue South and East 35th Street. Approaching this spot today, you can still feel the incline as you climb what's left of Murray's Hill. Back in 1776, however, it was an even more pronounced hill, which made it a strategic spot to hold if you happened to be the leader of the British forces, invading along the coast of Kips Bay (see Point of Interest #10).

A terrific legend about the day of the invasion, September 15, 1776, recounts the role of Mrs. Murray, who was left at the house with her daughters and domestic help. Washington's troops were still fleeing north up the island

Ladies to the rescue! Mrs. Murray and her daughters distract the enemy with their hospitality.

and could have been easily stopped by the surging British flank. The quick-witted Murray women, however, stopped the newly landed British officers and invited them in for refreshments, distracting the invaders with their conversation and grace, while giving Washington and his men time to escape. (Even with the tea party, British forces still managed to apprehend hundreds of rebels that day.)

Although much embellished, there is certainly a kernel of truth to the story. General Henry Clinton was indeed ordered to hold steady at the hill by his commander, General Howe. So who's to say that a little old-fashioned feminine charm didn't delay the British advance? (*Park Avenue South and East 35th Street*)

13 THE *MIAMI VICE* HOUSE What, another stable? Yes, we're visiting another former stable because this one is *insane*, inside and out. Ostensibly

built for horses in 1902, this kooky Dutch revival house was swiftly refitted as an automobile garage less than two decades later. Horse heads pop out from its exterior, and centered at the top is a churlish-looking bulldog.[18] All of this dates back nearly a century. So why is this place some-times called "the *Miami Vice* house"? Its interior was once the very pearl of mid-1980s design, with pink neon pillars that needed only a popped collar and a Huey Lewis record. (*149 East 38th Street*)

14 STATIONARY STONE SISTERS New York has always had its share of wealthy residents. You know, *ordinary* rich people. And then there was J. Pierpont Morgan (1837–1913), the financier, mogul, and collector whose influence over the American business sector during the Gilded Age would be hard to overstate. The lordly brownstone at the corner of Madison Avenue and East 37th is the only part of the original Morgan mansion that still remains today, for after Morgan's death in 1913 his entire property was retooled into a public institution that showcased his rich collection of books and art.

---

18 This may remind you of the old American Express building seen in Chapter 6.

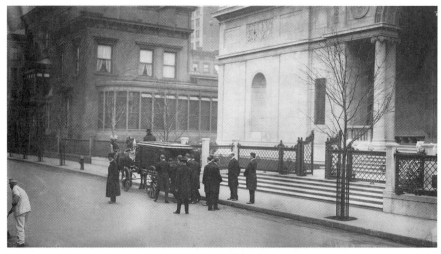

J. P. Morgan's funeral procession, 1913, in front of his library.

Today the Morgan Library and Museum dazzles with its splendid rooms filled with artistic treasures. You can almost whiff the ghosts of cigars past in Morgan's private study, while its hallowed library seems plucked from the set of an Indiana Jones film.

But our favorite part of the Morgan complex? Those Assyrian lady lions sitting out in front of the library building, constructed in 1903 with every ounce of mighty Classical pomposity possible. The library[19] is presented like a pagan temple, full of enigma and intrigue. And these tranquil beasts harbor a touch more

These cool cats, located in front of the Morgan Library, have seen it all.

grace than their younger brothers up at the New York Public Library (also sculpted by Edward Clark Potter). (*225 Madison Avenue, 36th Street side*)

---

19 Designed by Charles Follen McKim of McKim, Mead, and White fame.

Tastes of History: The Pizza Slice

Lombardi's coal-fired stove in the kitchen is the original, lugged up the street from the first bakery.

New York's love affair with a piping-hot slice of pizza began in a tiny grocery store in Little Italy. Here, at 53½ Spring Street, baker Gennaro Lombardi, watching his customers hustling to and from work, decided to toss together an easily transportable "tomato pie" that they could pick up in the morning for lunch. He baked this early form of fast food in his coal-fired stove, using a recipe passed down to him by his father. When he realized that not all customers could afford an entire pie (which cost five cents in 1905), Gennaro started slicing them up, and charged by the inch. He had unknowingly given birth to the pizza slice.

And so in 1905 Lombardi dedicated his entire store to selling only tomato pies. Lombardi's was a neighborhood mainstay for decades and even began attracting non-Italian tourists following World War II. In 1984, Lombardi's folded, another victim of the city's tough times, but a decade later Jerry Lombardi, Gennaro's grandson, reopened the store with his friend John Brescio at its current location: 32 Spring Street. While it no longer sells individual slices, the coal-fired stove in the kitchen is the original, lugged up the street from the first bakery, and the restaurant is treated like a shrine by pizza pilgrims everywhere.

Meanwhile, many of Gennaro Lombardi's kitchen crew went on to cook up their own now-legendary pizzerias, many with their own particular spin on the pie. These included Antonio "Totonno" Pero, whose Totonno's on Neptune Avenue in Coney Island opened in 1924 and is still operated by the family today. Another *pizzaiolo*, John Sasso, left to open John's Pizzeria on Bleecker Street in 1929, which still packs 'em in today.

But perhaps the most intriguing spinoff from Lombardi's pizza came from another former cook: Pasquale (or "Patsy") Lancieri. He left Lombardi's in 1933 to open Patsy's with his wife, Carmella, in the then-thriving Italian section of East Harlem at 118th Street and First Avenue. In 1991 the Lancieri family sold their Patsy's in Harlem, and today's owners operate several Patsy's pizza locations throughout the city.

But wait—there's one more Patsy's! Pasquale "Patsy" Grimaldi, nephew of Patsy Lancieri, learned pizza-making skills from his uncle in the 1940s before opening his own pizzeria in Brooklyn. When the Manhattan Patsy's became a franchise in the 1990s, this Patsy's switched over to using their last name: Grimaldi's. Got that?

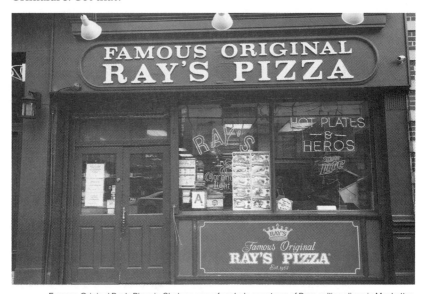

Famous Original Ray's Pizza in Chelsea, one of a whole spectrum of Rays selling slices in Manhattan.

Aside from Patsy, Ray is probably the most common name associated with pizza in Manhattan. Original Ray's, Famous Ray's, Original Famous Ray's... etc. But there may not even be a Ray at all. The real original Ray's opened in 1959 at 27 Prince Street in Little Italy near Lombardi's. Its owner's name? Ralph Cuomo. He allegedly found his name too feminine for a slice joint, and thus beefed it up as "Ray." In 1964, Rosolino Mangano opened Original Ray's Pizza at First Avenue and 59th Street (claiming his nickname was "Ray") and then opened numerous Original Ray's outlets. And it didn't stop there—other Ray's spread throughout the city in the '70s and '80s, leading to serious brand confusion and pie-in-the-sky lawsuits.

An excerpt from *Maggie: A Girl of the Streets* by Stephen Crane:

Everybody knows all about the Tenderloin district of New York. There is no man that has the slightest claim to citizenship that does not know all there is to know concerning the Tenderloin. It is wonderful—this amount of truth which the world's clergy and police force have collected concerning the Tenderloin. My friends from the stars obtain all this information, if possible, and then go into this wilderness and apply it. Upon observing you, certain spirits of the jungle will term you a wise guy, but there is no gentle humor in the Tenderloin, so you need not fear that this remark is anything but a tribute to your knowledge.

Tenderloin Police Station, 1908.

Chapter 17//

Herald Square and The Tenderloin:

27th Street to 40th Street, from Madison Square to the Hudson River

What a view! In the early 1900s, from the window of a Sixth Avenue elevated train, you could see Macy's, the New York Herald office, and One Times Square in the background.

SITUATE THE READER
~ Herald Square and The Tenderloin ~

With Washington Square Park as a starting line, Fifth Avenue was a veritable nineteenth-century racetrack upon which wealthy New Yorkers attempted to overtake each other, leaping farther northward to construct their increasingly ostentatious mansions. A major turning point in this money game came in the 1850s, when William Backhouse Astor, Jr. (married to society doyenne Caroline Schermerhorn Astor), built a house next door to his brother on Fifth Avenue between 33rd and 34th Streets— way out of town! The rivalry between these competing Astors would eventually give New York its most famous Gilded Age hotel—and, indirectly, its most famous skyscraper.

The glimmer of high society fades the farther west you get from Fifth Avenue. Just one avenue west of here, Herald Square and Greeley Square—plazas named for a newspaper and a newspaperman, respectively—attracted theaters, vaudeville houses, and, by the 1900s, department stores moving up from Ladies' Mile. A major elevated train station here made the square a busy and convenient middle-class destination round the clock.

The area farther west between Herald Square and the slaughterhouses and factories along the Hudson River earned the nickname "the Tenderloin" for its smorgasbord of vices and bawdy entertainment options. "I've been having chuck steak ever since I've been on the force, and now I'm going to have a bit of tenderloin," quipped Police Captain Alexander "Clubber" Williams in 1876, savoring the sweet smell of corruption. Many in the city rejoiced when the Pennsylvania Railroad built its colossal train station between West 31st and 33rd Streets in 1910, buying up and demolishing huge chunks of the Tenderloin.

But walk around the far west side at night. On occasion, the old Tenderloin comes back to life with the snap of a garter belt or the holler of a late-night poker game.

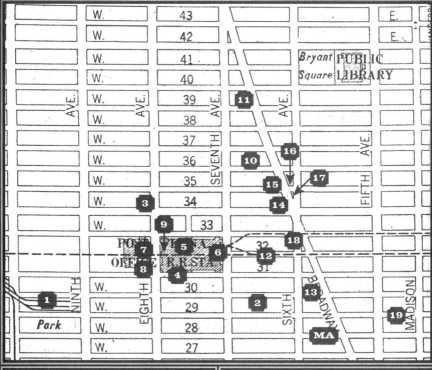

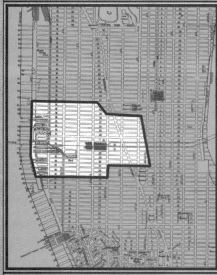

POINTS OF INTEREST

1 The Unsung Lincoln Memorial

2 To the Tenderloin Dungeon!

3 Birds of a Feather Flock Together Here

4 I've Got the Power

5 Sam's Place

6 The Mighty Eagles

7 Special Delivery

8 Read This Quote

9 Scenes from a Station Past

10 Ready to Wear

11 The Fat Lady Sings

12 The Skybridge of Yesterday

13 The Heyday of the Haymarket

14 The Million-Dollar Corner

15 Who Wants to See Some Sad Fish?

16 For Whom the Bell Tolls

17 The Owls Are Watching You

18 Greeley's Birds

19 The Church of Manda the Cat

MA Tin Pan Alley

The Echoes of Tin Pan Alley

The American music industry was born on a ragged and dingy street south of Herald Square that today is populated with perfume vendors, costume jewelry dealers, and wig shops. While that particular combination might still resemble a subset of today's music scene—Lady Gaga has certainly benefited from plastic trinkets and fake hair—all of American pop music, in fact, got its start here.

Music men: Song composers Gene Buck, Victor Herbert, John Philip Sousa, Harry B. Smith, Jerome Kern, Irving Berlin, George W. Meyer, Irving Bibo, and Otto Harbach.

Popular music was not magically invented the moment the phonograph started turning in 1877. Short and catchy tunes first entered people's homes in the late nineteenth century as sheet music to be played on family pianos. Tickling the ivories was crucial for keeping families entertained and up to date on the popular tunes of the times. But the skill was also seen as helpful for snagging a spouse. Homes were centered around their pianos— much like they are around their HD television sets today. (Cue: sad trombone.)

The American popular song was born[1] from a patchwork of musical styles, from African American spirituals to the folk ballads of Irish immigrants. But tunes became *popular* in the late nineteenth century via the stage—from their performances from vaudeville and minstrel shows to the concert hall. These tunes were eventually disseminated as sheet music and sold in department stores around the country, and even by door-to-door salesmen. Unlike much of the disposable pop music of today—which seems to evaporate into the ether almost from the moment of its first auto-tuning—a piece of sheet music at this time could take years to reach peak popularity, often after being featured in a stage production along the way.

---

1 We should stay "born and sometimes stolen," actually. There were no copyright protections at the time for composers and lyricists, so songs could be liberally and nonchalantly duplicated. Stephen Foster, often considered the inventor of the American popular song, died in New York in 1864 virtually penniless.

But New York song pluggers didn't have time to wait around for a song to become big. They'd write them, "plug them" to sheet music publishers, then run out and try to make them big. They'd compose numbers for big stars, lavishing them with gifts to get their attention, hoping that they'd incorporate their songs into their vaudeville acts and make them hits. For this reason, music publishers began flocking to New York's late nineteenth-century entertainment districts: the blocks surrounding Madison Square and Herald Square.

In 1893, the music publisher M. Witmark and Sons was the first to arrive on 28th Street,[2] a convenient spot midway between the two squares. Other

"My Jersey Lily" by Harry Von Tilzer was one of the catchiest tunes of 1900.

publishers followed and soon the once-tuneless block was packed with music publishers, their demo pianos plunking loudly from every open window. It was this astonishing cacophony that, legend has it, earned the street the nickname "Tin Pan Alley."

By 1906 the street was home to at least three dozen music publishers, bolstered by the popularity of variety revues and vaudeville theaters up and down Broadway and around town. Harry Von Tilzer, a former performer in a traveling circus, grew up to hammer out big hits like "A Bird in a Gilded Cage" (1899) and "Wait 'Till the Sun Shines, Nellie" (1905); he opened his own song shop at 37 West 28th Street. Jerome H. Remick churned out so many ragtime hits from his 45 West 28th Street office that he bought his own printing plant. Song pluggers sat with clients in charmingly small parlors, altering and inventing new melodies on the spot.

Legendary American songwriters would get their start in these shops. A precocious young George Gershwin reported to work for Remick, penning smash hits such as "Rialto Ripples Rag" before he turned 18. Harry Warren, an Italian immigrant who grew up in Brooklyn, also "plugged" along the street, years before he'd write "Lullaby of Broadway" (1935) and "Chattanooga Choo Choo" (1941).

---

2   49–51 West 28th Street to be exact. The sons in this case were vaudeville performers themselves. Young, sprightly Julius Witmark was called "the boy soprano."

Some of these songs would be used in minstrel acts, in which blackface performers would ham it up with offensive portrayals of African Americans. But Tin Pan Alley also employed black songwriters, such as Bob Cole and Chris Smith. In 1905 the Gotham-Attucks Music Company (at 42 West 28th Street) became the first black-owned and -operated firm on the street.

Tin Pan Alley still comes alive in the imagination. It's all sweat and snapping fingers and rolled-up shirtsleeves. Stroll this hardscrabble block today and imagine it as it must have been a century ago, a frenetic place with new melodies bouncing off the lampposts and passing carriages. And behind each of these peppy tunes is a plugger hoping to attract the attention of a producer or a star in need of her next signature song.

By the early 1900s composers had started writing tunes for recorded music. While early records were scratchy and difficult to make out, the recording industry would make quick advances and Tin Pan Alley hopped on the opportunities that emerged. Publishers made exclusive deals with manufacturers; record labels were soon created. Inside these cramped townhouses on 28th Street an entire music industry was born.

An industry that, unfortunately for West 28th Street, would not stay planted here. With the rise of Times Square as America's hottest entertainment

The former Tin Pan Alley: The buildings remain, although the music has moved on.

district in the first decades of the twentieth century, the old shops of West 28th Street quickly seemed rather inconvenient and outdated. Publishers soon relocated to the streets above 42nd Street, where they were now sharing office buildings with talent agencies, casting offices, and stage production companies. Hollywood too drew songwriters, especially after the advent of talking pictures in the late 1920s.

Fifty years later another industry had blossomed along 28th Street. The city's Flower District had once adjoined Tin Pan Alley — convenient if you were buying a bouquet for a diva — and when the music publishers left, it moved onto 28th Street. It remained there until well into the 1980s.[3] Today the street is not designated as a protected historic district, and the buildings are not landmarked. Its history is in perpetual danger of being cleared away for new condos. That is, unfortunately, a sad, familiar tune.

Herald Square and Penn Station

POINTS OF INTEREST

1 THE UNSUNG LINCOLN MEMORIAL The United States Postal Service mail processing facility is nothing to write home about architecturally, but visit the northern side of the building and you'll find a moving tribute: "On this site stood, in 1861, the station of the Hudson River Railroad. The first passenger to use it was Abraham Lincoln who came to New York on February 19, 1861, on the way to his inauguration as president of the United States. His funeral train left here on April 25, 1865, for Springfield, Illinois."

When Lincoln died on April 15, 1865, assassinated by Edwin Booth's brother John (see Chapter 16), his body was taken on a mournful tour of the United States aboard a funeral train. In New York, Lincoln lay in state at City Hall as an estimated 500,000 mourners paid their respects.

---

3   A few sweet-smelling remnants of the Flower District still exist south of Sixth Avenue.

Then, on April 25, a train with Lincoln's body left from the 30th Street Station here, the depot that served the Hudson River Railroad back when the train brought passengers down the western side of Manhattan.

Turn around with the plaque behind you, and you will face another (less poignant) way that New Yorkers pay their respects today: an entrance ramp to the Lincoln Tunnel, which opened in 1937. (*West 30th Street, between Ninth and Tenth Avenues*)

2 TO THE TENDERLOIN DUNGEON! The office buildings and warehouses surrounding Herald Square offer a unique mix of architectural styles, but two will surely jump out at you: medieval Gothic Revival and ancient Mesopotamian. Take a stroll around the district, and you'll see at least a dozen otherwise somber office buildings bursting forth with unusual ornamentation—even dragons and monsters are up there! Two structures that unabashedly exhibit this sit next to each other on West 30th Street.

Going medieval: The Tenderloin police station is literally a fortress.

The building at 130 West 30th Street has the loftiest pedigree—it was designed by Cass Gilbert of Woolworth Building fame. This peculiar loft building was finished in 1928 and decorated with bizarre Assyrian reliefs, which greet visitors like the world's most expensive welcome wagon. Next door sits the so-called Tenderloin Station House, a police precinct built in 1907. Its imposing castlelike facade must have driven fear into the hearts of every no-goodnik dragged in, certain that they were headed to an iron maiden in the dungeon.[4] (*130 and 134 West 30th Street*)

3 BIRDS OF A FEATHER FLOCK TOGETHER HERE The Hotel New Yorker—today the Wyndham New Yorker—is one of the city's art deco treasures. Opened in 1930, it exuded glamour during the big band era—imagine fur-wrapped starlets arriving in limousines.

So it might seem odd that we're focusing on the death of a lonely man with a deep love of pigeons.

Of course, that man happens to be Nikola Tesla (1856–1943), the genius inventor who championed the use of alternating current (AC) for electrical power. Tesla was treated poorly during his life—by Thomas Edison, among others—and he ended his days impoverished and living here in room 3327, obsessed with the care of various pigeons. He tended to one injured bird in particular in the room and kept it in an elaborate recuperating invention that he'd designed. Tesla died on January 7, 1943. A few days later, his personal possessions were seized by the FBI, who feared that his papers contained blueprints for a secret weapon. Alas, their efforts were for the birds. (*8th Avenue and 34th Street, plaque on the 34th Street side*)

Nikola Tesla.

4   Look for the arched ceilings done by Rafael Guastavino; the next chapter will feature a slew of Guastavino ceilings!

For this section, we're going to mostly ignore today's Madison Square Garden and the modern Pennsylvania Station hiding in its basement—two highly utilized, but uninspiring mainstays of the West Side. To be fair, this MSG,

Above lovely old Pennsylvania Station...

completed in 1968, has staged legendary performances and witnessed memorable sporting events inside its massive Bundt-cake container. The tight tunnels, narrow staircases, and twisting passageways beneath the arena provide access to a bevy of trains in an unfriendly and claustrophobic environment, its most interesting feature perhaps the digital arrival board for the Long Island Railroad.

This numbing but vital rail transportation hub is New York's busiest. It replaced one of the most magnificent buildings to have ever stood in Manhattan—the original Pennsylvania Station, the defining triumph of New York's renowned architecture firm McKim, Mead, and White.[5]

...and within, under its glass canopy.

Built for the Pennsylvania Railroad, the Beaux-Arts masterpiece opened in 1910 and was possible only because of an astonishing feat—the first tunnels constructed under the Hudson River, finally connecting New Jersey with New York by rail.

The station's grandeur and majesty allowed travelers—commuters on their daily slog, tourists on their first visit—a sense of wonderment upon arrival. Marble eagles graced the exterior, and there were nods to ancient Roman baths, St. Peter's

---

5 This entire book seems to build up to this particular achievement of theirs. Indeed, neither McKim nor White lived to see Penn Station's official opening on November 27, 1910.

Basilica, the Acropolis—if it was old and big, the architects were inspired by it. The whole place—foyers, waiting rooms, platforms, staircases—were majestic and bathed in natural light.

This was the greatest train station in the United States. And yet it all came crashing down in 1963, a victim of decreased train ridership and a city lacking any serious landmark protection. However, the station's destruction wouldn't be completely in vain, for it awakened a sense of urgency among preservationists and an awareness among the general public that architectural treasures deserved some sort of protection. The station is often credited with being the martyr that saved other jewels from a similar destruction.

You can still find small traces of the old Pennsylvania Station around and in the nooks and crannies of the neighborhood itself, including these:

4 I'VE GOT THE POWER Two years before Penn Station opened its doors, a power station was built on West 31st Street to provide electricity, refrigeration, light, and heat to the new structure. The Penn Station Service Building was intentionally designed with few embellishments; it was there simply to provide support for the temple of transportation across the street. Yet its invisibility came into play when the train station was torn down in 1963. As a functional but nondescript building, they simply left it alone. Today its imposing yet standoffish facade with its barred-off windows is a bit of a curiosity: It's the engine that survived the train. (*242 West 31st Street*)

5 SAM'S PLACE Countless statues of people who are unknown to us today stand about Manhattan. Well, let Samuel Rea no longer stand in obscurity! Rea,[6] who helped direct the construction of the Hudson River tunnels, was the president of Pennsylvania Station from 1913 to 1925. This statue of Rea once stood watch over hundreds of

Samuel Rea still watches thousands of people pass him daily.

thousands of daily commuters from a niche in old Penn Station's waiting room stairwell. Rea gets to witness even more people today (now including

---

6   Pennsylvania Railroad's previous president was Alexander Cassatt, a man who doesn't need a statue. He was the subject of paintings by his more famous sister, the impressionist painter Mary Cassatt.

sports and music fans) as they stream into the Garden. (*Outside 2 Penn Plaza, at Seventh Avenue and 32nd Street*)

6 THE MIGHTY EAGLES When Penn Station was demolished, fourteen of its twenty-two prized decorative eagles were saved and scattered to the

four winds: from the Smithsonian Museum to Valley Forge. But three remained in New York City and two of them still sit on this block in front of Madison Square Garden.[7] If we were to bring them back together, Mighty Morphin Power Rangers–style, do you think a beam of light would emanate from their bodies from which the original Penn Station might emerge? It's worth a try. (*West side of Seventh Avenue between 31st and 33rd Streets*)

The station might be gone, but a couple of stone eagles still guard their old roost.

7 SPECIAL DELIVERY But the most vivid reminder of the old Pennsylvania Station is probably its reflection—the James A. Farley Post Office, also designed by McKim, Mead, and White, and opened in 1912, two years after the station. The formidable row of columns was meant to echo those of the train station across the street. It was even originally named the Pennsylvania Terminal, but later renamed after Depression-era postmaster James Farley. There are long-gestating plans to convert the mighty old post

office into a new train station. (*Eighth Avenue between West 31st and 33rd Streets*)

8 THAT QUOTE ON THE JAMES A. FARLEY POST OFFICE "Neither snow nor rain nor heat nor gloom of night stays these couriers from the swift completion of their appointed rounds" is a loose translation of the words of Herodotus, linking the US postal system to that of ancient Rome. (Gotta match the architecture after all.) But more

The post office and some cool cars, 1920.

"superhuman" were the feats of the man who carved those words into the marble: engraver Ira Schnapp (1892–1969). He would later go on to design titles for DC Comics, including the original logo

---

7   The third eagle in Manhattan? For some reason, it landed on the eighth floor of 41 Cooper Square in Astor Place, one of the futuristic buildings that comprise Cooper Union.

for Action Comics, which gave the world Superman. (*Eighth Avenue between West 31st and 33rd Streets*)

9 SCENES FROM A STATION PAST It's a nice gesture, we suppose, but it's also almost too sad to witness. Head underground into the main Amtrak and New Jersey Transit waiting area (dominated by the main departures board), and hunt around for the jumbo-size photographs of the great old station in its prime. Marvel at the beams of sunlight in every black-and-white shot…and then try not to cry when you turn around to see the modern station in all its drop-ceiling grimness. (*Main departure hall, Penn Station*)

10 READY TO WEAR The Garment District, despite its ironically drab streetscape, is still the heart of the American fashion industry. Many of its factories and wholesalers moved here from the Lower East Side and the Ladies' Mile neighborhood, and many of the early designers and much of the workforce were Jewish immigrants. While you can still find fabric, zipper, and button stores along these streets today, most of the work is done upstairs in the outwardly rather dull office towers. One glamorous building stands out

Looking good at Emery Roth's Fashion Tower.

from the rest: the Fashion Tower, completed in 1922 by Emery Roth and Sons. Look for the colorful peacocks above the doors, emblems of the Jazz Age women's fashion industry. (*135–139 West 36th Street*)

11 THE FAT LADY SINGS (Vanished) The city's old and new money worlds sat cheek-to-cheek at the original Metropolitan Opera House, which opened here in 1883. Ostensibly built to present operatic works, the Opera House also functioned as a show-and-tell for the rich, who sat arrayed in their finest outfits in 122 private loges in the theater's "golden horseshoe." (The Vanderbilts alone held five

Picture the original Metropolitan Opera House (here in 1914) in yellow, lots of yellow.

loges at one point!) Its less-acclaimed exterior was nicknamed "the yellow brick brewery," and in time its stage became outdated for modern productions. The opera moved up to its new house at Lincoln Center in 1966, and this theater was deemed an unessential relic — and demolished the next year. (*1411 Broadway*)

12 THE SKYBRIDGE OF YESTERDAY Perhaps during your walks about the city you've noticed various "traverses" high overhead, skybridges linking two buildings together from many stories up.[8] We'd gamble that the Gimbels traverse, or skybridge, is the city's most interesting and most beautiful, with its green-oxidized copper veneer. Built in 1925 for Gimbels Department Store, it linked Macy's chief retail competitor in Herald Square to its annex across the street. The bridge is actually three stories tall, and was a teeth-cutting project for young architect William F. Lamb, who would soon go on to help design the Empire State Building. Gimbels left Herald Square in 1986, but the bridge hangs around like a friendly ghost, hovering high above the busy street. (*West 32nd Street, between Sixth and Seventh Avenues*)

The ornate Gimbels skybridge gives Herald Square a little class.

13 THE HEYDAY OF THE HAYMARKET (Vanished) No Tenderloin establishment was better known — or better beloved for its bawdiness — than the Haymarket, a wild three-story dance hall that was lit up like a Broadway

---

8 We highlight one at the old Nabisco factory near the High Line. Another beautiful one connects the Metropolitan Life Insurance Company Tower with the Metropolitan North building on 24th Street, near Madison Square.

theater and named after the lively London street. In 1887 New York's chief of police described it as "animate with the licentious life of the avenue." Where do we sign up?

With bands playing and high-kicking saloon girls swirling about the dance floor, owner Edward Corey maintained that his club was always legally "aboveboard." In fact, however, those girls were most often prostitutes. Nicknamed "the prostitutes' market," the Haymarket was a veritable shopping mall for sin, where patrons would shower ladies with champagne and gifts before, commonly, making their way to curtained-off rooms in the balcony and upper floors. If you preferred male prostitutes — no problem! — just head for the back

Dance hall dames: Miriam Carson and Florence Williams.

entrance. And although the working girls and boys were strictly forbidden by the management to rob their clientele, the Haymarket nonetheless became a paradise for thievery.

Is it any wonder artistic bon vivants such as Eugene O'Neill and Stephen Crane loved hanging out here? Artist John Sloan famously painted it. The Haymarket finally closed for good in 1911, and with it went a bit of Herald Square's joie de vivre. (*66 West 30th Street, main entrance was on Sixth Avenue*)

14 THE MILLION-DOLLAR CORNER The following is not meant as an advertisement for either Macy's department store or the Sunglass Hut. This particular corner, however, is certainly already familiar to anyone who has ever watched the Macy's Thanksgiving Day Parade or watched the 1947 classic film *Miracle on 34th Street*. Look closely and you'll see the ultimate in architectural trolling.

Macy's moved up from Ladies' Mile to this corner in 1902, signaling a major shift up the island for the city's retail scene. One of the many stores that would follow Macy's lead — the grand Siegel-Cooper — actually tried to dash Macy's grandiose plans by snatching up a tiny sliver of land on the corner of Macy's property. Siegel-Cooper's gambit cost them dearly — $375,000, or more than

$10 million dollars in 2016 money. No matter; Macy's simply built around it. It still seems odd now with a sunglass outlet there, although isn't it appropriate that it's responsible for one of the city's shadiest stories? (*151 West 34th Street*)

Cutting corners: 34th Street and Broadway.

15 WHO WANTS TO SEE SOME SAD FISH? (Vanished) On behalf of aquatic life everywhere, we hope that no venue the likes of the 1876 Great New York Aquarium ever exists on this corner again. The aquarium's

centerpiece was an enormous tank fit for a whale—too bad that the whale died in transit, leaving the tank empty for its opening day. Displays for porpoises, sharks, and sea lions were scattered around the gas-lit floor, and the poor creatures swam about in small tanks with painted backgrounds featuring their native habitats. Also on display were a set of fish hatcheries—you know, for educational *porpoises*—possibly the first such nurseries ever featured in a public aquarium. The aquarium closed in 1881 and its occupants were auctioned off. Poor guys.[9] (*35th and Broadway, northwest corner*)

---

9   The real New York Aquarium would open in 1896 in old Castle Clinton. See Chapter 2.

Broadway's diagonal defiance continued to wreak havoc upon the grid system as it cut north past Sixth Avenue and 34th Street, creating two symmetrical triangular plazas. These would become home to two great newspapers of the late nineteenth century: the *New York Herald* and the *New York Tribune*. Both publications have since vanished, but their imprint remains upon this popular public plaza today.

Three's Company: Minerva on her perch, 1921.

16 FOR WHOM THE BELL TOLLS The building on the northern end of Herald Square today houses a bank and a chain drugstore. (Really, this could be said of 70 percent of the city's buildings these days.) But here once sat the publishing offices of the *New York Herald*. Its presses were at street level, and the paper's publisher, James Gordon Bennett, Jr., installed large glass windows to draw audiences to the sight of the ink literally hitting the paper. Placed high atop the building was the ornate clock that sits within the park today, attended to by a curious trio. The goddess Minerva menacingly holds a spear, while wrapped in snakes and topped with miniature horses. She's in eternal command of the two enslaved bell-ringers, sometimes nicknamed Gog and Magog, for end-of-days biblical entities.[10] They were placed within a granite monument here in 1945,

Today Minerva and her bell-ringers greet office workers on their lunch breaks.

---

10 An alternative name for the duo is Stuff and Guff. But those are just silly!

just steps from their original location. Somewhat disturbing creatures to have gonging it up across from Macy's, eh? But wait, it gets weirder.... (*35th Street and Broadway*)

17 THE OWLS ARE WATCHING YOU James Gordon Bennett, Jr., inherited the *Herald*, as well as his comfortable, lavish lifestyle, from his father. While adroit at running a newspaper, his social behaviors were a bit more erratic and brash. So much so that the early twentieth-century expletive "Gordon Bennett!" actually meant surprise or alarm. (Try yelling that today— chances are nobody will turn around.) Among other obsessions, Bennett was

particularly taken with owls.[11] He even planned to be buried within a tomb that featured a 200-foot owl, but his proposed architect, Stanford White, would be murdered before it could be designed. White did, however, design the *Herald* offices in the 1890s and included more than two dozen owls in its facade, with eyes that glowed in the dark! Today those owls grace the southern entrance to Herald Square, their eyes coldly gazing at the pedestrian rush around them. Meanwhile,

Evidence of the owlish obsession of James Gordon Bennett, Jr.

behind the massive granite monument is a doorway with an unusual etching—another owl, this one accompanied by a French expression, *La Nuit Porte Conseil* (or, Let's Sleep On It). By the way, the owl of Minerva just happens to be the emblem of the mysterious Illuminati, the shadowy all-powerful organization with alleged ties to some of the darkest and most ancient secrets. Could their headquarters be contained within this custodian's closet? (*Herald Square*)

18 GREELEY'S BIRDS Staring at all this owl nonsense from the south in Greeley Square is a statue of Horace Greeley, installed here in the 1890s. Greeley was one of New York's most influential civic leaders. As the editor of

---

11 You might recall from Chapter 9 that this obsession was shared with Florence Nightingale.

the *Tribune*, he was one of Bennett's chief competitors.[12] Unlike the theatrical diorama of Herald Square, Greeley's image is rather casual, even a little sleepy. He counters those pesky owls with a set of eagles at the square's northern entrance, inspired by the birds on Greeley's own newspaper masthead. (*Greeley Square, Broadway between 32nd and 33rd Streets*)

19 THE CHURCH OF MANDA THE CAT The Church of the Transfiguration is the embodiment of a pleasant sigh, an 1849 country chapel that today is crowded, but never suffocated, by skyscrapers. Part of the charm of

the "Little Church Around the Corner" comes from its lychgate, a covered entrance that has welcomed those on the fringes of society during the direst of moments. African American New Yorkers found peace here during the Civil War draft riots of 1863, and starting

Saint of all cats: The mysterious Manda marker.

in the 1870s the church gained another nickname, the "Actors Church," for its acceptance of those in the theatrical community, many of whom were turned away by other churches, who found the profession to be immoral. Among the church's many mysteries is a memorial in its courtyard to a feline named Manda, who delighted parishioners during the Great Depression. (*1 East 29th Street*)

---

12 Both Greeley and Bennett might have been displeased to learn that their newspapers merged into the *New York Herald Tribune* after their deaths.

The Icons: Empire State Building

The opening of the Empire State Building in 1931 signaled a new era for New York City. It also signaled the end of old New York. It was built to be the best— or at least the tallest. It put an end to the quest for ultimate height in New

York; skyscrapers would blossom like daffodils (or multiply like weeds), but they'd never approach its height until the construction of the World Trade Center, nearly four decades later.

But that's not the only reason that the Empire State Building has become a New York icon. Its prominence is due to a number of traditions, circumstances, and ambitions that went into its conception and design. As an object of commerce and a symbol of defiance in the face of the Depression, its history can also be told by its numbers:

400 — The number of people who could allegedly fit into Mrs. Caroline Schermer-horn Astor's private ballroom (although many people believe that the number was a

Empire State of Mind: New York's most famous skyscraper in 1940 (courtesy MCNY).

much more modest 319). In **1862** she and husband, William Backhouse Astor, Jr., built an opulent mansion here at 350 Fifth Avenue, a northern outpost at the time for somebody so wealthy and the very spot on which the Empire State Building would later rise. Mrs. Astor's nephew William Waldorf Astor, with whom she regularly disagreed, later moved next door.

13 — The number of floors of the Waldorf Hotel, built in **1893** upon the site of William Waldorf Astor's former mansion, to the consternation of Caroline, who still lived next door. Hotelier George Boldt had been encouraged by his wife to build 13 floors; evidently she thought it a lucky number. By **1897** Mrs. Astor had moved out and their mansion was replaced with a companion hotel, the Astoria, built by her son John Jacob Astor IV. Together the Waldorf-Astoria epitomized luxury and fine dining, and became the most famous hotel in New York.

1,046 — The height of the Chrysler Building (in feet) upon its completion on **May 20, 1930**, when the rise of its antenna made it the tallest skyscraper in the world and the king of the New York skyline.

$200 — The price per square foot to purchase the Waldorf-Astoria property in **1929**. A group of investors, led by former New York governor Al Smith, envisioned constructing a more profitable skyscraper for this block.

$50 million — The projected cost of the new skyscraper — called the Empire State Building from the start — as announced by Smith at a press conference on **August 29, 1929**. It now had a lavish budget, a lofty name, and a former governor giving it some gravitas.

$14 billion — The amount of money lost on the stock market on **October 29, 1929**, "Black Tuesday," capping off days of market plunges and leading to the Great Depression. It was a terrible time to be constructing a grand skyscraper, and yet construction began soon thereafter, on March 17, 1930.

410 — The number of days that passed from the start of the Empire State's construction to the moment it surpassed the Chrysler Building as the world's tallest at 1,250 feet (or 1,454 feet from the tip of its antenna).[13] The sleek, sturdy structure, designed by William F. Lamb, steadily rose at a rate of about four-and-a-half stories a week, thanks to the diligence of 3,400 construction workers. It also came in way under budget—at just under $41 million. It officially opened on **May 1, 1931**.

A worker diligently laboring on the Empire State Building (photo: Lewis Hine).

200 — The size of the mooring mast in feet, easily the largest such device, used for the docking of dirigibles. Alas, the brisk winds at that height prevented any airship dockings from occurring.

56 — The number of floors, out of 102, in **1933** that were still unrented and sat completely empty. The Great Depression initially stole the thunder of the stellar skyscraper, and owners struggled to fill the hundreds of offices in the so-called "Empty State Building." Fortunately, by the following decade, nearly every office had been rented. In 1942 one occupant on the fourteenth floor was Timely Comics, the progenitor to Marvel Comics.

14 — The number of fatalities that occurred on **July 28, 1945**, when a B-25 bomber on its way to Newark Airport swerved off course, meandered over the foggy city, and smashed into the Empire State Building. Eight people working in the Catholic War Relief Office on the building's seventy-ninth floor were killed. An elevator operator named Betty Lou Oliver plummeted seventy-five stories inside an elevator car and managed to survive.

10118 — The Empire State Building's dedicated zip code, which it received in **1980**.

1,860 — the number of steps from the ground floor to the 102nd floor. Each year 1,576 of those — up to the 82nd floor — are climbed by athletes during the Run-Up race.

---

13 It held that title until the early 1970s with the completion of the World Trade Center.

NEW GRAND CENTRAL:
AN ENGINEERING MARVEL[1]

If twenty or even fifteen years ago some person had prophesied that in 1912 New York Central Railroad trains in the heart of New York would be operated far below the level of the earth to the number of 1,200 daily, that 70,000 outbound

An early sketch of the terminal, with almost no tall buildings north of it!

passengers alone could easily be handled each day, and that for a distance of twenty blocks railroad trains would run 100 feet or more below skyscrapers erected by the company operating the railroad system, he would quite probably have been regarded as a visionary, as were Cyrus W. Field when he first suggested the feasibility of laying the Atlantic cable, Alexander Graham Bell when he invented the telephone, Marconi when from the ether he caught the idea of wireless telegraphy, and hosts of other men whose inventions are considered indispensable throughout the world today.

With the rapid approach of the completion of the main station, or Grand Central Terminal, as it is to be known, of the New York Central and Hudson River Railroad which with other improvements in progress is to cost the sum of $180,000,000 culminates the chief section of one of the most remarkable illustrations of civil engineering in the world. In many ways it is more wonderful than the construction of the Panama Canal.

---

1   From the *New York Sun*, May 12, 1912.

Chapter 18///

Midtown East and Turtle Bay:

40th Street to 60th Street, from Madison Avenue to the East River

The little old shack of Anne Morgan, daughter of J. P. Morgan, on Sutton Place (photo: Berenice Abbott).

SITUATE THE READER
—Midtown East and Turtle Bay—

The Beekmans were among New York's oldest families, tracing their lineage to Dutch immigrant Wilhelmus Beekman, who arrived at the settlement of New Amsterdam in 1647. By 1765 his great-grandson James Beekman had built a majestic house overlooking the East River (at around today's East 51st Street and First Avenue), naming it Mount Pleasant. The house, we must assume, contained much pleasantness.

Alas, it was short-lived, for by the late nineteenth century, a mass of slums stretched from the Lower East Side all the way up the river. The Beekman home was but a genteel memory by the 1880s, the waterfront and blocks east of the tracks of the New York Central Railroad mostly given over to industry and working-class housing. Turtle Bay, an idyllic cove during the British era, had become one of New York's most polluted neighborhoods by the turn of the twentieth century, a morass of slaughterhouses, breweries, and, eventually, an Edison power plant.

When Grand Central Terminal was redeveloped in 1913, its old above-ground tracks were buried and covered by a new grand boulevard, optimistically named Park Avenue, and with it billions of dollars in new real estate appeared, just in time for the boom of Midtown Manhattan in the 1920s.

A more unusual force—an early sort of gentrification—arrived that decade with the development of exclusive family mansions for various Morgans and Vanderbilts on Sutton Place, which again took advantage of that commanding view. The elegant Turtle Bay Garden Colony rose in the 1920s out of a row of deteriorating tenements, their festive new faces drawing in movie stars and socialites alike. But it wasn't until the completion of the United Nations Headquarters in 1952 that a new identity for the neighborhood was forged and pleasantry, now of the diplomatic kind, returned to the old Beekman property.

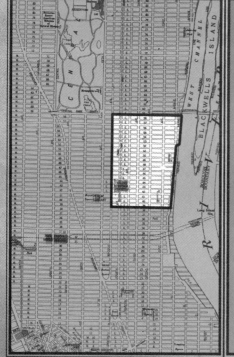

SOUTH PLAZA

E. 59 58 57

E. 56 E. 55 E. 54

PARK · FOURTH AVE. · THIRD AVE. · SECOND AVE. · FIRST AVE.

E. 53 52 51 50 49 48 47 46 45 44 43 42 41

FIFTH AVE. · MADISON AVE.

VANDERBILT AVE.

MA
GRAND CENTRAL TERMINAL

Bryant Park

BEEKMAN

PIERHEAD

BULKHEAD

6 9 7 8 4 5 11 1 2 3 10 12 13 14 15

POINTS OF INTEREST

1 The Regal Elegance of Old Goat Hill

2 The World Within

3 The Greatest Trick a Skyscraper Ever Pulled

4 The Magic Mirror

5 Rage Against the Machine

6 Read This Quote

7 The Other Chrysler Building

8 Park Avenue Pastiche

9 Stand Here

10 Vanderbilt the Stranded

11 Sex Secrets of the United Nations

12 The Ambassador of Music

13 The Boar of Sutton Place

14 Beauty Under the Bridge

15 Still Smokin'

MA Grand Central Terminal

The Constellations of Grand Central

Cornelius Vanderbilt, the king of ferries, railroads, and muttonchops.

Grand Central Terminal[2] might very well be the most important building in modern New York City history. Thanks to several canny decisions made over the course of a few decades, a dirty, sooty old train yard was transformed into the richest couple of blocks on the planet, figuratively molding modern Midtown out of wads of cash. The terminal itself is not only an icon of architecture and engineering, but of perseverance, so treasured by the public even the US Supreme Court would chime in to defend it.

So it should come as no surprise that strolling into its cavernous Main Concourse today, you can look up and see the heavens themselves, constellations twinkling upon a slightly sickly looking green atmosphere—it's like peering through a film negative of the universe.

Grand Central Depot was situated near a grazing pasture.

The original idea for the ceiling was a massive skylight like you might find in other train stations of the day; however, it was dismissed as too obvious. Why not bring a virtual sky to the concourse instead? The muralist J. Monroe Hewlett worked from renderings by the French belle epoque painter Paul César Helleu to create Grand Central's constellations out of 2,500 stars—from the Zodiac signs Aquarius and Gemini to the unmistakable Orion and Pegasus—each brought to life through the magic

---

2   The phrase "Grand Central Station" lives on in popular parlance as a metaphor for a bustling place, but the current structure is an actual "terminal," as trains start and end their journeys here. Except for the subways that run underneath it. Well, we suppose you could call that subway stop a "station." Grand Central Terminal Station?

of gold leaf and small light bulbs. The mural, first conceived in 1912, was intended to remind commuters of the simpler days of travel, of navigating before electricity, before steam, before Vanderbilt.[3]

In the early days of the railroad, small, independent train lines connected cities across the American landscape like the lines linking stars within a constellation. They were eventually united by Cornelius Vanderbilt (1794–1877), called simply "the Commodore," who had masterfully built his transportation empire from steam ferries all the way to interstate railroads. He consolidated regional railroads in the northeast, and by 1869 his New York Central Railroad controlled both rail lines into Manhattan—the Hudson River line, used mostly for freight, and the New York and Harlem Railroad for passenger travel.[4]

Model train: The first electric locomotive heads to Grand Central, pulling by the High Bridge (see Chapter 25) in 1906.

The Commodore lived to see the construction of Grand Central Depot here in 1871, a lovely if more modest prototype of today's building. This location, 42nd Street and Fourth Avenue, meant that the depot was far enough north of town at the time to avoid causing too many accidents—streets here were

---

3   In no way is the astronomical work accurate. In several places the universe has been rendered backward.
4   This would become a special frustration for his main competitor, Pennsylvania Railroad, and the reason they would dig tunnels under the Hudson River. (See Chapter 17.)

much less crowded, after all, and cows grazed in a pasture nearby. The tracks north of Grand Central along Fourth Avenue (later renamed Park Avenue) were dangerous to those cows and other street traffic, as they were sunken into a fissure and occasionally dotted with pedestrian bridges at intersections. On overcast days it looked like a river of soot and smoke.

Commodore Vanderbilt's children and grandchildren would ride the railroad into the age of electricity with the help of New York Central Railroad's master engineer, William Wilgus (1865–1949). By the early 1900s the tracks north of the station had been entirely covered and the depot was enlarged into a six-floor station (thus making it Grand Central Station), but the railroad's reliance on steam power created increasingly dangerous conditions. Under Wilgus, trains were converted to electric power by 1906, and the New York Central was given a massive new home—Grand Central Terminal, instantly hailed an architectural and engineering masterpiece[5] when it was completed and officially opened on February 2, 1913.[6]

The Main Concourse, 125 feet tall, buzzes with a cacophony of commuters, tourists, and Apple Store customers.

---

5 Three wonderful examples of drastically different architectural styles sit within mere blocks of each other: Grand Central (Beaux Arts), Chrysler Building (art deco), and the United Nations Headquarters (International Style).

6 The terminal was built in stages, from 1903 to 1913, and the station remained opened throughout the construction.

Designed by two firms—Reed and Stern, and Warren and Wetmore[7]—the terminal was a public space tricked out with upscale attractions, like a basement restaurant lined with Guastavino tile and an expensive Tiffany timepiece at the center of the concourse.

The electric trains, the state-of-the-art terminal—these were not even Wilgus's greatest claim to fame. That would be his ability to produce something incredibly valuable out of thin air. With the train tracks now buried north of the station along a new boulevard that stretched to the northern end of the island, an enormous new real estate opportunity opened up just as the city was swimming in cash. The area would attract wealth day and night—from the new office towers in the blocks north of the terminal to the elegant apartments farther uptown, and in a period when Times Square, the rising entertainment capital, was booming just west of here.

It was all new—and it was all right here in Midtown. A universe inside a train terminal doesn't seem so unusual now, does it? Unfortunately, the virtual heavens didn't get to enjoy their view for very long. The plaster began leaking in the 1920s, and specks of the universe started flaking off onto passengers below. In 1944 the entire ceiling was recovered in new tiles embroidered with a close approximation of the original constellation work.

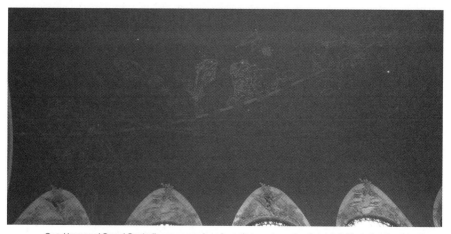

Good heavens! Grand Central's concourse is so busy that most passing through fail to notice the stars above.

By the 1950s, this new, lesser constellation gazed down upon a shrinking railroad industry, one that had been gravely affected by the suburban boom,

7 Both were connected to the Vanderbilts by either blood or marriage. This is how things were done in the Gilded Age. And, mostly, today too.

increased automobile usage, and the exploding costs of maintaining a network of train tracks. By 1968, the now-combined Penn Central Transportation Company had already thuggishly demolished the old Pennsylvania Station and was looking to wipe away costly and increasingly obsolete Grand Central as well, drooling over the development possibilities that would soon be theirs. Fortunately, the New York City Landmark Preservation Commission swooped in to block the bulldozers, granting the structure landmark status and kicking off a massive court battle between Penn Central and the commission. Bolstered by the participation of prominent activists, including Jacqueline Kennedy Onassis, and a public sentiment still stinging from the loss of Penn Station, the fight to save Grand Central went all the way to the Supreme Court in 1978. The justices ruled in favor of the landmark commission, and Grand Central Terminal, stars and all, was saved.

Today's Grand Central is in fabulous shape, despite the shadow of the Met Life Tower behind it. The ceiling, nicotine stained by decades of smoking commuters, was almost completely cleaned and restored in the 1990s. Almost, but not quite entirely, for a single blackened and uncleaned square was left behind in the northwest corner of the cosmos to remind those gazing up of just how far we've come.

Midtown East and Turtle Bay

POINTS OF INTEREST

1 THE REGAL ELEGANCE OF OLD GOAT HILL New housing developments make history, even as they wipe it away. It happens today, and it was certainly also true in the 1920s. Take Tudor City, for example, the beautiful if exaggerated Elizabethan housing complex that's perched high over the East River at East 40th–43rd Streets. Each of the development's 15 apartment buildings is garbed in flamboyant English drag; it might all seem rather outlandish in a more central location. Considered one of the great building projects of the late 1920s, this cluster of Shakespearean goofiness is so tucked away that few take notice of it.

More than 150 years ago, this elevation was called Goat Hill, named not merely for the animals that grazed here, but also for its disadvantaged poor, who raised them in a shantytown here. It was later known for its Irish population and called "Corcoran's Roost" after its rowdy community leader, Jimmy Corcoran (1819–1900), all of which makes developer Fred French's decision in the 1920s to turn it into a ritzy, English-themed upscale apartment complex especially unusual, if lucrative. (*North Park, East 43rd Street and Tudor City Place*)

The Chrysler Building, seen from a perch in Tudor City, 1935. (Courtesy of MCNY.)

2 THE WORLD WITHIN Tudor City, the Chrysler Building, and many other 42nd Street treasures came about because of the extraordinary ambition and imagination that fueled the late 1920s. Architecture of this era, like the music and literature of the time, embodied the Jazz Age, when traditional forms of art and architecture were fearlessly reconceived. The Daily News Building, built in 1929 and 1930 by Raymond Hood and John Mead Howells, is a stunning display of art deco theatricality, even more postured than the Chrysler, down the block.

The limestone frieze over the door, populated with busy figures, is a work of art. But you don't come to look at the walls! The famous indoor 12-foot globe,

the largest in the world, has slowly kept turning since 1930. Above and below, radiating outward from the floor and ceiling, are facts about astronomy and the locations of distant cities. (*220 East 42nd Street*)

The world revolves around (and within) The Daily News Building.

3 THE GREATEST TRICK A SKY-SCRAPER EVER PULLED Stand across the street from the Chrysler Building—any corner, just look up—and stare at that magnificent spire, that art deco top hat that graces one of the craziest, kitschiest, and most beloved buildings in New York City. It's the first moments of a romance, it's drama and comedy, it's champagne by the glass. (It makes us type crazy things like the previous sentence!)

But that spire? That's the dirtiest trick an architect ever played.

Sneaky spire: The evolution of the Chrysler Building's design.

The Chrysler Building, designed by the great William Van Alen (1883–1954), was completed in 1930 as both a literal and figurative showroom for Walter P. Chrysler's motor company.[8] Keep in mind that at that date automobiles were still relative newcomers to city streets, having made their debut just over a couple of decades before. Now look at the Chrysler, with its details that clearly evoke shiny automobile features, their grills, glass, and hubcaps shooting straight into the sky. Imagine a skyscraper today built as a tribute to Google or Facebook, festooned with artistically rendered computer screens and Wi-Fi signs from every floor. This was the Chrysler, sparkling with silver hood ornaments and radiator caps, a piece of beauty—and of promotion.

The spire was a last-minute addition, and it put the Chrysler in the history books. Locked in a heated competition with the builders of 40 Wall Street to become the world's tallest building, Van Alen decided to add an additional bauble to his tall drink of water. In another great moment of architectural trolling,[9] on October 23, 1929, a custom-built 185-foot spire was quickly affixed atop the Chrysler Building—in just 90 minutes. It took people several days to realize that Van Alen's little surprise accessory had now made the Chrysler the world's tallest building, at 1,046 feet.[10] (*405 Lexington Avenue*)

4 THE MAGIC MIRROR There are few serene spaces in Midtown East and fewer still that feel like the courtyard of *Sleeping Beauty*'s Maleficent, a place where you're free to gaze at yourself while cackling with insane laughter. While Amster Yard traces back to an eighteenth-century stage-coach stop, it's named for interior decorator James Amster, who laid out this quiet haven in 1944, to the delight of his artist friends. The idea for its most entrancing feature was provided by another iconic decorator, Elsie de Wolfe[11]—a large mirror at the end, which appears to open a portal into a parallel

Mirror, mirror in the alley, in charming Amster Yard we dally.

---

8 For many years, vehicles on revolving platforms graced the ground floor.
9 For another, see Macy's versus the Sunglass Hut, in Chapter 17.
10 It held that title for almost a year before the Empire State Building handily beat it in 1931.
11 She was the resident of the faux Washington Irving house near Gramercy Park.

dimension. Today the property is maintained by Instituto Cervantes, but you can pop in during business hours to visit the mirror…and cackle wildly. (*211 East 49th Street*)

5 RAGE AGAINST THE MACHINE (Vanished) The Civil War draft riots, a series of violent protests from July 13 to 16, 1863, were among the gravest and most tumultuous events in the city's history during the nineteenth century.[12] An army draft office at this corner is often considered to be the starting point of the riots. Led by some members of the volunteer fire department, protesters burned down the office here on the morning of July 13 and almost killed the superintendent of police, John Kennedy. (*East 46th Street and Third Avenue*)

6 THAT QUOTE ON THE TOWNHOUSE AT 124 EAST 55TH STREET "She Who Must Be Obeyed" is technically a quote from the 1887 novel *She* by H. Rider Haggard. ("I did not at all like the accounts of this mysterious Queen, 'She-who-must-be-obeyed,' or more shortly She….") So why is it here? The building once belonged to Donald L. Taffner, a television

In Eleanor's squad: A stern sign on East 55th Street with a lovable backstory.

producer who imported British programs, including *Rumpole of the Bailey*, whose main character, Horace Rumpole, stole that line to refer to his wife, Hilda. Eleanor was the name of Taffner's wife, which explains why it's also labeled "Eleanor's Building." Eleanor passed away in 2010, Donald in 2011, but the signs remain in their memory. (*124 East 55th Street*)

7 THE OTHER CHRYSLER BUILDING 570 Lexington has much of the flash and glamour of the Chrysler Building, but little of the fame. This is mainly the fault of Rockefeller Center. The Lexington building, designed by Cross and Cross, was built in 1931 with RCA in mind as a tenant, but the company got wooed away with an offer to occupy the central building of Rockefeller's massive project a few blocks west instead. So General Electric moved in—but they too, in 1988, would move to Rockefeller Center. (Sigh. Always the Jan Brady to Rockefeller Center's Marsha!)

---

12 See Chapter 20 (Hell's Kitchen) for more information.

This Lexington jewel accomplishes two difficult feats with panache. Its particular hue and hints of Byzantine design make it a perfect companion for its neighbor, St. Bartholomew's Church (see below). But the fanciful lightning bolts and electric rays that erupt periodically from the surface demonstrate true art deco literalness. So maybe Google and Facebook should move in *here*? (*570 Lexington Avenue*)

Give it time: The old General Electric building on Lexington Avenue is armed with kooky details.

8 PARK AVENUE PASTICHE If the tracks of the New York Central Railroad weren't covered up until the early 1900s, then where did St. Bartholomew's Episcopal Church come from? Its triple arched entranceways and famed bronze doors — cast by the hottest artists of the day — were built in 1902 and 1903 for St. Bart's at its former location on 44th Street and Fifth Avenue. They were moved to this new church by its opening in 1918, not merely because they were beautiful, but also as a tribute to parishioner Cornelius Vanderbilt II, the Commodore's grandson.

Not that the congregation has always resisted change. With the development of air rights along Park Avenue, St. Bart's tried to get in on the action in 1981, planning a 59-story glass skyscraper on the south side of its property. But plans were blocked by the Landmark Preservation Society, who had granted the structure landmark status in 1967. The church argued the millions made from rents on the

A study in contrasts: Art deco 570 Lexington looms over Byzantine Revival St. Bart's.

project could have helped the poor. And what's one more glass skyscraper, right? (*325 Park Avenue*)

9 STAND HERE: The plaza in front of the Seagram Building (375 Park Avenue, between 52nd and 53rd Streets). *Why?* A perfect sort of historical equilibrium can be experienced at this spot, with eras colliding to illustrate the various phases of Park Avenue's history. Old New York gives way to new New York here.

On the footprint of today's Seagram Building stood, back in 1860, a "piano forte finishing factory" owned by Steinway and Sons, its front door facing

the busy street-level railroad tracks of the New York Central Railroad. By the 1910s those tracks had been buried, which ushered in a boom of new construction in the area, including the Racquet and Tennis Club, still across the street from this spot.

Both the club and St. Bartholomew's are the remaining nontowering holdouts on a street that was later transformed by the selling off of air rights, which sent buildings hurtling toward the sky. The Seagram Building, which opened in 1958, inspired another Midtown innovation: plaza setbacks. The building's architect, Ludwig Mies van der Rohe, worked with the available open space to create

The Seagram Building: Park Avenue's tall, cool glass of modernism since 1958.

a slender monolith. Its glamour is echoed in an earlier building just a block up — the classy-and-glassy Lever House (390 Park Avenue), which brought International Style to Park Avenue when it opened in 1952.

Seagram (you know them for their booze) and Lever (you know them for their soap) are brands in the same way Chrysler and Woolworth are, but you won't find their products festooned upon their facades. Instead these structures are magnificent examples of the sleek glass-curtained International Style; the look is chill and austere. Unfortunately, the skyscrapers that appear up and down the block fail to inspire in the same way the Seagram and the Lever do. A glass curtain eats up the space above the racquet club, just as farther south the

MetLife hangs ominously over the Helmsley Building (built as the New York Central Building in 1929). Alas, how quickly they got bigger—and blander.

10 VANDERBILT THE STRANDED Cornelius Vanderbilt is one of the great tycoons of American history and a man instrumental in the development of New York. All of this is undisputed. He was also a monopolist—as was common with so many wealthy men of the Gilded Age—and a robber baron to boot. In 1859, the *New York Times* described him as one of "those old German barons who, from their eyries along the Rhine, swooped down upon the commerce of the noble river and wrung tribute from every passenger that floated by."

Vanderbilt was not bashful either. Atop St. John's Terminal, his train station in lower Manhattan,[13] the Commodore erected a frieze in 1869 that gave a statue

of himself center stage. That terminal was later torn down, but Vanderbilt's likeness was moved to a perch atop Grand Central. Today he stands in front of the Terminal's southern exterior, glaring down at the Park Avenue Viaduct, the elevated automobile roadway that surrounds the station. Keep in mind that Vanderbilt, the mogul of ferry and rail who died in 1877, never saw an automobile in his life. (*42nd Street and Park Avenue*)

Disturbed: Vanderbilt's statue moved from a quiet marble niche to a busy traffic island.

11 SEX SECRETS OF THE UNITED NATIONS After briefly shacking up temporarily (from 1946 to 1951) in Flushing, Queens, on the campus of the 1939–1940 World's Fair, the newly formed United Nations finally arrived in Midtown at their permanent home after much lobbying on the part of city bigwigs like Parks Commissioner Robert Moses and Governor Nelson Rockefeller. Their headquarters—the central Secretariat Building, completed in 1952—was designed by a consortium of International Style architects, led by Le Corbusier. Compared with the whimsy of the Chrysler Building and the grandeur of Grand Central, the UN headquarters is like an intellectual smoking a cigarette, a pensive and sleek little smarty-pants.

Several politically charged sculptures can be seen from outside the gates. One sculpture, however, is discreetly hidden. Near the northern side, camouflaged

---

13 In the former St. John's Park. See Chapter 6 for more information.

in shrubbery, sits a bronze African elephant by sculptor Mihail Simeonov, cast from an actual drugged elephant. Why is it not more prominently displayed? Dignitaries were aghast at its unveiling in 1998 when they noticed the male animal's sexual organ was rather, um, prominent in appearance. "The sheer size of this creature humbles us," said Secretary-General Kofi Annan at its dedication, referring to the animal's overall appearance, of course. (*First Avenue and 48th Street*)

12 THE AMBASSADOR OF MUSIC For a truly international scavenger hunt, nothing beats seeking out the UN missions and consulates along the side streets of Turtle Bay. Some countries took over old brownstones while others built new homes, often in the 1960s and '70s. But we've identified our favorite of them all: the Consulate General of Luxembourg. Their home on Beekman Place, built in 1929, was the home of songwriting legend Irving Berlin for more than 40 years.[14] The year after the composer died in 1989 — at age 101 — the Grand Duchy of Luxembourg purchased Berlin's home for use as their consulate. Buying a place of such profound inspiration for your UN offices seems like such a very *Luxembourgian* thing to do, don't you think? (*17 Beekman Place*)

Puttin' on the Ritz: The appropriately stylish Consulate General of Luxembourg.

---

14 While living here, Mr. Berlin wrote the music to such classic shows as *There's No Business Like Show Business* and *Annie Get Your Gun*.

13 THE BOAR OF SUTTON PLACE Vanderbilts did more than dictate the fate of Park Avenue; they changed the fate of a little street called Sutton Place. Anne Harriman Vanderbilt—along with other society mavens—had mansions built there in 1920, quickly turning it into a pocket colony for the wealthy. "You have to be way up in *Who's Who* to gain admission into this selected settlement," explained the *New York Evening World* in 1921.

So why does the little park tucked into proper little Sutton Place contain a garish bronze sculpture of a boar sitting next to a hideous frog-eating snake? Even the boar has a pedigree! It's a copy of Pietro Tacca's *Porcellino* from Florence, Italy, installed here in 1972.[15] Given the neighborhood's history with abattoirs and stockyards, we can't help but think that it was placed here as a bloody homage. (*Sutton Place South and 57th Street*)

Never boar-ing. It's just like out of a scene from a Woody Allen movie!

---

15 You may also know this particular park from a famous scene from the 1979 Woody Allen movie, *Manhattan*.

Is it the Ed Koch Queensboro Bridge or the 59th Street Bridge? It's both!

After constructing three bridges to Brooklyn, city planners decided it was high time to link Manhattan with the new borough of Queens. By 1909, the year the Queensboro Bridge was completed, Times Square and Grand Central were Midtown magnets, quickly raising the profile of the entire neighborhood. But the bridge didn't just bring people to Midtown; by the 1920s Queens was experiencing a population boom of its own. The bridge even made an appearance in that decade's most famous book, *The Great Gatsby*, "The city seen from the Queensboro Bridge is always the city seen for the first time, in its first wild promise of all the mystery and beauty in the world." Its allure unfolds in its spectacular design by Henry Hornbostel and Gustav Lindenthal, and along a couple of historic points on the Manhattan side:

Amazing mosaic: A touching memorial from husband to wife, 1919.

14 BEAUTY UNDER THE BRIDGE At the start of World War I, New York's grocery stores were facing some shortages. To fend off rising food prices, the city did something rather extraordinary: It opened its own direct food markets (or "open markets"), which cut out the middleman entirely. One such market was built under the new bridge, beneath the beautifully tiled ceilings designed by Rafael Guastavino (who was also working wonders in the Oyster Bar in Grand Central). The Guastavino ceilings are still there, as is the 1919 mosaic mural and ornate fountain dedicated to the memory of civic leader Evangeline Blashfield and created by her sculptor husband Edwin Howland Blashfield. (*59th Street, between First Avenue and Sutton Place*)

15 STILL SMOKIN' A solitary smokestack has stood guard over the bridge for most of its existence, a vestige of the New York Steam Heating and Power Company (incorporated in 1879),[16] an ancestor of Con Edison. The stack is a fitting reminder of the neighborhood's industrial past. It also marks a sudden change in the cultural landscape of the East Side. Or to quote a 1939 guide book, "At Sixtieth Street Sutton Place passes under the Queensboro Bridge and into the more plebeian world of York Avenue." (*59th Street and Sutton Place*)

Echoes of industry: Travelers along the bridge have grown familiar with the old steam company's smokestack.

---

16 It merged with the New York Steam Company a couple years later and helped popularize steam heat by the 1880s.

The Mysteries of Roosevelt Island

Roosevelt Island runs parallel to Manhattan like its "mini-me," a shadow island where New Yorkers live in smaller skyscrapers and have their own smaller landmarks. Alas, if only that were really the case with this island's peculiar history. It would make that tram ride even more delightful! The real story is far less amusing. For this was once Blackwell's Island, the dreaded destination of some of New York's most terrifying and depressing health and correctional institutions of the nineteenth century.

Had Robert Blackwell, the eighteenth-century owner of the island, realized what his name would come to represent, he would have fled this cursed rock immediately. By the 1830s, New York had begun to turn Blackwell's Island into a "city of asylums," a network of vital institutions deemed too unpleasant or too dangerous to be near the city. Situated in a row were a lunatic asylum, a workhouse, an almshouse, a penitentiary, and a smallpox hospital (later turned into a charity hospital).

Today there are six locations on the island where glimpses of this bleak but important history still exist:

The Blackwell Island Lighthouse Built in 1872, this lighthouse assisted ships as they navigated the treacherous waters of the East River. Legends abound about the lighthouse, including suggestions that it was constructed by patients from the nearby lunatic asylum.

Ruins of James Renwick's haunting and beautiful smallpox hospital cling to the island to this day.

The Octagon New "lunatic" patients were sometimes brought into the asylum via the Octagon Tower, which opened in 1839. Two wings of patients' quarters and treatment rooms emanated from this central chamber. Today the Octagon has been transformed into luxury apartments, although the spiraling staircase that patients once climbed still exists![17]

---

17 Intrepid reporter Nellie Bly didn't much like it here when she checked in as a patient in 1887 for a now-famous exposé on the facility's wretched conditions.

Chapel of the Good Shepherd Given all the suffering and strife on the island, a little blessed relief was provided by this Episcopal church, built in 1888. It originally served the poor and elderly occupants of the nearby almshouse.

The Blackwell House Here sits the 1796 home of the Blackwell family, the oldest structure on the island. The home was a later addition to the family's holdings, which included a "Barn, Bake and Fowl House, a Cyder Mill, a large orchard, stone quarries and running springs."[18]

Strecker Memorial Laboratory Disease anyone? The many medical institutions that remain on the island today trace back to research facilities like this unusual rock-faced lab, built in 1892 for pathological and bacteriological research. It closed in the 1950s and remains a most intriguing reminder of the island's medical importance.

The Smallpox Hospital, or "Renwick Ruin" Perhaps the island's best-known object of mystery is the crumbling ruin of the 1856 hospital designed by James Renwick, Jr.[19] It's a rather astonishing example of a historic structure frozen in a

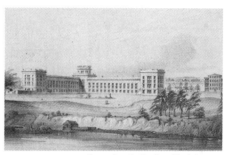

Unnerving destination: The infamous "lunatic asylum," pictured in 1861, gave Blackwell Island a very bad reputation.

state of decay. At night drivers along Manhattan's FDR Drive can observe the ruin, all lit up like something from the set of *Dracula*.

In 1921 the island's name was changed to Welfare Island—why sugarcoat it any further?—then changed again to Roosevelt Island in 1973 in anticipation of an expected monumental outdoor tribute to Franklin D. Roosevelt, designed by Louis Kahn. That monument—Four Freedoms Park—did finally arrive, almost four decades later, in 2012.

Today, Roosevelt Island is one of our favorite places in New York City. It holds one secret that often goes untouted: an unbelievable view of Manhattan, either from a strolling path along the water or from a compartment of the Roosevelt Island Tramway.

---

18 From a letter written by later descendant James Blackwell in 1784.
19 Also the architect for St. Patrick's Cathedral in Midtown and St. Bartholomew's Church, mentioned earlier in this chapter.

THE NAMING OF TIMES SQUARE

By the action of the Board of Aldermen, made effective yesterday by the signature of the Mayor, the open space formed by the intersection of Broadway and Seventh Avenue, and extending from Forty-Second to Forty-Seventh Street, hitherto popularly known as "Long Acre Square," received the name of Times Square.

Very likely the name would have been conferred by speech of people without official action. The action of the city authorities gives legal sanction to the name Times Square. It is a name that serves perfectly for identification and is one, we think, not likely to be forgotten in this community.

~ From the *New York Times*, **April 9, 1904**

Times Square and Rockefeller Center:

40th Street to 60th Street, from Fifth Avenue to Eighth Avenue

Your garden variety paradise: Rockefeller Center sits on the footprint of the long-forgotten Elgin Botanical Garden.

SITUATE THE READER
-Times Square and Rockefeller Center-

There once was an idyllic garden where Rockefeller Center is now planted.[1] The Elgin Botanical Garden, "the pride of New Yorkers of that day,"[2] was the first of its kind in America, planted in the early 1800s by Dr. David Hosack, best known as the physician who treated the gunshot wound that afflicted Alexander Hamilton during his fateful 1804 duel. Hosack was so passionate about his garden that he wildly overspent on it, and by 1814 its "flora exotica" had outgrown its environs and become something of a mysterious mess. The land was sold off to the state, who then handed it over to Columbia University, who managed to live off the real estate profits from the property (referred to as the "Upper Estate") for more than a century.

Columbia moved its campus from the City Hall area to one block east of this Upper Estate in the 1850s, a location it would call home for more than 40 years. Columbia's students were just a quick walk to New York's horse-and-carriage district, Longacre Square, named after a similar business district in London. The tumult of blacksmiths and carpenters, coachbuilders and tanners filled the wide plaza and surrounding streets at Broadway, Seventh Avenue, and 42nd Street.

But by the 1890s those who plied the carriage trade could see change galloping up Broadway from Herald Square — theater and other popular forms of entertainment were on the move north. For many years after Longacre Square changed its name to Times Square, descendants of the transportation trade — the first automobile dealerships — could be found on the side streets here, remnants of an earlier romantic (and aromatic) era of horses and hansom cabs.

---

1   47th to 51st Streets and Fifth Avenue to Sixth Avenue
2   From *The Elgin Botanic Garden, Its Later History and Relation to Columbia College*, 1908.

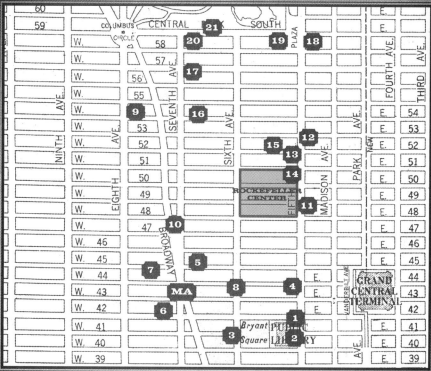

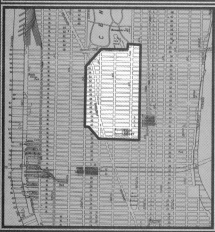

POINTS OF INTEREST

1 The Real Kings of the Book

2 Reservations About the Reservoir

3 What Lies Beneath (and Once Above!)

4 The Ugly Mob

5 The Oldest Girl on the Block

6 The Circle of Life

7 New York's Classiest Alley

8 "Be Sure to See the Hippodrome"

9 Television Disco Inferno

10 Stand Here

11 Awesome Sign Alert

12 The Abortion Queen

13 The Fifth Avenue Fancies

14 The Quiet Princess of St. Pat's

15 The Street of Jazz and Jockeys

16 The Club Kids

17 Midtown's Artsy Block

18 The Gleaming Cube

19 The Champagne Porch

20 The Crowned Salamander,
or the Building That Went Insane

21 Read This Quote

MA One Times Square

Poor Little One Times Square, Crossroads of the World

Almost nobody knows what the building at the crossroads of the world really looks like.

Few can describe the original appearance of the building that features centrally in the city's biggest party of the year. Its name is never included in New York's top ten most visited structures, despite its prominent placement in millions of photographs snapped by tourists. And despite sitting at one of the busiest intersections in the world, almost no one works inside the thing.

Such is the curious fate of One Times Square, the humble, disfigured building at the center of modern New York City.

Times Square in 1908, with nary an Elmo or Naked Cowboy in sight. The large building (right) is the Hotel Astor. The car dealership Garford appears on the left.

At the dawn of the twentieth century, the thrust of New York's growth had already ventured past 42nd Street, and splendid new mansions stretched up Fifth Avenue to St. Patrick's Cathedral at 50th Street and beyond. Longacre Square to its west served up carriage, saddle, and harness shops, which was convenient, given its proximity to the American Horse Exchange[3] on 50th and Broadway.

But a new force was steadily high kicking its way up Broadway — the musical theater district, which by the turn of the century was situated primarily along Broadway, between Herald Square and Longacre Square. The first theater jumped the 42nd Street frontier in 1895,[4] ensuring the district's theatrical legacy up to today.

It is Grand Central to the east along 42nd Street, however, that's to thank for bringing the city's new subway system to Longacre Square. Because of the valuable properties lining Broadway between Union Square and Herald Square — from Ladies' Mile shops to luxury hotels — landowners objected to messy subway tunnels being dug up under their street. So instead, the first subway line was pushed east of here, up Fourth Avenue (today's Park Avenue) to Grand Central on 42nd Street. It would then cut west to Broadway (at Longacre Square) before continuing uptown under Broadway. This decision would essentially define 42nd Street as one of New York's most important roads.

All this excitement would pique the curiosity of young Adolph Ochs, who in 1896 had become the new publisher of the *New York Times*. While their offices were down on Park Row with many of the city's other dailies (along "Newspaper Row," which faced City Hall), publications were getting larger, outgrowing their offices and printing facilities, and readers were steadily moving uptown. The *New York Herald* had moved offices to 34th and Broadway in 1894, a gamble that turned out to be so successful that the plaza would eventually be named for it. Certainly the same could be done for the *Times* at the next major intersection up Broadway?

One problem: Another building already occupied the triangular plot of land at 42nd Street and Broadway. In fact, it had *just* been built in 1899 — the Pabst

---

3   Owned, of course, by a Vanderbilt: Cornelius's grandson William.
4   The Olympia Theatre, operated by Oscar Hammerstein I, which opened on Thanksgiving 1895 with a show called *Excelsior Jr.* by Robert Ayres Barnet.

Building, a nine-story "modern steel skyscraper." Ah, but that's not an issue if you got the money. *Get rid of it!* And so the Pabst Building goes down in history as the first skyscraper ever dismantled, in this case, by the George A. Fuller Company.[5]

The architect Cyrus L. W. Eidlitz, no stranger to Beaux-Arts frillery, leaned heavily on the Italian Renaissance in his design for the new Times building, creating the impression that one was standing next to a Venetian palazzo, except, of course, that his building was much taller and more out of proportion

One Times Square today: A flashy, hi-tech mash-up of electronic advertisements has replaced its original beauty.

than almost anything you'd find in Venice. And at its feet lay the new 42nd Street subway station. Upon its completion in 1904, the twenty-five-story building became the second-tallest building in the world, after Joseph Pulitzer's New York World Building downtown.[6]

Both the new office building and the newly named plaza in front of it—Times Square—were feted by a massive fireworks celebration at midnight on December 31, 1904. The building's narrow silhouette overlooking such a large open plaza made it a natural and picturesque spot for such a party; however, the ash that dropped from the fireworks upon the 200,000 people crammed into the square was less pleasant, and city officials banned the fiery practice two years later. Looking for a new and less dangerous way to signal the stroke of midnight, Ochs turned to the "ball drop," an old English maritime time-keeping tradition developed to help ships accurately set their navigational chronometers. The newspaper hired Strauss Signs to use electricity to light one hundred 25-watt bulbs on a giant "electric ball," which during the last minute of 1907 "fell in accordance with the prearranged plan," the newspaper noted on January 1, 1908.

5   The Fuller Company would soon build a triangular-shaped building for themselves in 1902—the Flatiron Building.
6   See Chapter 5.

By then, Times Square had become the hottest destination in town, brimming with champagne and lobster palaces,[7] Ziegfeld showgirls, and that most glamorous and clever invention, the electronic sign. Ochs's newspaper quickly outgrew its wedge-shaped headquarters and in 1913 moved to nearby offices at 229 West 43rd Street. But they still owned the old triangular building, and in 1928, slapped something on there that would change the look of Times Square forever: an electronic news zipper, or as they called it, a "Motogram"—a 5-foot-tall message board that used more than 14,000 light bulbs to create a ribbon of information scrolling across the front of the building, illuminating the day's headlines. The fate of One Times Square had been sealed. It would not only wear an electronic sash from here on out, but it would soon be completely covered by electronic knickknacks.

The Motogram announced the results of the 1928 election (Hoover won), although probably its most well-known bit of "breaking news" was many years later when it triumphantly announced the surrender of Japan, ending World War II.[8] Other elaborate advertisements soon clung to its surface, and have included everything from stock quotes to a steamy Nissin Cup Noodles advertisement affixed in 1996. In 1961 the Times sold the building to Allied Chemical, which promptly replaced its splendid Beaux-Arts facade with futuristic white marble. But hey, who could even see it?

It's a truly weird concept if you stop to think about it. Every year, millions of people gaze at One Times Square on their televisions during the annual New Year's Eve celebrations, momentarily breaking their gaze from TV host Ryan Seacrest to focus on a shimmering ball that (in some form) has lowered nearly every year since 1907.[9] The building has become so synonymous with celebrations and electronic razzle-dazzle that the structure supporting the party is literally superficial; there are no tenants in its upper floors, and its windows are completely blocked today by giant LED billboards. To say history has been stripped from One Times Square is an understatement. The years have turned this glorious building—responsible for the very name of Times Square—into the architectural equivalent of a mannequin, sporting the latest in electronic fashions...and the most famous headgear in town.

---

7   Lobster palaces like Rector's and Murray's Roman Gardens set the table for Times Square's tourists restaurants today, with their lavish dining rooms, late hours, and partylike atmospheres.
8   It was on August 14, 1945, that Alfred Eisenstaedt's iconic "V-J Day in Times Square" photo, depicting a sailor kissing a woman in a white dress, was taken.
9   Except for two years during World War II.

Times Square

NEW YORK PUBLIC LIBRARY (STEPHEN A. SCHWARZMAN BUILDING)

The cavernous and marble-lined hallways, foyers, and grand staircases of the most famous modern library building in the world echo other great monumental structures, even St. Peter's Basilica in Rome—as though architects Carrère and Hastings had constructed a house of worship for millions of volumes when it was completed in 1911. From its rare maps to its sequestered trove of ancient manuscripts, the New York Public Library is the city's brain, a combined intellectual and archival powerhouse. But it's not just the books and documents that are loaded with breathless tales, for the building next to Bryant Park holds a few stories of its own.

1 THE REAL KINGS OF THE BOOKS The two resolute lions who sit at the entrance of the New York Public Library—named, like precious Park Slope children today, Patience and Fortitude—are rendered in pink Tennessee marble, bestowing upon the institution a sense of permanence.

The library's gorgeous facade in 1907, its lions not yet protecting its front steps.

But the real lions, the real foundations of the library, are chiseled along the top of the building: Astor, Lenox, and Tilden. Before the founding of the New York Public Library in 1895, library collections in the city were privately owned by wealthy residents, who opened their doors only to select visitors. The John Jacob Astor Library[10] was the most impressive book collection in town, but struggled financially, as did the collection of wealthy bookworm James Lenox. Samuel J. Tilden, a former governor of New York and very nearly the president of the United States in 1876, died in 1886[11] and left his fortune to the creation of a public library. These initial collections—stirred together with the financial muscle of Andrew Carnegie[12]—created New York's first public library system.

As for the marble lions, they will leap from their perch and dismember you if you garner too many late book fees. (*Fifth Avenue and 42nd Street*)

2 RESERVATIONS ABOUT THE RESERVOIR (Vanished) The fountains bubbling forth on the library's Fifth Avenue side are a fitting reminder that a whole hell of a lot of water was long ago stored on this spot. The library, you see, sits upon the footprint of the old Murray Hill Reservoir, a mammoth Egyptian-style reservoir that held 20,000,000 gallons of the city's drinking water.[13] Finished in 1842, the reservoir became a popular date spot, as visitors could stroll its perimeter, at ground level or way

One last drink: The Murray Hill Reservoir in 1900, before demolition.

up along its upper edge, taking in the views of the growing city and of the water that would later flow into their homes. It was dismantled beginning in 1898 to make way for the library; however, an inspection of the lower levels will reveal a bit of the reservoir's original stone foundations. (*Fifth Avenue and 42nd Street*)

---

10 Its original building off Astor Place is today home to the Public Theater.
11 His home in Gramercy Park is the National Arts Club today.
12 Carnegie poured $5.2 million into building dozens of branch libraries throughout Manhattan, Staten Island, and the Bronx. He later funded branches for the separate library systems in Brooklyn and Queens.
13 The reservoir was a critical part of the Croton Aqueduct system and also called the Croton Distributing Reservoir. We'll dive in further in Chapter 25.

3 WHAT LIES BENEATH (AND ONCE ABOVE!) Spacious, formally lovely Bryant Park is named for famed poet and newspaper editor William Cullen Bryant (1794–1878), who sits at the eastern end of the park, looking out over the lawn as though trying to find a word that rhymes with "fabulous." The park is indeed once again fabulous today, finally, after decades of deterioration and renovation.

The Crystal Palace burned to the ground in just thirty terrifying minutes on October 5, 1858.

Bryant stares over a lawn that holds two incredible secrets. In 1853 the grounds were home to the New York Crystal Palace, a magical world's fair, housed in an immense glass-and-steel steampunk castle that brought together dazzling inventions (including the elevator) and a superb collection of sculptures and paintings to the New York public. It was America's stage for technology and invention, a celebration of an industrious new age—until it burned to the ground on October 5, 1858.

Today an equally impressive collection sits below the park—120,000 square feet of library shelving, accommodating more than 3.2 million books. This makes Bryant Park the smartest park in the universe. (*Sixth Avenue between 40th and 42nd Streets*)

4 THE UGLY MOB (Vanished) And now for a depressing reminder of the ugly powers of mob mentality. On Monday, July 13, 1863, the first violent day of the Civil War draft riots that rocked the city, an angry, racist throng swarmed the Colored Orphan Asylum, which stood at this site and burned it down. From *Harper's Weekly* the following week: "Hundreds, and perhaps thousands of the rioters, the majority of whom were women and children, entered the premises, and in the most excited and violent manner they ransacked and plundered the building from cellar to garret....There is now scarcely one brick left upon another of the Orphan Asylum."[14] (*West side of Fifth Avenue between 43rd and 44th Streets*)

The Colored Orphan Asylum in 1861.

BROADWAY AND THE THEATER DISTRICT

Broadway is both a busy thoroughfare and a category of theatrical production. More important, it is a benchmark for the American theater, not only in price, but in production standards. Musical shows and revues were already big business by 1895, when Oscar Hammerstein I built the first playhouse above 42nd Street—the Olympia at Broadway and 44th Street. By the time this district became Times Square a decade later, the industry had transformed itself into a lucrative cultural force, thanks to powerful promoters and theatrical innovations. The theater district is having one of its greatest moments today, a great revival that's playing out on stages packed along

14 Chapter 20 will have more about the Civil War draft riots.

the side streets just west of Times Square. Most of these are among the oldest structures still standing in Times Square.

The Lyceum Theatre's greatest hits have included *Born Yesterday*, *Steel Magnolias*, and *"Master Harold" ... and the Boys.*

5 THE OLDEST GIRL ON THE BLOCK The Lyceum Theatre is the oldest continuously operating Broadway theater,[15] high kicking its doors open on November 3, 1903, with everybody's favorite play, *The Proud Prince* (starring E. H. Sothern, later to be known for his Shakespearean roles). The Lyceum's striking row of columns and undulating marquee have welcomed millions of theatergoers over the years. It's been a Shubert house since 1950. (*149 West 45th Street*)

The New Amsterdam in 1914.

6 THE CIRCLE OF LIFE We wish we could say that Peter Stuyvesant once thumped across the stage of the New Amsterdam Theatre, as it is named for the company town he so vociferously defended. Alas, it opened much more recently, in 1903. One of Broadway's narrower stages, it's also one of its best known, thanks to the many years of *Ziegfeld Follies*, which delighted audiences here from 1913 to 1927. During the 1970s it descended into a home for grindhouse and porn films, just one of many along this stretch of 42nd Street, which was converted for these less dignified purposes. Prince Charming came

15 The New Amsterdam is actually older than the Lyceum but closed for a few decades to get her beauty sleep.

to the rescue in 1997, when Disney swooped in to clean up its acts, and make it their 42nd Street playhouse. (*214 West 42nd Street*)

7 NEW YORK'S CLASSIEST ALLEY Consider Shubert Alley a private little Times Square just for theater folk. This alley is named for the Shubert

brothers, Sam, Lee, and Jacob — since the 1920s, theirs has been the management company most responsible for the creation of Broadway's biggest hit shows. And that's not just because one of the theaters along the alley is the Shubert. The powerful producers

Shubert Alley: Where dreams are made (or not).

Lee and J. J. Shubert had offices in the Shubert and Booth theaters that overlooked the alley; hopeful actors would gather outside with résumés, headshots, and dreams. (*Cutting between West 44th and West 45th Streets, Seventh and Eighth Avenues*)

8 "BE SURE TO SEE THE HIPPODROME" (Vanished) The massive Hippodrome was no mere Broadway theater. It was like Madison Square Garden as it might appear in your wildest dreams: a 5,300 seat, jumbo-size

The New York Hippodrome once featured Harry Houdini making a 10,000-pound elephant disappear.

theatrical behemoth that opened in 1905 equipped with, among many other fanciful features, an aquatic tank that emerged from the stage for water ballets. A typical show included an international music extravaganza called "Around the World," which featured elaborate production numbers set in Egypt, Constantinople, Venice, India, Ireland, and the islands of Hawaii (well before they joined the United States). Unfortunately, the Great Depression killed ticket sales and it closed in 1939. The glass office tower that stands here today is respectfully called the Hippodrome Building. (*1120 Sixth Avenue, between West 43rd and West 44th Streets*)

9 TELEVISION DISCO INFERNO A number of today's biggest Broadway stages actually survived the middle of the twentieth century as television sound studios.[16] Several theaters are, in fact, more important to the beginnings of the early TV industry than they are to theater history. This theater on West 54th Street was built in 1927 as an opera house, only to immediately hear the fat lady sing and shutter. CBS then took over the space, producing radio shows here and, later, some of its most beloved early television programs from the 1940s to the early '70s, including *Captain Kangaroo, To Tell the Truth*, and *The $64,000 Question*.[17] In the 1970s the space was again transformed, this time into Studio 54, one of New York's most infamous nightclubs. Disco dancers snorted cocaine where the Captain and Mr. Moose once talked about Ping-Pong balls! It only recently returned to staging theatrical productions, thanks to a massive restoration by new owners, the Roundabout Theater, in 1998. They still call it Studio 54, and traces of its glamorous past can still be found. (*254 West 54th Street*)

10 STAND HERE In front of the George M. Cohan statue at the southern end of Father Duffy Square (between 45th and 47th Streets), just north of Times Square. *Why?* Cohan (1878–1942) was Broadway's leading showman, a virtuoso performer and producer, as important to the enduring popularity of the Broadway musical as the inventor of the jazz hand. His statue overlooks Times Square from his perch on triangular Father Duffy Square,[18] and comes be-sashed with some of his biggest tunes, including "Over There" (1917) and "Yankee Doodle Boy" (1904).

---

16 The Ed Sullivan Theater, home to *The Late Show with Stephen Colbert*, is perhaps the most-beloved holdout to this particular sort of transition.
17 A television show best known for the part it played in the notorious quiz show scandals of the 1950s.
18 More on Father Duffy in Chapter 20.

But if Cohan could come to life and hop down from his pedestal, would he recognize anything in today's Times Square? The electronic signage engulfing the square obscures any view of the buildings underneath. Old structures, some with notable architectural features, have become mere supports for the dazzling LED advertisements that blanket them. The sight might be enough to scare the showman silly; however, he'd find comfort in the many familiar Broadway theaters that line the side streets—many that were there in his time, including the Richard Rodgers (opened as Chanin's 46th Street Theater in 1926) down the street.

Cohan wrote his biggest hit, "Yankee Doodle Boy," in 1904 for the musical *Little Johnny Jones*.

But if he needed some real revival, you'd just need to drag him across the way to I. Miller's shoe store, to the left of Cohan at Broadway and 46th Street, with its 1929 statues of beloved film actresses Mary Pickford and Rosa Ponselle, and two stage beauties Cohan would know quite well: fellow stage stars Ethel Barrymore and Marilyn Miller. (*West 46th Street and Broadway*)

11 AWESOME SIGN ALERT Astride the glorious 1894 headquarters and bookstore for publisher Charles Scribner's Sons you'll spot a large, attractive sign—"Charles Scribner's Sons, Publishers and Booksellers, Founded 1846"— that makes you want to run in and give somebody your manuscript. Unfortunately, it's a cosmetics store now, so they might turn you away (or just give you a makeover). Among the visages pressed into medallions over the storefront are those of iconic printers like Benjamin Franklin and the O.G.: Johannes Gutenberg. (*597 Fifth Avenue*)

12 THE ABORTION QUEEN (Vanished) Here sat the sublime five-story home of perhaps the most notorious woman of nineteenth-century New York: Madame Restell, America's leading abortionist. Its location, close to the rising St. Patrick's Cathedral, was an intentional and defiant decision by Mrs. Restell. But this is also the place where Madame, following an arrest and incarceration

Madame Restell, depicted menacingly in an 1847 *Police Gazette*.

in the Tombs,[19] killed herself on April 1, 1878, cutting her own throat in the bathtub. (*Northeast corner of Fifth Avenue and 52nd Street*)

13 THE FIFTH AVENUE FANCIES Oh, what would the turn-of-the-century Fifth Avenue doyennes think of their grand avenue today? Those ladies with plumed hats and diamond brooches, with husbands who created vast monopolies (while often breaking up union rallies and exploiting child labor). In the early twentieth century, this avenue was a dense concentration of mansions and ritzy townhouses, stretching from its base at Washington Square all the way up into the Upper East Side. By the 1920s, most of the preposterously large mansions (including those of the Astors at 34th and the Vanderbilts' "Triple Palace" at 52nd) had already been demolished to make room for high-end retail establishments and luxurious hotels. But some of the more "modest" homes were simply converted into shops. What an affront! Clutch the pearls! Once the home of gadabout and professional heir Robert Goelet (1841–1899) (not to be confused with dashing star of stage and screen Robert *Goulet*), 647 Fifth Avenue is now home to the silk-patterned treasures of Versace. Interesting that Goelet died in Italy. Coincidence? (*647 Fifth Avenue, between 51st and 52nd Streets*)

14 THE QUIET PRINCESS OF ST. PAT'S St. Patrick's Cathedral, a favorite of popes and tourists alike, defines Midtown in an unusual way.

It took decades to complete — from placing the cornerstone in 1858 to the finishing touches on its eastern section in 1900 — and its construction took place during periods of swelling anti-immigrant (read: anti-Irish and anti-Catholic) sentiments. Yet St. Patrick's helped define the culture of Fifth Avenue too as a beacon of godliness that seemed to condone the lifestyle of the wealthy residents surrounding it. In the early twentieth century, as the mansions gave way to upscale stores, St. Pat's became Fifth Avenue's elder statesman.

St. Pat's Cathedral took forever but was worth the wait.

---

19 See Chapter 6 for more information on the Tombs.

Inside its splendid sanctuary are chapels and niches populated by a host of saints. St. Patrick's is so filled with hallowed and sacred figures that even its 9,200-pound bronze door gets in on the act. Here you will see depictions of Frances X. Cabrini (1850–1917) and Mother Ann Seton (1774–1821).[20] But if we're allowed to have a favorite saint, it would have to be Saint Kateri Tekakwitha (1656–1680), a Native American woman captured in a state of ecstasy at the bottom of the door.

Tekakwitha was an Algonquin-Mohawk who converted to Catholicism as a teenager; it's said her body was cleansed of its smallpox scars at the moment of her death.

Walk through that doorway, past the sanctuary to the entrance of the crypt to view one of St. Patrick's most intriguing guests of honor: the Venerable Pierre Toussaint, the first

St. Patrick's bronze door gives praise to an unconventional saint.

nonordained person ever interred in this resting place for bishops. (See Chapter 8 for more information on this fascinating man.) (*Fifth Avenue, between East 50th and 51st Streets*)

15 THE STREET OF JAZZ AND JOCKEYS Virtually nothing remains of the moody blocks of West 52nd Street, which not long ago percolated with the rhythms and heat of late-night jazz music. From the end of Prohibition

Aces: The legendary "21" Club is a throwback to the days of three-martini lunches.

---

20 Her home is mentioned in Chapter 2.

until Midtown's 1950s office building boom, 52nd Street was the heart of the city's jazz scene, lined with neon-lit nightclubs with hepcat names: The Onyx, The Famous Door, Club Downbeat, 3 Deuces. "Swing Street" stretched from Fifth to Seventh Avenue, offering nightly audiences of cigarette-puffing, gimlet-swilling aficionados the world's greatest jazz musicians.

And yet the only "club" that remains from this line of legendary nightclubs is one with relatively little jazz in its history—the 21 Club, home to an unusual collection of lawn jockeys beckoning you to enter (or run away, depending on your opinion of lawn jockeys). Two more extraordinary collections await inside: the famous toys and pop culture objects dangling from the ceiling in the bar (including gifts from Presidents John F. Kennedy and Bill Clinton) and the divine assortment of wines in the legendary cellar. Unsurprisingly, "21" has been a private lair for the rich and famous since Prohibition. (*21 West 52nd Street*)

16 THE CLUB KIDS (Vanished) Texas Guinan was New York's most infamous Prohibition-era provocateur, an entertainer and entrepreneur whose brass and sass infused her speakeasies. In 1920 she opened the 300 Club on

The sassy and saucy Texas Guinan, film star and speakeasy queen.

54th Street, conveniently compact enough to force her 40 fan dancers— occasionally accompanied by George Gershwin on piano—to dance in the aisles quite close to those tippling the bar's illegal sauce. Texas was always on hand to greet customers with her signature slogans: "Hello, suckers! Come on in and leave your wallet on the bar!" and "Give the little ladies a great big hand!" The 300 Club has long since dried up, but at least the hotel standing in its place today has a cocktail bar. (*151 West 54th Street*)

17 MIDTOWN'S ARTSY BLOCK While today the art scene is hopping downtown in Chelsea, for many years New York's hottest art district was actually in Midtown, along West 57th Street. Andrew Carnegie's Music Hall— only later signage call it "Carnegie Hall"—is world renowned for its musical performances, but its studio apartments in the adjoining tower have housed thousands of artists, composers, and writers since its construction in the 1890s. Two additional towers exclusively for artists exist nearby: the landmarked Studio Building (130 West 57th Street, 1908) and the Rodin Studios (200 West 57th Street, 1916–1917), named for sculptor Auguste Rodin. One reason for this creative concentration of residents? The building across the street from the Rodin Studios is the American Fine Arts Building, home since 1892 to one of America's greatest arts institutions, the Art Students League. (*881 Seventh Avenue and locations along 57th Street*)

Carnegie Hall hosted more than music. Pictured here, the 1908 New York State Republican Convention.

18 THE GLEAMING CUBE On May 19, 2006, New York met one of its newest tourist attractions: the Apple Cube, the city's "smallest skyscraper," a

32-foot-tall glass enclosure in the plaza of the General Motors Building along Fifth Avenue, which beckons crowds to its subterranean retail store. But what stood here before the Apple Cube? It started as the Savoy Hotel in 1890, then was replaced in 1927 with the slightly more elegant Savoy-Plaza, where the city's most celebrated folks were known to sometimes check in with someone other than their spouse. It was also home to New York's most infamous library — film producer

The borg have landed: Apple's most famous New York store is more than a decade old.

Adolph Zukor's curious collection in his 22nd-floor apartment. Thousands of notable books, every one of them a fake…except for the phone book. They tore the hotel down in 1964 to make way for the GM Building and its dreary plaza, now enlivened by the glassiest act in town. (*Fifth Avenue, between 58th and 59th Streets*)

19 THE CHAMPAGNE PORCH One imagines, standing in the illustrious Grand Army Plaza at the southeast corner of Central Park (stretching from 58th to 60th Streets on Fifth Avenue), that it was created in tandem with the famously ritzy Plaza Hotel across the street. However, some of the square's most celebrated features predate the hotel, such as its gold-leafed statue of General Sherman, standing north of 59th Street. This stretch of Fifth Avenue was nothing but indulgently large mansions in the late nineteenth century, and this was the carriage entrance into Central Park.[21]

Pop the cork! The Plaza's former champagne porch brought high society and chorus girls together.

---

21 The Soldiers' and Sailors' Monument on the Upper West Side was originally slated to sit at the southeast corner of the park.

The Plaza Hotel, designed by Henry Hardenbergh and completed in 1907,[22] quickly became a favorite for high society parties and those seeking high-profile accommodations (famous guests over the years would range from Enrico Caruso to the Beatles). The hotel's eastern side, facing Grand Army Plaza with its gilded awning, was not the Plaza's main entrance in 1907, but rather a "champagne porch," where chorus girls and robber barons could enjoy music and sip bubbly in style. Prohibition killed off the champagne porch, and it's been the hotel's photogenic entrance ever since. The Plaza underwent a high-profile refurbishment from 2005 to 2008, during which many of its hotel rooms were converted into private condos for the super-rich. Today the Plaza operates as a hotel–luxury condo hybrid. (*Grand Army Plaza, Fifth Avenue and 59th Street*)

20 THE CROWNED SALAMANDER, OR THE BUILDING THAT WENT INSANE There is only one word that can accurately describe Alwyn Court: "bonkers." Completed in 1909, it's the Beaux-Arts version of your eccentric aunt, or perhaps an over-the-top cake that the baker couldn't stop frosting. Of the many luxury apartments built south of Central Park, this is the most ostentatious. The architects, Harde and Short, went to town with an

Fit for a king: The excessive terra-cotta madness of Alwyn Court, built in 1909.

22 The architect's other major New York treasure, the Dakota apartments on the Upper West Side, is like a smaller prototype of the Plaza.

explosion of terra-cotta in the French Renaissance style. The overwhelming facade even features salamanders, the emblem of French king Francis I, crawling all over it. Call it all "too much," but the decoration saved the building from destruction when other apartment houses (such as the regal Navarro Flats, once located a block away) were demolished to make way for larger buildings. In 1966, the Alwyn Court was among the first buildings to be landmarked by the city. The salamanders saved the day. (*180 West 58th Street*)

21 **THAT QUOTE ON THE HAMPSHIRE HOUSE** "Dedicated to Yesterday's Charm and Tomorrow's Convenience 1937" is from the very glamorous New York interior decorator Dorothy Draper, who designed the whole place in exchange for her apartment there. Another of her bon mots: "Never look back, except for an occasional glance, look ahead and plan for the future." (*150 Central Park South*)

The Icons: Rockefeller Center
Tells Its Own Story

Rockefeller Center was planned as an upper-crust entertainment palace, but it would wind up a commercial hub for the masses, funded by the philanthropic son of America's greatest oil monopolist. This mostly uniform ensemble of Depression-era office towers means something different to everyone who views it; Rockefeller Center is a busy subway station, it's the Rockettes at Radio City, it's home to the Christmas tree, it's the place where they broadcast *Saturday Night Live*. While its 22 acres of skyscrapers, public spaces, and pedestrian tunnels have a particular nostalgic charm—call it post-*Metropolis* art deco—the complex embodies almost 200 years of history, intentional or not, from almost every corner.

Live from New York: The RCA Building in 1935 (photo: Berenice Abbott).

1 THEN: The real story starts on this spot in 1801 as the Elgin Botanical Garden, a lifelong project of Dr. David Hosack that featured hundreds of American plants located inside three buildings on 20 acres.

TODAY: The Fifth Avenue entrance to Rockefeller Center continues Hosack's tradition more than 125 years later with the planting of the Channel Gardens, a sumptuous grove of fountains and flowers, populated with whimsical sea

The buildings lining the Channel Gardens are topped with gardens as well.

nymphs. One of the planters honors the memory of Hosack, a "citizen of the world." The gardens get their name from their location—between the British Building and La Maison Francaise. (Get it?)

2 THEN: In 1810 Hosack sold off his gardens to the state, which promptly deeded the land to Columbia College. They soon chopped up the property (calling it the "Upper Estate") and leased it out to dozens of tenants. Columbia would eventually move its campus close by at East 49th Street and Madison Avenue.

TODAY: The sliced-and-diced Hosack property became a headache in the 1930s to Rockefeller and investors, as they went millions of dollars over budget to piece (most of) it back together. Think of today's complex not as solid blocks of office buildings, but rather as hunks of cheese with corners nibbled off by stubborn mice.

Paul Manship's golden Prometheus statue heats things up near the ice rink.

Even today, the touch of Columbia is evident. Rockefeller Center feels a bit like a college campus, a world unto itself. It even has its own cheerleading squad (the Radio City Rockettes) and a mascot (Prometheus, hanging out at the skating rink)!

3 THEN: By the 1880s, an elevated train line rumbled up and down Sixth Avenue. While Ladies' Mile made do with this calamitous soot machine, the Upper Estate was less enthusiastic about its presence, and businesses below the tracks were often associated with less respectable endeavors, even vice. The whole thing was torn down by 1939.

TODAY: The IRT Sixth Avenue Elevated wasn't demolished until many years after most of Rockefeller Center had been completed. Radio City Music Hall, which opened in 1932, actually faced into the tracks. Today you can imagine where the elevated train once ran by looking at Radio City's Sixth Avenue marquee.

The entrance to 10 Rockefeller Plaza features a blockbuster lobby mural depicting the history of transportation

Radio City Music Hall (above); the transportation mural at 10 Rock (below).

painted by Dean Cornwell in 1946, a far more heavenly experience than the subway station rumbling far beneath it today.

4 THEN: The Metropolitan Opera, displeased with their hideous brick "brewery" of an opera house at 39th Street,[23] beseeched their boxholders to build them a new home. The idea intrigued John D. Rockefeller, Jr., enough to purchase the present lots in the late 1920s at great cost. But after the stock market crash of 1929, Rockefeller changed course, instead envisioning a colossal retail and office concourse.

TODAY: Although opera never came to Rockefeller Center, the entertainment industry would still dominate the complex, as its principal tenant became the Radio Corporation of America (RCA), and two of its other chief developments included Radio City Music Hall and the RKO Roxy Theatre (1230 Sixth Avenue, at 49th Street), both operated by impresario Samuel "Roxy" Rothafel. Opening in 1932, Radio City would prevail, becoming Midtown's most recognizable performance venue. The RKO Roxy, on the other hand, was demolished in 1954, the only Rock Center building to come down.

5 THEN: J. D. Rockefeller, Jr., a devout Baptist, might have been the towering figure during the construction of Rockefeller Center, but it was a family affair. His ambitious son Nelson Rockefeller became the project's principal adviser, and John's wife, Abby Aldrich Rockefeller, dictated many of the Center's finest artistic embellishments.

TODAY: It would be a stretch to say Rockefeller's religious beliefs were imprinted upon the building, but there is a surprising amount of Christian symbolism to be found, in itself a playful wink to its neighbor, St. Patrick's Cathedral. Mosaic angels sweep through the loggia of 250 Sixth Avenue, Saint Francis of Assisi feeds birds at 9 West 50th Street, and the Bible verse from Isaiah 2:4 is explicitly called out in a gilded carving above the doorway at 19 West 50th Street.

Lee Lawrie's "Atlas" is often associated with Ayn Rand.

Abby's particular (some might say "subversive") tastes in art were reflected throughout, most notably in the handsome depiction of Atlas at 630 Fifth Avenue. For years people thought it looked like Benito Mussolini. Abby would be able to more freely express her artistic vision nearby at the Museum of Modern Art (1929), which she helped found with other art lovers.

---

23 See Chapter 17 on Herald Square.

The *New York Tribune*, an excerpt from the article "Hell's Kitchen Passes," September 7, 1919:

"The neighborhood has all gone t'hell," said the flagman, as he soulfully waved a freight train past Thirty-ninth Street on its way down Eleventh Avenue. The flagman said that his name was Danny. Being a bachelor, he said, his last name hadn't been spread about much. He laughed and showed both his teeth.

"Yip," he reflected, "there ain't much to this neighborhood any more. We had one killin' last year, and that was a mistake."

Thirty-ninth Street and Eleventh Avenue, where the flagman bemoaned the decay of the community, was the sink of Hell's Kitchen.

"It was interestin' here before the place cleared out," he said, ruminatively. "There was always somethin' cookin' in Hell's Kitchen. I remember the time, right in the middle of the street, when One Lung Curran bet he could take a cop's coat home to his dame—an' he did. She made some kind of a military coat for herself and soon all the dames on Eleventh Avenue were wearin' 'em. They would send out their guys to get 'em cops' coats to show that their love wasn't dead."

Hell's Kitchen and Columbus Circle: 40th Street to 60th Street, from Eighth Avenue to the Hudson River

High and low: McGraw-Hill Building in 1935, Ninth Avenue Elevated station at its feet (photo: Berenice Abbott).

SITUATE THE READER
–Hell's Kitchen and Columbus Circle–

"Hell's Kitchen" is too good a name for a neighborhood to have just one origin story. Newspapers in 1881 used the name to describe a particular tenement on 39th Street[1] where all manner of misdeeds and squalor were frequently reported. The vice that filled the Tenderloin district just south of here swiftly spread north in the late nineteenth century, as did affordable housing, mostly for African Americans and newly arrived Irish and German immigrants. Life was tough on these western outskirts. Another legend has it that a cop named Dutch Fred coined the term when he remarked upon patrolling the area, "Hell's a mild climate. This is Hell's Kitchen." The devilish slur applied to the rampant crime overwhelming the slums along the West Side, but it could have also referred to the far western streets and avenues themselves, with their jagged piers and the dangerous street-level Hudson River Railroad.

Most New Yorkers in the mid-twentieth century knew Hell's Kitchen for its star attraction: Madison Square Garden, which moved up from Madison Square to Eighth Avenue, between 49th and 50th Streets, in 1925. In the 1950s Puerto Rican immigrants began to join the neighborhood's Irish working class, pushing back against a growing criminal underworld that reigned well into the 1980s.

Today the Hell's Kitchen of the Marvel superhero Daredevil—the blind rogue who swings from tenements while stamping out organized crime—is mostly gone, as rent hikes, rezoning, and the Times Square cleanup of the 1990s have made it distinctly unhellish.

---

1   553 West 39th Street, an address (perhaps intentionally) eradicated by the Lincoln Tunnel.

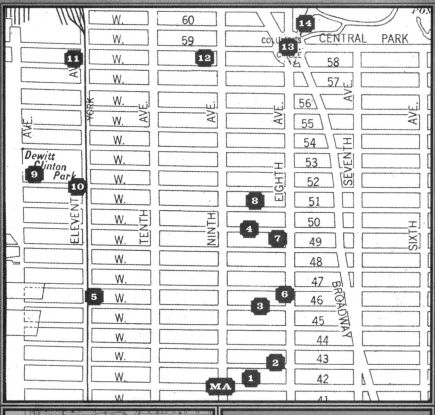

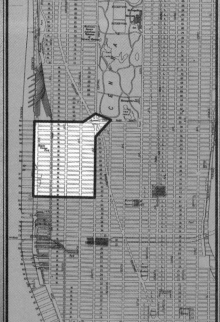

POINTS OF INTEREST

1 The Duff Man

2 Read This Quote

3 New York's Most Famous Mustache

4 Forever Valentino

5 The Sweetest Perfection

6 Truly a Fire Sale

7 Stand Here

8 Awesome Sign Alert

9 There's a What in DeWitt Clinton Park?!

10 Blood of the Bloom

11 Power to the People

12 The Cleanest Place in Town

13 Discovering Columbus

14 Remember the *Maine* (and the Mayor)

MA The Ninth Avenue Barricades

The Ninth Avenue Barricades: The Civil War Draft Riots

Certainly there are worse intersections in New York than Ninth Avenue at 42nd Street. Sure, the buttocks of the Port Authority bus terminal is a block away, with its steady stream of buses and weary passengers flowing to and fro. Automobiles race in and out of the Lincoln Tunnel to its south, creating an unpleasant congestion. But at the same time, there are great off-Broadway theaters down West 42nd Street and fine restaurants running up Ninth Avenue, and a flurry of new construction projects prepare to bring new residents and hotel guests to the area.

But this spot was a place of unimaginable horror in the summer of 1863, a macabre scene of war and strife. A half-mile-long barricade made of barrels, carts, and other street detritus separated armed residents from police and militia, and "the combined forces…fought from block to block, forcing the protected defenders to retreat, leaving the dead and the wounded at the barricades."[2] Along the rooftops, citizens fired at infantrymen as women and children along the sidelines cheered on the pandemonium.

Had New Yorkers lost their minds?

Police and rioters clash on Ninth Avenue, separated by a makeshift barricade.

The Civil War had divided America into the blue and the gray, but in New York, both colors were flying for all to see. New York's maritime and trading economy tied it to the profits produced by Southern plantations and their rueful institution of slavery. The powerful Democratic machine Tammany Hall

2   From *Riots, U.S.A., 1765–1965* by Willard A. Heaps.

fueled antagonism toward President Abraham Lincoln. Mayor Fernando Wood, a Democratic politician and scoundrel, even waxed on in 1861 about New York joining the South in seceding from the nation. Later, in 1863, as a New York congressman, he would embody Southern sympathies as if he wore the Confederate insignia under his trousers.

But these alone did not explain the riots that erupted in the streets of New York from July 13 to 16, 1863. More than two years of war had tempered the enthusiasm of even the most ardent Union supporter. The US Congress, hoping to refresh the frontlines, passed the Enrollment Act, drafting Northern men into service through a lottery system. Any able-bodied young man could be called. But there was a catch: If chosen, you could pay to get off the hook by purchasing an exemption for $300 (the equivalent of about $6,000 today). The rich had an "out."

Removing the wealthy from the draft left only the poor to serve, and many were from families that clearly needed their husbands and sons working at home to get by. Worse yet was the luck of the newly arriving immigrants, mostly Irish, who were often recruited right as they landed in New York. Imagine sailing

Rioters hang an African American man on Clarkson Street.

to America in search of a better life for you and your family, only to be drafted immediately into a civil war that you didn't even understand.

The street violence began on Monday, July 13, at the provost marshall's office on Third Avenue.[3] Crowds, including the volunteer fire department, torched the building and nearly killed the police commissioner. The unrest soon spread throughout the city, spilling down almost every street above 14th Street. Burning buildings dotted the landscape by the late afternoon. What had started as a vigorous protest against authority devolved into an uncontrollable wave of violence against anyone opposing the mob—this included the police, of course, but also Republicans and wealthy families who chose, unwisely, to stay in the city.

---

3   See Chapter 18.

But things were even more dangerous for those who competed for jobs with many of those in the mob: black New Yorkers. As many African Americans lived in neighborhoods just next to where the riots were unfolding, they quickly found themselves easy targets. Angry crowds destroyed black-owned businesses and homes throughout the week, but the attacks turned brutally violent as mobs hanged men from lampposts and struck down innocent residents in the streets. Among the worst atrocities committed during the three-day reign of terror was the destruction and burning of the Colored Orphan Asylum, near the Murray Hill Reservoir.[4]

The city was under attack by its own citizens, from Gramercy Park to Park Row (where Republican newspaper editors at the *New York Times* shot back at rioters with Gatling guns). While the state militia was successful in pushing back against the violent mob, the militia's progress was halted at several makeshift barricades that had been thrown together throughout the city.

The most infamous barricade was here at Ninth Avenue, stretching between 32th and 43rd Streets. An infantry captain later reported the following:[5]

"In front of me on Ninth Avenue, I observed what appeared to be a formidable barricade, guarded by a strong force of rioters. After waiting a short time, endeavoring to procure a field-piece, I concluded to storm the barricade with

the small force I had, and wheeled into the avenue, advancing rapidly to the first barricade, which I found composed of empty wagons, carts, telegraph poles, and wires."

The infantry dismantled the barricades and subdued rioters despite being "assailed with a terrific shower of brickbats, thrown by unseen hands." Militia picked off

The provost marshal's office burns on Third Avenue and 47th Street.

snipers on rooftops, and their bodies fell to the street. What had been an unassuming neighborhood — near the small industries and warehouses of the Hudson River — had been transformed into a scene of mayhem and death.

4   See Chapter 19.
5   From *The Great Riots of New York* by Joel Tyler Headley (1873).

Similarly disturbing scenes played out throughout the city until late that first night—then on Tuesday, and again on Wednesday. By Thursday thousands of federal troops had arrived on the scene and overwhelmed the streets, stamping out the last disturbances. Mind you, these were troops that could have been contributing to the war effort, perhaps bringing the national crisis to a quicker end had they not been battling civilians in the nation's largest city.

No remembrance: Life goes on at Ninth Avenue and West 42nd Street, site of the barricades.

In the end, the tragic riots saw the destruction of millions of dollars of property and nearly 200 casualties. As a result of these days of terror, New York's African American population mostly relocated to safer, more remote communities like Weeksville in today's borough of Brooklyn. And then, a month later, the draft resumed in New York. The violence had done nothing but reinforce New York's allegiance to the Union cause.

The draft riots are an incredibly tragic and violent episode in the city's complicated history; it would be unfortunate if they distracted from the sacrifice of the thousands of New Yorkers who gave their lives in the service of the Union Army. New York is rightfully proud of its reputation as a melting pot, a place where people of different ethnicities coexist, usually peaceably. Yet the sad realities of the draft riots—families fleeing the city in terror, lynched bodies hanging from trees and streetlamps—tell a different story.

At Ninth Avenue today there are no markers or historical plaques that commemorate this event. Who wants to remember some of the worst days in New York City's history? And yet, can we ever learn from tragedy if we're always rushing by without taking note?

Hell's Kitchen

POINTS OF INTEREST

1 THE DUFF MAN While the northern portion of the Times Square triangular plaza is technically named Father Duffy Square, the lasting legacy of Father Francis Patrick Duffy (1871–1932) is actually this old church across 42nd Street from the Port Authority bus terminal. Considering that during recent decades sin and sleaze dominated 42nd Street, we're surprised that Holy Cross Church didn't just pick up its bricks and run for its life. Built in 1870, the church was led by Reverend Francis Duffy during the dry Prohibition years. Duffy's exploits as an army chaplain during World War I — for which he was decorated — lent him a tough, no-nonsense air. In a way, Holy Cross has been on the frontlines as well, attracting some unconventional leadership, like the recently retired Father Peter Colapietro, known as the "saloon priest" for his previous career as a bartender. (*329 West 42nd Street*)

Holy Cross Church, built in 1870 (making it the oldest existing building on 42nd Street), stands strong in Hell's Kitchen.

2 **THAT QUOTE IN THE MOSAIC MURAL AT THE MARTIN LUTHER KING, JR., LABOR CENTER** "If there is no struggle, there can be no progress" is an excerpt from Frederick Douglass's West India Emancipation speech, given in 1857 in Canandaigua, New York. The lines following this in his speech are equally stirring: "Those who profess to favor freedom and yet deprecate agitation are men who want crops without plowing up the ground; they want rain without thunder and lightning. They want the ocean without the awful roar of its many waters." (*310 West 43rd Street*)

3 **NEW YORK'S MOST FAMOUS MUSTACHE** Restaurant Row, which transformed a line of old townhouses along 46th Street into a pre- and post-theater feeding frenzy, feels like a quaint old institution, something that developed over time out of necessity and convenience. And yet, it wasn't officially recognized as Restaurant Row until 1973. "Where else in the world, except possibly Paris, could you get sixteen of the best restaurants collected in such a short strip of land?" proclaimed hungry mayor John Lindsay during the block's dedication. While the cabaret Don't Tell Mama and the jazzy throwback Swing 46 tend to be the liveliest tenants on the block, Barbetta Restaurant is the most historic. Opened in 1906, Barbetta means "little beard" and was named after founder Sebastiano Maioglio's brother's facial hair. (A very 2016 thing to do, if you think about it.) Today, the restaurant is run by Sebastiano's daughter, Laura, and offers an old-fashioned elegant dining experience.

During Times Square's downswing in the 1970s, Restaurant Row was also known for the drug addicts and prostitutes who loitered outside the eateries. Needless to say, they're long gone. (*321 West 46th Street*)

Main course: Restaurant Row features great eateries in nineteenth-century brownstones.

4 FOREVER VALENTINO Dashing Rudolph Valentino was one of the silent film era's biggest sex symbols, but many today don't realize that his

Debonair: Rudolph Valentino bundles up for an ocean voyage.

tragic story actually ended in New York. The young Italian dancer–turned–smoldering "Latin lover" collapsed at a Midtown hotel and was taken to Polyclinic Hospital at 345 West 50th Street, where he died of pleuritis on August 23, 1926. Due to its close proximity to the third Madison Square Garden (which opened across the street in 1925), the Polyclinic was known for treating entertainers, athletes, and even mobsters. In the days leading up to Valentino's death, hundreds of young women attempted to infiltrate the hospital to visit the actor. Among the last faces he saw was that of a bodyguard stationed outside his room.[6] (*345 West 50th Street*)

---

6   Another historic spot in the history of Valentino's death can be found in the following chapter.

5 THE SWEETEST PERFECTION "Hey, guys! Let's go to work at the candy factory!" is something that hundreds of New Yorkers should be saying

to themselves every day, even if they don't work in the confection industry. D. Auerbach and Sons, once famous for its chocolate marshmallow and pineapple bars, built a massive factory in 1913 on 11th Avenue and West 46th Street. While candy manufacturers thrived during Prohibition (Can't reach for a drink? Reach for a Charleston

Pay day: Working in an old candy factory.

Chew!), the Auerbachs were not able to profit from the booze-free cravings and sadly melted out of business in 1931. Today the spruced-up building is home to the Ogilvy and Mather advertising agency—who must certainly count a couple of candy bars among their clients. (*636 11th Avenue*)

6 TRULY A FIRE SALE Hell's Kitchen is not especially well known for

its architectural treasures. (Look, every snowflake is precious in its own special way!) But there are some interesting exceptions, like this perky little former firehouse on West 47th Street. This 1888 home for Fire Engine Company 54 was designed by Napoleon LeBrun & Sons, and is one of the firm's forty fire stations constructed in the late nineteenth century. Off-Broadway theater companies have been a savior to many of Hell's Kitchen's most beautiful buildings, and that is the case here.[7] The Puerto Rican Traveling Theatre has made this their home since 1977. The rent they paid the city that year for this awesome firehouse: $210 a month. (*304 West 47th Street*)

Fire Engine Co. No. 54: This old station still puts on a good show.

---

7 The famed Actors Studio, for instance, is in the old Seventh Associate Presbyterian Church at 432 West 44th Street, built in 1859. However, James Lipton has uttered the line "Tell me about your craft" thousands of times on *Inside the Actors Studio*, from a studio at a separate location.

7 STAND HERE: The "Four Seasons" Fountain at One Worldwide Plaza (West side of Eighth Avenue, between West 49th and West 50th Streets). *Why?* One of the greatest sporting venues in history once stood on this spot.

Between wistfully remembering the first two Madison Square Gardens (located downtown at Madison Square) and begrudgingly accepting the current MSG (plopped atop today's Pennsylvania Station), many overlook the "Madison in the Middle." Boxing promoter and extravagant sports fanatic Tex Rickard leased the downtown Madison Square Garden in the 1920s, returned its focus to popular, lucrative, and more working-class sporting events, then picked it up and moved the whole venue up to Hell's Kitchen.

This third Madison Square Garden was a blockier, less ornate venue, designed by an architect famous for his theaters and "movie palaces," Thomas W. Lamb,[8] who gave it a glitzy marquee to compete with those of the Broadway theaters nearby. From the moment it opened on December 15, 1925, the Garden was a temple for boxing. Soon orbiting the Hell's Kitchen Garden would be popular and raucous taverns, restaurants, and hotels, all of which would be left stranded when the sporting venue would again move, this time about twenty blocks downtown, in 1968.

Marquee events: On deck at Madison Square Garden in 1944—a boxing match and a Sonja Henie ice revue! (Courtesy of MCNY.)

---

8   Another Thomas Lamb delight awaits you in the following chapter.

While famous today for many iconic boxing matches, the Hell's Kitchen Garden is also the birthplace of the New York Rangers ice hockey team. (Their name is actually a pun—"Tex's Rangers," after Tex Rickard.) Perhaps the Garden's most famous cultural event took place here on Saturday, May 19, 1962, when Marilyn Monroe cooed "Happy Birthday" to President John F. Kennedy. The ultimate knockout!

Today hardly a ghost of the classic venue hangs about bricky One Worldwide Plaza, which was developed by William Zeckendorf, Jr., from 1986 to 1989 to reenergize the flagging Midtown West neighborhood. (*Between Eighth and Ninth Avenues, West 49th and West 50th Streets*)

8 AWESOME SIGN ALERT Perhaps no sign sums up the neighborhood better than the neon crucifix of St. Paul's House on West 51st Street, promising that "Sin Will Find You Out." The ministry moved to this block in 1945, founded by Reverend J. J. D. Hall, the so-called "bishop of Wall Street" for his street sermons there. (*335 West 51st Street*)

9 THERE'S A WHAT IN DEWITT CLINTON PARK?! Hell's Kitchen has several small green spaces but only one large park: DeWitt Clinton Park, opened in 1906 way over on 11th Avenue to honor New York's former mayor and governor, and the man who oversaw the planning of the Erie Canal.[9] The park gave residents some fresh air—and gave Hell's Kitchen's leaders the opportunity to rechristen the neighborhood with a less foreboding name: the less colorful but more respectable Clinton. Unfortunately for their efforts, it seems that nobody really prefers calling it that. But the park's most striking feature—indeed, the most astounding detail in all of Hell's Kitchen—is older than the river itself: the rock formations that still jut out just west of the sports field. This unique outcrop, dating back 450 million years (that's right: read that again!), is called exotic terrane, meaning that a portion of the earth's crust formed by two tectonic plates grafted together to create a rock composition unlike anything that surrounds it. Over the past couple of centuries, most

---

9   The canal was completed in 1825, and connected the interior of the growing United States with the Atlantic Ocean via a canal that linked Lake Erie and the Hudson River. It led to a manufacturing and import/export boom in the city and made many New Yorkers absurdly wealthy.

of Manhattan's unique geological features have been smoothed over by the city, which hired workers to push plows and drive dump trucks filled with dirt. Thankfully, this extraordinary feature was left in place to remind us of how very young we all are. (*11th Avenue, between 52nd and 54th Streets, west side of the park*)

School of Rock: Toy horses in DeWitt Clinton Park await children who play upon old Manhattan stone.

10 BLOOD OF THE BLOOM Here is one of New York's most touching

In Flanders Fields: A doughboy offers a poignant remembrance.

World War I memorials, a lonely doughboy with a rifle slung over his shoulder holding, wait, what is that? He's offering up a handful of poppies, flowers that held a decidedly different meaning during the statue's dedication in 1930 than they have today. Poppies grew in abundance in the Flemish town of Ypres, site of multiple battles during the war, and the bright-red variety came to symbolize the fallen. A quote from the famed World War I poem "In Flanders Fields" by poet-surgeon-Lieutenant Colonel John McCrae hugs the base, explaining the mysterious imagery: "If Ye Break Faith / With Those Who Died / We Shall Not Sleep / Though Poppies Grow / On Flanders Fields." (*11th Avenue and 52nd Street*)

11 POWER TO THE PEOPLE The architectural icons that were the second Madison Square Garden and the original Pennsylvania Station might be gone today,[10] but several other mammoth structures designed by the same architect, Stanford White, still stand in Manhattan. Included on this list is the oft-overlooked Interborough Rapid Transit Powerhouse, which provided the juice for New York's first subway system back in 1904. With its startling scale and Beaux-Arts drama, it's a surprise that 1) it's still standing and 2) it hasn't been turned into a mall. The remaining five smokestacks — there used to be six — must have fit in seamlessly with the steamships docked along the waterfront a block away. (*11th Avenue and 58th Street*)

12 THE CLEANEST PLACE IN TOWN Roosevelt Hospital was born out of the generosity of James H. Roosevelt (1800–1863), a wealthy philanthropist who was confined to his manor by illness for most of his life. Upon his death he bequeathed his entire fortune to the creation of a new hospital, which opened in 1871. Many years later, another wealthy benefactor — gun merchant

William Syms (1818–1889) — benefited from a successful operation at Roosevelt Hospital and donated most of *his* fortune there as well, with the specific purpose of building a new operating room. When the William J. Syms Operating Theatre opened in 1891, the press trumpeted its sleek and sanitary innovations, which included a brightly lit, aseptic environment very different from those found in other city hospitals of the day.

New standards of cleanliness were observed within the surgical theater. "[The visitor] will see everywhere signs of the most exquisite cleanliness. [He or she] will see no sign of haste or confusion, of dirt or litter, of human pain or suffering." It was probably the cleanest place during all of New York's Gilded Age. Today it's home to the private Speyer Legacy School, so chances are it can no longer claim that distinction. (*925 Ninth Avenue*)

---

10 See Chapter 17.

13 **DISCOVERING COLUMBUS** Christopher Columbus is rather passé these days, a symbol of Eurocentric imperialist attitudes and the patronizing belief that people and their cultures can be "discovered." So it may seem a bit old-fashioned that one of New York's most prominent intersections plays tribute to Columbus the explorer.

Now get this: In the late nineteenth century, Christopher Columbus actually represented cultural diversity! By the 1880s, thousands of Italians were arriving in New York weekly, and this number would hold steady well into the 1910s. They looked upon this statue with pride (and many Italian Americans still do today). In fact, the Columbus statue by Gaetano Russo was funded entirely by Italian Americans — or, at least, by readers of the Italian American newspaper *Il Progresso*.[11] Its dedication on October 12, 1892, commemorated the 400th anniversary of Columbus's "discovery" and accompanied the intersection's increased prominence as a place for late-night entertainment, and a northern extension of Times Square's theater and restaurant activity. (*Columbus Circle*)

14 **REMEMBER THE *MAINE* (AND THE MAYOR)** The Maine Monument, located at the southwestern corner entrance of Central Park, pays tribute to the 266 American soldiers who perished aboard the USS *Maine*, which exploded in Havana, Cuba, on February 15, 1898. But some feared another conflict would break out 15 years later at its dedication on Memorial Day in 1913.

The Spanish-American War, which started during the spring of 1898, was fueled by New York publishers who, following their yellowest journalistic instincts, featured stories of trumped-up Spanish aggression that were outlandishly exaggerated or outright fabricated in order to sell newspapers. The papers were also behind the construction of war monuments too. Within days of the *Maine*'s explosion, the *New York Morning Journal* publisher William Randolph Hearst appealed directly to his readers, young and old, for donations to build a memorial to the *Maine*'s fallen crew.[12]

---

11 And he's not the only statuesque figure on the West Side to be funded by the newspaper. See Chapter 21.
12 Given the wall-to-wall coverage of the war that year and the ample profits from newspaper sales, it's strange that Hearst couldn't just fund the whole thing himself. It took well over a decade to raise the money.

The memorial was unveiled with a grand military parade and accompanied by ten warships in the harbor, including one sent from Havana. There was, of course, one great conflict on everyone's mind that day when, in the official ceremony, sworn enemies Hearst and Mayor William Jay Gaynor met at the unveiling. (In addition to their other grievances, Hearst had unsuccessfully run against Gaynor for mayor in 1909.) With utmost restraint, Gaynor managed to shake Hearst's hand without punching him in the face. (*Columbus Circle, entrance to Central Park*)

The *Maine* Event: The memorial's 1913 dedication was not without a little drama.

Tastes of History: The Tavern

New Yorkers have always been in the mood for a drink. While other New World settlements were rooted in lofty and religious ideals, New Amsterdam was started as a company town, attracting those more interested in jobs than religious liberty. Beer and wine were flowing as early as the 1640s at the City Tavern ("Stadt Huys"), a spot so popular with the Dutch settlers that it became the city hall.[13] By the 1880s, there were an estimated 10,000 places to get a drink in New York.[14] As the city's richest Gilded Age drinkers lifted their spirits in posh hotel bars and extravagant restaurants, taverns in less affluent residential neighborhoods served the enormous waves of immigrants eager for an escape from overcrowded tenements. Many of these were operated by German or Irish immigrants themselves, offering a community for the new arrivals, many of whom had left their families thousands of miles away.

Prohibition shuttered the city's taverns (or saw them transform into illicit speakeasies), and the law's repeal a decade later revealed a city whose tastes had moved on to other kinds of drinking establishments. Still, there are a few old-fashioned taverns left in town today, including the following:

MCSORLEY'S OLD ALE HOUSE

You can't drink just one beer at McSorley's, a legendary divey tavern of the sawdust-on-the-floor variety in the East Village. (Literally, you can't. They're served by the pair.) Claiming to be the city's oldest bar in continuous operation, since 1854 (a claim disputed by many who follow this sort of thing), McSorley's, like most taverns in town, didn't allow women for most of its history. *New Yorker* writer Joseph Mitchell highlighted McSorley's scruffy charm in a series of stories surrounding the bar in the 1940s, and it's remained popular with thirsty tourists ever since. (And yes, women are allowed today. They were the last bar in town to change their policy—in 1970.) (*15 East 7th Street at Third Avenue*)

PETE'S TAVERN

Another bar clinging to the "city's oldest watering hole" claim, Pete's started pouring in 1864[15] at its cozy spot on Irving Place, south of Gramercy Park. Given its swanky locale, Pete's has long attracted its share of artists and writers, including, most famously, bar regular O. Henry, who penned his

---

13 See Chapter 4.
14 According to *The Encyclopedia of New York City*, Kenneth Jackson, editor.
15 Pete's claim to being the oldest is based on liquor being sold in the building as early as the early 1850s.

classic "The Gift of the Magi" at the bar in 1905. In rooms adjacent to the bar, Pete's serves pub-style classics in dark wooden booths. (*129 East 18th Street*)

LANDMARK TAVERN

Opened in 1868 by Patrick Henry Carley near the shores of the west side, the Landmark Tavern poured pints for those working the nearby docks. Some of the upstairs rooms were turned into a speakeasy during Prohibition and others rented out to lodgers—some of whom, if you believe the ghost stories, have never left. The tavern today still retains the look of an old Irish pub, with its prominent carved mahogany bar, tin ceilings, and convivial management. (*626 11th Avenue at 46th Street*)

P. J. CLARKE'S

The Midtown East stalwart P. J. Clarke's is virtually surrounded by skyscrapers today, although its history goes back to 1884, when it quenched the thirsts of the Irish laborers working in the neighborhood's early industries. Irish immigrant Patrick Joseph Clarke started working as a bartender in 1902 and purchased the saloon a decade later, naming it for himself. As Midtown developed and engulfed the saloon (accelerated by the demolition of Third Avenue's elevated railway in the 1950s), the small brick saloon refused to budge, earning its reputation as a true New York "holdout." (*55th Street at Third Avenue*)

EAR INN

See page 137. (*326 Spring Street*)

WHITE HORSE TAVERN

Boasting one of the best old-school neon signs in the West Village, the White Horse Tavern has been pouring pints since 1880, when the neighborhood was decidedly more working class than it is today. A century ago the tavern was popular with sailors taking a break from the nearby docks, a scene that later attracted poet Dylan Thomas in the 1940s, when he frequented the bar and increased its popularity with other downtown artists and writers. The White Horse has expanded over the years into two adjacent buildings, although the original corner structure is notable for its wood-frame construction, a rarity in any Manhattan neighborhood these days. (*567 Hudson Street at West 11th Street*)

OLD TOWN BAR

Located north of Union Square, the legendary Old Town Bar offers a sudsy time machine to 1892, when it opened in the predominantly German neighborhood. Virtually nothing has changed in the past century—the 16-foot tin ceilings, 55-foot mahogany and marble bar, wooden booths, snapshot-worthy urinals (so large you could fall in), white tiled floors, and still-cranking dumbwaiter (the kitchen is upstairs, next to a second dining room) are all more than 100 years old. (*45 East 18th Street*)

UPWARD MOBILITY

New York Tribune, January 3, 1901

Introduction to a real estate article called "Modern City Dwellings":

An architectural transformation process is constantly at work in New-York, and this is nowhere more pronounced than in the residential parts of the city. Whole sections of the upper West Side have within the last few years assumed a new and variegated aspect. Rows upon rows of attractive dwelling houses have made their appearance where only a very short time ago unsightly landscapes of rocks and rubbish greeted the eye.

Upper West Side and Riverside Park:

60th Street to 110th Street, from Central Park West to the Hudson River

Riverside Park and Drive in the 1910s, separating the city from the river's edge.

SITUATE THE READER
–Upper West Side and Riverside Park–

The Upper West Side boasts one of the loveliest collections of residential buildings in the world—lavish apartment buildings and hotels along its main stretches, and handsome row houses lining its side streets. But as late as the mid-nineteenth century, even as lower Manhattan was overcrowded, there was virtually no development up here.

The Dutch called the west side "Bloemendaal," later corrupted to "Bloomingdale" in honor of a tulip-rich region in the Netherlands. Its relatively high elevation attracted farms and estates along Bloomingdale Road (later Broadway), most notably the 300-acre farm of British loyalist Charles Ward Apthorp from 89th to 99th Street.[1]

The area has often been used as a conduit—first by the Croton Aqueduct, which brought water to New York when it opened in 1842, and then the Hudson River Railroad, which started shipping commodities down Manhattan's West Side in 1846.

While verdant Central Park and Riverside Park certainly gave the area a new *leaf* on life, it wasn't until the elevated railroad laid tracks here in 1879 that residents finally had a convenient way of coming and going. By the following decade, New Yorkers had begun moving into the neighborhood's apartment buildings and increasingly opulent homes.

More than a half century later a different fate awaited San Juan Hill, a neighborhood just north of Columbus Circle. In the 1950s, this mostly African American and Puerto Rican neighborhood was almost completely wiped away by the construction of Lincoln Center for the Performing Arts. Much more on that drama to come....

---

1   The Apthorp at 2201–2219 Broadway pays homage to this farm owner—he would have appreciated its pricy apartments.

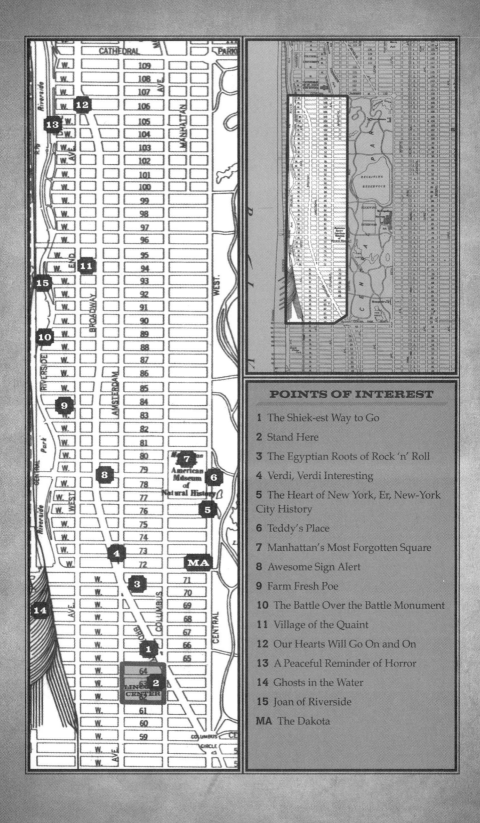

CATHEDRAL PARKWAY

109
108
107
106
105
104
103
102
101
100
99
98
97
96
95
94
93
92
91
90
89
88
87
86
85
84
83
82
81
80
79
78
77
76
75
74
73
72
71
70
69
68
67
66
65
64
61
60
59

Riverside
Dr.
W. END AVE.
BROADWAY
AMSTERDAM
Central Park West
RIVERSIDE
WEST
MANHATTAN AVE.
CENTRAL PARK WEST
COLUMBUS
COLUMBUS CIRCLE
LINCOLN CENTER
American Museum of Natural History

POINTS OF INTEREST

1 The Shiek-est Way to Go

2 Stand Here

3 The Egyptian Roots of Rock 'n' Roll

4 Verdi, Verdi Interesting

5 The Heart of New York, Er, New-York City History

6 Teddy's Place

7 Manhattan's Most Forgotten Square

8 Awesome Sign Alert

9 Farm Fresh Poe

10 The Battle Over the Battle Monument

11 Village of the Quaint

12 Our Hearts Will Go On and On

13 A Peaceful Reminder of Horror

14 Ghosts in the Water

15 Joan of Riverside

MA The Dakota

The Dakota and the Birth of the New York Apartment

The Dakota is one of the most famous apartment buildings in the world, known not only for its dark, striking architecture but also for its horrors, both imagined (as the setting of the film *Rosemary's Baby*) and real (the 1980 murder of John Lennon, who resided here). There are certainly larger apartment

Upper Vast Side: The Dakota in 1890, with nary a neighbor to its west or north.

buildings on the Upper West Side, and even more extravagant ones, but none that equal it as a pioneer — as the first in the neighborhood and of this peculiar urban-centric style of living in the city.

Before the 1870s very few middle- or upper-class New Yorkers lived in what we'd call apartments. The richest of the rich were still building fine mansions and stately homes: the row house, the townhouse, and their sandstone-covered cousin, the brownstone. But as real estate prices increased and available properties dwindled, most of these homes would be quietly divided in half, with one family on the first two floors, and another on the upper floors. If you had money but didn't want to bother with that, you could also live in a hotel, an acceptable, if costly, way to live that caught on during the Gilded Age. For those with less money to spend, there was the boardinghouse, which was like a hotel but a bit more transient.

However, none of these types of structures could accommodate the thousands of poor immigrants who had been flowing into the city daily, starting in the 1830s. And thus was born another, now infamous, form of housing: the tenement. These were constructed quickly and cheaply on the Lower East Side and other poor neighborhoods to house multiple families per floor, with small rooms with very few amenities, windows, fresh air, or sunlight.

The rise of the city's middle class in the mid-nineteenth century required a different approach to housing. A lavish hotel life or the purchase of a spacious townhouse was out of the question, but the lifestyle of the boardinghouse or tenement were also unsuitable.

The answer was found in Paris, in the new, very French-looking dwellings referred to as French flats, multistory constructions that included several independent living units for families, with units that were larger than anything found in the tenements. These Parisian apartments had well-decorated parlors, private kitchens, and private bathroom facilities—all hallmarks of wealth—and shared large communal courtyards. More important, the apartments awarded privacy. Residents didn't seem bothered by living in such close proximity to complete strangers.

Back in America, some thought these French flats scandalous and improper for families, and imagined them filled with blowsy, licentious women—*French* women! But New York–based architects like Calvert Vaux and Richard Morris Hunt took to the idea and eventually convinced New Yorkers of their potential.

Dominating the skyline: Skating in the park near the Dakota, 1893.

New York's first apartment building is commonly considered to be the Stuyvesant Apartments near Gramercy Park, built in 1870 by Hunt for the well-connected Rutherford Stuyvesant.[2] He lured a famous, if unusual, assortment of residents to his experimental project, most notably Elizabeth Custer, wife of the fallen George Custer.

Within a decade several more apartment buildings were under construction in the city, including many cooperatives (where the occupants own a share of the building, rather than their physical space). If you were a real risk-taking developer, it was no longer enough to merely live in a "wacky" European-style flat; now you needed one in an up-and-coming neighborhood!

2   He was born Stuyvesant Rutherford. When he was a child, however, his childless great-uncle Petrus Stuyvesant died and left all his money to the young man, with the stipulation that the boy *flip* his name in order to keep the Stuyvesant name alive. So from that point on, Stuyvesant Rutherford became Rutherford Stuyvesant.

Singer Sewing Machine[3] mogul Edward Clarke was a consummate risk taker, and saw the undeveloped Upper West Side as a no-brainer investment. In 1880 he broke ground at West 72nd Street and Central Park West on what would be the most eclectic residence in town, one that faced the park on one side and almost literally nothing else on the other three.[4] It worked so well for its architect, Henry Hardenberg, that a later project of his, the Plaza Hotel (constructed in 1907), seems almost like the Dakota's kid sister.

Many considered the Dakota's name a clever joke on the building's pioneering "middle of nowhere" western location. However, judging from its architectural details, the name more likely suggests Clarke's love of Native American history. At its completion in 1884, the Dakota's exotic appearance stunned New Yorkers: "Probably not one stranger out of fifty who ride over the elevated roads or on either of the rivers does not ask the name of the stately building which stands west of Central Park."[5]

Winter Wonderland: The Dakota and a snowy Central Park in the 1910s.

More important, the Dakota waved the checkered flag, starting a race of ever more spacious and extravagant apartments and hotels on the Upper West Side. The magnificent Ansonia, built in 1904 at Broadway and 73rd Street, had

---

3 We've seen two other buildings related to the sewing machine company in this book: the Singer Building (see Chapter 3) and the Little Singer Building (see Chapter 8).
4 You would have been able to see the first home of the American Museum of Natural History, built in 1877 a few blocks north.
5 *New York Daily Graphic*, October 27, 1884.

cows grazing on its rooftop farm to provide its guests with fresh milk. The 1920s brought changes to apartment zoning laws, allowing for superstructures along Central Park West—the Eldorado at 300 Central Park West (1929), the Majestic at 115 Central Park West (1930–1931), and perhaps the most recognizable building on the Upper West Side: the two-towered San Remo at 145 Central Park West (1929–1931).[6]

They're grand, expensive, ambitious—but they can never be the Dakota, a building whose mythical allure has inspired volumes of ghost stories, its spirits and sprites wandering the central courtyard and bothering residents in the hallways. More enigmatic than these alleged ghosts have been the many celebrities (like Judy Garland and Lauren Bacall) who have chosen the Dakota as their home. It's so possessed with lingering memories that Jack Finney's 1970 novel, *Time and Again*, uses a room at the Dakota as a time machine. "Then it's back to the Dakota," one character says. "Come on, you lucky bastard, I'll drive you."

Upper West Side

POINTS OF INTEREST

1 THE SHIEK-EST WAY TO GO (Vanished) The world's most famous funeral home…wait, can funeral homes be famous? They can be when they're the Frank E. Campbell Funeral Chapel, the safe haven for celebrated deceased New Yorkers since 1898. Campbell pretty much invented the idea of the "funeral chapel," a place with the reverence of a church but without all the angels and confessionals. They took the funeral out of the home—always a cramped place for something so reverent—and into a tastefully decorated space on West 23rd Street. By 1915 they'd moved up to Broadway and West 66th Street, coincidentally (and conveniently) near rowdy restaurants and glamorous theaters. It was here that Campbell's would host the final tributes to celebrities such as Anna Held (1918), Frank W. Woolworth (1919), and Enrico Caruso (1921). But it was the funeral of Rudolph Valentino on August 24, 1926, that made headlines worldwide as thousands of hysterical mourners stormed the streets and smashed the funeral home's windows. Their passionate displays elevated both Valentino's fame and Campbell's

---

6 The San Remo, located between West 74th and West 75th Streets, took so long because construction crews had just dug in when the stock market crashed.

business. It still operates today at Madison Avenue and 81st Street on the Upper East Side. (*1966 Broadway, West 66th Street*)

2 STAND HERE: At the center of Josie Robertson Plaza near the fountain, Lincoln Center. *Why?* Lincoln Center draws together several of the city's most cherished performing arts institutions, all of which had been scattered about Manhattan in various locations, before being grouped here in the 1960s to reside in an austere and modern (if somewhat clinical) trio of performance halls. But like any great project—including Civic Center, Rockefeller Center, and the World Trade Center—something occupied the space before it, and had to give way for its construction. Although the city had given the intersection the name Lincoln Square in 1907, it was adjacent to San Juan Hill, a largely African American and Puerto Rican neighborhood. While the neighborhood had its share of crime, it was no Five Points.[7] But the influence of New York's cultural heavy hitters, with fightin' Robert Moses firmly on their side, brought the curtain down on the impoverished neighborhood. Its tenements were handily demolished in the early 1960s and most of its residents relocated to Harlem or poor neighborhoods in the outer boroughs. (The western part of San Juan Hill did become home to the Amsterdam Houses development in 1974.) (*10 Lincoln Center Plaza*)

3 THE EGYPTIAN ROOTS OF ROCK 'N' ROLL What the Tutankhamen is this building on West 70th Street? The Pythian, an apartment building since 1982, is like a trunk of Egyptian-themed Halloween costumes

A pyramid scheme: Flamboyant Egyptian decor at the Pythian.

---

7 That said, the gang life was active enough along its tenement-lined streets to warrant it as the setting of the musical *West Side Story*.

come to life, wild and campy. Pharaohs chill out on the roof while bulls, sphinxes, and assorted monsters gallivant above the doors. The Pythian was unsurprisingly home to the Knights of Pythias, a free-wheeling Freemason-like fraternal order based on the Greek friendship fable of Damon and Pythias, the original "bros." If it seems like an old-timey movie theater, that's because it was constructed in 1926 by Thomas W. Lamb, the master of the silent movie house.[8] Decca Records, home to music legends like Billie Holiday and Judy Garland, moved here in the 1940s. Then, on April 12, 1954, the rock 'n' roll era was kicked off with "Rock Around the Clock" by Bill Haley and the Comets, recorded here at the Pythian. (*135 West 70th Street*)

4 VERDI, VERDI INTERESTING It's no coincidence that the statue of Giuseppe Verdi, nineteenth-century opera composer extraordinaire, stands nearly in line with that of Christopher Columbus, about thirteen

blocks south. Verdi's was funded by the same Italian American newspaper, *Il Progresso,* and given its very own plaza when the sculpture by Pasquale Civiletti was finished in 1906, five years after the composer's death. (A third statue was planned for the middle of Times Square — this one for Dante Alighieri — but they could never get the infernal thing funded.[9]) Around Verdi dance characters from his most famous operas; most captivating is Otello, his hand striking his breast. But life around the statue has not always been so harmonious. In 1937, a mysterious poisoner killed off the plaza's pigeons, leaving dozens of dead birds scattered by a fowl and cold-blooded act. In the 1960s and '70s this plaza,

Othello sings Verdi's praises on West 73rd Street.

along with Sherman Park on the other side of West 70th Street, were derisively known as "Needle Park" for the drug addicts and dealers who called the parks home. Verdi looks especially handsome from the south, with the mighty Ansonia apartments (2109 Broadway) rising just behind him. (*Verdi Square, West 83rd Streets, between Broadway and Amsterdam Avenue*)

---

8   Lamb also designed the third iteration of Madison Square Garden, discussed in Chapter 20.
9   There is, however, a Dante Park with a tiny Dante statue, in front of Lincoln Center.

5 THE HEART OF NEW YORK, er, NEW-YORK CITY HISTORY
The New-York Historical Society[10] not only collects and recounts history, it *is* history, having been founded in 1804, a mere two decades after the British left New York. Among its inaugural members was DeWitt Clinton, one-time mayor, governor, and chief proponent of the Erie Canal project. The current

incarnation of the society, housed along Central Park West since 1908, holds some the city's greatest historical treasures in its front lobby, from the only remaining fragment of King George's statue[11] to the wooden leg of Gouverneur Morris. Head here for a few hours to witness relics of many of the people, places, and events mentioned in this book.[12] If merely passing by outside, at least stop to say hello to the sculptures of Abraham Lincoln and Frederick Douglass. It's unfortunate they're on separate staircases, for they were friends in life. Douglass helped promote the memory of Lincoln after the president's death in 1865. They belong to every American's historical society. (*170 Central Park West*)

Frederick Douglass greets visitors at the New-York Historical Society's north entrance.

AMERICAN MUSEUM OF NATURAL HISTORY

Has any museum had to navigate the precarious changing winds of public opinion and political correctness more often than New York's American Museum of Natural History? While the museum is packed with splendid specimens of the natural world (like the "Ahnighito" fragment of the Cape York meteorite), they have also put forth some controversial presentations (as in 1906, when an Eskimo boy named Minik lived in the museum while his father's bones were on display). Yet its tremendous dinosaur and stuffed

---

10 New York was commonly written as "New-York" in 1804 and, let's be honest, if anyone is gonna uphold that tradition, shouldn't it be them?
11 The tail of the horse, actually. See Chapter 2.
12 Our podcast, it should be noted, would often be at a loss without the help of the society's vast research collection and knowledgeable librarians.

animal halls still attract more than 5 million visitors each year, and the Hayden Planetarium brings the heavens to a grateful Upper West Side.

Unnatural! The original museum-castle looked quite a bit different in the early twentieth century.

6 TEDDY'S PLACE Theodore Roosevelt (1858–1919) is the only US president born in New York City, so naturally he deserves a fabulous memorial, right? Oh, he doesn't get just a memorial, he gets the entire eastern entrance of the American Museum of Natural History, plus a dedicated rotunda *and* memorial hall! After all, he was a nature lover and creator of national parks. He filled this institution with countless exotic animals that he himself had hunted and killed—from Tigger to Dumbo!

A captivating yet problematic sculpture of Roosevelt at the museum's entrance.

But we can't help but feel a little weirded out by New York State's Theodore Roosevelt Memorial, completed in 1936 by John Russell Pope (best known for his Jefferson Memorial in Washington, DC). While the museum's lovely eastern facade includes depictions of much of the animal kingdom heading for the museum's front door, Roosevelt's equestrian statue by James Earle Fraser presents him leading an American Indian and an

African "courageously" into the future. *That* plays well in the twenty-first century! We can only guess that the European and the Asian have already galloped away. (*West 79th Street and Central Park West*)

7 MANHATTAN'S MOST-FORGOTTEN SQUARE Theodore Roosevelt Park, which contains today's museum, is the oldest developed section of the Upper West Side, purchased by the city in 1840 as a possible strolling park to be called Manhattan Square. Central Park was but a gleam in the eye! Unfortunately, the city forgot all about Manhattan Square, and it was soon surrounded by shanties. Samuel Ruggles, developer of both Union Square and Gramercy Park, squawked, "It is a disgrace to the city. It is in some places forty feet below the grade and well characterized as 'a pestilential hole of stagnant water.'" *Suh-nap!* Luckily, Manhattan Square would get its moment to shine when the museum was built here in 1877 and apartment developers later flocked to the park's edges. (*77th and 81st Streets, between Central Park West and Columbus Avenue*)

8 AWESOME SIGN ALERT The stunning harp sign of the Dublin House is one of the finest old-school neon gems in Manhattan today, hung here in all its multicolored tubular glory in 1933. The bar below it has been Irish-owned since the days of Prohibition. It's not as high-strung as it seems: Its doors open for thirsty patrons at 9 a.m. Breakfast anyone? (*225 West 79th Street*)

9 FARM FRESH POE Why are there a couple of blocks named for Edgar Allan Poe in Manhattan? His most famous New York residence, after all, is

his ramshackle yet storied little cottage in the Bronx. But in 1844, Poe and his sickly young wife, Virginia, lodged at a dairy farm somewhere near today's West 84th Street. (While blocks would have been marked by the Commissioners' Plan of 1811, there was little development here for many decades.)

It's widely believed that it was here that Poe worked on his poem "The Raven," although to be fair, pretty much every Poe-related site in America makes the same claim. Although he lived here for only a short time, the street was ceremonially christened Edgar Allan Poe Street in 1980 (although the city misspelled the honor for many years on street signs—"Edgar Allen Poe Street"). Look for a couple of competing plaques near Broadway marking the supposed location of the farm. "Over here!" quoth the Raven. But don't listen to ravens, for no one really knows. (*West 84th Street, between Riverside Drive and Broadway*)

10 THE BATTLE OVER THE BATTLE MONUMENT The Soldiers' and Sailors' Monument is a solid, serene temple of columns, one of many built

in the United States during the 1890s to honor the military sacrifices of the previous generation who had fought in the Civil War. But its location inspired a bit of a *civic* war from the moment it was first proposed in 1893.

Neighborhood associations on both the Upper East and Upper West Sides wanted it, and brawled over it like Black Friday shoppers. After all, in 1895, didn't it make sense to place it on Fifth Avenue at 59th

The Soldiers' and Sailors' Monument almost docked on Fifth Avenue.

Street, one of the classiest spots in the world? But naval officers bristled at the Fifth Avenue site—it was, after all, almost as far from water as you could get in Manhattan, and thus, the West Side won out.

The monument was planned for a spot in the newly developed Riverside Park known as Mount Tom (at 83rd Street), which was believed to have been a spot of quiet contemplation for Edgar Allan Poe during his quick residential

stop in the neighborhood. But that too was deemed inadequate, and the temple once again moved up to 89th Street, and was officially dedicated on Memorial Day, 1902. (*89th Street and Riverside Drive*)

11 VILLAGE OF THE QUAINT Down the slope from Symphony Space is an enclave of twenty-seven buildings so unusual that you'd be forgiven for thinking you'd stumbled onto the set of a fantasy film. Is that Elijah Wood with pointy ears over there? No, it's an enchanted residential hideaway called Pomander Walk, named for a 1910 play that featured a set of an eighteenth-century London street. That feel was emulated here in 1921 by restaurateur Thomas J. Healey, who built a theatrical village in which theatrical people could live. Brightened with flamboyant paint jobs, the gated little street is one of New York's most secretive and sought-after cooperatives. If you find one of these on the market, sell your firstborn and make a bid. (*94th to 95th Streets between Broadway and West End Avenue*)

12 OUR HEARTS WILL GO ON AND ON The most ornate Manhattan memorial to the 1912 sinking of the RMS *Titanic* was built specifically to honor the memory of just two victims: Isidor and Ida Straus. Isidor, a generous philanthropist to Jewish causes, was best known as the co-owner of Macy's Department Store. Straus Park, near their home on 105th Street, was dedicated in 1915 and at its centerpiece is a reclining bronze woman (modeled after Audrey Munson, the "It Girl" of the day) in front of a Bible verse. Ida stood by her husband on the *Titanic* when, as a society woman, she could have been first on the rescue boats. The verse reads, "Lovely and pleasant were they in their lives and in their death they were not divided."[13] (*Broadway and 106th Street*)

The Straus Memorial is dedicated April 15, 1915, on the third anniversary of the *Titanic* disaster.

13 Second Samuel 1:23.

13 **A PEACEFUL REMINDER OF HORROR** Riverside Park today seems to embody a sense of peace and reflection—it's surprising then to learn that one of its residents witnessed unspeakable tragedy more than 70 years ago. The statue of Shinran Shonin,[14] which sits in front of the squat, square headquarters of the New York Buddhist Church, once stood in Hiroshima, Japan. It was located just 1.5 miles from the epicenter of the atomic explosion on August 6, 1945, which killed at least 100,000 people. Somehow unscathed, the statue was moved to New York and placed here on September 11, 1955. You can still see the reddish burns on it. It reportedly still gives off a slight trace of radioactivity today. (*322 Riverside Drive, between 105th and 106th Streets*)

A silent witness to horror stands on Riverside Drive.

RIVERSIDE PARK

It's such an odd bird, ol' Riverside Park. Strange to think that this ribbon of a park is related to Central Park, but they do have the same parents: Frederick Law Olmsted and Calvert Vaux. However, it was Robert Moses who finished the job in the 1930s, extending the park to the water, tucking it in between roadways (of course!) and concealing the very untranquil railroad tracks and their trains (you can hear 'em, but you can't see 'em!). The southern part of the park has developer-turned-politician Donald Trump to thank—well, kind of. In the 1990s, he put an artificial park extension over the old rail yard, although he would have much preferred a shopping mall here. Fantastical statues pop up at random intervals to the delight of wanderers.[15]

14 **GHOSTS IN THE WATER** So far we've pointed out several Manhattan ruins that still exist—for example, Beth Hamedrash Hagodol (Chapter 9) and the Smallpox Hospital of Roosevelt Island (Chapter 18). To

---

14 Shonin (1173–1262) was the founder of Jōdo Shinshū Buddhism.
15 The park continues north into Harlem and will be discussed in Chapter 24, as well.

find one of the city's most dramatic ruins, head over to immaculate Hudson River Park, in the shadow of an elevated West Side highway. Jutting out of the water you'll find the remnants of the 69th Street Transfer Bridge, which opened in 1911 as a dock for railroad cars floated from New Jersey to the former New York Central Railroad tracks here. There have been plans for years to turn it into something — a ferry terminal, a pedestrian walkway. For now, however, it languishes in the water, almost haunted, a truly stunning vestige of the past. (*69th Street, Hudson River Park*)

15 JOAN OF RIVERSIDE The mighty teenage warrior Joan of Arc (1411–1431), triumphantly posed on horseback, is one of the few women depicted

Wonder Woman: Joan of Arc makes her Upper West Side debut on December 6, 1915.

in sculpture in all of New York City.[16] The windswept "Maid of Orléans" was the first, designed by Anna Hyatt Huntington (1876–1973) and unveiled in a 1915 ceremony attended by the French ambassador and Mina Edison, the wife of Thomas Edison. At the statue's feet are inset stones from the Tower of Rouen, where Joan was imprisoned in 1430. There is almost no reason for this statue to be situated at this precise spot, but perhaps it is significant that it was placed here in the second year of World War I, when America was not yet in the conflict, but New Yorkers had battle and triumph very much on their minds. (*Riverside Drive and 93rd Street*)

NOTE: Walking along? Jump to Chapter 24 for more Points of Interest on the Upper West Side and in Riverside Park.

---

16 Eleanor Roosevelt welcomes visitors to Riverside Park to the south, Harriet Tubman sits in Harlem, and Alice of *Alice in Wonderland* is chilling out in Central Park.

Tastes of History: Old-School Restaurants

When it comes to restaurants, New Yorkers are spoiled. Today nearly 20,000 eating establishments can be found within the five boroughs, dishing up a riotous mix of cuisines that are as deliciously diverse as the city's population.

But for much of its history, eating wasn't exactly considered something you did in public. In the eighteenth and early nineteenth centuries, some taverns served meals, but these were often based upon what ingredients the tavern owner could acquire that day. Everyone ate the same thing, and, most likely, it all tasted pretty foul.

In 1837, the Delmonico brothers made culinary history when they opened a restaurant near Wall Street that imported refined Continental cuisine and Parisian-style service to a city experiencing an economic boom. Sumptuously decorated, the restaurant boasted private dining rooms, live music, and the city's largest wine list (16,000 bottles!). It was a sensation, attracting a who's who of rich locals and visiting notables, and was the most famous restaurant in the United States for much of the nineteenth century. (See Chapter 4 for the ancient secret of its present facade.)

As the city's economy boomed at the turn of the twentieth century, lavish new restaurants attempted to lure in moneyed diners with a flurry of innovations. Meanwhile, enterprising foreign-born restaurateurs were cooking up dining options that were familiar to the thousands of immigrants arriving daily. Italian restaurants opened in Little Italy, German and Jewish spots opened on the Lower East Side, and Chinese eateries opened near Mott Street.

The restaurant business was hit hard by Prohibition (alcohol, after all, is a cash cow) and, coupled with the Depression that followed it, many old-fashioned restaurants were wiped out. Some persevered, however, and are still serving today, often in the same vintage settings. These include the following:

DELMONICO'S
Famous for inventing now "classic" dishes (including lobster Newburg and eggs Benedict), Delmonico's, mentioned above, operated in several locations during the Gilded Age. The sole surviving location, which dates back to 1891, was reopened and closed by various owners a few times in the twentieth century (the current iteration opened in 1998). A little trivia: Delmonico's— along with the restaurant at the Astor House Hotel[17]—received the very first restaurant review in the *New York Times*, on January 1, 1859. (*56 Beaver Street*)

RUSSIAN TEA ROOM
Opened by former members of the Russian Imperial Ballet in 1927 as a hangout for Russian immigrants, this famously glitzed-up eatery boasts

---

17 See Chapter 5 for more on the Astor House.

an unforgettable modernist Russian decor (gold ceilings, red banquettes, theatrical partitions). During much of the twentieth century, the Tea Room attracted a notable lineup of artists and performers; its location next to Carnegie Hall made it a convenient postconcert spot. The Tea Room's recent history reads like a Russian drama, with a threatened demolition, a $36 million renovation, a bankruptcy, and a 2006 reopening. If the Russian-themed cuisine is too rich for you, at least push through the 1920s revolving doors to take a free glimpse of the decor. (*150 West 57th Street*)

SARDI'S

The stars gaze down upon Sardi's—quite literally. Famous for the caricatures of stage stars that line its walls, this Theater District institution dates back to

1921, when Vincent Sardi, Sr., and his wife, Eugenia, opened their first restaurant in a brownstone down the block from the current location. Six years later, when that building was set for demolition to make way for the St. James Theater, Sardi's set up shop here, across from the Shubert Theater. Sardi's has worked with notable artists from its early years to sketch the exaggerated likenesses of more than 1,200 actors appearing on stages nearby, a tradition that artist Richard Baratz keeps alive today—he adds 20 new portraits to the walls each year. Since the beginning, Sardi's has drawn a theatrical clientele, mixing actors, producers, and their biggest fans, and still offers a highly discounted "actor's menu" to anyone showing an Actor's Equity card. (*234 West 44th Street*)

GRAND CENTRAL OYSTER BAR

This city has always been a bit oyster crazy. When Grand Central Terminal opened with great fanfare in 1913, its dramatically arched basement (with terra-cotta tiles designed by Rafael Guastavino) was handed over to the Oyster Bar. Its location, just under New York's busiest transit hub, kept its tables and lunch counter packed for decades, although by the 1950s the restaurant (like the terminal) had gone a bit stale. After closing briefly in the 1970s, restaurateur Jerome Brody reopened the Oyster Bar with a new emphasis on fresh oysters and seafood. Its adjoining cocktail bar is a fabulous *Mad Men*–esque spot to throw one back before catching a train—if you can find a spot before catching a train. (*Under Grand Central Terminal*)

THE SEED OF CENTRAL PARK

In 1845 while on a tour of Europe, William Cullen Bryant, editor of the *New York Evening Post*, became enamored with the large public parks of London and Paris. In a letter published in his newspaper on June 24, Bryant first mentioned the idea of a "central" park for his growing city, a notion that eventually led the *Evening Post* to hold a competition in 1857 to choose a suitable park design. It was this contest that produced Olmsted and Vaux's Greensward plan. From Bryant's letter:

> The population of your city, increasing with such prodigious rapidity, your sultry summers, and the corrupt atmosphere generated in hot and crowded streets, make it a cause of regret, that, in laying out New York, no preparation was made, while it was yet practicable, for a range of parks and public gardens along the central part of the island or elsewhere, to remain perpetually for the refreshment and recreation of the citizens during the torrid heats of the warm season. There are yet unoccupied lands on the island which might, I suppose, be procured for the purpose, and which, on account of their rocky and uneven surface, might be laid out into surpassingly beautiful pleasure-grounds; but, while we are discussing the subject, the advancing population of the city is sweeping over them, and covering them from our reach.

Chapter 22//
Central Park

Bethesda Terrace, pictured here in the 1860s, is one of the oldest components of the park. The majestic angel in the terrace's fountain, by sculptor Emma Stebbins, was the only sculpture included in the original plan by Olmsted and Vaux.

SITUATE THE READER
–Central Park–

Central Park is one of the great unnatural wonders of the modern world. It's New Yorkers turning to God and saying, "You know, good effort and all, but we think we can make nature look a little bit more, you know, *breathtaking*."

Mind you, the Commissioners' Plan of 1811, which laid out most of the city's streets north of Houston Street had no interest in a large park hogging up all that real estate. But by the 1840s, two forces combined to create it: the popularity of nouveau European city planning, which featured lavish public spaces, and a swelling city population in need of fresh air. Always game for a civic competition, city leaders launched a contest to design a park in Manhattan that would be centrally located and conveniently reached by residents on both the east and west sides of the island. The winners, in 1858, were Frederick Law Olmsted and Calvert Vaux with their Greensward plan. The design replaced the commonplace topography of the existing land (read: nature) with fanciful, dreamlike vistas, grand promenades, enchanted forests, and artificial lakes. The hottest thing in painting at the time were the lush landscapes of the Hudson River School; Central Park bested it—it brought paintings to life.

The construction challenges facing the park's landscape architects, engineers, and gardeners were considerable—not the least of which was the fact that the proposed parkland was already, quite inconveniently, home to farms and about 1,600 residents, many of them freed black slaves living in an area called Seneca Village. Furthermore, the proposed park's natural topography was far less interesting than those of those of Olmsted and Vaux's bucolic designs. Hills were flattened in some places and entirely constructed in others. The park-in-progress attracted curiosity seekers, and the finished product was an instant tourist attraction upon its completion in 1873, its magical assortment of paths, bridges, and waterways defining the development of upper Manhattan.

Central Park is loosely divided into three sections: the sculpted, manicured, and theatrically staged southern section; the large, tranquil reservoir; and the forested, more wildly natural northern area. The Metropolitan Museum of Art arrived at the park's eastern edge in 1880 with its priceless collection of Western masterpieces, proving that a bit more beauty could, in fact, fit inside the city's new playground.

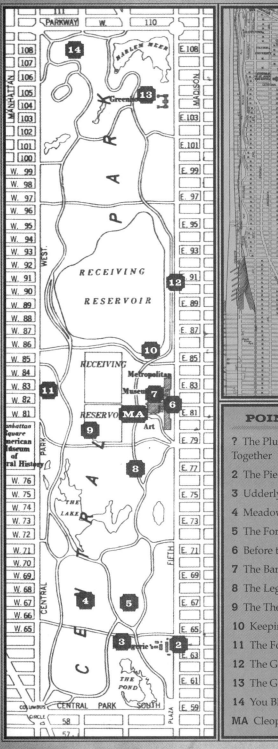

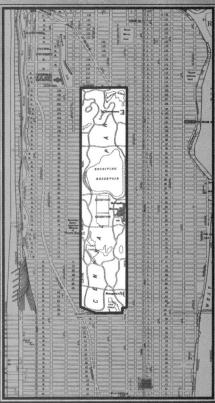

POINTS OF INTEREST

? The Plug That Holds Manhattan Together

2 The Pied Piper of Central Park

3 Udderly Essential!

4 Meadow Lands

5 The Forgotten Icon

6 Before the Facelift

7 The Bank of America

8 The Legend of the Mad Cat

9 The Thermostat of New York

10 Keeping the Faucet Running

11 The Former Village People

12 The Golden Boy

13 The Glorious Nuns of Central Park

14 You Blockhouse!

MA Cleopatra's Needle

Cleopatra's Needle and the Secret of the Freemasons

Cleopatra's Needle, a 224-ton obelisk that today resides outside the back door of the Metropolitan Museum, was somehow carved, crafted, and erected in the ancient Egyptian city of Heliopolis sometime in 1460 BCC (Before Construction Cranes). More than 1,400 years later, Cleopatra met both the obelisk and its twin when the two massive monuments were hauled to Alexandria to decorate the Caesareum, a temple she had built and dedicated to her old lover, Julius Caesar. They are no more her needles than the Washington Monument is.

As we've already seen in this book, there's just something about obelisks. And we're not just engaging in phallic talk here—there's something seemingly mystical about them. For centuries, they've been the West's ultimate trophy and symbol of dominance (and would remain so until the invention of an even more durable "obelisk," the skyscraper). New Yorkers would go wild over these ancient marvels due in part to one of the world's most secretive organizations: the Freemasons.

One of two Alexandrian obelisks, depicted here in its original home in 1822.
One was carried off to France, the other to New York.

You'll find that the Freemasons seem to pop up all over the place in American history. Robert Livingston (1746–1813), Grand Master of the Great Lodge[1] of New York, gave the first presidential oath of office to another Freemason, George Washington, swearing him in with a Bible owned by (you guess it!) the Freemasons.[2] Theirs is a fraternal order tracing back to seventeenth-century Europe, and depending upon your love of conspiracy theories, they're either a long-lasting community organization focused on charitable endeavors,

The empty pedestal of Cleopatra's Needle at right, as carriage riders gallop by.

or a devilish cabal orchestrating every facet of American life. (It's undoubtedly the former, but we can't resist at least entertaining the latter.)

With the persistence of Veruca Salt in Willy Wonka's chocolate factory, the city of New York wanted an obelisk, needed an obelisk, demanded an obelisk… now! After all, Paris had received its obelisk in 1836, and London had received one half of the twin obelisks from Alexandria in 1878. All the important cities had a massive granite shaft on display — and New York, in the late nineteenth century, its population booming, was important and deserving of one too.

So who better to go retrieve an obelisk than a Freemason?

The Egyptian khedive gifted America the remaining Alexandrian obelisk in 1877, and an American contingent arrived in 1879, led by Henry Honychurch Gorringe, a naval officer, intrepid engineer, and ardent Freemason. Gorringe's task was tricky and treacherous. Six men had died in the transportation of the London obelisk, and that massive object, strapped to a cylindrical barge, had even been lost at sea for several days.

Gorringe and his crew succeeded — barely — in lowering the obelisk to the ground, and carted it seven miles over land before loading the massive structure onto a ship by employing a makeshift conveyor belt fashioned from cannonballs…and off it sailed.

---

1 He was among the drafters of the Declaration of Independence and served as the U.S. minister to France during Thomas Jefferson's presidency, among other things.
2 Return to Chapter 4 to visit this interesting chestnut.

And so in the summer of 1880, this ancient Egyptian artifact, more than 3,000 years after its mysterious construction, crossed the Atlantic Ocean and arrived in New York Harbor in one piece.

And here's where the story becomes a wee bit mysterious: The endeavor was almost entirely funded by William Henry Vanderbilt (1821–1885), son of "Commodore" Cornelius Vanderbilt. William was (surprise, surprise) a Freemason too. Naturally, he and many others believed that the hieroglyphics

carved into the obelisk held secret messages from the ancient world meant only for the fraternal organization. After all, weren't the Egyptians the original stonemasons? And wasn't America, entering the Gilded Age full steam ahead, the new Egypt?

A grand Masonic parade in 1875. The obelisk procession five years later would be far larger!

Vanderbilt had selected a home for the obelisk in Central Park, which had been completed just two decades earlier. But it didn't seem to make sense — it was in a strange and out-of-the-way area called Greywacke[3] Knoll, hidden behind the newly built Metropolitan Museum of Art. The spot was neither special nor prominent enough for such an important monument. Vanderbilt refused to explain himself.

On October 9, 1880, more than nine thousand Freemasons arrived in New York for a grand ceremony — one that was shrouded in mystery, of course, as it wasn't intended to bless the obelisk (which was still moored in the harbor) but rather its massive seven-ton pedestal, already planted in Central Park. During the ritualistic blessing the organization buried a time capsule beneath the pedestal, a curious package that included, among other items, a set of US coins, a copy of the Declaration of Independence, a volume of *Webster's Dictionary*, and literature from the Society for the Prevention of Cruelty to Animals (for some reason).

Hauling the obelisk to its unusual new home required some serious heaving and ho-ing. From its dock on the East River at 96th Street, thirty-two horses

---

3   Greywacke is a form of sandstone and clay sediment.

worked tirelessly, slowly dragging the monument from the hull, lugging the ancient cargo block by block to Central Park. At the point where the procession hit the New York Central's train tracks,[4] the path had to be cleared of traffic until the obelisk rolled over and made its way past. (Fortunately, Vanderbilt also owned the trains and their tracks, so he could basically do whatever he liked.)

At Fifth Avenue, the horsepower was replaced by steam, as a train engine along a trestle bridge slowly pulled the object into Central Park and to its eventual destination. The obelisk was methodically hoisted up and mounted on January 22, 1881, again with mysterious and solemn Freemasonry pomp and ceremony. The trip from the East River to Central Park had taken more than 110 days.

On February 22, a gala at the Metropolitan Museum of Art celebrated its new neighbor, linking it with the museum's already impressive Egyptian collection. Although the obelisk is not officially a part of the museum, it no doubt informs and even trumpets the museum's collection, which now also

includes the Temple of Dendur, which made a similar journey to Central Park from its Egyptian home in 1978. Even still, the ancient temple, marked by graffiti scratched over the course of several centuries, is 1,445 years younger (or so) than the needle.

But why did Vanderbilt place the obelisk at precisely this spot in the park? Take out a map and a ruler: If you draw a line connecting the Central Park obelisk south to the oldest obelisk in the city — the gravestone of Thomas Addis

Mystical mystery: Is there a reason why Cleopatra's Needle sits behind the Metropolitan Museum?

Emmet at St. Paul's Chapel[5] — the line cuts straight through the site of a second obelisk, the grave marker of General William Jenkins Worth[6] at Fifth Avenue and 25th Street. Three obelisks, lined up perfectly in a row.

---

4   See Chapter 23.
5   Mentioned in Chapter 3.
6   Mentioned in Chapter 15.

And what, pray tell, is located one block away from General Worth's obelisk, at Sixth Avenue, between 23rd and 24th Streets? The headquarters of the New York Freemasons.[7]

Central Park

POINTS OF INTEREST

? **THE PLUG THAT HOLDS MANHATTAN TOGETHER** Sorry, but we're not going to tell you where this one is located. You'll just have to search

for it yourself. Embedded in a piece of rock somewhere in the southern portion of Central Park is a small, rusty spike, barely noticeable. It was discovered by geographers in 2004 and is believed to be a bolt used in the original survey of Manhattan by John Randel, Jr., in the 1810s—the survey that created New York's grid.[8]

Randel and his team spread out over the island, marking along a delineated grid spots that would become the intersections of streets and avenues. Indeed, this spot was slated to become just another intersection had Central Park not

Nailed it! This little spike may hold the entire city grid together.

been carved out of the plan in the 1850s. If this random little bolt is indeed part of that original survey, then it's truly an extraordinary link to the city's history. Unfortunately, it's not protected, and we'd hate to see it disappear, so you'll have to hunt it down on your own. If you do find it—mum's the word! (*Somewhere in Central Park—we won't tell you where.*)

2 **THE PIED PIPER OF CENTRAL PARK** Only two structures predate the existence of the park that surrounds them: the Blockhouse (see page 425) and the Arsenal. When it was constructed in 1851, the latter did indeed hold ammunitions, but it seemed a bad idea to have guns lying around in a park once work began on Olmsted and Vaux's plan in 1858. Then, sometime in 1859, New Yorkers began leaving animals at the Arsenal's front door.

---

7   This tantalizing theory courtesy of author Martin Langfield.
8   See the entry on "This Is the Beginning" in Chapter 10.

The mid-nineteenth century was an experimental period in America's relationship with domesticated animals, as families raced to bring home animals for pets that would today be considered wildly exotic. These adventurous collectors rather quickly came to terms with the fact that city dwellings were not ideal habitats for, say, monkeys. Abandoned pets from South America, horses and oxen from faraway farms, four-legged freak show deposits, and yes, even monkeys cast out of apartments were dropped off at the Arsenal's front door.

The environs around the building quickly developed into a proper menagerie, and soon iron cages had to be constructed to contain the wild animals (who, by the way, were often given derogatory Irish names, an embarrassing custom that hung around until 1893). For a time, the skeletal remains of other animals — dinosaurs — were contained inside the Arsenal within the original home of the American Museum of Natural History (from 1869 to 1877).

Today the Arsenal serves as the headquarters for the Department of Parks and Recreation and stands watch over the Central Park Zoo. Make a monkey out of yourself and ask a ranger when the rooftop is open, as it provides an interesting view of the zoo. (*At the Fifth Avenue and 64th Street entrance*)

The Arsenal, 1862.

3 UDDERLY ESSENTIAL! The Central Park Dairy actually did serve park visitors milk — a lot of it. In 1870, "[t]he Commissioners of the Central Park…determined to erect and open next Spring a dairy for the supply of pure, wholesome, and unadulterated milk for the special use of invalid and

delicate ladies and their infant children visiting the Park."[9] Its completion in 1871 marked a key turning point in the park's history. Although the elite considered it their own personal playground, Central Park would soon become a park for all New Yorkers, including (naturally) young children. Quality milk, a staple that was missing from the diets of poor children in tenement neighborhoods, was hard to come by in New York. The dairy

The park's dairy served children in the nineteenth century.

building, fairytale-like in appearance, appealed to the park's growing working- and middle-class visitors; when it opened, a small restaurant also served affordable meals. It was certainly no place for the Fifth Avenue socialites, living a short distance away! (*Midpark, between 64th and 65th Streets*)

4 MEADOW LANDS Perhaps no other section of the park is as important to American history as Sheep Meadow, which has been the location of innumerable rallies, protests, concerts, sit-ins, love-ins, general outrages, making ups, and making outs. But when the meadow was designed by Olmsted and Vaux, it was not intended for any human lollygagging whatsoever.[10] Among the most challenging terrains for construction, given its rocky formations (and, of course, the people already living there!), Sheep Meadow was, through great effort, transformed into a picturesque tribute to simpler times. And yes, for several decades sheep actually did graze upon the grass here — until Parks Commissioner Robert Moses banished them from the park in 1934.[11] Alas, the sheep have missed the good times; notable events in

---

9 *New York Times,* February 18, 1870.

10 Actually it was originally intended to be a military parade ground, but the influential designers quickly dispelled with that notion.

11 Moses was a grouch, sure, but in this case, his decision was prudent; during the Great Depression, officials feared hungry New Yorkers would eat the animals!

the Meadow postgrazing have included a postwar speech by President Harry Truman in 1945, large-scale peace rallies in the 1960s, and a legendary 1968 concert by Barbra Streisand (or is that *Baaaa*-bra Streisand?). (*West side of the park, 66th to 69th Streets*)

5 THE FORGOTTEN ICON The park's Literary Walk isn't too literary — Christopher Columbus is here, always getting in the way! — but its wide path and its magnificent leafy views will probably put you in a studious mood. It's here that you will find the first statue ever placed in Central Park — that of William Shakespeare in 1872[12] — as well as the first statue of an American placed here. Granted, Fitz-Greene Halleck (1790-1867) is decidedly less famous than ol' Shakes, but he's considered the American Byron and notable, partly, because he's considered to be America's first homosexual poet.[13] He's almost completely unknown to the general public today, and most people

One of Halleck's most famous poems is about Robert Burns, whose statue sits nearby.

race past his statue to get to other, more famous, monuments. (Seriously, another Columbus?[14]) As Fitz would say (in the poem "Fanny"), "Yet, on the whole, they thought him — a poor devil." (*Midpark, parallel with 70th Street, right side of Literary Walk, right after the statue of Walter Scott*)

METROPOLITAN MUSEUM OF ART

Before the Met was founded in 1870, almost all of the city's fine nonreligious art could only be found hanging in the opulent homes of New York's wealthiest families. Even after the museum's creation, its earliest homes were mansions themselves, with little effort made to beckon commoners inside.

---

12 The very same Shakespeare statue that Edwin and John Wilkes Booth raised money for in 1864!

13 Speculation, of course, but certainly noticed even in his time. Halleck's work was often infused with homoerotic themes that may explain why he fell way out of favor in later, more masculine eras.

14 See Chapter 20 for its reason for being.

Placing the first museum structure, completed in 1880, within Central Park was a symbolic gesture toward openness and democracy.

Even so, the state legislature had to force the Met in 1891 to open its doors — on Sunday — to nonartists and nonsocialites (i.e., the rest of us). Thousands of years of history and billions of dollars' worth of art are contained inside its walls, but in a couple of instances, it's not the Grecian urns or the Caravaggios that tell the story, but the museum building itself....

The old museum, tucked behind the new, pictured here in the early 1900s.

6 BEFORE THE FACELIFT Fashion is so fickle, and architecture is not immune to the public's changing tastes. By the time a structure is completed, it could be immediately deemed passé. Such was the case with the original 1880 Metropolitan Museum of Art building, designed by Vaux and his new collaborator, Jacob Wrey Mould. Its redbrick Gothic facade was quickly considered hokey, and plans were later hatched to conceal the building behind dramatic Beaux-Arts frill (designed by Richard Morris Hunt, among others). "Our first building was a mistake," said the Met's founding president, John Taylor Johnston, "there must be none about the second."

However, bits and pieces of the original 1880 structure occasionally peek out like a frilly undergarment under a ball gown. The museum's original front facade — in all its ruddy red glory — can be seen from the European Sculpture

Court. Another glimpse is possible atop the museum's grand staircase in the Robert Wood Johnson, Jr., Gallery. (*Fifth Avenue at 82nd Street*)

7 THE BANK OF AMERICA American art was not highly regarded among critics—or deemed worthy of museum exhibition—in the late nineteenth century, which could explain why the present American wing was relegated to the back of the museum. But the American collection is separated from the old-world finery in a surprising way: with a bank. The Branch Bank of the United States, erected in 1825, once sat at 3 Wall Street and was a next-door neighbor to Federal Hall. The museum brought the entire facade of the building uptown to grace their new American wing in 1924. It's a curious old thing, facing a sculpture garden filled with nude nymphs and other fanciful creatures. And no, there's no ATM inside. (*Metropolitan Museum, American Wing*)

The Branch Bank's (1825) facade was so handsome that they just lifted it off and stuck it in the Met!

8 THE LEGEND OF THE MAD CAT If you think about it, it seems counterproductive to place statues inside Central Park. After all, the park was meant to be a respite from civilization and all its responsibilities and pressures. How are you supposed to relax and unwind if you keep running into overachievers like Alexander Hamilton (placed near the obelisk in 1880) or the sled dog Balto (near the Children's Zoo, placed in 1925) or the formidable King Wladyslaw II Jagiello of Poland with his massive crossed swords (overlooking Turtle Pond, 1945)? Olmsted and Vaux didn't want *any* statues sullying their carefully planned gardens and hills, but twenty-nine have sneaked in over the years.

The best sculptures either amuse you (such as that of Alice in Wonderland) or terrify you, as in the case of the quiet but deadly bronze by Edward Kemeys

Invasion! By the 1860s, statues were already making themselves at home in Central Park.

called "Still Hunt," which depicts a cougar hunting its prey. "Still Hunt" is the only sculpture in Central Park that absolutely does not feel like a sculpture. It's been perched on a rock at the edge of the Rambles since 1883, ready, at any moment, to spring to life. (*West side of East Drive, Midpark at 76th Street*)

9 THE THERMOSTAT OF NEW YORK "Follies," architecturally speaking, are fake ruins or whimsical structures meant to evoke some forgotten storybook era. They're like predistressed jeans, remains of good times you never knew. Perhaps the biggest folly in New York City is Belvedere Castle, built atop old Vista Rock in 1869, high above the Great Lawn. It makes a fantastical discovery for those who have navigated the tricky paths of the Rambles. While mostly decorative—like a sunken object in an aquarium—the castle actually has a very important task, one that New Yorkers couldn't live without: Since 1919, it has been an official weather station for the National Weather Service. When you hear on the radio that it's "65 and windy in Central Park," they mean it's 65 and windy atop this crazy little folly! (*Midpark at 79th Street*)

10 KEEPING THE FAUCET RUNNING The largest feature of Central Park—the Jackie Onassis Reservoir—was also once its most important. Don't call it a lake! The reservoir was an important link in the Croton Aqueduct water distribution system, built from 1858 to 1862 to bring water from north of the city down into the Murray Hill Reservoir,[15] from where it would be distributed to residences and businesses. The reservoir is no longer part of

---

15 See Chapter 19.

the water system, of course, but the two gatehouses are great reminders of its invaluable link to New York City life. The South Gate (1864) features a history of the Croton water system, among the greatest civic works ever built for a major American city. The reservoir's most important responsibility today is to provide a most picturesque track for the hundreds of joggers who circle it daily. (*East side of Central Park at 86th Street*)

The Jacqueline Kennedy Onassis Reservoir is the largest body of water in Manhattan.

11 THE FORMER VILLAGE PEOPLE (Vanished) Even after the Commissioners' Plan of 1811 carved a street grid onto Manhattan, many northern sections of the island continued to develop according to their own designs. In 1825 a small settlement named Seneca Village, home to hundreds of people, formed here, well north of the center of New York (at the time still below 14th Street). Seneca Village was notable for being one of New York's first settlements of freed blacks, although new German and Irish immigrants soon moved to the area as well. They built churches, a school, and even their own cemetery.

A few decades later, however, the village found itself, unluckily, in the way of the planned park development. By 1857, all the residents had been bought out and the town demolished. Recent excavations have unearthed traces of the former village. You really never know what lies underfoot, even in America's most famous park! (*West side of Central Park, between West 81st and 89th Streets*)

12 THE GOLDEN BOY John Purroy Mitchel (1879–1918), the Bronx-born grandson of an Irish revolutionary, became the mayor of New York in 1914.

He was called "the boy mayor" for his youthful good looks and youthful age (34) when he took office. He was not a particularly effective mayor and was swiftly voted out four years later by a wide margin. In 1918, Mitchel tragically fell from an airplane during military training in Louisiana and died. Ten years later New Yorkers paid tribute to the former mayor with a most curious monument—a gilded bronze bust of Mitchel greeting visitors at the park's Engineers Gate. Easily one of the strangest memorials in New York, Mitchel's bust looks both gleaming and robotic today, an almost futuristic tribute to the

John Purroy Mitchel, the sharply dressed "boy mayor" of New York.

man.[16] (*Fifth Avenue and 90th Street*)

13 THE GLORIOUS NUNS OF CENTRAL PARK (Vanished) Long before the creation of Central Park, an embankment called McGowan's Pass figured into the Revolutionary War. George Washington, the British forces hot on his tail, guided his men through this land to find safety in upper Manhattan. In 1814, under threat of another possible war with the British, New Yorkers built forts around this area: Fort Clinton, Fort Fish, and Nutter's Battery. But even *that* is not the most extraordinary thing about McGowan's Pass.

In 1861, the gracious old home of the Sisters of Charity was pretty much all there was to see up here.

---

16 Mitchel Square Park in Washington Heights is also named for the former mayor.

It was here in 1847 that the Sisters of Charity of St. Vincent de Paul arrived and opened the Academy of Mount Saint Vincent, a school and convent. The bucolic surroundings were perfect for a nunnery then (and almost impossible to imagine today). While the nuns took off when the area was incorporated into the park, the building remained standing and was utilized for several purposes, including as a Civil War hospital and as a restaurant. The stone chapel was even refashioned as an art gallery for "stuffed specimens of animals of considerable value."[17] The structure was destroyed in a fire in 1881; otherwise it might still be there, overlooking the Harlem Meer. (*East side of Central Park, between 106th and 107th Streets*)

14 YOU BLOCKHOUSE! The northeastern end of the park once contained the fortifications listed in #13, which were built for the War of 1812 — a war that never arrived in New York. There is one fortification, however,

that remains: the Blockhouse, on the northwestern corner of the park. This sturdy, rocky cube is intentionally difficult to get to; it would have been a fine fort had the occasion arisen. Today it has a romantic, even forgotten, feel to it, but that is not by design. Plaques have been placed here to honor the significance of the blockhouse over the years, but they keep getting stolen. Perhaps the British are still here! (*West 109th Street and Central Park West*)

Like a rock: The War of 1812-era blockhouse.

---

17 *New York Times*, January 3, 1881.

THE DELIGHT OF JONES'S WOOD

Published in 1893, *A Tour Around New York, and My Summer Acre: Being the Recreations of Mr. Felix Oldboy* is actually not by Felix Oldboy at all, but rather John Flavel Mines, who recalls old New York from behind an amusing pen name. This is the mysterious wonder that was Jones's Wood in the nineteenth century:

What a place of delight Jones's Wood used to be in the olden days! It was the last fastness of the forest primeval that once covered the rocky shores of the East River, and its wildness was almost savage. In the infant days of the colony it was the scene of tradition and fable, having been said to be a favorite resort of the pirates who dared the terrors of Hell Gate, and came here to land their treasures and hold their revels. Later, its shores were renowned for its fisheries, and under the shadow of its rocky bluff and overhanging oaks the youth of a former generation cast their lines and waited for bites. The ninety acres which composed the wooded farm that was known in olden times as the Louvre passed through many hands until it came into the possession of the Provoost family in 1742, and here they built and occupied for nearly sixty years. Then they deeded their broad acres to Mr. John Jones, reserving the family vault and the right of way thereto. The old graves are there yet, but the ancient chapel has been transformed into a club-house, and the youthful athletes of to-day play leap-frog among the tombstones.

Chapter 23///

Upper East Side and Yorkville

Yorkville in 1916, during a streetcar strike. A beautiful elevated train station stands at the corner of East 86th Street and Second Avenue.

SITUATE THE READER
–Upper East Side and Yorkville–

If Wall Street is the place where you make money, then the Upper East Side is where you live it. Since the late nineteenth century, no other neighborhood in New York has been so defined—and refined—by wealth.

Two centuries ago, a few members of elite society built their mansions here, blessed with spectacular views of the East River. (They often also owned the ships upon the waters, not to mention the cargo held within those ships.) The Commissioners' Plan of 1811 and the subsequent planning and construction of Central Park in the 1850s and 1860s cleared away the shantytowns and small settlements just in time for the rise of Fifth Avenue society. The most prosperous families moved uptown, building their mansions and townhouses along this magnificent avenue and the streets leading to it. Among the most opulent palaces of the "Millionaire's Row" was that of Andrew Carnegie, who constructed his family's compound at Fifth Avenue and East 91st Street in 1903.

One of the catalysts for the neighborhood's million-dollar makeover was a bit of housekeeping performed by the New York Central Railroad. When it finally covered its filthy railroad tracks from Grand Central all the way up to 97th Street, it prompted an unprecedented race of ritzy residential development. New York society, which had settled comfortably at the foot of Fifth Avenue in the early nineteenth century, took hold of these new expanses of the Upper East Side—Park, Madison, and Lexington—by the beginning of the twentieth century.

And yet the neighborhood hasn't been simply a stomping ground for the rich. After the *General Slocum* disaster of 1904, much of the city's German American community moved from the East Village to the Yorkville neighborhood, joining Eastern European immigrants in creating a vibrant community that would stick around for decades. Southern Italians would settle north of Yorkville, to be replaced in later years by Puerto Rican arrivals. In time, this area would find itself a part of Spanish Harlem, now more commonly called East Harlem or El Barrio.

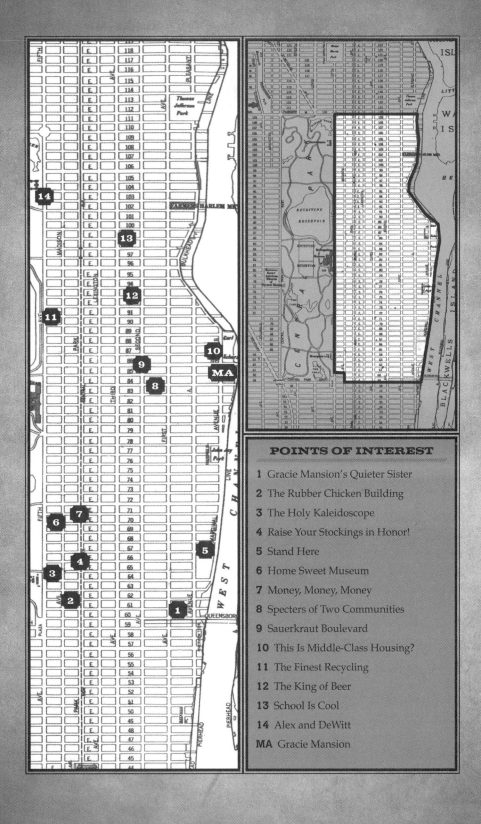

POINTS OF INTEREST

1 Gracie Mansion's Quieter Sister

2 The Rubber Chicken Building

3 The Holy Kaleidoscope

4 Raise Your Stockings in Honor!

5 Stand Here

6 Home Sweet Museum

7 Money, Money, Money

8 Specters of Two Communities

9 Sauerkraut Boulevard

10 This Is Middle-Class Housing?

11 The Finest Recycling

12 The King of Beer

13 School Is Cool

14 Alex and DeWitt

MA Gracie Mansion

Gracie Mansion and the Treacherous Views of Hell Gate

Gracie Mansion, today the mayor's official residence, overlooks a convergence of New York waterways, where the East River meets the Harlem River and slashes its way between Queens and Randall's Island.[1] For almost half of the existence of Archibald Gracie's 1799 mansion, its residents had an unblemished view of the brave sailors who ventured into this tidal strait, with its turbulent currents and churning whirlpool, fantastically labeled the "Hell Gate." Thousands of ships were either turned to shore or smashed against the rocks. Countless lives were lost here, including, in 1904, the 1,021 passengers aboard the *General Slocum* steamship (see Chapter 10).

Gracie Mansion, once surrounded by farmland, now sits inside a park, lined with apartment buildings.

The Hell Gate is relatively safe for boats passing through today, thanks to many decades of explosive work performed by the US Army Corps of

---

1   Technically it's Randall's Island and Wards Island, two separate entities until the mid-twentieth century when landfill finally united them. That body of water that once separated them was called Little Hell Gate.

Engineers.[2] The real dramas now take place on land, in the corridors of Gracie Mansion itself, one of the most unusual centers of local government in the city.

The Hell Gate, as seen behind an actual gate, in this early nineteenth century illustration by Joshua Shaw.

The house sits on an unusually high elevation that the Dutch called Horn's Hook.[3] Naturally, such a height could prove quite advantageous during the Revolutionary War, and it did — for the loyalists. The original home on this lot featured an underground tunnel that led to the river's edge. (What New York mayor hasn't dreamed of rebuilding this dramatic escape route?) Washington's army threw up a defensive battery here in 1776, but were run off the land by the British, who then promptly occupied it. Today a cannonball from this period rests on the mantle inside the mansion. (Yes, an *actual* Revolutionary War cannonball. And here you thought it was from Crate and Barrel....)

After the Revolution the land was sold to Archibald Gracie (1755–1829), a prosperous merchant and ship owner who amassed a fortune during the city's shipping boom. Gracie's new home, built in 1799 atop the ruins of the old battery, would have granted excellent views of his own ships, perhaps at times tussling with the waters of the Hell Gate. Gracie was Scottish by birth, so the ascent of this "outsider" into New York society is especially unusual. He planted his home near those of the Schermerhorns, the Beekmans, and, somewhat later, another new money name, the Astors.

The Gracie family entertained an early nineteenth century who's who at their mansion, including Alexander Hamilton, Washington Irving, and John Quincy

---

2   The first planned detonation in the Hell Gate was in 1851, and work would not be completed until the 1920s!

3   Named by Dutch settler Sybout Claessen for the village of Hoorn in the Netherlands.

Adams. "It is a charming, warm-hearted family," wrote Irving in 1813, "and the old gentleman has the soul of a prince. From the porch the guests could enjoy wine and take in the troubled waters below, an extraordinary sight when no vessels lurked."

Gracie Mansion in 1910: Weathered and a bit worn, but the old girl's still standing.

But shipping disruptions during the War of 1812 and financial mismanagement by his sons sank Gracie's fortunes. Gracie sold his home to Rufus King in 1823, and his firm was promptly dissolved. He died of St. Anthony's Fire[4] six years later.

The house then passed through the hands of a few families—the Foulkes, the Wheatons, and then, through marriage, the Quackenbushes. In the 1870s, during the final years of the Foulkes's residency, city engineers resumed setting off explosions[5] in the Hell Gate, further attempts to smooth out the waterways to make them passable. Those explosions would continue throughout the lives of the Wheatons and the Quackenbushes, and long after they were gone, into the 1920s.

By then, the Upper East Side had been radically transformed. The farmland had been parceled into blocks, and the streets rolling west from the mansion were filled with the rollicking German culture of Yorkville. With the arrival of

---

4   Today we know it as erysipelas.
5   Their objective was to blast apart the rocks underwater. The powerful explosions actually made the front page of the *New York Times* on September 25, 1876.

the elevated railroad in the 1880s and then the subway in the 1910s, settling in the neighborhood became increasingly practical for carriageless families, and row houses and apartment buildings quickly arrived to fill the new demand. So how did Gracie's old house, now more than a century old, manage to survive?

Fortunately for the old house, the Department of Parks and Recreation began buying up land near it in 1876. When the mansion lost its final residents fifteen years later, the park's borders were enlarged to include it. In 1910 the park was renamed for Carl Schurz, the first German-born member of the US Senate.

Park life: Carl Schurz Park hides the FDR Drive from view.

Yet the old mansion remained neglected. Who would come to its rescue?

Naturally, a lively bunch of old ladies! It was here in 1922 in the parlor of the downtrodden mansion that a feisty society dame named May King Van Rensselaer, dressed in head-to-toe lacy realness, launched a fight to preserve the house as a museum. In 1923, another group of well-connected doyennes would form the Museum of the City of New York here, and would eventually open the house as a museum. They'd furnish it with the Gracie household's original pieces, as well as other treasures from New York's golden years.[6]

In 1936 tenacious parks commissioner Robert Moses decided to spruce up the old house, and must have thought to himself, "New York needs its own White

---

6 For a time, the house held the card table of Dr. David Hosack, whom you met in Chapter 19 as the owner of New York's first (and failed) botanical garden on the spot of today's Rockefeller Center.

House." In 1942 it was proclaimed the official residence of the mayor, and Fiorello La Guardia moved right in after living for years in a private residence at Fifth Avenue and 109th Street.[7] Every mayor since La Guardia, with the notable exception of Michael Bloomberg, has resided there during his tenure.

None of them, however, has seen a shipwreck in the Hell Gate, a relatively calm body of water today. Moses fixed that too with the opening of the Triborough Bridge in 1936. No force of nature was ever a match for Moses.

Upper East Side

POINTS OF INTEREST

1 GRACIE MANSION'S QUIETER SISTER It's not very pretty just north of the Queensboro Bridge—or rather the "59th Street Bridge"—whoops, make that the Ed Koch Queensboro Bridge—where an inordinate number of concrete apartment complexes cluster around the ramps leading to the FDR Drive. But in the shadow of a storage warehouse, a surprise awaits—the Mount Vernon Hotel Museum and Garden, a post-Colonial vestige of the Upper East Side's peaceful days of yore.

Lovely Mount Vernon, surrounded by massive (and decidedly unlovely) gas tanks.

The old residence boasts a roundabout connection to the Founding Fathers, as it was built in 1799 on land owned by Colonel William Stephens Smith and his wife, Abigail Adams Smith, the daughter of the second president of the United

---

7   23 East 109th Street, to be precise.

States. It was turned into a hotel in 1826, back when escaping overnight to this area was considered "getting out of town." Today it offers all our favorite features of a "historic house museum": interesting artifacts, mannequins in curious poses, that "old house smell," etc. The backyard garden provides a whiff of simpler times—as modern apartment blocks glower down. (*421 East 61st Street*)

2 THE RUBBER CHICKEN BUILDING The Upper East Side contains perhaps the greatest collection of Queen Anne revival architecture in the city, all of it embodying turn-of-ye-olde-century English style with a formal, purse-lipped dignity. The upscale apartment building at 40 East 62nd Street, however, is just plain goofy. It was built in 1911 with dashes of bold color to bring its royal details to life. The row of noble griffins, over time, have unfortunately morphed into the shape of rubber chickens, comedy props that might come in handy at Dangerfield's Comedy Club over on First Avenue. (*40 East 62nd Street*)

Wocka Wocka Wocka! These Queen Anne griffins have morphed into rubber chickens.

3 THE HOLY KALEIDOSCOPE The congregation of one of the largest synagogues in the world got its start in the Lower East Side in 1845. During the nineteenth century, Temple Emanu-El moved up the island and became the preferred synagogue of wealthy Jewish New Yorkers during the Gilded Age. In 1929 a massive new worship space was built on the former site of Caroline Schermerhorn Astor's final home on East 65th Street and Fifth Avenue.

The hypnotic window of Temple Emanu-El.

The synagogue is more spectacular than anything Caroline might have imagined; nothing seems to be holding up its magnificent 103-foot ceiling. Its stained glass windows and mosaics are among the finest in the world. Yet for all its glamorous art deco touches, the temple's facade holds an ancient secret. Straddled by lions on pedestals, the wheel window recalls the traditional symbols of the Holy Land with twelve spokes (the twelve tribes) emanating from a Jewish star (Jerusalem). The glass webbed between the spokes creates a kaleidoscopic mix of colors when seen from the inside. (*1 East 65th Street*)

4 RAISE YOUR STOCKINGS IN HONOR! Park Avenue is a thoroughfare better known for its financial muscle than its military might. However, during the Gilded Age, members of New York's Seventh Regiment Militia were known for both their bravery *and* their wealthy Fifth Avenue families. (They were sometimes known as the "Silk Stocking Regiment," a nickname that holds a slightly different connotation today.[8]) So naturally, they needed a suitably luxurious armory. The imposing Seventh Regiment Armory—today the Park Avenue Armory—was built in 1880, when the tracks of the New York Central Railroad were still exposed, if sunken into the street. Many famous names of architecture and fine arts were called upon to contribute to its construction, including Louis Comfort Tiffany, whose two rooms are still intact. Today it's home to the nonprofit cultural center Park Avenue Armory; you're more likely to see art installations than artillery here. (*643 Park Avenue*)

5 STAND HERE: East 68th Street, between York Avenue and the FDR Drive, and between Rockefeller University and NewYork-Presbyterian Hospital. *Why?* These two institutions and their respective campuses and complexes, an anchor of medical care and research in the

---

8 "Its distinctive dress uniform—gray swallow-tail coats, white cross-belts, gray trousers and black shakos—have been a familiar sight in New York City since 1806, when the regiment was organized." *New York Times*, June 7, 1940.

United States, make up the most important sector of the Upper East Side. The university, founded by John D. Rockefeller in 1901, specializes in biological and medical sciences, which are on display next door at NewYork-Presbyterian Hospital, an institution that traces its roots to the city's first hospital in 1771.

But imagine if these weren't here at all. For alas, this was the proposed location of a not-so-Central Park.

The tomb of David Provoost (who died in 1781) was a haunting feature of Jones's Wood.

Back in the eighteenth century this was one of the most densely forested areas of the island, located miles north of the city. At the heart of this forest was a small 90-acre farm artfully called the Louvre. Later, two of New York's most famous old families—the Schermerhorns and the Provoosts—built manors and placed family crypts here. For decades afterward, adventurers would find broken tombstones in the brush, inspiring a host of ghost stories.[9]

By the nineteenth century, the woods had become a popular day trip for nearby city dwellers. Stories of its mysterious past drew those seeking a little recreation and fresh air. So many were drawn into the woods, in fact, that it became, according to one account, the "first major U.S. amusement park," complete with beer gardens, sporting events, and immense spaces for large gatherings.

In the mid-nineteenth century, as city planners were debating where to plant their enormous new park, the forest emerged as a natural candidate. Its proponents claimed that its lush riverfront and "dense growth of forested

---

9   Later on the land was sold to one John Jones for which the forest gets its name.

trees" made it an ideal, logical, and convenient choice. However, Olmsted and Vaux's plan for a much more "central" park won out, and old Jones's Wood, over time, was almost entirely deforested. (*East 68th Street, between York Avenue and the FDR Drive*)

6 HOME SWEET MUSEUM Imagine waking up tomorrow and thinking, "My apartment is going to be a museum, so I think I'll keep it exactly as it is right now!" For many of us, that would result in a museum of

Henry Clay Frick's home pictured in 1913, when it was still a home.

haphazardly constructed IKEA furniture, a dying fern, and a dusty (if well-intentioned) bookshelf. For industrialist Henry Clay Frick, his elegant surroundings were a logical fit. In fact, when he had his Fifth Avenue mansion built in 1912, he already intended that one day it would be turned into a museum. Providing some sort of justification

for this was the fact that he had an extraordinary collection of paintings, including works by Monet, El Greco, and Vermeer. His mansion, already so similar to an art museum during his lifetime, was remade into one following his death in 1919.[10] Only a few alterations were made. The museum's dazzling courtyard, itself like a dreamlike Maxfield Parrish painting, was Frick's former driveway! (*1 East 70th Street*)

Movin' on up to the East Side.

7 MONEY, MONEY, MONEY The Park Avenue canyon can best be observed from this spot on the Upper East Side, as luxury apartment buildings simply cascade down the incline toward the glass office towers, screeching to a halt at the Helmsley Building. From here, the importance of William Wilgus's decision to cover the busy New York Central train tracks seems evident; this has become one of the richest streets in the world.

---

10 Work on the transformation didn't really begin until 1931, following the death of his wife Adelaide, who had continued to live in the home.

The burying of this filthy crevice, completely concealed[11] by 1910, created a wide-open field that had luxury apartment developers licking their lips. Apartment living was now in vogue, the city's economy was booming, and all the super-rich were already living just west of here, near the park. Now there was suddenly room for the rest of them!

The art deco apartment building at 740 Park Avenue, while hardly the most beautiful along this stretch, has the distinction of drawing the absolute wealthiest names in town, with notable residents ranging from John D. Rockefeller, Jr., to David H. Koch. But how many knew about the very curious crime that took place here in 1931 when $75,000 worth of jewelry[12] was burgled in a highly publicized heist that captivated the city? No fingerprints were left behind, and the police assumed the thief a master "Jimmy Valentine."[13] The culprit? A seventeen-year-old boy from the Bronx. (*740 Park Avenue at East 71st Street*)

8 SPECTERS OF TWO COMMUNITIES The tale of the *General Slocum* disaster (see Chapter 10) ended here at Zion St. Mark's Evangelical Lutheran Church. Most of the 1,342 passengers aboard that ill-fated steamship were members of the congregation of St. Mark's in the East Village. Many of the survivors eventually relocated to the German enclave in Yorkville, where many attended Zion, which opened in 1892. More than fifty years later, in 1946, the remaining congregation of St. Mark's in the East Village officially merged with Zion. Its combined name is a reminder of rebirth after tragedy, although interestingly, no significant German community remains in either old Kleindeutschland or in Yorkville. That said, although the church serves the entire community, a German service is still held here. (*339 East 84th Street*)

9 SAUERKRAUT BOULEVARD In 1937 the delicatessen Schaller and Weber opened its doors selling one product: pork! While that might be the *wurst* business plan today, in 1937 it fit right in, as the neighborhood was already home to delicatessens and eateries that catered to German American tastes. The center of social activity in Yorkville's "Germantown" was East 86th Street, which was packed with cafes, social clubs, and beer halls. It was very

---

11 The trains finally emerge at 97th Street. It is no coincidence that 97th Street is where housing developments for the less-than-opulent begin.

12 That's almost $1.2 million in 2016 dollars!

13 The press named him Jimmy Valentine — for a character in an O. Henry story — but his real name was Frederick Potter.

much a pocket universe of its own, as Germans were heavily scrutinized and under much surveillance during the World Wars.[14] World events did touch the neighborhood, however, from pro-Nazi organizations that met here in the

early 1940s to the German Jewish refugees who settled here after the war. German American efforts to assimilate into postwar America and the pull of the suburbs eventually whittled down "Sauerkraut Boulevard," but a bite of it survives here at Schaller and Weber,[15] next to the salami and spätzle. (*1654 Second Avenue at 86th Street*)

10 **THIS IS MIDDLE-CLASS HOUSING?** Yet another block seemingly

The charming homes of Henderson Place.

lifted from the set of a Harry Potter film is Henderson Place, twenty-four row houses[16] with a unique rustic aesthetic and their own private street. Keeping in mind that the really pricey housing was over by Central Park, a developer named John Henderson built a set of Queen Anne–style houses here for "persons of moderate means." Today these redbrick beauties represent some of the most attractive homes on the Upper East Side. Hardly moderate by any means. (*Henderson Place, off East 86th Street at East End Avenue*)

11 **THE FINEST RECYCLING** The Upper East Side was synonymous with the ultra-wealthy in Manhattan for much of the twentieth century. Many of today's super-rich have actually hit the geographical reset button and started anew in lower Manhattan, driving up the price of everything their gilded fingers touch. But when financier Andrew Carnegie built his "simple" little

---

14 Yorkville takes its name from York Avenue, which is named for decorated US Army hero Alvin York, who fought during World War I against the Germans.
15 The Heidelberg just down the street (1648 Second Avenue) is your other link to Yorkville's past; its present incarnation dates to 1964.
16 There used to be 32 in total.

megamansion up at 91st Street in 1903 (equipped with such indulgences as central heating), its location was perceived as being so far north that it might as well have been in Canada.[17] His mansion eventually defined the Upper East Side so completely—with the rest of the city moving up on Carnegie's coattails—that the surrounding area became known as Carnegie Hill.

But—let's be honest—this is way too much house. Why, the dusting alone! Eventually, almost all of these palatial palaces were taken over by (or deeded to) cultural institutions. For example, the Jewish Museum (at 92nd Street) moved into the mansion of German banker Felix M. Warburg in the 1940s. Following their example, the Cooper-Hewitt, Smithsonian Design Museum took over the Carnegie palace in 1976. (*2 East 91st Street*)

A modest abode: Carnegie's Upper East Side home in the early 1910s.

12 THE KING OF BEER (Vanished) An impressive number of breweries bubbled up in the neighborhood after the Civil War, attracting German immigrants with beer-making skills. The factory plants of Doelger, Schaefer, and Ruppert[18] employed hundreds of local residents, and their product was on tap in taverns throughout the city.

But the biggest brewer in New York—in the United States, actually—was George Ehret, whose massive Hell Gate Brewery, opening in 1866, was

---

17 Carnegie lived in this house until he died in 1919.
18 Jacob Ruppert, Jr., as an incentive to sell more beer, bought the New York Yankees in 1915. He would eventually move them to Yankee Stadium in 1923, a couple years after hiring their most famous player, Babe Ruth.

eventually topped with a clock tower that seemed plucked from a German *Rathaus*. (Ehret was born in Hofweier, Germany, in 1835.) Ehret's suds were poured in beer halls throughout the area, and by the 1870s he had become New York's most famous beer maker.

After Prohibition was repealed, Ruppert bought Ehret's brewery, but Midwestern brewers quickly proved themselves to be more effective at bottling and distributing their product than the New York producers. The Ehret brewery was torn down in 1965 and its famous clock tower destroyed. Now everybody had a reason to drink. (*91st to 94th Streets, between Second and Third Avenues*)

Just getting started: Ehret's original brewery in 1876, surrounded by vast open land.

13 SCHOOL IS COOL Going to school should feel like a quest where adventure and dragons wait around every corner. (Arithmetic is easy by

An artsy new direction for P.S. 109.

comparison.) The architect Charles B. J. Snyder knew this well, designing playful and mighty school buildings throughout New York and granting Gothic sophistication to schools like Public School 109, built in 1898–1899. Exactly one hundred years later, demolition began on P.S. 109, and another marvel of architecture was prepped for the garbage heap. But a last-minute entreaty—post-last-minute actually, as the roof had already been knocked in—saved the school, and today it's the home of El Barrio's Artspace PS109, an affordable housing initiative for artists. They even put the green turrets back on top, because what's a knight without his shining armor? (*215 East 99th Street*)

14 ALEX AND DEWITT The Museum of the City of New York keeps the torch of history burning along Central Park's eastern edge while the New-York Historical Society, flaunting their hyphen, girds the west. MCNY, which formed in 1923 at Gracie Mansion, has been a close observer of city life ever since a major 1926 exhibit called "Old New York" proved that New Yorkers just can't get enough of their own history.[19] When kicking around for a permanent home, a site near Washington Square Park was briefly considered before they plunked it down on Central Park's eastern border—Fifth Avenue, yes, but at 103rd Street—far north of the storied avenue's opulent mansions. Since its opening in 1932, the museum has lured New Yorkers here with glorious secrets from their past, as well

Hamilton at MCNY: The Founding Father has found his niche.

as some genuine oddities (like the mysterious dollhouse of Carrie Walter Stettheimer, filled to its tiny brim with 1920s avant-garde artwork). It's worth a visit just to check out the two guardians of the museum, frozen in demure poses within niches facing the street—favorite sons Alexander Hamilton and DeWitt Clinton, unveiled by Mayor Fiorello La Guardia in 1941. (*1220 Fifth Avenue and East 103rd Street*)

---

19 Which we pay a little nod to in our book title.

THE SEGREGATION OF HARLEM

Harlem was a predominantly white neighborhood in 1900, but as African Americans began settling here at a rapid pace, landowners feared a sudden drop in their property values and financial futures. A disturbingly blunt article ran in the February 1, 1914, edition of the *New York Sun* under the headline "Harlem Owners to Save Property Values by Segregating and Uplifting Negros." An excerpt:

> Owners or their agents, representing more than $400,000,000 invested in real estate in the district north of 110th Street and east of Morningside, Bradhurst, and St. Nicholas Avenues met one night last week and took initial measures to stop the spread of Negroes throughout Harlem. It was the first meeting of this kind held within the memory of the oldest real estate man in the city and it marks the high tide of fear on the part of owners that their investments will be destroyed and their interests wiped out unless something radical is done to prevent the spread of what Harlem calls its blight.

> For a starter the white people have formed an incorporated association which will have a capital of $500,000 to be used for defensive purposes. Their next step will be to force out Negroes from streets where only a few families have settled and gradually to work into the heart of the Negro belt, reclaiming so far as possible the principal streets and avenues now occupied by blacks up to 135th Street. With valuations constantly falling throughout the district, and even the prestige and value of 125th Street, the shopping place of Harlem threatened, owners and agents who have not yet given way to the Negro invasion find themselves confronted by one of the greatest problems they have had to face and they propose sparing no effort to save Harlem from literal destruction. Their efforts will be entirely along peaceful lines and their programme includes radical measures for the social and physical betterment of the Negroes.

Chapter 24///

Harlem and Morningside Heights: 110th Street to 145th Street, Harlem River to Hudson River

The Harlem plains in 1814, undeveloped and rugged, would be tamed by development in the following decades.

SITUATE THE READER
–Harlem and Morningside Heights–

Harlem has had a certain magnetism, a pull, in its combination of desirable physical traits, ever since the days of Manhattan's earliest European settlers. In 1658, Peter Stuyvesant authorized a group of wealthy residents to develop this northern outpost as Nieuw Haarlem, named for the Dutch city of Haarlem and dedicated to "the promotion of farming."[1]

The island's topography rises significantly higher here, which made it a strategic spot to hold during the Revolutionary War, but also a natural home base later for the mansions of those who had fought in it. Its winding rural roads were popular with wealthy daredevils on their winter sleds, and it was situated far enough from the center of New York to open Bloomingdale Insane Asylum here in 1821.

When the New York and Harlem Railroad was extended here in 1837 via Fourth Avenue (Park Avenue), Harlem was poised to become an early sort of commuter town. By the mid-nineteenth century, significant urban development had arrived in Harlem, drawing middle-class Jewish immigrants from the East Side tenements to the blocks around bustling 125th Street, and later, Italian immigrants to an enclave farther east.

Meanwhile, to the west, the quiet charms of Morningside Heights (named for Morningside Park[2]) were disrupted in 1896, when university president Seth Low relocated Columbia University here from its Midtown campus. Columbia's new Beaux-Arts campus, one of McKim, Mead, and White's crowning achievements, was ready for students in 1897.

Extraordinary changes were soon happening down the hill in Central Harlem, which became a mecca for African Americans in the 1920s after the area had been settled for two decades, both for New Yorkers escaping racial tensions downtown and for new arrivals from the South in search of a friendlier home. Influential black churches like Abyssinian Baptist Church and resourceful entrepreneurs like Madam C. J. Walker[3] would further define Harlem as a black capital, culminating in the 1920s with the Harlem Renaissance, a cultural explosion of brilliant writing, art, and music.

---

1 From a Common Council ordinance, March 4, 1658.
2 The park's unique contouring, sloping down to the east, made it an ideal place to watch the sun rise, and thus the name "morning side."
3 The Louisiana-born Walker (1867–1919) became the first self-made female millionaire in the United States through the sale and marketing of hair care products.

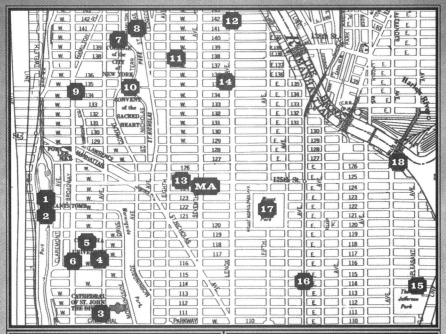

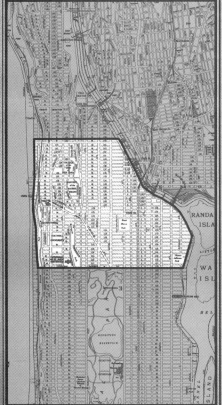

POINTS OF INTEREST

1 Read This Quote

2 Amiable Grant

3 The Hallowed Secrets of St. John

4 Psychiatrics 101

5 One Owl to Rule Them All

6 Don't Blow Your Fox Horn at Me

7 Gargoyle City

8 Home on the Grange

9 Still Ready for Its Close-up

10 The Water Works

11 A Very Stable Neighborhood

12 New York's Greatest Nightclub

13 The Sacred Stump

14 Langston Lives On

15 Your Table Is Ready—Ha, Ha, Just Kidding

16 Whole Foods

17 In the Heights of Harlem

18 The Other African Burial Ground

MA Hotel Theresa

Hotel Theresa: The Waldorf of Harlem

Should you ever find yourself hungry for a miniature hamburger served on the site of a great cultural landmark, head to 125th Street and Adam Clayton

Checking in on the Hotel Theresa in 1913 (pictured here in *Architecture and Building* magazine).

Powell Jr. Boulevard (Seventh Avenue) to the gleaming terra-cotta castle on the southwest corner. An actual White Castle restaurant, it turns out, sits on the ground floor of a once-magical hotel, on the very spot where the greatest icons of Harlem once threw back a few cocktails.

The Hotel Theresa was easily one of the most glamorous places in New York in the 1940s and '50s. Musicians, movie stars, politicians, and athletes flocked here, turning this 300-room hotel of limited architectural interest into a lively

nightly spectacle, and transforming this intersection of Harlem (conveniently located near the Apollo Theater, and the ballrooms and nightclubs of the neighborhood) into a focal point of American black culture.

However, behind the party there rested another less-glamorous reason that the Theresa attracted this A-list crowd: Most of New York's most famous hotels at the time denied them entry because of their race. In fact, for the first two decades of its existence, so too did the Hotel Theresa.

A men's collars and cuffs salesman named Gustavus Sidenberg built the Theresa as an apartment hotel in 1913. An ad in the *New York Tribune* called it a "refined family and transient hotel" with "unexcelled cuisine, perfect service, breakfast 50 cents, lunch 60 cents, dinner a dollar."[4]

What may not have been immediately evident to Mr. Sidenberg was the incredible change to Harlem life that was just about to occur. In the South, the persistence of racial segregation through Jim Crow laws and the cruel treatment of African Americans by whites saw more than a million black Americans move north in the first decades of the twentieth century. Black families settled into the most affordable neighborhoods of cities from Philadelphia to Chicago. In New York, Harlem, with its reasonably priced housing, soon became a nucleus of African American life. Imagine the relief of finally living in a place surrounded by thousands of others with shared cultural experiences, thriving and developing an alternative to an otherwise hostile mainstream. And just in time for the Jazz Age.

By 1930, nearly 70 percent of the Harlem population identified as black. However, many of the businesses in Harlem, and those along 125th Street, were still white-owned. While the spending power of the neighborhood's new African American residents certainly eased

Look at those rates! An advertisement for the Theresa in the *New York Tribune*, 1917.

some racist policies—and the speakeasies at night certainly saw black and white patrons intermingle—many stores and businesses remained steadfastly segregated. This included the Hotel Theresa.

By the 1940s, however, the neighborhood had developed a real need for high-end accommodation. Black guests, including wealthy African American businesspeople, tourists, celebrities, and musicians (often whole orchestras of musicians) were not welcomed by most downtown hotels.

---

4   Who was Theresa? His wives. That's not a typo: Mr. Sidenberg had not one, but *two* wives named Theresa. The first Theresa died in 1910, and the following year he married the second Theresa.

The Theresa (now an office building) still gleams today, but little remains of its illustrious past.

Little by little, black celebrities shunned by other hotels made the Theresa their home in New York—sometimes for months at a time—creating an atmosphere of desirability and cool. When downtown hotels began loosening their discriminatory policies, even those who had the option of staying elsewhere chose the Theresa. By the late 1940s it had became known as the "Waldorf of Harlem," although really, doesn't it sound *better* than the Waldorf?

Better because, after all, the Theresa fit a diverse group of people—everyday visitors, but also showgirls, tourists, actors, athletes, socialites, politicians, even gangsters—into just 300 rooms. The hotel was booked months in advance for most of the 1940s. *Ebony* magazine called the hotel the "social headquarters of Negro America," and *Ebony* should know, for John Harold Johnson—the founder of both *Ebony* and *Jet* magazines—developed *Ebony* in 1945 while staying at the Theresa!

Sitting in the middle of it all at 125th Street and Seventh Avenue, the Theresa bustled with guests coming and going from the Apollo or the Savoy, cabs lined up day and night under its divine emerald marquee. The first thing to catch the eye inside was the hotel's lounge, with its 51-foot, J-shaped bar, packed nightly with celebrities and a roomful of others wanting to get close to them. According to gossip columnist Billy Rowe, "The bar was so crowded, a man could lose his pants and walk the length of the place without anybody noticing."

If cocktails weren't your thing, you could walk over to the Theresa's coffee shop, where you might see boxer Joe Louis enjoying a mushroom omelet. In the lobby of the Theresa, you could really witness the clash of permanent versus transient residents — wealthy, well-dressed tourists following bellboys to the elevator, passing socialites, a cluster of people tending to a starlet, and maybe a few less desirable characters as well, like gamblers or even prostitutes (especially in later years).

Perhaps you might head up to the mezzanine level to the exclusive boutique of Etienne Johnson, outfitter of black chanteuses, from Ella Fitzgerald to Lena Horne. The club room was on this floor, as was the orchid-decorated dining room, an upscale restaurant that hosted literary parties, like one in 1940 for Richard Wright upon the release of his novel *Native Son*.

In the 1950s the Theresa became a stop for presidential candidates looking to connect with the black vote, and it was not a stop without consequence. In late October 1952, just days before the election, both Dwight D. Eisenhower and Adlai Stevenson used the backdrop of the Hotel Theresa to drum up support. (Eisenhower was eventually successful.) But perhaps the most infamous guest at the hotel was Fidel Castro, who stayed here in 1960 during a visit to the United Nations.

In a way, the triumphs of the civil rights movement hastened the Theresa's decline, as downtown hotels and restaurants gradually did away with their segregationist policies and the brightest stars of Harlem opted to stay in the fancier, more fashionable hotels downtown.

Left behind was a neighborhood that was slowly deteriorating and a hotel past its prime. In 1966, the final guests checked out of the Theresa and the famed hotel was converted into an office building called the Theresa Towers. Its ground floor space, once a hopping nightspot, was converted to retail use. In July 1993, the Landmark Preservation Commission granted landmark status to four significant buildings in Harlem. Three of them were churches, and the other was the Theresa. Chew on that next time you snack on a slider.

Harlem and Morningside Heights

RIVERSIDE PARK

The park stretches along the Upper West Side and well into upper Manhattan to 125th Street. See Chapter 21 for more information.

1 THAT QUOTE ON THE FUNERAL URN NEAR GRANT'S TOMB "Erected to the memory of an amiable child St. Claire Pollock, died 15 July 1797, in the fifth year of his age." The Amiable Child Memorial has touched and intrigued New Yorkers for decades, inspiring wistful poets and

thinkers. The present urn dates from 1967, and is the third that has marked his grave. The boy's father wrote in 1800 to the new owner of the property: "There is a small enclosure near your boundary fence within which lie the remains of a favorite child, covered by a marble monument. You will confer a peculiar and interesting favor upon me by allowing me to convey the enclosure to you so that you will consider it a part of your own estate." (*Just north of Grant's Tomb, along Riverside Drive*)

2 AMIABLE GRANT Ulysses S. Grant was a first-rate Civil War general but a less successful US president. This was graciously forgotten when he died on July 23, 1885, and the city set out to create the greatest tomb in New York.

In 1900 the tomb of Ulysses S. Grant had few neighbors.

So painstaking was the process — thousands of designs were considered before John Hemenway Duncan's was selected — that his tomb wasn't completed and dedicated until nearly twelve years after his death. It is still today North America's largest mausoleum.

But remember that there are *two* bodies in Grant's Tomb; his wife Julia Grant died in 1902, knowing where she'd be interred. By the 1990s the tomb had deteriorated to such a degree that lawmakers from Illinois threatened to transport the president's remains back to his home state if New York couldn't clean up its act. The tomb is thankfully in better shape today, and Grant, um, remains. (*West 122nd Street and Riverside Drive*)

3 THE HALLOWED SECRETS OF ST. JOHN The Cathedral of St. John the Divine is New York's largest and most unusual house of worship, a cavernous unfinished space bathed in rich colors from medieval-style stained glass windows. This Episcopal retreat was built to trump the Roman Catholic St. Patrick's on Fifth Avenue and has taken far longer to construct. St. John's, after all, began construction in 1892 and is technically *not* finished, as it's been hampered by fire damage, changing tastes, and other disruptions. Their website offers a rather modest explanation

The church interior, sometime between 1915 and 1920.

for the delay: "Like the great Medieval cathedrals and churches of the world, St. John the Divine will continue to be constructed over many decades."

It's also a *cultural* cathedral. Its captivating interiors burst forth with curiosities—a poet's corner, marble niches featuring luminaries like William Shakespeare and Abraham Lincoln, and stained glass depictions of great inventions, from locomotives to the RMS *Titanic*.

Outside, a macabre surprise awaits in the courtyard—Greg Wyatt's 1985 Peace Fountain, which features the Archangel Michael decapitating Satan upon the shell of a crab. You're not on drugs! If you can pull yourself away from all of this drama, turn to the seemingly incongruous Greek Revival columned building, which long predates both the cathedral and the beheaded Satan. This was part of the Leake and Watts Orphan Asylum, built in 1843 on open countryside for the care of 300 abandoned children. Remember the ostentatious green statue of John Watts standing in the churchyard of Trinity Church?[5] He would certainly be pleased, if slightly puzzled, by his orphanage's present surroundings. (*1047 Amsterdam Avenue, 111th Street entrance*)

---

5   See Chapter 3 for the tale of Trinity Church's graveyard.

Speaking of Trinity Church, King's College—the educational institution it spawned in 1754—lives on, more than two-and-a-half centuries later, and is situated today on a former patch of farmland transformed into an academic oasis. Its name changed following the Revolutionary War, Columbia College moved from its original home downtown near Trinity Church to buildings near its Upper Estate property (near today's Rockefeller Center; see Chapter 19) in 1857. But watching the city encroach upon his campus (and distract his highly distractible pupils), Columbia's president (and later mayor of New York), Seth Low,[6] decided in the 1890s to once again relocate the school farther outside the action. He desired a more formal setting, and hired Charles McKim to design a collection of lovely Beaux-Arts buildings, which were completed in 1896.

Fortunately, you don't need to head off on an odyssey to discover some of its more interesting particularities. Check these out:

4 PSYCHIATRICS 101 Columbia students driven mad by the demands of the college's famous core curriculum (a set of required courses covering the greatest works of Western arts, literature, and philosophy) find cold comfort

in knowing that most of the area's former occupants were actually clinically insane.

The Bloomingdale Hospital Centenary, as it was called, began operations at 116th Street and Bloomingdale Road (Broadway) in 1821 and remained open until the university moved in. Employing the latest advances in psychiatric treatment, the hospital announced

It's a lovely day for a stroll around the Bloomingdale asylum!

in 1821, "This institution has been established with the express design to carry into effect that system of management of the insane, happily termed *moral management*." One building still exists from those days: Buell Hall, located next to Low Memorial Library, is noticeably different from its neighbors. This

---

6 Low Memorial Library was actually named by Seth for his father Abiel Abbot Low. And it's not a library, but the main administration building. The library, Butler Library, faces it to the south and was constructed in the early 1930s.

building, which today houses La Maison Française, was once Bloomingdale's exclusive asylum for wealthy male patients who could afford to keep themselves from the general asylum population. So yes, it was essentially for the insanely rich. (*Buell Hall, Columbia Campus*)

5 ONE OWL TO RULE THEM ALL Columbia's central campus is filled with ghosts, the names and likenesses of former graduates affixed to the brick and sandstone walls of Charles McKim's design. Pupin Hall, for instance, is named for Mihajlo Idvorski Pupin, the Serbian innovator of long-distance communication.[7] Hamilton Hall, home to many of the college's core courses, and John Jay Hall, home to the undergrad dining hall and a dorm, refer to some of the most famous early graduates of King's College. Statues of these Founding Fathers, Alexander and John, face each other on the south lawn in quiet seething.[8]

But perhaps the most visited statue on campus is the open-armed figure of Alma Mater, sculpted in 1903 by Daniel Chester French (whose Lincoln Memorial in Washington, DC, keeps his arms relaxed). Nestled within the folds of her robe is a very small owl, and great and wondrous things are rumored to bless she who succeeds in locating it.[9] (*Center of campus, in front of Low Memorial Library*)

6 DON'T BLOW YOUR FOX HORN AT ME If students sitting in on a lecture in one of Columbia's western halls—say, Dodge or Lewisohn—find the material challenging, they should find some relative comfort in the fact that their challenges are not nearly as daunting as those facing General Washington and his Continental Army, who fought a battle at this spot in 1776. The Battle of Harlem Heights, waged on September 16 of that year, wasn't a major skirmish, but it's notable for being a victory for Washington's forces as they were fleeing New York.

Scholars attribute his success to a bit of outrage; British troops had mockingly blown their fox horns to taunt Washington's men. As a result of the battle,

---

7 In 1939 Enrico Fermi split an atom in the basement, thus ushering in both the atomic age and civilization's heightened anxiety.

8 Both worked on the Federalist Papers together, but later in their careers Alex (first Secretary of the Treasury, among many other things) and John (first chief justice of the Supreme Court, among, you know, tons of other stuff) had several disagreements. They all did.

9 Or perhaps we should say "he," as Columbia College didn't accept female students until 1983.

hundreds of British troops were killed or gravely injured. You do not wave your finger in Washington's face! (Interestingly, Alexander Hamilton, alumnus of this fair institution, was present at that battle.) Today, just north of the gate at 117th and Broadway, you can find a rather melodramatic plaque commemorating the altercation. (*West 117th Street and Broadway*)

It's clobberin' time! Washington's troops get revenge at the Battle of Harlem Heights, September 16, 1776.

Alexander S. Webb, second City College president, stands proud.

7 GARGOYLE CITY Columbia inspired other educational institutions to make Upper Manhattan their homes, most notably the City College of New York, which built a campus on a bluff on Convent Avenue in 1906. Like Columbia, they also had a superior architect in charge: George B. Post. Whereas the architecture of the university to the south bristles with seriousness, City College's neo-Gothic campus has a playful and melodramatic feel, like a bawdy Shakespeare production. Hanging from nearly every nook are goofy gargoyles and grotesques, faces you might see in a Disney film or your nightmares (or both!). Wander about here, taking in the grinning stone musicians and court jesters. Because over at Compton Hall, more evil creatures—demons and harpies—issue forth from the tower. Sorry, professor, a monster ate my homework! (*West 140th Street and Convent Avenue*)

8 HOME ON THE GRANGE New Yorkers have treated Hamilton Grange, the greatest surviving connection we have today to Alexander Hamilton, like a leather ottoman, just scooting it around as they saw fit. The Hamilton Estate, believed to be the only home that Alex ever owned, once sat approximately midblock at West 142nd Street, between Amsterdam and Convent Avenues. Possessing incredible views at the time, the stately home nearly bankrupted Hamilton and would be his final residence—he was living here when he took part in the fateful duel with Aaron Burr in 1804.[10]

House at home: Hamilton's home in its original spot in the early eighteenth century.

The Grange was in poor condition in 1889 when St. Luke's Episcopal Church across the street saved it by moving the entire shebang and then incorporating it into its new church (at 141st and Convent). In 2008 the house was carefully moved again, this time across West 141st Street to St. Nicholas Park. While technically farther from the location where Hamilton had it built, its four sides finally at least get to breathe and are well worth a visit today. (*414 West 141st Street*)

---

10 The house was later sold by Hamilton's son to purchase a townhouse on St. Mark's Place (see Chapter 10).

9 **STILL READY FOR ITS CLOSE-UP** Sorry, LA, but New York made movies first. Hollywood was but a rural farm town when the movie industry developed in New York; the fundamental language of American narrative film was established here and in production studios in New Jersey. Few traces of this fleeting moment in the film industry exist today—not only have the studios largely disappeared, but so too have the earliest theaters.

Lights, camera... A surprising cinematic tribute at 135th Street.

But the Golden Age of pictures still flickers upon a fancy two-story structure in Manhattanville. The old Claremont Theater, opened in 1914, brought the great "photoplays" to upper Manhattan. In 1915 the theater was even featured in an Edison short.[11] Gracing the cornice where normally a goddess or cherub would recline, is the low relief of a movie camera on a tripod. The theater closed in 1933 and became an automobile showroom. (*3338 Broadway, southeast corner of 135th Street*)

10 **THE WATER WORKS** The Croton River water system was responsible for producing a number of notable, even unusual, structures, from the old Murray Hill Reservoir (the site of today's New York Public Library main branch at 42nd and Fifth) to the Central Park Reservoir (presently passing itself off as a lake in Central Park). But more tangible evidence of this extraordinary system still exists the farther north you climb in Manhattan.

At West 135th Street and Convent Avenue, you'll find an old water gatehouse, completed in 1890 for the New Croton Aqueduct Water System. (See Chapter 25 for more information.) They could have just built a large container, but no. The 135th Street Gate House features a medieval-style octagon tower, as though the water it watched over were a moat, not a basin. Even better? Today it houses a theater operated by Harlem Stage, a performing arts group. (*150 Convent Avenue*)

11 **A VERY STABLE NEIGHBORHOOD** The city has called it the "St. Nicholas Historic District" since 1967, but everybody else still calls it, quite fabulously, "Strivers' Row." This impressive lineup of row houses on West

---

11 The unnamed short depicts audiences leaving the theater after a showing of *On the Stroke of Twelve*.

138th and 139th Streets was designed between 1891 and 1893 by the city's leading architects[12] for moneyed families. Three decades later, in the 1920s, the families living here were now mostly African American and were enjoying gracious homes that, due to a range of unjust reasons, probably wouldn't have otherwise been constructed in one of New York's black neighborhoods.[13]

No horseplay: Instructions for chauffeurs along Strivers' Row.

The homes along Strivers' Row share a curious feature, most beautifully expressed on the western end of West 138th Street: private alleyways, with entrances still marked "PRIVATE ROAD. WALK YOUR HORSES." Legendary entertainers like Scott Joplin and W. C. Handy lived here during the 1920s, and the block remains a sumptuous remnant of the Harlem Renaissance. (*Between 251 and 253 West 138th Street*)

12 NEW YORK'S GREATEST NIGHTCLUB (Vanished) The most unbelievable irony of Harlem nightlife in the 1920s—at the height of the neighborhood's creative boom, mind you—is that the biggest nightclubs featured the world's top African American musicians, but only white patrons were admitted inside to hear them perform. This string of music venues soon became the hottest spot of Jazz Age New York and took on the racially charged moniker "Jungle Alley."

A 1925 advertisement for the Cotton Club.

Concentrated on 133rd Street between Lenox and Seventh Avenues, Jungle Alley was a place where white patrons could dabble in the saucy, "dangerous" sounds of jazz as performed by some of the world's greatest musicians. Elegant new Pontiac and Franklin sedans lined the street, delivering partygoers

---

12 Stanford White designed the homes on the northern side of 139th Street.
13 See "The Segregation of Harlem," page 444.

to the likes of Connie's Inn (2221 Seventh Avenue at 131st Street) and Smalls Paradise (2294 Seventh Avenue, near 135th Street).

But the most famous club was slightly north of them at the northeast corner of 142nd and Lenox: the Cotton Club—opened in 1923 and owned by gangster Owney Madden—which didn't shy away from employing racist stereotypes in its decor and themes. Guests were entranced by the top-tier performers— including Duke Ellington, Lena Horne, Louis Armstrong, Cab Calloway, and Dorothy Dandridge. The Cotton Club became so popular that after Prohibition it moved to Times Square, where it lost much of its luster. (*644 Malcolm X Boulevard/Lenox Avenue at West 142nd Street*)

13 THE SACRED STUMP Before the Apollo Theatre was known as one of America's great music stages, it was a burlesque house—the 1914 Hurtig and Seamon's New Burlesque Theater, to be precise. Twenty years later, as the Apollo, it began its famed amateur nights, which have since introduced the world to such "amateurs" as Billie Holiday, James Brown, Gladys Knight, Marvin Gaye, and Aretha Franklin.

For good luck, performers today are often told to rub a piece of heavily laminated wood (that looks like something out of a rural craft fair). But this

The Apollo, between 1946 and 1948 (photo: William Gottlieb).

is no ordinary wooden souvenir! It's a sliver from the famed Tree of Hope, an actual elm tree that once stood at Adam Clayton Powell Jr. Boulevard (back when it was just "Seventh Avenue") and 131st Street. Harlem's Jazz Age entertainers were also known to have rubbed the actual tree for good luck.

In 1934, the year the newly renamed Apollo opened for black audiences, the tree was pulled down to expand the avenue, but a portion was saved by the Apollo's owner, Ralph Cooper, Sr., as a fine gimmick to tie into his amateur competitions. Given the talents who have rubbed against this odd artifact, who are we to think otherwise? (*253 West 125th Street*)

14 LANGSTON LIVES ON The passion and creativity that produced the Harlem Renaissance can be described in a single word: liberty. At the start of the twentieth century, as African Americans got a foothold in Harlem—something they couldn't do in Five Points, Hell's Kitchen, or other neighborhoods that pushed them out—black writers and artists began to feel at liberty to speak and express themselves in their own voices and with a new-found

Paying respects at the Schomburg Center.

directness. Langston Hughes (1902–1967), a poet from Joplin, Missouri, became one of the best-known writers of the Harlem Renaissance because he spoke with simple honesty: "Hold fast to dreams / For if dreams die / Life is a broken-winged bird / That cannot fly."

You can visit and pay tribute to Hughes today in central Harlem. His ashes are interred at the Schomburg Center for Research in Black Culture, in the foyer, beneath an African cosmogram, which contains an excerpt from his first published poem, "The Negro Speaks of Rivers." (*515 Malcolm X Boulevard/ West 125th Street*)

15 YOUR TABLE IS READY—HA, HA, JUST KIDDING Let's pause to remember the rich legacy of East Harlem's Italian heritage, which was at its peak in the early twentieth century. Most of the area's Italian American residents had moved to the outer boroughs and Long Island by the 1960s and '70s, but a few hints of the old neighborhood remain, including the Church of Our Lady of Mount Carmel (448 East 115th Street), where the Giglio Society of East Harlem continues its annual feast tradition.

But the most famous *taste* of Italian Harlem is a place whose interior (and whose food) most of us mere mortals will never know: Rao's Italian Restaurant, located off of Pleasant Avenue at Thomas Jefferson Park. Charles

Rao opened his modest eatery here in 1896; over the years it has developed a reputation for being mythically exclusive, offering only a handful of tables for reservations—which, by the way, are never available. Why, some guests from 1896 are still waiting! (*455 East 114th Street*)

16 **WHOLE FOODS** "El Barrio," a nickname used today for East Harlem,[14] is a neighborhood that saw populations shift in the mid-twentieth century as Italian businesses closed and were slowly replaced by newly arriving immigrants from Puerto Rico, Mexico, and Central America. Today more than a million New Yorkers have Puerto Rican ancestry, and most are related to immigrants who arrived here in the 1930s and '40s.

East 115th Street east of Park Avenue's elevated train tracks became a haven for food vendors, who often specialized in Puerto Rican, West Indian, or South American dishes. In 1936 Mayor Fiorello La Guardia, on a tirade against unregulated "pushcart peddlers," authorized the construction of a covered market under the tracks called the Park Avenue Market.[15] Still operating today as "La Marqueta," the market continues to serve up dishes that reflect the changing tastes of the neighborhood. (*La Marqueta, 1606 Park Avenue at East 115th Street*)

Still keeping watch: Harlem's historic fire tower.

17 **IN THE HEIGHTS OF HARLEM** We might take modern communication for granted these days, but it certainly makes us all much safer. Consider, for example, the days before the telegraph, when the only warning for a blazing fire could come from observers perpetually watching over the land, ready to ring fire bells to rally volunteers to douse the blaze. In the mid-nineteenth century, before the building boom saw larger "fire-proofed" structures constructed, wooden homes lined the streets of

14 Previously known as "Spanish Harlem."
15 It was the model used for "cleaning up" the streets of the Lower East Side, when La Guardia pushed for the formation of the Essex Street Market.

Harlem. In 1857 a cast-iron fire tower was erected on Harlem's highest point, Mount Morris, and was equipped with a bell to alert the neighborhood (and other fire towers). The bell was also a reliable timepiece, ringing at noon and 9:00 p.m. to help locals synchronize their timepieces. Despite the spectacular development of Harlem over the decades, Mount Morris is still around (contained today inside Marcus Garvey Park), and so too is that fire tower.[16]
(*The highest point of Marcus Garvey Park, Madison Avenue and East 122nd Street*)

18 **THE OTHER AFRICAN BURIAL GROUND (Vanished)** In Chapter 6 we visited the African Burial Ground National Monument, which marks the spot where thousands of early black New Yorkers were buried (and promptly built over). But there is another African burial ground—and this one isn't marked. Elmendorf Reformed Church[17] is a congregation that traces its founding all the way back to 1660 during the Dutch New Amsterdam days. A church burial ground on this site permitted the interment of European settlers and of African slaves and freedmen. When the church moved, so too did the remains—or rather, the white ones. The rest of the old church land was developed, and in 1947 a bus depot was constructed at the foot of the Triborough and Willis Avenue Bridges upon this site. Bodies were discovered during a 2008 excavation, and the bus depot has since closed. (*2460 Second Avenue at East 126th Street*)

---

16 Well, usually. As of press time, it's being repaired.
17 Its current incarnation is located at 171 East 121st Street, next to an interesting little private half-street named Sylvan Court.

A Short History of the Bronx

The Bronx is New York City's link to the mainland. Without it, the city would just be a bunch of funny-looking islands, adrift off the coast of New Jersey and New York State. Before Robert Moses's tenure, the Bronx was known for its serene and natural qualities; after Moses, for its dysfunctional ones.

The Lenape tribes held tight to this land even as European settlers whittled it away. The Dutch settler Jonas Bronck (1600–1643), for whom the river and then borough would be named, most likely fell victim to fighting between the New Amsterdam settlers and the Lenape. As did Anne Hutchinson (1591–1643), who fatefully settled here in 1642 and would die here (with most of her family) in an attack the following year.

By the eighteenth century, the rocky cliffs and forested elevations here appealed to aristocratic farmers like the Van Cortlandts and the Pells,[18] whose Revolutionary-era homes still stand in the major Bronx parks that bear their names. And the family of Gouverneur Morris (1752–1816), one of the most intriguing Founding Fathers, settled the southern area that still holds their name: Morrisania.

Squad goals: High school girls picnic in Bronx Park, June 23, 1911.

---

18 As found in the name of New York City's largest park: Pelham Bay Park = Pell + ham (or "hamlet" or "settlement").

By the early nineteenth century, much of the area surrounding the Bronx River was part of the town of Westchester. But as industries found the river useful—sons of tobacco king Pierre Lorillard built a mill here in 1840—towns began splitting off. The area's fortunes improved with the arrival of the railroad in the 1830s and again with the construction of the Croton Aqueduct in the 1840s, which streamed millions of gallons of water daily into New York along the High Bridge, which crossed the Harlem River. In 1841, with the development of Fordham University (then St. John's College) in old Rose Hill Manor, Westchester could now claim an educational institution on par with those in New York.

And then, little by little, pieces of the Bronx became part of New York. In 1874 New York officially brought three towns (Morrisania, West Farms, and Kingsbridge) into its "Annexed District" and soon connected it to Manhattan with an elevated train. Other sections soon joined the party, even the village of Westchester (for whom the county is named). Thus Westchester is in the Bronx, Sleepy Hollow is in Westchester, but Sleepy Hollow is not in the Bronx. Got that?

The consolidation of New York in 1898 created the borough of the Bronx, which notably excluded Yonkers, whose residents specifically voted to stay independent. With the expansion of the subway lines starting in 1905, great development arrived in the area, especially along the Grand Concourse (which opened to traffic in 1909), an artery of fabulous apartment complexes, joining the public amusements that had sprouted along the river shores in the previous decade: the Bronx Zoo (opened 1899) and the New York Botanical Garden (opened 1891).

The African American and Hispanic populations in the southern parts of the Bronx were the hardest hit by Robert Moses's decision to plow his Cross Bronx Expressway through the South Bronx when it was constructed from 1948 to 1972, cleaving off neighborhoods entirely. The resulting combination of urban decay and crumbling infrastructure turned the South Bronx into a symbol of New York's decline in the 1970s.

But ask any non–New Yorker about the Bronx, and chances are they'll associate it with another New York icon: the Yankees. The team moved from Manhattan to the borough in 1923 and have never left (although they did switch to a fancy new field in 2009).

SALE OF MANHATTAN

In 1626, Peter Schagen, a high-ranking member of the Dutch West India Company, made a report to his directors of the contents of an arriving vessel from New Amsterdam. Tucked within that letter is the first report of the "sale" of the entire island for the company. This would be one of the earliest reports of life in the fledging outpost, which had just been founded a year earlier, in 1625.[1]

Rcvd. 7 November 1626

High and Mighty Lords,

Yesterday the ship the *Arms of Amsterdam* arrived here. It sailed from New Netherland out of the River Mauritius on the 23d of September. They report that our people are in good spirit and live in peace. The women also have borne some children there. They have purchased the Island Manhattes from the Indians for the value of 60 guilders. It is 11,000 morgens in size [about 22,000 acres]. They had all their grain sowed by the middle of May, and reaped by the middle of August. They sent samples of these summer grains: wheat, rye, barley, oats, buckwheat, canary seed, beans, and flax. The cargo of the aforesaid ship is:

7246 Beaver skins

178½ Otter skins

675 Otter skins[2]

48 Mink skins

36 Lynx skins

33 Minks

34 Muskrat skins

Many oak timbers and nut wood. Herewith, High and Mighty Lords, be commended to the mercy of the Almighty,

In Amsterdam, the 5th of November anno 1626.

Your High and Mightinesses' obedient,

P. Schaghen

---

1 Translation courtesy of the New Netherlands Institute.
2 Yes, otter skins was listed twice. That's a lotta otter skins!

Chapter 25 ///

Washington Heights and Inwood: 145th Street to Spuyten Duyvil, Harlem River to Hudson River

Traffic jam in Washington Heights in the mid-nineteenth century. From *History of New York* by Mary L. Booth.

SITUATE THE READER
–Washington Heights and Inwood–

We've come to the end of the world—at least for the nineteenth-century city planners who created New York's street grid. The Commissioners' Plan of 1811 stopped at 155th Street, the steepest elevation on the island and a physical obstacle for development at the time. While a semblance of the grid plan was eventually extended up to West 193rd Street east of St. Nicholas Avenue, the rest of the district is wild and wonky, with clusters of apartment complexes crawling up hillsides helter-skelter.

A few freestanding homes remain in the neighborhood, most notably the former home of Roger Morris, which got a fast-and-furious makeover for General Washington's troops during the final New York battles of 1776. A fort named for Washington that once stood upon Manhattan's highest point gives the neighborhood its name. In Sugar Hill, the famed African American neighborhood between 145th and 155th Streets, old estates reside casually next to dazzling row houses. Dozens of apartment buildings gather along the heights of the west side, many offering postcard vistas of the Palisades and the George Washington Bridge.

The hilly three-mile hike from the eastern edge of Sugar Hill to the northern point of forested Inwood Hill Park would challenge even the most athletically inclined urban walkers. In Inwood there are a few pockets where you can still imagine Manhattan as it looked back in 1626 when New Amsterdam Director-General Peter Minuit "purchased" the island from the Lenape. But today the area holds treasures that hearken back to even older times—like the Cloisters, strung together from medieval European monasteries, or the High Bridge, crafted to resemble an ancient Roman aqueduct. The past refuses to hide in Upper Manhattan.

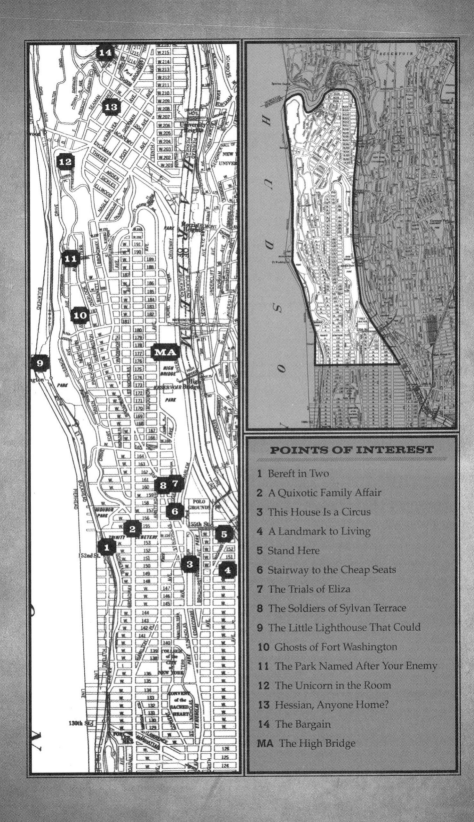

POINTS OF INTEREST

1 Bereft in Two

2 A Quixotic Family Affair

3 This House Is a Circus

4 A Landmark to Living

5 Stand Here

6 Stairway to the Cheap Seats

7 The Trials of Eliza

8 The Soldiers of Sylvan Terrace

9 The Little Lighthouse That Could

10 Ghosts of Fort Washington

11 The Park Named After Your Enemy

12 The Unicorn in the Room

13 Hessian, Anyone Home?

14 The Bargain

MA The High Bridge

The High Bridge: Water for New York

The thirst for water has transformed New York. The Dutch were sold on the island's placement in the harbor at the mouth of the mighty Hudson River, making it a convenient waypoint for explorers and traders. Soon its ports had built the foundation for New York's—and later America's—financial sector. The city's most influential nineteenth-century businessman, Cornelius Vanderbilt, got his feet wet in business first with ferries and steamships before

building his mighty railroad empire. Manhattan is surrounded by water, and yet early New York would almost be undone due to a lack of it.

Traces of the city's centuries-long quest for clean drinking water can be found from the island's tip to its top—from the site of springwater

The High Bridge in 1849, like a vision of ancient Rome.

wells down in Bowling Green to the relics of old water systems that we've visited in the past few chapters. But no monument to freshwater dominates quite like the High Bridge, the Romanesque wonder linking Manhattan to the Bronx over the Harlem River. For many decades this majestic artifact, seemingly plucked from the hills of ancient Gaul, was a vital link in that great engineering triumph: the Croton Aqueduct.

With the dense river traffic below and the icky-brackish composition of the surrounding rivers, early New Yorkers had to look beyond their waterways for drinking water. They dug cisterns and hunted down springs, but these couldn't support the growing city. By the late eighteenth century, Collect Pond, a so-called freshwater source located northeast of today's City Hall, had become polluted by the industries that surrounded it, and valiant efforts to bring water from other sources during the Colonial era were dampened by debt and war. In 1799 future vice president/murderer Aaron Burr hatched a grand business plan to construct a reservoir system that would distribute water via an elaborate network of hollowed-out logs. Unfortunately for parched New Yorkers, he ended up using most of the funding for his Manhattan Company to establish a successful bank instead.[3] His water distribution efforts ended up being woefully inadequate, and left Manhattan high and dry.

Wet and wild: New Yorkers celebrated the arrival of water from the Croton River in 1842.

By the 1830s the city was on the verge of a health crisis, as putrid water, poor sanitation, and all-around squalid living conditions culminated in a series of health epidemics and breakouts—which only heightened the urgent need for clean water. In April 1835 New Yorkers were so desperate for a freshwater supply that they voted in favor of a seemingly impossible plan: a pipeline that would bring the pure waters of the Croton River, forty miles north in Westchester County, down to city residents. Only underscoring the emergency, eight months later the Great Fire of 1835 (see Chapter 4) would ravage the city. The aqueduct couldn't be constructed quickly enough.

The elaborate project employed thousands of mostly Irish immigrants for many years (1837–1842). They constructed a sophisticated system of iron piping and brick masonry, which drew upon gravity to run the water through pipes and over arches, across the lush terrain of Westchester, and through the small towns that would later form the nucleus of the Bronx.

---

3   More than a century and a half later, Manhattan Company merged with Chase National Bank to become Chase Manhattan, known today simply as "Chase," one of the largest banks in the world.

But how would the water get into the island of Manhattan? The aqueduct's architects would need to find a way to keep it flowing across the Harlem River. Drilling technologies were not advanced enough in the 1840s to allow for a tunnel, so planners thought bigger—and higher.

The High Bridge, at an elegant 1,450 feet long, is the oldest surviving bridge in New York. Completed in 1848, it not only brought the Croton water into the city, but it also made one heck of a statement noticed around the world. New Yorkers had pulled off a technological miracle, borrowing engineering and architecture principles not attempted, on this scale, since the glory days of the Roman Empire. They were changing the course of one river forty-one miles away and sending its waters high above another.

"Water! Water!" wrote diarist and former mayor Philip Hone on October 12, 1842, "is the universal note which is sounded through every part of the city, and infuses joy and exultation into the masses." When the water was finally turned on—flowing on October 14, 1842[4]—the city threw a bash bigger than any since the expulsion of the British in 1783.[5] The water flowed through pipes across the

The High Bridge.

High Bridge and to a receiving reservoir in the area of today's Central Park, and from there to a distributing reservoir at 42nd Street and Fifth Avenue. From there it moved through the city, eventually to City Hall Park, where good, clean water shot high into the air and down into the City Hall fountain, to the delight of the public. Imagine— enough water to waste in a fountain!

But the celebrated new system struggled to keep up with the demands of the growing city. In 1872, as masses of new arrivals from far-off lands crammed into tenements, an attractive water tower was constructed near the High Bridge to help increase the water pressure into the city. By this time the High

---

4 The High Bridge wasn't completed at this time, so Croton water crossed a temporary low bridge.
5 There was even an official song called "The Croton Ode," which included the jaunty lyric, "Water leaps as if delighted / While her conquered foes retire! / Pale Contagion flies affrighted / With the baffled demon, Fire!"

Bridge itself had turned into an attraction, a festive promenade where young gentlemen and their parasol-clinging lady companions could stroll, taking in the striking views of the still-forested landscape that surrounded them, while millions of gallons of clean water coursed beneath their feet.

A View from the Bridge: The newly opened walkway again links Manhattan with the Bronx today.

But New York, growing larger every day, would need *more* water. Much, much more. The introduction of indoor plumbing would require an entirely new and much larger Croton system to be built, which opened in 1890 and employed the massive Jerome Park Reservoir in the Bronx to satisfy the demand.

But alas, with a million flushes came the end of the High Bridge as an active part of the water system. Its function replaced by unromantic pipes buried underground, the bridge and water tower were retired from service by 1949, and soon these structures modeled after antiquity became historical relics themselves.

In a surprising twist given the unforgiving tendencies of city planners of the day, it was probably the beauty of the bridge and the tower that kept them from being ripped down in a bit of "progress." Motorists along the Major Deegan Expressway took moments from their traffic jams to reflect on the possible story behind these strange and magnificent artifacts, which grew more incongruous as the modern highway system developed around them.

In 2015 the High Bridge was restored, not for the movement of water but for those visitors and their parasols (replaced by headphones, we imagine) to enjoy a one-of-a-kind perspective on their buzzing metropolis. If you go, reflect upon the water that once passed below you—it helped this city grow.

Washington Heights and Inwood

POINTS OF INTEREST

1 BEREFT IN TWO In 1842, with the city rapidly growing and new burials banned from lower Manhattan, Trinity Church constructed a second cemetery, way, way out of town upon property owned by naturalist John James Audubon (1785–1851). The burial ground was once an uninterrupted place of quiet hills, marked with broken and overgrown marble tombstones and sepulchres, a place of reflection and mourning. It was a spot for quiet contemplation—until they plowed Broadway through it in 1871, splitting Trinity's peaceful cemetery in two (and disinterring dozens of bodies in the process).

A Gothic stroll: A thousand stories hidden in Trinity's uptown cemetery.

Many of the colorful characters featured in this book can be visited today by stopping by this cemetery, preferably on a blustery autumn afternoon for full dramatic effect. Clement Clarke Moore, the lord of Chelsea (Chapter 14), was interred in the western burial ground in 1899, as was wealthy landowner and budding hotelier John Jacob Astor in 1848 (Chapter 5) and scandal madam Eliza Jumel in 1865 (featured on page 478). The eastern burial ground contains slightly newer arrivals, including those rapscallion nineteenth-century mayors Fernando Wood (buried in 1881) and A. Oakey Hall (buried in 1898). A more recent addition to the cemetery, buried in 2013, is former mayor Ed Koch. (*770 Riverside Drive*)

2 A QUIXOTIC FAMILY AFFAIR The Audubon Terrace features the most wonderfully misplaced set of structures in New York, majestic Beaux-Arts palaces surrounding a sculpture garden that would look at home in the Metropolitan Museum of Art or the Frick Collection. The Audubon Terrace's remoteness is a big part of its charm. Audubon owned twenty acres of rolling hills, ideal for his naturalistic obsessions, and when he died in 1851, the land was parceled off into a shaded neighborhood named Audubon Park.

El Cid welcomes you to Audubon Terrace.

Philanthropist Archer Milton Huntington (1870–1955) envisioned a haven for arts and culture when he purchased lots and developed Audubon Terrace to house his favorite endeavors, including the Hispanic Society of America (for his love of Spanish art), the American Numismatic Society (for his love of coins), and the Museum of the American Indian, among others. It was a family affair; his cousin Arthur Huntington designed most of the buildings, and his wife, Anna Hyatt Huntington (1876–1973), crafted the extraordinary statues of El Cid, Boabdil, and Don Quixote in the courtyard. (*Broadway and West 155th Street*)

3 THIS HOUSE IS A CIRCUS Sugar Hill has more than its share of mansions and elegant homes, looking dubiously at their row house neighbors like disapproving dowagers. The mansions were loners when constructed in the 1880s, and their views were unparalleled. (Can you blame them for being so aghast at more recent developments?) The festive home of James Anthony Bailey (1847–1906), completed in 1888, has an appropriately delightful air about it, given that he was a famous circus man. Bailey had worked in circuses since he was a teenager and eventually became the John Oates to P. T. Barnum's Daryl Hall, launching the world-famous Barnum and Bailey Circus in 1881. "He Is the Creator of the Modern Circus," touted the *New York Times* ten years later. Bailey died in 1906, but his circus—and his fanciful house—live on. (*10 St. Nicholas Place*)

4 A LANDMARK TO LIVING The Dunbar Apartments, completed in 1928, were a garden apartment cooperative funded by John D. Rockefeller, Jr., and built to absorb Harlem's expanding middle-class African American population. The Dunbar's 536 apartments became a bit of a sensation;

Between the buildings at the Dunbar Apartments.

residents back in the day included W. E. B. Du Bois and Paul Robeson. In the following decades, dozens of garden apartment complexes were built throughout the city, in part due to the Dunbar's success.

The complex is named after African American poet Paul Laurence Dunbar (1872–1906), perhaps most famous for his 1899 poem "Sympathy" and its final resonant line, "I know why the caged bird sings!" (*West 149th to 150th Streets, between Frederick Douglass and Adam Clayton Powell, Jr. Boulevards*)

5 STAND HERE: The pedestrian walkway at West 154th Street and Adam Clayton Powell Jr. Boulevard, across the river from Yankee Stadium. *Why?* You've just read about New York's oldest bridge (the High Bridge) and you've *definitely* heard of its second oldest bridge (the Brooklyn Bridge). The third oldest bridge, the Washington Bridge, lies farther up the Harlem River at West 181st Street. But the *fourth* oldest is no slouch in the historical legends department: Macombs Dam Bridge, a modest swing bridge over the Harlem River at this spot. While it might not boast groundbreaking architecture, the bridge holds a secret tie to the past within its name.[6]

---

6   Or, more precisely, its nickname. The official name was originally Central Bridge, but tenacity of the past connection won out over that blah designation.

The wealthy merchant Robert Macomb[7] built a dam and bridge here in 1814, collecting tolls on the bridge and charging for boats to pass through a small lock. By 1839 citizens were so angered by the dam—willfully blocking an active waterway!—that a hundred men attacked it with axes over the course

Macombs Dam Bridge in 1861 (artist: G. Hayward).

of a few days. This vicious act of civilian vigilantism had the desired effect: A new bridge, now operated by the city, opened in 1861, and its replacement, still swingin' today over the Harlem, arrived in 1895.

The most violence you'll see here these days are the curses of Yankees fans erupting from the nearby stadium after a losing game. (*West 154th Street and Adam Clayton Powell Jr. Boulevard*)

6 STAIRWAY TO THE CHEAP SEATS Upper Manhattan contains many sites important to early sports history. New York-Presbyterian Hospital today sits upon the spot where Hilltop Park (1903–1912) hosted games by the New York Highlanders, the precursor to the New York Yankees. Polo Grounds Towers, a housing project on West 155th Street, marks the former spot of the Polo Grounds (1890–1964), the legendary stadium that was home to three major baseball teams (Yankees, Mets, and Giants) and the first home to football's New York Jets.

The housing towers may have replaced the Polo Grounds in 1968, but a surprising vestige remains: a staircase, linking the low-lying east side to the high promontory called Coogan's Bluff. The stairs were installed in 1913, linking public transit on the bluff to the stadium. An even more romantic image to ponder: fans with empty pockets often watched games from these stairs, which are named for John T. Brush, the owner of the Giants from 1890 until he died in 1912. The team's adoring tribute to Brush can still be seen in rusted metal on one of the staircase platforms. (*Edgecombe Avenue and West 158th Street*)

---

7   The home of his father Alexander Macomb is featured in Chapter 2, as it was George Washington's first official residence as president of the United States.

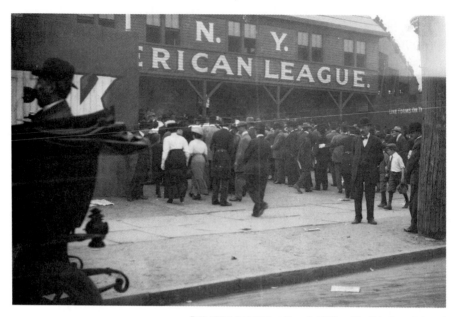

Both Hilltop Park (pictured here in 1912) and the Polo Grounds turned Washington Heights into a major sports destination.

7 THE TRIALS OF ELIZA Perhaps Manhattan's richest concentration of unspoiled history is contained on a plot of land uphill from the Harlem River Drive. Built in 1765, the Morris-Jumel Mansion is the oldest surviving house in New York, and was the home of British sympathizer Roger Morris, who wisely decided to bid New York adieu during the war. (Washington, in a practical if shady move, briefly used his home as a headquarters.)

Worth writing home about: Morris-Jumel Mansion on a vintage postcard.

But it's the tales of Eliza Jumel that give its Colonial hallways a jolt of saucy sex appeal. Her wealthy husband, Stephen Jumel, bought the house in 1810, as Eliza tried in vain to enter New York's snooty social circuit. (Her previous unfortunate stint as an actress and rumors of early years in prostitution held her back.) Stephen died in 1832, and Eliza managed to snag former vice president Aaron Burr the following year, but his squandering of her estate led to a quick divorce. When she died in 1865, she was regarded as one of the most notorious women in the city's history. Some say her ghost still inhabits the house (now a fascinating museum, well worth a visit). If you see her, say hello from us.

But the historical finds are not limited to the home's interiors. Out back, in the garden, is an ancient mile marker that once alerted carriages and stagecoaches of the distance to the city, which is eleven long miles to the south. (*65 Jumel Terrace at West 160th Street*)

8 THE SOLDIERS OF SYLVAN TERRACE In the mid-nineteenth century, most of New York's modest homes were constructed of wood. After all, it was cheap, as much of Manhattan was still wooded, and thus simple structures dotted the newly laid-out streets before more substantial stone and steel structures were erected. But terrors like the Great Fire of 1835 forced city leaders to revise and enforce stricter building standards, which abolished wooden structures from most parts of town.

Sylvan Terrace seems like a row of Victorian-era dollhouses, cobblestoned street and all.

But waaaaay up here in upper Manhattan, things were a little more free-form. In 1882, a row of identical wooden houses was built along Sylvan Terrace, the former carriage trail leading to the Jumel Mansion. They look like toy soldiers or dolls all lined up, their staircases rising high off the cobblestones like lifted petticoats. (*St. Nicholas Avenue, between West 160th and 161st Streets*)

9 THE LITTLE LIGHTHOUSE THAT COULD The George Washington Bridge, a marvel of enormity and simplicity, is a Jazz Age trophy in a league with the Empire State Building, both of them projecting modern American ingenuity and its unflinching audacity. Bridge engineer Othmar Ammann (1879–1965) originally planned to cover the bridge's latticework skeleton with a stone facade fit for a cathedral (think: Brooklyn Bridge[8]), but the plan ultimately proved to be too costly.

The George Washington Bridge: A mighty Tinker Toy.

The bridge, which opened in 1931, takes its name specifically from George Washington's decisions in 1776 to have forts built at the highest points on both sides of the river: Fort Washington in Manhattan and Fort Lee in New Jersey. Today more than 300,000 people a day follow a similar route to that which was first charted by Washington and his men as they fled the British.

Dwarfed by the bridge's might, tiny as a peg as you drive past it into Manhattan, is the quiet red Jeffrey's Hook Light far below. Manhattan's only operational lighthouse when it was placed here in 1921, it was quickly made obsolete by the very bright new bridge that opened high above it in 1931 — the new structure cast plenty of light down to help guide vessels along the Hudson. Fortunately for the lighthouse, it became the subject of a popular 1942 children's book, *The Little Red Lighthouse and the Great Gray Bridge* by Hildegarde Swift. Demolishing it would have been like killing off Pinocchio, and so it remains to this day. (*178th Street and the Hudson River*)

---

8   Or, better yet, the Woolworth Building, as the stone facade, later abandoned, was designed by the Woolworth's architect, Cass Gilbert.

10 GHOSTS OF FORT WASHINGTON The highest point on Manhattan Island was, unsurprisingly, also the site of a Revolutionary War fort. Nothing remains of it; the spot, now surrounded by apartment buildings, instead holds

Bennett Park today, named for newspaper publisher James Gordon Bennett, Sr.,[9] because he happened to own this land when he died in 1872.

Bennett Park features both swing sets and cannons.

But with a little imagination and a wave of patriotism, you can piece the site together from its tributes. Its height, represented by a marker upon an outcropping of stone, 265.05 feet above sea level, made it a natural choice for Washington and his men for building a fortress in 1776 from which to keep watch for British vessels. A decorative cannon still adorning the park is a stern reminder of the day, November 16, 1776, when the fort fell into British hands. It was (seemingly) Washington's last stand. A marble memorial from 1901 reminds us that the site was "REPOSSESSED BY THE AMERICANS UPON THEIR / TRIUMPHAL ENTRY INTO THE CITY OF NEW YORK / NOVEMBER 25, 1783." And nearby, to commemorate the bicentennial of Washington's birth in 1732, grows an American elm, planted in 1932. (*Fort Washington Avenue, West 183rd Street, Pinehurst Avenue*)

11 THE PARK NAMED AFTER YOUR ENEMY Ask any New Yorker at random where the site of Fort Washington once stood, and chances are your query will be met with a furrowed brow, followed by frantic tapping on a smartphone. But ask about Fort Tryon, and chances are better that they could point it out on a map.

Fort Tryon Park not only hosts the renowned Cloisters museum, but it's also one of the lushest and most romantic spots in Manhattan, with dramatic outlooks over the Hudson River and sweeping views of the Palisades.[10] Curiously, the name refers to Sir William Tryon (1729–1788), one of the last

---

9 The newspaper he founded, the *New York Herald*, already has its own quite-prominent plaza downtown.

10 The view is no accident. Along with buying the Cloisters *and* the land that would become Fort Tryon Park, J. D. Rockefeller, Jr., also bought hundreds of acres along the New Jersey waterfront to preserve them—and the view.

governors of the Province of New York, who led British forces to burn and plunder civilian outposts throughout New England during the Revolutionary War.

Fancy people milling about the ruins of Fort Tryon (depicted in 1858).

He was a debonair monster. And yet the name has, by tradition, stuck, a haunting reminder of the violence of 1776, which once marred this land. Wander the meandering paths and you'll come across several other mementos of long-ago times, including a bronze plaque to the memory of Margaret Corbin (1751–1800), considered the first woman to see active battle in the Revolutionary War and the first to receive a military pension after the war.[11] (*190th Street and Fort Washington Avenue*)

Hasta la vista: The best views in Manhattan are very likely at Fort Tryon Park.

---

11 The road leading up to Fort Tryon Park is called Margaret Corbin Circle.

12 THE UNICORN IN THE ROOM The Cloisters museum, an offshoot of the Metropolitan Museum of Art, specializes in medieval European treasures and is filled with spectacular examples of Middle Ages paintings, reliquaries, tapestries, and tombs. But nearly as amazing as its collection is the actual museum structure itself, its walls, corridors, and apses cobbled together from five European holy sites and cloisters.[12] Parts of the Cloisters are among the oldest structures standing in the United States—although of course, they weren't made here. They were brought over, stone by stone, in an ambitious scavenger hunt that could only have been the pet project of one of the richest New Yorkers who ever lived: John D. Rockefeller, Jr.

So imprinted is Rockefeller's personal touch upon the Cloisters—perhaps even more so here than at Rockefeller Center—that some old tapestries that had been hanging around his apartment are now permanently installed at the museum. Granted, these weren't the sort of tapestries that your great-aunt might weave; these are the famed Unicorn Tapestries, crafted in Belgium between 1495 and 1505.

But while Rockefeller may have bought them over—and the Met now owns the seven hangings—they will forever be the property of "A.E.," whose initials are stitched into the bottom corner of the medieval works. The identity of this individual is unknown to this day. (*99 Margaret Corbin Drive*)

13 HESSIAN, ANYONE HOME? Not all of the surviving Colonial-era homes in New York are elegant mansions. The Dyckman Farmhouse, built in 1784, wouldn't look out of place on the Midwestern prairie. However, it

The Dyckman Farmhouse, before it had neighbors. Date unknown.

---

12 The cloisters are from the following French monasteries: Bonnefont-en-Comminges, Froville, Saint-Michel-de-Cuxa, Saint-Guilhem-le-Désert, and Trie-en-Bigorre.

could not be farther from an actual farm today, as it is boxed in by apartment buildings and locked into place by the traffic of Broadway. Two additional features set it apart from the urban reality that surrounds it: 1) It has a backyard, blooming with flowers, and 2) that backyard also has rugged Hessian barracks. Hessians were German mercenaries hired by the British to fight Washington's troops during the Revolutionary War. The excavated hut — thrillingly rebuilt in 1916, when the home became a museum — predates the house. This dank, low-slung abode would make an excellent listing for tourists on Airbnb. (On second thought, scratch that; the Hessians didn't install Wi-Fi in their huts.) (*4881 Broadway*)

14 THE BARGAIN And, here at the end, we go back to the beginning. Inwood Hill Park is quite possibly New York City's most underappreciated treasure, a series of breathtaking postcards come to life, where earth, foliage, and water return Manhattan to "Mannahatta."

Made a park in 1916, its woods are the opposite of southern Central Park, naturally wild and rugged, as if no European had ever crossed this forested landscape. Who knows what ancient secrets lurk along the banks of Spuyten Duyvil[13] Creek or cling to the anchors of the Henry Hudson Bridge?

Nearly 400 years ago, in 1626, next to a tulip tree here, Peter Minuit, the director-general of New Amsterdam, reportedly purchased the island from the Lenape for a grand total of 60 guilders. While that's generally considered a steal on an island where today a guilder couldn't buy you a hot dog, it's not clear that either party understood the arrangement. (The Lenape were not encumbered by the European concept of "ownership.") Today you can find the location of the old tulip tree near a boulder named Shorakkopoch Rock.

If the legends are true, then the journey to old New York actually starts here. (*Dyckman Street, farthest north on the island*)

---

13 Its curious name is Dutch — *Spuitende Duivel* or "Spouting Devil." Early Dutch folktales did indeed place the devil as lurking in the waters' depths.

Afterword: Marble Hill

And finally we come to perhaps the most unusual place in all Manhattan, so unusual, in fact, that it's not even on Manhattan island.

Neighborhoods have certainly been known to change their allegiances. For instance, Ridgewood switched to Queens when things got rough in Brooklyn in the 1970s. But Marble Hill still remains Manhattan both in spirit and in law, even though it now physically resides across the river in the Bronx.

As the dislocated northern tip of Manhattan, Marble Hill traces its history to the earliest days of Dutch occupation, and during the eighteenth century its renowned marble was extensively quarried for new constructions in New York. It resides on a protrusion into Spuyten Duyvil Creek and effectively increased the routes of sea vessels moving between the Hudson and Harlem Rivers. So in 1895 a canal was plowed through Marble Hill's southern section, severing it from the Manhattan mainland and leaving it as an island. But wait, it gets weirder: In 1914 this island was then joined to the Bronx by filling in the old waterway north of it. Like an island amoeba, it broke from one creature and joined another.

Today Marble Hill borders the Kingsbridge neighborhood, named after the first bridge constructed by the British in 1693, and the Bronx neighborhood of Spuyten Duyvil, located high on a bluff overlooking its mystical namesake waters. From here it's onto Riverdale, and then Van Cortlandt Park, and then to more treasures of the Bronx, the area's Dutch and Colonial past left behind and remembered only as names.

BOWERY BOYS BOOKSHELF

Looking to dive deeper into New York's story? Here's a selection of our favorite New York City history books:

AIA Guide to New York City by Norval White, Elliot Willensky, and Fran Leadon. 5th ed. New York: Oxford University Press, 2010.

Alexander Hamilton by Ron Chernow. New York: Penguin Books, 2005.

Biography of a Tenement House in New York City: An Architectural History of 97 Orchard Street by Andrew Dolkart. Charlottesville, VA: University of Virginia Press, 2006.

City on a Grid: How New York Became New York by Gerard Koeppel. Boston: Da Capo Press, 2015.

The Complete Poems of Paul Laurence Dunbar by Paul Laurence Dunbar. New York: Dodd, Mead, and Company, 1922.

Conquering Gotham: Building Penn Station and Its Tunnels by Jill Jonnes. New York: Penguin Books, 2008.

The Death and Life of Great American Cities by Jane Jacobs. New York: Random House, 1961.

The Devil's Own Work: The Civil War Draft Riots and the Fight to Reconstruct America by Barnet Schecter. New York: Walker Publishing Company, 2006.

The Encyclopedia of New York City, edited by Kenneth Jackson. New Haven, CT: Yale University Press, 1995.

The Epic of New York: A Narrative History by Edward Robb Ellis. New York: Kodansha America, 1997.

The First Tycoon: The Epic Life of Cornelius Vanderbilt by T. J. Stiles. New York: Knopf Publishing Group, 2009.

Five Points: The 19th-Century New York City Neighborhood That Invented Tap Dance, Stole Elections, and Became the World's Most Notorious Slum by Tyler Anbinder. New York: Plume, 2002.

The Flatiron: The New York Landmark and the Incomparable City That Arose with It by Alice Sparberg Alexiou. New York: Thomas Dunne Books, 2010.

Footprints in New York: Tracing the Lives of Four Centuries of New Yorkers by James and Michelle Nevius. Guilford, CT: Lyons Press, 2014.

Forgotten New York: Views of a Lost Metropolis by Kevin Walsh. New York: Collins Reference, 2006.

The Gangs of New York: An Informal History of the Underworld by Herbert Asbury. New York: First Vintage Books, 2008.

Gay New York: Gender, Urban Culture, and the Making of the Gay Male World, 1890–1940 by George Chauncey. New York: Basic Books, 1994.

Gotham: A History of New York City to 1898 by Edwin G. Burrows and Mike Wallace. New York: Oxford University Press, 1999.

Grand Central: How a Train Station Transformed America by Sam Roberts. New York: Hachette Book Group, 2013.

The Great Bridge: The Epic Story of the Building of the Brooklyn Bridge by David McCullough. New York: Simon & Schuster, 1972.

Great Fortune: The Epic of Rockefeller Center by Daniel Okrent. New York: Viking Adult, 2003.

Guide to New York City Landmarks by the New York City Landmarks Preservation Commission. Hoboken, NJ: John Wiley & Sons, 2009.

Harlem: The Four Hundred Year History from Dutch Village to Capital of Black America by Jonathan Gill. New York: Grove Press, 2012.

The Historical Atlas of New York City: A Visual Celebration of 400 Years of New York City's History by Eric Homberger. 2nd ed. New York: Holt Paperbacks, 2005.

How the Other Half Lives: Studies Among the Tenements of New York by Jacob Riis. New York: Charles Scribner's Sons, 1890.

The Island at the Center of the World: The Epic Story of Dutch Manhattan and the Forgotten Colony That Shaped America by Russell Shorto. New York: First Vintage Books, 2005.

Low Life: Lures and Snares of Old New York by Luc Sante. New York: Farrar, Straus and Giroux, 1991.

Meet Me at the Theresa by Sondra Kathryn Wilson. New York: Atria Books, 2004.

New York: An Illustrated History by Ric Burns and James Sanders. New York: Knopf Publishing Group, 1999.

New York Burning: Liberty, Slavery, and Conspiracy in Eighteenth-Century Manhattan by Jill Lepore. New York: First Vintage Books, 2006.

The Power Broker: Robert Moses and the Fall of New York by Robert Caro. New York: Knopf Publications, 1974.

Robert Moses and the Modern City: The Transformation of New York edited by Hilary Ballon and Kenneth Jackson. New York: W. W. Norton & Company, 2007.

Scenes from the Life of a City: Corruption and Conscience in Old New York by Eric Homberger. New Haven, CT: Yale University Press, 1994.

Show Boat: The Story of a Classic American Musical by Miles Kreuger. New York: Oxford University Press, 1978.

Supreme City: How Jazz Age Manhattan Gave Birth to Modern America by Donald L. Miller. New York: Simon & Schuster, 2014.

Triangle: The Fire that Changed America by David Von Drehle. New York: Grove Press, 2004.

Up in the Old Hotel by Joseph Mitchell. New York: First Vintage Books, 2008.

The Village: 400 Years of Beats and Bohemians, Radicals, and Rogues, a History of Greenwich Village by John Strausbaugh. New York: Ecco, 2013.

When the Astors Owned New York: Blue Bloods and Grand Hotels in the Gilded Age by Justin Kaplin. New York: Penguin Books, 2007.

The Works: Anatomy of a City by Kate Ascher. New York: Penguin Books, 2007.

The WPA Guide to New York City: The Federal Writers' Project Guide to 1930s New York by Federal Writers' Project. New York: The New Press, 1995.

Wrestling with Moses: How Jane Jacobs Took On New York's Master Builder and Transformed the American City by Anthony Flint. New York: Random House, 2009.

FAVORITE WEBSITES

Daytonian in Manhattan, **daytoninmanhattan.blogspot.com**

Ephemeral New York, **ephemeralnewyork.wordpress.com**

Forgotten New York, **forgotten-ny.com**

Inside the Apple, **blog.insidetheapple.net**

Jeremiah's Vanishing New York, **vanishingnewyork.blogspot.com**

New-York Historical Society Blog, **blog.nyhistory.org**

New York Neon, **nyneon.blogspot.com**

New York Times Article Archive, **www.nytimes.com/ref/membercenter/ nytarchive.html**

NY Songlines, **www.nysonglines.com**

OldNYC: Mapping Historical Photos From the NYPL, **www.oldnyc.org**

The Retrologist, **theretrologist.com**

Untapped Cities: New York, **untappedcities.com/category/globe/new-york**

PHOTO CREDITS

The photographs in this book come from the following sources:

© javarman/shutterstock.com: pages *xviii–xix*, 2–3, 18–19, 32–33, 48–49, 68–69, 88–89, 104–105, 124–25, 140–41, 162–63, 180–81, 198–99, 218–19, 236–37, 256–57, 280–81, 300–301, 322–23, 344–45, 370–71, 390–91, 410–11, 428–29, 446–47, 468–69

New York Public Library: pages *vii, xii*, 1, 4–7, 9–10, 12–13, 17, 20–22, 27, 29, 31, 34–35, 40, 46–47, 50, 52–53, 55, 57 (top), 63–64, 67, 70, 74–78, 80, 85, 90, 97 (top), 98 (top), 101, 103, 108, 111, 114 (top), 116, 119, 123, 130, 132 (top), 135, 142–43, 148, 151, 152 (top), 160–61, 165–66, 174–76, 179, 182–85, 189 (top), 190–91, 192 (top), 194, 197, 200, 202, 204, 206–207, 217, 222, 224, 225 (bottom), 227, 230, 232 (bottom), 233, 235, 242, 245 (bottom), 247 (bottom), 251–53, 255, 258–60, 262, 266, 268 (bottom), 269, 271, 273–274, 276, 279, 282, 285, 290–93, 295 (top), 299, 303, 308, 310 (bottom), 311 (bottom), 313, 314 (bottom), 315 (top), 321, 324–25, 330, 333 (bottom), 335, 338 (top), 340–41, 343, 350–353, 354 (bottom), 355 (bottom), 357 (top), 358, 360, 365 (top), 369, 372–374, 392, 399, 409, 412–14, 417–22, 424 (bottom), 431, 437, 445, 452 (bottom), 454 (bottom), 456 (top), 457, 459 (bottom), 467, 470–72, 477, 478 (bottom), 480, 481 (bottom), 482 (top), 483

Greg Young: pages 8, 11, 14, 24–26, 28, 36–39, 41–43, 45, 51, 56, 57 (bottom), 58–61, 79, 81, 83–84, 92–96, 99–100, 110, 113, 114 (bottom), 117–18, 120, 126, 129, 131, 132 (bottom), 133–34, 136–37, 144, 146–47, 149, 150 (bottom), 152 (bottom), 154–56, 158, 164, 168–73, 186–88, 192 (bottom), 203, 205, 208–209, 211–14, 220, 225 (top), 226, 228–29, 231–32, 241, 244, 245 (top), 246, 247 (top), 248–49, 261, 263, 265 (top), 267, 275, 284, 287–89, 294, 295 (bottom), 296–97, 304–306, 309, 310 (top), 311 (top), 312, 315 (bottom), 316–17, 326–27, 331, 332, 333 (top), 334, 336–37, 338 (bottom), 339, 348, 354 (top), 355 (top), 359, 361 (bottom), 362–63, 365 (bottom), 366–67, 375–77, 378 (top), 379, 381–83, 386, 397–98, 400–402, 403 (bottom), 407, 415–16, 423, 425, 433, 435–36, 438 (bottom), 440, 442 (bottom), 443, 450, 452 (top), 456 (bottom), 458, 459 (top), 461, 473–76, 479, 481 (top), 482 (bottom)

Library of Congress: pages *ix–x, xiii, xv–xvi*, 44, 97 (bottom), 106–107, 112, 115, 127, 139, 150, 153, 195, 210, 238–39, 243, 265 (bottom), 268 (top), 270, 272, 283, 298, 302, 307, 314 (top), 320, 346, 361 (top), 378 (bottom), 385, 389, 394, 403 (top), 405, 424 (top), 427, 430, 432, 434, 438 (top), 441, 449, 453, 460, 462, 464, 478 (top)

Internet Archive Book Images: pages 54, 71, 87, 189 (bottom), 215

The U.S. National Archives: pages 98 (bottom), 319

The British Library: pages 128, 393, 442 (top)

Brooklyn Public Library: page 166

Museum of the City of New York: page 318 © Wurts Bros./Empire State Building ca 1940; page 329 © Wurts Bros./Chrysler Building from a roof in Tudor City ca. 1935; page 380 © United States Office of War Information/Madison Square Garden exterior 1944.

U.S. National Library of Medicine: page 357 (bottom)

Google Books: page 448

Benjamin Stone Photography: page 510

INDEX

ACKNOWLEDGMENTS

We are greatly indebted to the many New York City institutions that have provided historical resources, insights, and inspiration ever since we started recording the *Bowery Boys: New York City History* podcast in 2007.

Institutions that have offered guidance include the Brooklyn Historical Society, Brooklyn Public Library, Green-Wood Cemetery, the Guides Association of New York, the Landmarks Preservation Commission, the Library of Congress, the Municipal Art Society, the Museum of the City of New York, the National Parks Service, the New-York Historical Society, the New York Public Library, the Tenement Museum, the Victorian Society of New York, the City of New York (nyc.gov), and many, many others.

This book would not have been possible without the contributions of many talented individuals, including our fearless editor, Casie Vogel, and Keith Riegert, who brought us in to Ulysses Press in the first place. We'd be a formless mess without the cover design and Bowery Boys logo designed by Thomas Cabus (thomascabus.myportfolio.com). Special thanks to our interns, Kirby Pate and Daniel Plumer, for always catching our mistakes.

A huge thanks is also due to our friends and family who have encouraged us to soldier on this past year (even when they didn't see or hear from us). In particular we'd like to thank Guillaume Meyers-Normand, Elizabeth Meyers-Hendrickson (there would be no podcast without her), Chip Pate, Mitch Paluszek, and Tom's grandma Eileen Detlefsen, who introduced him to the music of George Gershwin and Tin Pan Alley long ago. Greg would like to thank his sister Tamara for standing in line at a Walmart during Black Friday sales to purchase the camera that was used to take the photographs in this book.

Thank you to our listeners and readers, some of whom have spent literally hundreds of hours listening to our stories. And finally, to our favorite subject, New York City, and the countless small and personal histories that comprise it—we offer our deepest gratitude. You continue to surprise, intrigue, and inspire us.

Tom Meyers (left) and Greg Young (right)

ABOUT THE AUTHORS

Greg Young was born in Springfield, Missouri, the Queen City of the Ozarks and former home of Bob Barker. He moved to New York City in the mid-1990s. In 2007, he cofounded the *Bowery Boys: New York City History* podcast and blog, along with Tom Meyers. He's worked for many years in the music industry and has also written for *New York Magazine*, *Entertainment Weekly*, and *Esquire*. He once wrote music reviews for a prison magazine. He currently lives in Brooklyn and is certain to get priced out of his apartment at any moment. He dedicates this book to Kent Alexander.

Tom Meyers was born and raised in Bellevue, Ohio, and moved to New York in 1993 to attend Columbia College. In 2001, Tom launched the budget travel website EuroCheapo.com, for which he still serves as editor and chief hotel reviewer. In 2007, he cofounded the *Bowery Boys: New York City History* podcast and blog, along with Greg Young. In 2015, after 17 years in the Lower East Side, Tom moved to Maplewood, New Jersey, with his husband, Guillaume, two cats, and a really sweet beagle.